Praise for *Endeavour*

'An extraordinary book about an unlikely ship that defined an age... Like the period it recounts, this book has enormous energy, creativity and self-confidence'
The Times Books of the Year

'Beautifully constructed, Moore's book is not just the history of a single vessel, but a window into the intellectual and political life of the Age of Enlightenment, from the thrill of botanical discovery to the horror of Cook's last moments on the beaches of Hawaii'
Sunday Times Books of the Year

'Fascinating and richly detailed... Peter Moore has brought us an acute insight into the ship that carried some of the most successful explorers across the world. A fine book'
Michael Palin

'An engrossing love letter to a word, an attitude and a ship: it is an endeavour that honours *Endeavour*'
Guardian

'*Endeavour* was more than merely the first English vessel to reach New Zealand and Australia's east coast. She was also a floating laboratory, a vast seed-bank and an international observatory'
The Econ

'Elegant and entertaining... A deeply satisfying book. It represents an intelligent, diverse, fresh and challenging approach to writing the history of exploration'

Literary Review

'Pays brilliant tribute to what was arguably the most significant ship in the history of British exploration'

Daily Mail

'Written in an engaging literary style... Engrossing'

Times Literary Supplement

'Truly remarkable... Moore has brought us a book that is entirely fresh and original. In lucid prose, he shows how this stalwart, unpretentious little coal bark came to embody the Age of Exploration, of Enlightenment, of Empire, and of Revolution'

Professor Iain McCalman, author of *Darwin's Armada* and *The Reef*

PETER MOORE

Peter Moore is a writer, journalist and lecturer. He teaches creative writing at the University of Oxford. His first book, *Damn His Blood*, reconstructed a rural murder in 1806. His second, *The Weather Experiment*, a *Sunday Times* bestseller, traced early efforts to forecast the weather. He lives in London.

www.peter-moore.co.uk

ALSO BY PETER MOORE

Damn His Blood
The Weather Experiment

PETER MOORE

Endeavour

The Ship and the Attitude that Changed the World

VINTAGE

To Claire

5 7 9 10 8 6 4

Vintage
20 Vauxhall Bridge Road,
London SW1V 2SA

Vintage is part of the Penguin Random House group of companies
whose addresses can be found at global.penguinrandomhouse.com

Penguin
Random House
UK

First published in Vintage in 2019
First published in hardback by Chatto & Windus in 2018

penguin.co.uk/vintage

A CIP catalogue record for this book is available from the
British Library

ISBN 9781784703929

Front jacket details from top to bottom: *The Moonlight Battle: The
Battle off Cape St Vincent* by Richard Paton from the National
Maritime Museum, London/Bridgeman; illustration from *A Journal
of a voyage to the South Seas: in His Majesty's Ship, the Endeavour*
by Sydney Parkinson from Dixon Galleries, State Library of New
South Wales/Bridgeman; *Earl of Pembroke, later HMS Endeavour,
Leaving Whitby Harbour in 1768* by Thomas Luny from the
National Library of Australia, PIC Screen 98 #R3397. Spine detail:
Naval Battle of the Saintes by Nicholas Pocock from the National
Maritime Museum/Bridgeman

Printed and bound in Great Britain by Clays Ltd, Elcograf S.p.A.

Penguin Random House is committed to a sustainable future for our
business, our readers and our planet. This book is made from Forest
Stewardship Council® certified paper.

MIX
Paper from
responsible sources
FSC
www.fsc.org FSC® C018179

It is pleasing to contemplate a manufacture rising gradually from its first mean state by the successive labours of innumerable minds; to consider the first hollow trunk of an oak, in which, perhaps, the shepherd could scarce venture to cross a brook swelled with a shower, enlarged at last into a ship of war, attacking fortresses, terrifying nations, setting storms and billows at defiance, and visiting the remotest parts of the globe.

SAMUEL JOHNSON, *The Rambler* (17 April 1750)

Contents

A map showing the voyage of HM Bark *Endeavour*, commanded by Lieutenant James Cook, adapted from an original chart by Henry Roberts of His Majesty's Royal Navy

Prologue: Endeavours of the Mind

In February 1852, the British writer John Dix stepped on board the *Empire State*, a steamship bound from New York to Newport, Rhode Island. About forty years old, Dix had spent several years roaming across the United States, scenting out colourful stories that he could write up as travel sketches. Many of these were printed in article form by the *Boston Atlas*, while collections were packaged together and sent back to Britain under the byline 'A Cosmopolitan' or, enticingly, 'an eminent literary gentleman on the other side of the Atlantic'.[1]

Dix had spent the winter in Brooklyn, New York. A tireless wind had blown south from the Great Lakes, cutting about the shoulders of walkers on the street. For the second consecutive year the East River had frozen, becoming a carpet of ice that capped the black waters where the herrings and harbour seals swam. Several brave souls had ventured across to Manhattan Island, that 'great wilderness of marble and mortar, the abode of merchant princes and millionaires'.[2] Dix had been charmed. It was 'beautiful', he wrote, 'beautiful even in its robes of frost and snow, and every street of it musical with the sound of jingling sleigh bells'.[3]

Only in late February were the biting northerlies replaced by the soft thaw winds of spring. It was around then that Dix read in a New York paper that the ice in Long Island Sound was breaking apart. At last presented with a chance of escape, Dix had walked to the harbour and purchased a ticket to Newport. His plan was to seize the earliest opportunity of visiting a friend in the coastal state and, hopefully, root out some fresh copy. At four that afternoon, as the sun was sinking behind the Hudson, he heard the merry chime of the pier bell. A loud 'twang' rang out from the *Empire State*'s engine room, a puff of black smoke filled the air, 'and, almost noiselessly, the huge double-chimneyed vessel glided from the shore'.[4]

Dix had come to America to start anew. His promising early career in literary London – launched by a 'heart-touching' biography of the child poet Thomas Chatterton – had been blemished by addiction to alcohol. This vice had cost him friends and injected an erratic quality into his journalism, bringing him a reputation as a fabulist. His revival had begun well. In the United States he had embraced the temperance movement and exploited his position as an outsider, casting a wry English eye over a youthful nation. In 1850 he had published *Loiterings in America* and in early 1852 was embarking on a fresh collection of traveller's tales. This would turn out to be a compendium of 'American scenes', accounts of hearing Daniel Webster address 100,000 in Philadelphia ('he forcibly reminded me of Sidney Smith's pithy description of him ... a steam engine in breeches');[5] a trip to Connecticut, 'the Yankee state – *par excellence*', to meet Samuel Griswold Goodrich; then an interview with Harriet Beecher Stowe, author of *Uncle Tom's Cabin* – a book so successful, Dix estimated, that sales in its opening nine months had outstripped those of *Waverley*, *The Sorrows of Young Werther*, *Childe Harold*, *The Spy*, *Pelham*, *Vivian Grey*, *Pickwick*, the *Mysteries of Paris* and Thomas Babington Macaulay's *History of England* put together.

All this lay ahead as the steamer ploughed through Long Island Sound. The *Empire State* was a paragon of modern luxury, as different from the old square-rigged sailing ships as could be. Not two decades before Charles Darwin had been forced to tolerate the conditions on HMS *Beagle*: the nauseating swinging and jerking of his hammock, the decks and hatches beating and pattering with feet, the reek of turpentine and tar. Now Dix was allotted his own apartment, furnished with sofas, ottomans, chairs and marble-covered tables. In the saloon a lady played piano while a gentleman sang in accompaniment. 'I never should have dreamed that I was "afloat on the ocean wave"', Dix wrote. To him the steamers were 'indeed floating Hotels! From the barber's shop to the bed all is perfection.'[6]

A day later Dix was ashore at Newport. The climate, he decided, reminded him of the Isle of Wight. Newport was an old town nestled within the complex geography of Narragansett Bay. The bay – a vast expanse of water dotted with islands the locals used as stop-offs on fishing trips – was once of strategic consequence, but over the last decades Newport's significance had dwindled. Trade had moved north to Providence, and what life remained blossomed only briefly. 'Only once, during the year, does the old town show any signs of vitality, and that is during "the season", when, from all parts of America, there flock to it, Fashion and Beauty, to enjoy the unrivalled sea-bathing and the lovely scenery in the vicinity. This spasmodic prosperity continues for about two months, and then Newport is its own dull drowsy self again.'[7]

Out of season and with little to entertain him, Dix strolled over the town. He found a curious old mill and several unusual rock formations in the cliffs. Investigating one he discovered many spires of stalactites, forgotten fingers of frozen water that brought to mind the 'glittering palaces' of the Arabian Nights. But Dix was to find his best story at the wharves. There he fell into conversation with 'an English gentleman'. After talking for a time this man surprised him by revealing 'a very interesting naval relic was standing in a store hard by'. He led Dix to the counting house of an oil merchant. There the man pointed out an apparently mundane object: a large wooden post, splintered and wizened but still upright and entire.

'This piece of wood was a part of the stern of the "Endeavour"', Dix wrote in *Transatlantic Tracings* – the 'identical vessel' in which the celebrated James Cook had sailed on his first navigation of the globe a century before. Dix scribbled the story down as he was told it. After her famous voyage *Endeavour* had been sold at Dunkirk to an American merchant, who intended to have her refitted for the whaling industry. With this in view she had been sailed to Newport for repairs. She had proved old and feeble. Whether before or after she had reached port, the vessel had been 'broken up by the equinoctial gales'. All that remained, the man told Dix, was this old post that had once formed part of the vessel's structural timbers.

The object stirred something within Dix. He responded, as he so often did at such a moment, in verse. Dix's poem, titled 'An Ocean Fragment', appeared in *Transatlantic Tracings*:

> A simple bit of old brown wood,
> Worm-eaten and decayed,
> Recovered, waif-like, from the flood—
> Is all that's here surveyed;
> And yet in it the thoughtful mind
> A history, like romance, may find.
>
> Within some English forest dim,
> It grew a stately tree;

> Waving, when breezes woke the hymn
> Of natural minstrelsy:
> Bright birds amid its foliage glanced
> And village folk beneath it danced.

Dix's poem sweeps on, in full picaresque verve. It charts the felling of the tree, the sculpting of the hull, the arrival of Cook, the imperial hero who 'fearless, paced his vessel's deck' as the world spun in contrasts about him.

> On, onward still, by Science urged,
> The Endeavour speeds her way,
> Until her anchor lies submerged
> In Otaheite's Bay!
> Half-round the globe her course has been,
> And now she rests near islands green.

The poem then blackens. Palms and mangos in Otaheite are replaced by daunting Pacific waves. It hurries towards its conclusion, Cook's murder in Hawaii and *Endeavour*'s conversion into a whaler. Then, at last 'her timbers shrank, And rotted upon Newport's bank'.[8] The poem closes as it has begun, with the ship disintegrating, separating once again into her constituent parts, until nothing was left but the stern post.

'An Ocean Fragment' was a typical Dix performance. It was cleverly conceived, woven with lasting images, and several forceful rhymes. But again, if it wasn't half a truth, it was a truth and a half. Most of those whom Dix met at Newport harbour that day, and the vast majority of his readers in Britain, would have known that Cook was sailing in his second great ship, *Resolution*, and not *Endeavour*, on Valentine's Day 1779 when he was killed in Hawaii. Dix probably knew this too. But never one to let cold facts stifle a rousing tale, he ignored this. 'Any relic of the dead is precious', Emily Brontë had recently written in *Wuthering Heights*.[9] Here Dix must have known he had found one of the most evocative relics of all.

Dix was an instinctive writer, but not a careful one. He did not stop to check his facts, which would betray him in more ways than one. He did, though, detect the narrative power of the object before him. Dix knew what most good writers do. He knew that objects like that stern post are time machines. They shrink years, decades and centuries into inconsequence, levelling time. The more commonplace they are, the more strongly they operate. To see them, or even better touch them, unlocks layers of meaning or moments of personal interaction. The shard of wood was a stern post that was once a tree; carried to the wharf by a whaler; fetched from the sea by a diver; mended by a carpenter. Before that it was set in place by a shipwright, who collected it from a woodsman who cut it from a tree that had grown from a sapling.

This was the theme of 'An Ocean Fragment'. Dix had a narrative sequence soaked in meaning. From that old stern post, Dix knew he could evoke the whole golden age of the Georgians. And it was not the distant courtly world populated by kings and queens, prime ministers or parliaments, rather it was an earthy place of oak wood, salt water, Pacific sunshine, the grind and crunch of coral rock, the stink of sulphur, the clatter of carriage guns, hempen sailcloth, a stiff northerly breeze.

In that one surviving wooden post, Dix saw all this. As for *Endeavour* herself, a Whitby-built collier, stout, steady, in her own rugged way an icon of the Enlightenment, Dix would have done well to check his facts – for the truth was richer than he could ever have imagined.

'Endeavour' is a word that is rarely spoken nowadays. Occasionally a politician will slip it into a speech to inject their sentiments with purpose, but otherwise it seems antiquated and overblown, tinged with a colonial past that Britons, at least, prefer to avoid. But it is a word with a rich history. It travelled to England with the Normans in the years after 1066, having its root in the French verb *devoir* – to do one's duty or to perform an obligation. The meaning of 'endeavour' is even deeper than that. Like the Finnish *sisu*, the Yiddish *chutzpah* or the Polynesian *mana*, it is difficult to catch its full vibrancy in translation. According to the *Oxford English Dictionary*, to endeavour is to 'exert oneself to the uttermost', an endeavour being 'a strenuous attempt or enterprise'.[10] Even that is only a beginning. To endeavour is to quest after something not easily attained, perhaps verging on the impossible. It is something one feels impelled towards or duty-bound to pursue nonetheless. You would not 'endeavour' to learn the guitar but you might speak of space exploration, clean energy or medical technology as 'collective endeavours' to 'make better ... the world in which we live', as Theresa May did in her Brexit Speech of January 2017.[11]

The earliest recorded use of the word came in 1417 when Lord Furnyval wrote of his 'great laboures, travels, and endevoures made by your said Lifetenaunte'. The word increased in popularity over the centuries that followed. Shakespeare made liberal use of it in his plays – 'Every man that means to live well, endeavours to trust to himself' (*Richard III*) – and court scribes would often mention en-devoirs, ende-voyres, endevyrs and indevors in their histories and communiqués. For dramatists and chroniclers the word was so useful because it implied movement, action and progress in a time that was increasingly alive with all of these. Those who endeavoured were engaged in an effort against the odds, fighting forwards to noble ends. The endeavourers were the heroes, the explorers, the commanders, the kings or queens. In the seventeenth century, the word found new resonance in the philosophy of Thomas Hobbes, who chose 'endeavour' as his transla-tion of the Latin *conatus*. *Conatus* was a central, unifying concept for Hobbes, the 'innate inclination of a thing to continue to exist and enhance itself', from the heartbeat of a human, to the motion of air, or the dynamic force which ignites gunpowder. For Hobbes, all matter was instilled with endeavour, a bottled-up, latent energy that was at the beginning and end of motion. 'For what is the *Heart*, but a *Spring*; and the *Nerves*, but so many *Strings*; and the *Joynts*, but so many *Wheeles*, giving motion to the whole *Body*.'[12] Endeavour was the intangible ingredient propelling the human machine into animated life.

By the mid-eighteenth century, the word had come to saturate the language. It is difficult to read a work of consequence from this time without soon finding an endeavour sparkling somewhere in the text. 'Endeavour' appears in the fourth paragraph of Adam Smith's *Wealth of Nations*. It is used nine times in Thomas Paine's short, explosive polemic *Common Sense,* and seven times in Catharine Macaulay's *Address to the People of England, Scotland, and Ireland, on the Present Important Crisis in Affairs.* It features in King George III's 1775 *Proclamation for Suppressing Rebellion and Sedition.* In reply it was used twice in the *Declaration of Independence.* It's right there in the dedication in *Tristram Shandy,* forty-three words in. It's the third word of the second edition of Edmund Burke's *Philosophical Enquiry into the Origin of our Ideas of the Sublime and Beautiful.* When despatched to Bencoolen to observe the Transit of Venus in 1761, Charles Mason and Jeremiah Dixon wrote dutifully to the Royal Society, 'We shall to our best Endeavours make good the trust they have pleas'd to confide in us.'[13]

'Endeavour' was one of Samuel Johnson's pet words, too. He used it four times in his opening *Rambler* column, five times in the *Plan* for his *Dictionary of the English Language*, where his definition for the word spanned the best part of a folio column. The word was so prominent because it chimed with the aspirations of the age. This was a time of enormous, ambitious projects, Johnson's *Dictionary* being a prime example. Setting off in 1746, he aimed to provide a definition, a quotation and an etymology for each word in the English language. Johnson embarked on the task with swaggering conviction. When Dr Adams, his old Oxford friend, called at Gough Square in 1748 he found the harassed Johnson at work on his *Dictionary* with a few of his amanuenses:

ADAMS: This is a great work, sir. How are you to get all the etymologies?
JOHNSON: Why, sir, here is a shelf with Junius, and Skinner, and others; and there is a Welch gentleman who has published a collection of Welch proverbs, who will help me with the Welch.
ADAMS: But, sir, how can you do this in three years?
JOHNSON: Sir, I have no doubt that I can do it in three years.
ADAMS: But the French Academy, which consists of forty members, took forty years to compile their Dictionary.
JOHNSON: Sir, thus it is. This is the proportion. Let me see; forty times forty is sixteen hundred. As three to sixteen hundred, so is the proportion of an Englishman to a Frenchman.[14]

Johnson would go on to complete his *Dictionary*, filled with 42,773 entries, although the job took him nine years instead of the expected three. But Johnson was not an outlier. During these years David Hume would publish his six-volume *History of England*. Other equally vast histories would be written by Tobias Smollett, Catharine Macaulay, William Robertson and Edward Gibbon, who produced his monumental six-volume *The Decline and Fall of the Roman Empire*. Thomas Warton spent several decades on his *History of English Poetry* and in 1766 Thomas Pennant produced the hefty first edition of *British Zoology*, printed in folio on sumptuous imperial paper – a largesse that almost bankrupted him. In France Denis Diderot led the compilation of the enormous *Encyclopédie* of all knowledge, to which Britain would reply in 1769 with the debut edition of the *Encyclopaedia Britannica*.

Each of these could be classed an endeavour: bold projects, undertaken with conviction, often for the benefit of the public and at high speed. 'Lost time is never found again', as Benjamin Franklin's Poor Richard put it. These projects were not confined to the literary world. The same feeling of rushing forward can be found in the radical MP John Wilkes's campaign for Liberty in the 1760s, the beginnings of the Industrial Revolution, the voyages to discover the fabled southern continent, the pan-European attempt to measure the dimensions of the universe and the stirrings of rebellion in America. A zest for endeavour is embedded in Jefferson's luminous phrase 'Life, Liberty and the pursuit of Happiness', and perhaps the endeavouring spirit was never more alive than on that unseasonably mild night of 4–5 March 1776, when General George Washington's army worked tirelessly to fortify Dorchester Heights at Boston. The next morning the British army woke astonished in their encampments to find twenty cannon pointing at them where before there had been none. 'Perhaps there was never so much work done in so short a space of time', muttered General Heath. Another marvelled at the 'expedition equal to that of the genie belonging to Aladdin's wonderful lamp'.[15]

Endeavour, then, was a fundamental component of the Enlightenment approach and it was in the years 1750–80 that the impulse was at its strongest. Mid-century marked a point for population growth and mercantile expansion from which, as Roy Porter has written, 'there was no looking back'.[16] Allied with the fresh impetus provided by the accession of the young, earnest George III in 1760, it provided the base for an endeavouring age more confident and impulsive than the decades it followed and the consolidating years that came after. The culture is not merely demonstrated by the use of the word, or by the literary, social and engineering enterprises but also by people's questing, give-it-a-whirl attitude to everyday life.

The mid-Georgian decades brim with tales of people seduced by what Sir George Lyttelton called 'that destructive fury, the spirit of Play!'[17] Lyttelton was referring to gambling, an addiction for those who had the funds (or not) in the Pall Mall gaming den Boodle's, and the Old Club at White's nearby. 'Extravagance, Luxury & Gaming' might have been flourishing in Westminster, but the same attitude found different expression across the country. Newspapers of the time are littered with reports of lotteries, wagers laid for fights, races and tests of stamina or courage. In 1761 dispatches detailing the progress of the Battle of Belle-Île during the Seven Years War between Britain and France were crowded out by news of a 'great Wager' between the racehorse owner Jennison Shafto and the master fox-hunter Hugo Meynel for 2,000 guineas. Both Meynel and Shafto had engaged jockeys in a contest to ride the unlikely distance of a hundred miles a day 'for twenty-nine days together', on any number of horses 'not exceeding twenty-nine'.*[18]

It was all the better if these feats were carried off with an element of fanfare or éclat. It seems a very 1760s news item, for instance, to find on the front page of the *Newcastle Courant* for 20 February 1768, 'A noble Lord has, we hear, engaged to eat six Pounds of Pork sausages in Half an Hour, for a Wager of 600 Guineas.' John Wilkes, who became one of the era's great popular heroes, understood this need for show all too well. During his insurgent campaigns against the establishment, he was carried through the streets of London on a sedan chair and feasted on roasted turtles in the King's Bench Prison. Once he would pronounce that he wrote his 'best' edition of his subversive paper, the *North Briton*, 'in bed with Betsy Green'.[19]

In awe of Wilkes's high-risk, spontaneous, populist brand of action, Voltaire wrote from the Continent, 'You set me in flames with your courage, and you charm me with your wit.'[20] This is a quote that catches the verve of the time, the impulse to move forwards, the indiscretion and impetuosity, the charged intellectual atmosphere as well as the desire to carry it all off with an air of bravado. In these years 'endeavour' became more than a word. It became a force as people strove for a better way of doing things. Voltaire's image of a person aflame is a defining one. Britain was a country burning with purpose; and from her fire was flung a spark, a spark that travelled further than any had ever done before. It emitted a glowing, scorching light. Only it wasn't a spark at all. It was a ship.

*

---

*   Shafto would prevail, along with his jockey John Woodcock, 'who started
on Newmarket-Heath, the 4th of May, 1761, at one o'clock in the morning,
and finished (having used only fourteen horses) on the first of June,
about six in the evening'.

His Majesty's Bark *Endeavour* was a Whitby-built collier. Round and sturdy rather than sleek and graceful, she had no dashing figurehead on her bows and no gingerbread work – those ornamental carvings that brought life to the sides of men-of-war. As a sailer she made a maximum seven or eight knots with an even wind abaft her beam, about half the rate of a frigate at full tilt. She would behave well at single anchor in the shallows, but otherwise she had no particularly noteworthy sailing qualities. Cook himself preferred the *Resolution*, his second ship, a vessel he sailed twice as far.

Endeavour was a touch smaller than *Resolution*. Her burthen was a middling 368 tons. She measured ninety-seven feet seven inches from stem to stern and was twenty-nine feet three inches across her beam. People often talk of ships as worlds with the captain as their absolute monarch. But if the *Endeavour* was Cook's kingdom, then she was a very modest one. To stride her length from taffrail to catheads would take perhaps twenty seconds. Cook might dash from the starboard to the larboard gunwales in a handful of seconds and a skilled hand might mount the shrouds and haul their way to the tops in less than a minute. The longest journey of all would have been to the bread room in the stinking depths, but even that, navigating the tangle of backstays and bowlines, can hardly have taken long. Yet *Endeavour* cannot be understood by statistics alone. She was at once utterly ordinary and completely extraordinary. There had never been a ship like her in the Royal Navy. With the most commonplace of attributes, she would go on to become the most significant ship in the history of British exploration.

In her short life she visited Pacific islands unknown to European geographers and played a major part in the early histories of New Zealand and Australia, carrying historical figures of true gravitas like James Cook and Joseph Banks. She transported thousands of plants, animals, watercolours, ceremonial and everyday objects back to London. In Charles Darwin's estimation, she helped add a hemisphere to the civilised world. This is *Endeavour*'s context. To hear her name is to conjure, as it did for John Dix, pictures of her riding at anchor in the twinkling waters of Tahiti, rounding the capes of New Zealand's North Island or running alongside the Australian coast towards the infamous accident when she ran aground on the Great Barrier Reef.

But there are other pictures from this bark's life that are less well known: of her drawing alongside the coal staithes on the Tyne, approaching the Port Egmont settlement in the Falkland Islands, or crossing the Sandy Hook bar at the treacherous entrance to New York harbour. She carried not only explorers, botanists and Polynesian priests, but Newcastle coal, colonial settlers and Hessian soldiers. She was there at the Wilkes Riots in London in 1768. She was part of one of the greatest invasion fleets in British history. She was present during the iconic battles at New York in 1776. Her biography roams across the history of the time, binding into a single narrative diverse moments of true historical significance.

Endeavour's memory is treasured by many, but for others she is a toxic symbol. She is the object that made possible the dispossession of the oldest continuous human society and brought disruption to many more. The moment her topgallant masts pierced the horizon marks the end, or at least the beginning of the end, of 'olden times', an age of innocence, and the beginning of a long, painful struggle. During her life, responses to her were equally contrasting. Some saw a Whitby collier or a navy transport. To others she was an exploration vessel, a spy ship, a smuggler, a market stall, a prison, a barricade. Further interpretations are harder to get at. She was a floating island, a mythic bird, a bad water spirit; a sand crab, a nest of goblins. Even today the idea of *Endeavour*'s cruise up Australia's east coast engages the imagination. Neil Murray, the Australian singer-songwriter, has pictured her through the eyes of Aboriginal and Torres Strait Islander peoples, gliding over the water like 'a huge canoe with a tree sprouting clouds'; 'a giant pelican crewed by possums!'; 'A sea-ship filled with little white men.' 'Pale skinned strangers – Ghosts! The walking dead!'[21]

These are the outsider's images. As Greg Dening wrote of the *Bounty*, 'The Ship, for the insider – in all its spaces, in all its relationships, in all its theatre – was always being re-made, was always in process.'[22] Truer words could not have been written of *Endeavour*, whose decks and holds had constantly changing purposes. For a long time I have been drawn to *Endeavour*'s shape-shifting identity, her striking mutability. Once afloat in 1764, she lived three distinct lives, under three distinct names, in three theatres of history. There are many histories of *Endeavour*'s voyage and they usually tell the story through the arc of her circumnavigation (1768–71) or the biographies of Cook or Banks. But I want to follow a different thread: the unfolding existence of the ship herself, the endeavouring culture that clung to her, the 'endeavours' of those she carried. By doing so, I hope to present a familiar story afresh.

Endeavour still has a place in many people's hearts today. More than 250 years after her launch she is remembered and commemorated in the names of bays and straits. The few known artefactual relics – her cannon and ballast – are treasured museum pieces. At Darling Harbour in Sydney there is an ongoing process of historical reanimation on the exquisite HMB *Endeavour* replica, with voyages that see the square-rigged bark glide into the harbour among yachts and cruise liners and beneath skyscrapers and aeroplanes, as out of time as a Roman chariot on a Formula One circuit.

But the original ship retains an elusive character. Barely any contemporary images of her survive. One that does is a line sketch by Sydney Parkinson, the young artist who formed part of Joseph Banks's voyaging party. Parkinson freezes a moment of high drama, perhaps in the Pacific. *Endeavour* lies under assault from a wicked sea that foams all about her. Waves wash and dissolve over her forecastle as she lurches to starboard. But for a taut mizzen staysail, all her masts are bare. There's no hint of human life. It is a contest. Fluid nature pounds the rigid vessel.

And yet here, in this moment of maximum struggle, the ship was already dead. Dead in the sense that dead things comprised her: dead plants, dead wood. Just like the seat you might be sitting on as you read this, or the floorboards under your feet, or the table you eat at, *Endeavour* was a dead object long before Cook set eyes upon her in April or May 1768 at Deptford Dockyard. As he well knew, the ship he saw had not been assembled in a few days in the King's Yard, or even at Whitby before that. Instead *Endeavour* had been infused with a character all of her own by the tough oak timber that accounted for ninety per cent of her body. *Endeavour* was, like many Whitby-built ships, uncommonly strong. This came both from her design and from the timber that made her. This had been the ship's first life, her lived-life, and it had begun long before 1764 when she was launched. Her story, and ours, begins not on the beating oceans of the Pacific, but sometime much earlier, in the subdued light and racing winds of an even-deeper past.

PART ONE

Life

I

Acorns

Endeavour's life starts in an unrecorded time, in a subterranean space several inches deep. There, as summer fades into autumn, an oak tree begins life as an acorn.

An acorn is a capsule, protected by a waxy skin. Inside is stored a genetic code and enough nutrients, tannins and essential oils to sustain it during its fragile early weeks. In September, it begins to grow, slowly, until after a fortnight its shell bursts open. For the first time, the acorn's insides can be seen. The ochre hue of the kernel contrasts sharply with the mahogany-brown of the shell, which cracks under the strain. A root dives downward, a tiny probe, seeking water and nutrients. By November, as the earth above gets a coating of frost, the husk of its shell has been pushed clear. In its place are the earliest signs of a stem, which ventures up, seeking light.

After four months the acorn's shell is shattered and discarded and gone. The stem is now the central feature of the tiny plant. It continues to rise. At six months, as the April sun begins to strengthen, it breaks through the soil. It seems other-worldly, blanched, ethereal, like a skeletal arm in a clichéd horror film reaching from the grave. Within days this pallor subsides and a vibrant, joyous green over-spreads it. The acorn of the previous autumn is gone. In its place is a seedling oak, an oakling, two inches tall, capped with a pair of helicopter leaves that tilt and turn and thrill to the sun. The plant has no longer to rely on its inbuilt store of energy. Now it photosynthesises in the sunshine, the newest addition to a woodland floor, hidden among brambles, bluebells and wood anemone. More leaves appear and already for those who study it closest they display their familiar, lobed form. As summer progresses these leaves emit a golden glow. Soon the oakling stands out among the flowers, exposed to rabbits, voles, browsing cattle or deer, but otherwise filled with promise for the future.

No one can say for certain just where the oaks that made *Endeavour* grew. Thomas Fishburn, the Whitby shipwright in whose yard she was built in 1764, left no records. Perhaps they have been lost or destroyed. Perhaps they did not exist to begin with.

Some might say that the trees grew in the snow-carpeted forests of central Poland. Cut with axes in the bitter continental winter, the timber would be floated down the Vistula to Danzig where it would be sold and loaded into the holds of merchantmen bound for Britain. Plying the old sea paths, those once sailed by the portly cogs of the Hanseatic League, the merchantmen would cross the Baltic, thread through the strait that separated Denmark from Sweden before entering the subdued mass of water called the German Ocean that conducted them to England's eastern shore.

Roger Fisher, a shipwright from Liverpool, voiced a different theory. In 1763 he wrote that the eastern shipbuilding ports of 'North Yarmouth, Hull, Scarborough, Stocton, Whitby, Sunderland, Newcastle, and the North coast of Scotland' sourced their oak chiefly from the fertile lowlands that bordered the rivers Trent and Humber.[1] Writing at the moment *Endeavour*'s oak would have been reaching the Whitby yards, Fisher's opinion cannot be discarded. But, equally, it seems more flimsy the more that it is examined. Fisher was a west-coast man. He confessed to having little knowledge of the ways of the eastern ports. All that he had gathered had come second- or third-hand.

Fisher was writing to a different purpose, too. His book on British oak, *Heart of Oak: the British Bulwark*, was published in 1763, a loaded year in history. This was the year the Treaty of Paris concluded the Seven Years War. During this conflict England's woodlands had suffered violent incursions from foresters, determined to supply the growing navy. Like so many before him, Fisher had been left cold by the destruction. He saw it everywhere. The forests, woods, hursts and chases of Old England were vanishing and he filled his *Heart of Oak* with evidence of this. Contacts in the timber trade had told him, 'fifteen parts out of twenty' of England's woodlands had been 'exhausted within these fifty years'.[2] The axe had been thrown indis-criminately. In the river valleys and sunny southern fields, in Wales and the ancient Midland forests, the story was the same.

To Fisher's mind the country stood as a pivot between the virtuous homespun past and a bleak treeless future. To underscore his theme Fisher evoked a vision of yesteryear. He pictured a landowner, at one with nature, 'a little cloyed with enjoyment', and wishing 'to retire from business, or for the sake of meditation', taking a saunter in his spacious woodlands. This was the Horatian ideal, liberty from the cares and distractions of the city. Using the present tense to enhance the sense of loss, Fisher described how:

> The variety of the scene revives his drooping spirits. On the branch of a full topt oak, at a small distance, the blackbird and thrush warble forth their notes, and, as it were, bless their benefactor. A little farther, the turtle dove, having lost his mate, sends forth his mournful plaint, till, by means of echo from a neighbouring wood, passing through the silent air, the happy pair are again united. Variety of changes draw on the pleasing hour amongst the massy bodies of the full-grown oaks and thriving plants. The prospect of his country's good warms his heart.[3]

Anticipating Rachel Carson's *Silent Spring* by two centuries, Roger Fisher was depicting the same vision of a paradise lost. Recent scholarship has indicated, though, that the oak problem was not as grave as he believed. Fisher may well have suffered a form of environmental panic, half seen, half felt, a type that would become increasingly prevalent in times ahead. In the 1760s attitudes like his masked a historical truth. In the mid-eighteenth century, as Thomas Fishburn went searching for faithful timber, there might not have been an abundance of oak – but there was still plenty left.

Ancient, twisted, vast, with their goliath limbs outstretched, almost every English parish had its own loved oak, a timeless presence on the landscape. When the clergyman and naturalist Gilbert White started to document the natural history of Selborne in Hampshire in the 1760s, he set out with a description of the village oak. He wrote mournfully of a 'venerable' tree that had stood in the centre of Selborne on a green by the church. The oak had a 'short squat body, and huge horizontal arms extending almost to the extremity of the area'. For centuries it had been 'the delight of old and young'. Parishioners had surrounded it with stone steps, and had erected seats around it so that it had become 'a place of much resort in summer evenings'. The village elders had made it their custom to congregate at the Selborne oak 'in grave debate', while the young parishioners 'frolicked and danced before them'.[4]

A similar story came from White's contemporary, Reverend Sir John Cullum, who included a description of the parish oak in the opening paragraph of his *History and Antiquities of Hawsted, and Hardwick* (1784). Cullum wrote of 'a majestic tree' named the Gospel Oak that 'stood on an eminence, and commanded an extensive prospect'. On his annual 'perambulations' Cullum and his congregation would pause in the shade of the tree, and 'surveying a considerable extent of a fruitful and well-cultivated country, repeat some prayers proper for the occasion'.[5] This image of the worshipful parishioners under the village oak is a vivid one, and Cullum was only doing what generations had done before him. A millennium before, the Anglo-Saxons had been buried in hollowed-out trunks of oak. People had pinned oak leaves to their jackets as signs of fealty and carried acorns in their pockets for luck.

If people recognised the oak's potency as a symbol, they venerated the tree equally for its strength. No tree could compete. A favourite classical tale told of Milo of Croton in ancient Greece. 'Renowned in history for his prodigious strength', explained a book in the 1760s, Milo was six times victor at the Olympic Games, 'he is said to have carried on his shoulders the whole length of a stadium an ox four years old; to have killed it with a single blow of his fist; and to have eaten the whole carcass in one day'.[6] The story was subverted by Milo's demise. Having found an old oak, to flaunt his strength Milo had tried to rip it open with his hands. As he grasped the tree, it closed around him. In an instant the oak had transformed Greece's strongest man into its most tragic victim. Unable to free himself, a pack of wolves had emerged, tearing Milo to pieces.

People did not need to know Milo's story to recognise the oak's strength. They only had to look around them, to the great manor houses and cathedrals that adorned the landscape, to the towers and bridges and a hundred everyday objects from mill wheels to casks, cudgels, daggers and poles. To look at the parish oak as Cullum and White did during these years, was to stir associations of quiet, brooding might. Both intrigued by nature, the clergymen may have realised that an oak derives its strength from its shape. A mature specimen can be three times as wide as it is tall. On a January day when the tree is stripped of its leaves you can absorb this. There it stands, serpentine limbs outstretched. When winds whip through these branches they sway and strain like levers, gathering up elemental energy. The forces are channelled backwards, from the budding tips, to the smallest branches and back along the boughs to the trunk. The motion creates massive stress forces. When 60 mph winds gust against the tree, it is equivalent to a weight of 220 tons. Oaks, like all nature, seek equilibrium. They respond by fortifying their wood and stiffening their fibres.

This is what the oaks would have done at Hawstead and Selborne, as would the other cherished English oaks: the Darley Oak in Cornwall, the Bowthorpe Oak in Lincolnshire or the Major Oak in Sherwood Forest. In a society changing fast, these oak trees provided powerful links with the past. They were the perpetual survivors, the time-hallowed, stoic relics of a medieval age. But these were not the trees that had made the country great. Those that had were the young oaks, aged between 50–150 years old, felled in a continuous harvest to build anything that had to last and needed to be strong. As the Cambridge ecologist Oliver Rackham later put it, this left England a place 'of young or youngish trees, like a human population with compulsory euthanasia at age thirty'.[7]

It has been estimated that 200 mature oak trees were used in the construction of *Endeavour*, providing the raw materials for the great structural timbers inside her hull: her floors, futtocks and knees, all of her outer planking and most of her inner embellishments. In *Heart of Oak*, Roger Fisher may not provide a reliable location for the source of the *Endeavour* oaks, but he does offer a formula to suggest their age at the time they were felled. 'It is generally taken for granted, that an oak tree is at least one hundred years before it comes to its perfection', he writes, 'continues in that position one hundred years more, and gradually decays another hundred.'[8] This rule of thumb would subsequently be sharpened by Robert Greenhalgh Albion in his *Forests and Sea Power* (1926):

The time for felling the great oaks was one of the chief problems of the timber grower. There was a 'psychological moment' for cutting, when the tree would yield a greater profit than at any other time. Oaks, it will be remembered, grow very slowly. The period of maturity is reached between the ages of eighty and a hundred and twenty years, when the tree attains a diameter of fifteen or eighteen inches. Up to that time it was not profitable to cut oaks for ship timber because of the additional value of a large-sized tree. Beyond that period of maturity, the risk of decay was great.[9]

This dislocates *Endeavour*'s story at its very beginning. It jolts the story from mercantile Britannia of 1764 to the more religiously fervent age of a century earlier: the reinvigorated England of Charles II, the Merrie Monarch, and his louche, extravagant Restoration court.

Always beloved by the English, at no time in the nation's history were oaks so idolised. Everyone knew the story of Charles II's – then Charles Stuart's – hair's breadth escape from the Parliamentarians following the Battle of Worcester in 1651. Chased from the battlefield, Charles concealed himself in the branches of an oak in the grounds of Boscobel House on the border between Shropshire and Staffordshire. The day passed in suspense as Oliver Cromwell's soldiers prowled beneath. At Charles's bleakest moment the oak lent a providential hand. When restored as king in 1660, Charles exploited the story to its maximum. He appointed 29 May, the date of his return to London in 1660, as a national day of celebration, Oak Apple Day. Great processions marched through the City of London, the people dressed in costume as oak trees, representing 'a greate Wood, with the royal Oake, & historie of his Majesties miraculous escape at *Bosco-bell* &c'.[10] In the years that followed the towns across England filled with Royal Oak taverns, where people could drink Burton ale, eat Cheshire cheese, damn the French and feel more English than anywhere else.

It's a striking thought, the idea of the *Endeavour*'s acorns germinating at the time that oak trees were being elevated as patriotic, national symbols. And if the 1660s brought a general celebration of all oak trees, it equally saw the beginning of modern attempts to scientifically understand what it was that made them so special. This movement was led by John Evelyn, the clever, inquisitive, founding fellow of the Royal Society. Today Evelyn is chiefly remembered for his diary – the cold-blooded twin to the warm-blooded diary kept by Samuel Pepys – but in the 1660s his reputation came from the book that would make his name: *Sylva, or a Discourse of Forest Trees* (1664).

Sylva was a fresh and eloquent blend of classical thought, wood-manship, folklore and careful observation. When gathering the materials for *Sylva* Evelyn drew on his own personal knowledge and on the collective wisdom of a network of philosophically inclined correspondents. His ambition was to create a survey of English trees, emphasising utility, explaining the characteristics of various species and demonstrating how they could be raised and turned to practical advantage. Evelyn began, naturally, with the oak. He toyed with several scientific names for the tree. One was *Robur* from the Latin, signifying strength. Next was a second Latin term, *Quercus*. Whichever was best, Evelyn divided British oaks into a few distinctive 'kinds'. There was *Quercus sylvestris*, with its 'hard, black grain, bearing a smaller *Acorn*'. Evelyn glided over a type called *Cerris*, 'goodly to look on, but for little else'. Most interesting, he thought, was the *Quercus urbana*, which 'grows more up-right, and being clean, and lighter is fittest for *Timber*'.[11]

Wanting to encourage the growing of oaks, Evelyn set out the space required for the tree to grow or 'amplifie'; ideal conditions for planting, raising and transplanting; and the importance of surrounding young trees with thorns or stakes to defend them from cattle or protect from the 'concussions of the *Winds*'. How they grew, he advised, very much depended on their setting. He warned that 'the *Air* be as much the *Mother* or *Nurse*, as *Water* and *Earth*', and so advised growers to be wary of 'unkindness' of various '*Aspects*' like the windy brow of a hill. Trees grew 'more kindly on the *south* side of an *Hill*, than those which are expos'd to the *North*, with an hard, dark, rougher, and more mossie *Integument*'.[12] But sown with foresight and left with patience, an oak tree with its arms outstretched in welcome would one day become a 'ravishing' sight.

Evelyn's chapter 'Of the Oak' preceded others on elm, beech, ash, chestnut, and forty or so other species. Combined with other sections on soils, seeds, seminaries and infirmities, *Sylva* was published in 1664, exactly a century before *Endeavour*'s launch. It was the first book produced under the aegis of the new Royal Society of London for Improving Natural Knowledge. The book tapped into the mood of the times, capitalising on the vogue for oaks and blending it with a patriotic cause – the regeneration of English woodlands – after the destructive Civil War. Such was the anticipation, 700 private citizens subscribed, and within two years more than 1,000 copies of the first impression had been '*Bought up, and dispersed*', which, Evelyn immodestly noted in the preface to the second edition, *'is a very extraordinary thing in* Volumes *of this bulk'*.[13]

Sylva would have many legacies. It provided a model for a learned, empirical work of popular science with a practical, patriotic edge. Furthermore it demonstrated that an oak tree was as susceptible to its environment as any other living being. This led, inevitably, to the notion of the 'ideal' oak. That England was so densely stocked with oaks had long been regarded as incontrovertible proof of God's providential goodness to English people. But it went beyond that. Something existed in the climate that invested the tree with unrivalled qualities. 'Our *English* oak is infinitely preferable to the *French*', Evelyn had affirmed, 'which is nothing so *usefull*, nor comparably so *strong* … wanting that native *spring* and *toughness*, which our *English* Oak is indu'd withall'.[14] For centuries such silvicultural xenophobia would persist. 'Privateer Captains are more cautious than to venture their Egg shells Sides against our *English Oak*', announced one book during the Seven Years War in the 1750s.[15]

But where were the finest trees of all? In *Sylva* Evelyn had made his preferences clear. 'If I were to make choice of the place, or the Tree', he had asserted, 'it should be such as grows in the best Cow-Pasture, or up-land Meadow, where the mould is rich and sweet (Suffolk affords an admirable instance).' Here, perhaps, was the germ of a bias that would take hold in the navy. For Stuart and Georgian naval administrators, it became an article of faith that a golden belt of the trees stretched across southern England, commencing in the Forest of Dean, then progressing east across Gloucestershire, Somersetshire, Hampshire and Kent, with the finest specimens of all being 'good, sound Sussex oak'.[16]

'To an English shipwright', Robert Greenhalgh Albion would affirm, 'there was no wood in the world superior to Sussex oak', and along with this favouritism tagged a prejudice. Naval contracts not only specified southern oak, but they 'constantly discriminated against the oak of Yorkshire and other counties of the north'. In the northern counties the *Quercus* genus was believed to be ruined by the heavy soils that strangled the oaks rather than nourishing them. But in Yorkshire, very few agreed.

In 1782, a land surveyor called William Marshall returned to his native Yorkshire to begin an agricultural survey of the county. Marshall had already authored two dense reports, *Minutes of Agriculture* and *Experiments and Observations on Agriculture and Weather*. These were productions of a man with a sharp eye and an independent mind. Marshall had lately studied rural Norfolk and in years to come he would extend his scheme into the Midlands, but in 1782 he was happy to be at home in Yorkshire, 'as my early youth was spent among it; and my acquaintances with its present practitioners of course extensive.'

Marshall's survey would expand into a five-year project, with him receiving 'an influx of fresh information I did not expect'. It eventually led to his *Rural Economy of Yorkshire* (1788), which began with typical regional conviction:

> YORKSHIRE has always been spoken of as the first Province of these kingdoms. If we consider its superior magnitude; the variety and strength of its natural features; the fertility of its soils; and the industry of its inhabitants; the abundance and copiousness of its rivers; the richness of the views on their banks; and the wildness of those which are found among its mountains; – it is well entitled to pre-eminence.[17]

It was a trenchant opening, but perhaps a justified one. Yorkshire – subdivided into its various ridings – was England's largest county. Anyone who climbed the tower of York Minster and turned 360 degrees could appreciate the diversity Marshall alluded to. To the east of York, the Wolds, chalk downlands, swelled in long elegant curves all the way to the coast at Flamborough Head. To the south and west were fertile grassy plains, while northward lay the Vale of York. 'The fens at its base, and a healthy plain', wrote Marshall, 'If we estimate the Vale of York by the number and copiousness of its rivers, and by the richness of its marginal banks, it would perhaps be difficult, in any country, to equal it.'[18]

But not all the county was so inviting. In the north-eastern corner, kennelled away beyond the luxuriant lowlands, lay the moors. A foreboding landscape, most avoided these moorlands unless they had an unavoidable reason to cross them. William Camden, the Elizabethan topographer, had written of burnished hills animated solely by a few 'wandering beakes [streams] and violent swift brookes, which challenge the vallies everywhere as their owne to passe through no memorable thing'.[19] Wolves were still rumoured to skulk in the hollows and throughout winter they were treacherous, even for locals. Eight years before Marshall began his survey, a man called Nicholas Harker had been caught in a blizzard on the moorland paths outside Scarborough. Days had passed before Harker and his wife had been dug, stiff as lead, from the gullies.

Marshall walked these same paths and visited Whitby, where Harker had worked as a roper before his death. Whitby stood at the end of the moors. It was a curious place. Once just a small fishing port, in the seventeenth century it had undergone a brisk period of growth fuelled by the start of alum mining. Loads of the alum were dug out of the surrounding cliffs, burnt in pits and boiled to create a crystal used to dye wool. In the seventeenth century a fleet of merchant ships had developed to ferry the alum crystals to outside markets, even as far as London, 'whither nobody belonging to Whitby before that time had ever gone without first making their wills'.[20] From this beginning, by the time Marshall was at work in the 1780s, 'the sea-ports of Whitby' and neighbouring Scarborough had become renowned 'as nurseries of hardy seamen', to which 'the nation at large owe much'.[21]

The hardiness of Whitby's sailors was matched by the durability of its ships. In merchant shipping the shorthand 'Whitby-built' had become a stamp of quality. There was a toughness to them that came from some element in their construction. While the Royal Navy were pleased to get thirty years' service for one of their vessels, Whitby merchantmen or colliers would last twice or three times as long. A collier called *William and Jane* launched in 1717 had still been afloat in the 1780s when Marshall was compiling his research. Another, *The Sea Adventure*, built in 1724, would remain in service until 1810 when she was eventually wrecked on the Lincolnshire coast. Nor 'did she go to pieces even at the last, but was carried up by the violence of the wind and of the flood tide into the midst of a field, where she was left high and dry, a good way from the sea'.[22] Another called the *Happy Return* would survive a century, while the whaling vessel *Volunteer* would spend seventy-five years plying the northern seas, making fifty-four voyages to the Greenland fisheries.

Marshall knew that Whitby's shipwrights had long made use of local oak. Years before, Whitby's timber had come from a place four miles away called Egton, a derivative of 'Ochetun', 'so called from the oak trees that surrounded it'.[23] But as time passed and supplies dwindled, the shipwrights had begun to look further afield. A bill of sale from 1707 shows one Whitby shipwright buying 239 oak trees from a location near York for £850 and ten guinea pieces of gold. This transaction was typical of the early trade which involved bargains directly between shipbuilders and landowners. As the 1700s wore on this process evolved to include specialist wood-buyers, middlemen who scoured the countryside, negotiated and sold the choicest pieces direct at the port at prices up to three guineas a ton. This was the system Marshall found in operation in the 1780s. The agents supplied the principal markets, the ports of Whitby and Scarborough, 'who take off the larger timber'.[24]

Marshall learned that the primary source of timber was the Vale of Pickering, which lay at the opposite side of the moors to Whitby. He declared this 'a singular passage of country'. 'Nature, perhaps,' he wrote, 'never was so near forming a lake without finishing the design.' As an example of the extreme flatness of the vale, he described the 'sluggard pace' of its rivers. One, the Rye, took 'four or five days in passing from Helmsley to Malton', a distance of fourteen miles, while the Derwent was 'not less than a week' covering the fifteen miles from Ayton to Malton. These rivers flowed over land once covered by the Royal Forest of Pickering, a deciduous woodland where in ancient times kings had hunted stags and boars. By the eighteenth century the forest had vanished as an entity, but distinct 'oak, ash and elm' woods survived, with many thriving in the valleys. 'Were the extensive woodlands which these vallies contain scattered on the bottom of the surrounding hills', Marshall contended, 'the Vale of Pickering would be a passage of country as singular in point of beauty as it is in natural situation.'[25]

Twenty miles of moorland separated Whitby from the Vale. This had never been an easy distance to cross. But in 1759 a subscription had been collected by Whitby's merchants and 'a very good turnpike-way' had been built. It ran direct from the town, across the moorlands to the northern opening of the Vale at Dalby.[26] The turnpike had been in operation by 1763, at about the time a sustained period of felling had commenced. An advert in the *Newcastle Courant* on 15 August 1767 lays bare the scale of this: 3,543 oaks were advertised in a single lot 'mostly fit for ship Timber', just '17 miles from Whitby'. Though none of these oaks could possibly have been used in *Endeavour* – she was at sea by then – the sheer availability of timber is significant. In the mid-1760s there was enough oak timber in Whitby's neighbourhood to build Henry VIII's flagship *Mary Rose* twice over, or fifteen of Fishburn's colliers.

Another advert in the *Newcastle Courant* on 10 April 1762 offered oak from the west side of the moors:

To be SOLD
Standing and growing in Colemandale, in the Parish of Guisborough, in Cleveland, Yorkshire;

A Parcel of fine OAK WOOD, marked and numbered, consisting of upwards of 500 Oak Trees, all full grown, fit for Ship Timber for Vessels of the largest size; amongst which are many large CROOKS, and other choice and valuable TIMBER.[27]

This is just one of a number of adverts that appeared of this kind. But this lingers in the memory for its timeliness. It was published two years before *Endeavour*'s launch.

John Tuke was the second agricultural surveyor to investigate the North Riding of Yorkshire immediately after Marshall in the 1790s. Tuke agreed with Marshall's assessment of the Vale of Pickering – an area he termed 'Ryedale' – as the chief source of timber for the shipbuilders. He noticed an unusual richness on the fringes of the moors, where black peaty soils gave out to a red clay or hazel loam. In these borderlands there was a richness in the earth, a quality Tuke supposed was 'evidently washed down by the floods of many former ages, from the higher country'. It made a soil bed of 'extraordinary fertility'.[28] Though the climate was hard, this soil was rich enough to support mature deciduous trees, oaks, elms, ash and broad-leaved or witch elm. They grew slowly. Their roots clutched the rocks. The annual rings of mature oaks were not spaced in the regular half-inch intervals; instead they clustered tight.

The oaks that grew in this landscape were dyed with a northern character – swart, savage, permanent – that came from the air as much as the earth. The weather in the North Riding was 'extremely cold and bleak' for as much as nine months of the year, wrote Tuke, with the summer season at least three weeks behind that of the south. Throughout winter snow stood yards deep, lit by a pale sun which slanted low over the slopes. Only the strongest trees could survive in this environment, and throughout the seventeenth and early eighteenth centuries, the winters were as hard as ever. The years 1650–1800 comprise the major part of what some climatologists now call the

Little Ice Age, a time of frost fairs on the River Thames that lasted for weeks at a stretch. The cold was if anything magnified in Yorkshire, with snows that in years like 1698 endured from December until April.

Whatever the climate, the North Riding was subject to the vicious northerly air that blew all the way from the Shetland Islands without interruption. Marshall, the surveyor, wrote of the 'cold, pinching winds', and 'smart frosts'.[29] Between October and February, gales were feared. Sheets of livid cloud would slide in from the north, swallowing the moorlands. Sometimes north-easterly storms arrived from Scandinavia to terrifying effect. The most violent came on 20 November, 1740. So extreme were the consequences, reports made it as far as the Scottish newspapers:

> By the late Storm the Town of Whitby in Yorkshire has suffered vastly: Many of their Ships of 500 Tuns coming from Southwark in Ballast, were obliged to ly up in sight of the Harbour, and being suddenly caught, some foundered at Sea, others dash'd to pieces on the Rocks, and many run on Shore; the Damage already known amounts to 40,000 l. But the Deaths of many expert Commanders and stout Sailors renders this a National Loss, since Whitby has now long employed 200 large Ships in the Coal Trade, and was a Nursery of Seamen. The whole Town is in Mourning; of 1,200 Families scarce one but has suffered in Relations or Fortunes, and too many in both.[30]

Another gale hit in April 1743. Then one more in January 1752. While reportage remained fixed on the human suffering in the towns, these storms shaped the landscape behind too. And, as many people suffered in the storm, oaks, oddly enough, gained something from this weather. The classical thinkers had speculated about this. Didymus had written how oaks 'being continually *weather-beaten* they become hardier and tougher' – a notion that had appealed to Seneca too: '*Wood* most expos'd to the *Winds* to be the most *strong* and *solid*.' This was a question Francis Bacon had turned over in the seventeenth century. Where Evelyn had favoured warmth over the wet and cold, Bacon had preferred 'that which grows in the *moister* grounds for *Ship timber*, as the most *tough*, and less subject to *rift*'.[31]

This was a truth the shipwrights of Whitby had doubtless absorbed too. Quite the opposite of the navy's view, Yorkshire oak was not inferior, rather it was dependable, strong and versatile. These qualities were also noticed by the surveyor Tuke. His verdict was unequivocal:

> The oak timber grown in great part of this Riding, though not large, is most excellent; produced as it chiefly is, upon sound and often rocky ground, its growth is very slow, which renders it extremely hard and durable; and probably to the use of much of it the ship-builders of Whitby owe their riches, and the ships they build their great celebrity.[32]

Tuke does not mention any 'celebrity' ship by name. But in 1794 when he was writing, there can only have been a few he had in mind. Of those *Endeavour* is most prominent. Four years earlier the artist Thomas Luny had travelled to Whitby to research a historically themed seascape, *The Bark 'Earl of Pembroke', Later 'Endeavour', Leaving Whitby Harbour in 1768*. No other ship in Whitby attained the pre-eminence of being painted by a professional artist for an exhibition at the Royal Academy in Piccadilly.

The Yorkshire landscape provided the Whitby shipwrights with one further advantage. It produced what was known as compass timber. Compass timber came from oaks that did not belong to a particular plantation or wood. These trees lived solitary existences on the side of highways, in hedgerows or on the borders of fields. Shipwrights and foresters recognised the crucial importance of compass timber in the making of ships, and they knew that these trees were most often found near heaths and on moorland.

These oaks grew as best they could, but their existences were destined to be fraught. Exposed to the atmospheric tumults of the open countryside, and the destructive behaviour of cattle and deer that would repeatedly maul their tops, they grew disfigured. Their limbs slanted, jutting in baffling directions. They grew slowly, and responded to the stresses they were forced to bear by reinforcing areas of their wood. To shipwrights these were a prize. In the puzzle of construction they offered ready-made pieces, especially suited to fit specialised sections of a ship's hull. Bent trunks formed catheads and futtocks. Oaks that forked in a Y near the ground made transom knees. Those whose trunks swayed one way and then another in an S were incorporated as floor pieces. No matter the skill of a carpenter, the strength of a single piece of compass timber would always outstrip that of several fastened together. As Tuke the surveyor recorded, Yorkshire was filled with a 'considerable quantity of timber in the hedge-rows, particularly in those of the Vale of York, the Howardian Hills and Ryedale'. And the advert in the *Newcastle Courant* in 1762 specifically mentioned 'many large Crooks, and other choice and valuable Timber'.

The Yorkshire moorlands and vales were a natural factory for the Whitby shipwrights, forging materials unique to their corner of the country. Tuke and Marshall knew this. To look at a tree was not just to study its form and colours. It was also to consider its past. The more a tree is forced to withstand, the stronger it becomes, which is why withered oaks standing in isolated ground survive gale after gale for a thousand years, while young, supple, apparently healthy other examples do not. In the hundred years an oak takes to mature, it becomes an archive or repository for everything it encounters, an archive not only captured in annual rings, but in zones of massive tensile and bending strength.

Again, no one can say for certain just where the oaks that made *Endeavour* grew. Materials were sourced as opportunities arose, to meet specific needs. But it can be said that in the early 1760s there was plenty of local oak in Whitby's neighbourhood for Thomas Fishburn to buy if he wished. Spring was the felling season in Yorkshire. Foresters would run their eyes over the shape of a tree. Was it straight and true, or gnarled and bent? They might run the palm of their hand over the bark or tap it with a hammer. Anything to divine the quality of the wood inside. For as Evelyn scolded in *Sylva*, 'There is not in *nature* a thing more obnoxious to deceit, then [*sic*] the buying of Trees *standing*, upon the reputation of their *Appearance* to the *eye* ... so various are their *hidden*, and conceal'd *Infirmities*, till they be *fell'd*, and *sawn* out ... A *Timber*-tree is a *Merchant Adventurer*, you shall never know what he is *worth*, till he be *dead*.'[33]

Really there was only one way for a forester to test the quality of a tree. Half an hour with an axe and soon enough the blemishes or the brilliance of the timber was clear.

Oaks never do anything quickly. Life ebbs out of them just as it ebbs in. But few things have afterlives like oak trees. Nearby at Whitby, in the early months of 1764, the oak timber seasoning in Thomas Fishburn's yard was turned to a new purpose. A new life was poised to begin.

PART TWO

Trade

2

Enigmas

The town of Whitby stands at the mouth of the River Esk on the north-eastern corner of the Yorkshire coast. Bordered by the moors to the south and west and the North Sea to the north and east, for centuries Whitby had existed like an island community, a secluded outpost from the society of York or markets at Pickering. But for the sanctuary of its inner harbour, Whitby may have had few visitors at all. Yet here the Esk, a cold salmon river, wound its way off the heights and broadened as it threaded between two steep cliffs to meet the sea. In the shallows beyond, fishermen had worked since ancient times, casting for cod, mackerel or haddock. Over the centuries Whitby had become known as a haven on a dangerous coastline.

In 1764 it was half a century since Whitby's harbour piers had been extended. Now they stretched north into the sea, the west pier longer by a third than the east so they took the form of a crab's claw. It was out of the bleak northern horizon, a millennia before, Norsemen had come. Townsfolk would have watched from Whitby's Saxon monastery on the east cliff: sleek, sharp-prowed longships, dragonheads on their bows, forty or fifty oars swinging as one, cutting white holes in the slate-grey water. The Norsemen had left their mark. Their legacy survived a thousand years on in the flinty local character and a dialect marked with hard consonants. A beck was a stream. A hagg was a sloping parcel of woodland. A carr was marshy ground, dangerous underfoot. Ghauts – pronounced 'goats' – described the alleys that cut between Whitby's houses, diving to the shore. Whitby folk dug with a mattock, but graved with a spade. A donnaught was an idler who skulked by the piers. Food was either plentiful or scarce. 'A Scarborough warning' meant no warning at all, but 'a sudden surprise'.[1]

There was an other-worldliness about Whitby. On hallowed earth on the east cliff stood the crumbling walls of its monastery. Long ago Benedictine monks had prayed here seven times a day, between cockcrow and vespers, and Cædmon the first English poet had been blessed with the gift of song. Beneath, the foot of the east cliff had long been a favourite site for hunting ammonites, known as 'sea snakes' by locals. John Leland, Henry VIII's antiquary, had heard of them and possibly collected some himself. 'It is a wonderful thing to see the Serpents', he wrote, 'twisted into circles, and by the mercy of heaven, or as the monks relate by the prayers of St Hilda, converted into stone.'[2]

This tale, that St Hilda – the monastery's founding abbess – had turned serpents into stone, was a well-rooted one. But it did not account for the many other curiosities to have been pulled from the scaur or scarr, the local name for the rocky foreshore. In about 1710 the petrified arm of a man had been dug up, 'in which all the bones and joints belonging to the hand and arm were very visible'.[3] In 1743, an entire petrified human skeleton was unearthed. Then in 1758, one of the town's sailing masters, William Chapman, felt impelled to write to the Royal Society with the news that the bones of an 'Allegator' had been chanced upon. The remains – ten feet in length – had been entombed in the black, flaky rock. They were, Chapman observed, certainly those 'of the lizard kind'.[4]

This mysterious world, revealing itself by degrees, fascinated some. Lionel Charlton, a schoolmaster in the town, was among those who felt a latency in Whitby. The crocodile was 'an animal that was never known in our seas', he wrote, baffled. Charlton – a self-styled 'philomath', or lover of learning – knew science offered no settled answer. Some, Charlton later recorded, believed the petrified remains in the scaur were produced by a fermentation in the alum shale that abounded on the coast. Others considered them 'antediluvian animals' imprisoned in the earth's crust at the Flood. Charlton remained unconvinced by either explanation. Hearing several pieces of petrified wood had been found, he examined them himself. 'These are not to be distinguished by the eye from real wood', he wrote, 'and that species of wood generally appears to be oak. In some of it I have observed, very distinctly, the bark, the inner rind, the fibres, the grain, the knots, and every thing else pertaining to oak timber.'[5] Just how the oak had come to be there, old and hard and cold as stone, Charlton could not say. But in touching the objects he felt a divine force. Looking at the neat strata of the cliffs, seeing 'the most exact symmetry and order', he concluded, 'the whole fabric has in it the marks and characteristics of an Almighty Architect where nothing has undergone any considerable change since its first creation'.[6]

At the beginning of 1764 Charlton was forty-four years old. He had lived in Whitby for sixteen years, supporting himself with jobs as a land surveyor and schoolmaster. But he retained the eye and the status of an outsider. He had been born further north, near the hamlet of Hesleyside on the banks of the River Tyne, into an old Northumbrian family. The Charltons had inhabited their land since the reign of Edward IV and recently a Charlton had served as High Sheriff of Northumberland. After a grammar school education he travelled to Edinburgh where he enrolled at the university for several terms' tuition. He soon crossed the border to England, settling at Whitby in 1748, a man of twenty-eight. Coming from the north, avoiding the moorland tracks, the romantic picture has Charlton arriving by water, climbing timorously from a collier into the rolling belly of a harbour boat. Soon he would step ashore and enter a place he grew to love.

Among the fishwives, the footloose apprentices and well-heeled merchants, Charlton stood out in Whitby. He brought 'the guttural accent, and pronunciation of his native country' to the town with him.[7] The sight of him shambling through the streets around the market square was memorable. One of his hands was lame, 'shrunk up', wrote a resident, 'a circumstance which probably induced his parents to procure him a classical education'. One of Charlton's legs, too, was 'halting', giving him a sloping, heaving gait.[8] Soon after arriving, Charlton leased a premises called the Toll-booth or 'Town's House' from the Lord of the Manor, and established a day school. He advertised himself as a 'Teacher of Mathematics', and the early pupils at the Toll-booth school would long remember the presence of their dominant master at the head of the class. He 'had a harsh and withered countenance, and was (at that time) of a severe disposition as a pedagogue', wrote one.[9] A hint, perhaps, of Charlton's asperity is to be found in a poem written later by another of his pupils:

> No longer trudge with shining face to school,
> There to be call'd a blockhead, and a fool;
> The formidable birch no longer dread,
> That oft has threatened this devoted head.[10]

Hostilities between Charlton and his pupils travelled in both directions. His 'peculiarities', one of them later confessed, 'offered a
constant fund' to their satirical talents. And if the strict, disfigured,
chiding schoolmaster was to be compared with anyone, then perhaps
his contemporary Samuel Johnson – who established an academy at
Edial in Staffordshire a decade earlier – would be a better choice.
Johnson, who like Charlton mellowed as he aged, would respond
memorably to the question of 'how' he had come to such an 'accurate
a knowledge of Latin'. 'My master whipt me very well. Without that,
sir, I should have done nothing', he shot back.[11]

Charlton would prove more successful than Johnson as a schoolmaster. In the 1750s he established himself at the Toll-booth as not
merely the geographical centre of the port but also its lucent, intellectual heart. His surveying work is also significant. With it he brought
to Whitby a fashion for mapmaking that was spreading throughout
the Western world (across the Atlantic George Washington was
striking out as a land surveyor at this time). One such survey survives
today. *An exact Plan and Survey of a Farm of Land lying in the Cars near
Ruswarp belonging to Mr J Mellar* (1761) shows Charlton bringing
geometric precision to the undulating landscape. Charlton divides
the property eleven ways, into various pastures, closes, carrs, garths,
banks and gardens. Despite the irregular dimensions of these zones,
Charlton reconciles each into acres, roods and perches. The confidence of his penmanship is striking. There's something seductive,
elegant and fresh in his execution of a task that must have attracted
attention in the neighbourhood: the schoolmaster, knocking his flags
into the wet earth, hobbling up an incline and defining an angle with
a theodolite. There, too, is the picture of Mr Mellar, absorbing the
survey; experiencing a pang of pride that he knows his 'Hollow Car'
is not merely a fair-sized field, but is 'three acres, three roods and
seven perches' in all, the fifth largest of his plots.[12]

Charlton's skills did not stop at this. In addition to mathematics,
he knew Latin and 'had some acquaintance with the French'.[13] In a
town where many remained illiterate, these skills opened up new
worlds, ancient Rome or enlightening Paris. By the 1760s the earliest
of Charlton's alumni would be graduating into the world, among
them the writers Francis Gibson and William Watkins. In the years
to come 'a number of excellent scholars' followed.[14]

*

If Charlton's school on the eastern bank of the Esk symbolised intellectual enquiry, then the western side was an earthier, practical place. Here was the centre of Whitby's shipbuilding industry. A chain of busy yards clustered on the edge of the river around a tidal stretch of ground called Bell Island. Dry at half ebb, Bell Island afforded Whitby's shipbuilders all they needed. It was close to the harbour, yet sheltered from the barrel swell of the sea behind a bridge, in a tidal stretch that acted as a natural lever for lifting heavy objects.

It was here at Bell Island, next to a moorland stream called Bagdale Beck, that Jarvis Coates had established his yard in the early 1700s. Coates was Whitby's first shipbuilder of any scale, and for four decades he had dominated the trade. Coates's vessels were tough, weatherly and pragmatic. They were designed as vehicles to transport huge volumes of coal from the mines at Newcastle to the markets in London and as more pits had been sunk in the north and more coal was needed in London, Coates had thrived as a go-between. By the 1730s he had been firmly established among Whitby's leading gentlemen with a property at 23 Baxtergate in the commercial centre of town, a minute's walk from his yard.

Jarvis Coates had three boys who followed him into the family business: Jarvis Jr, Francis and Benjamin. The boys had been raised as the Coates's fortunes rose, and when the elder Jarvis died in 1739 it must have seemed that he had bequeathed a lasting legacy. Now their own masters, Jarvis Jr had proved the most ambitious. He converted the Baxtergate property into an elegant townhouse, four bays wide and three storeys high, and expanded the old shipyard into adjoining land. As he concentrated on the new yard, the younger son, Benjamin, assumed control of the old one. Ostensibly the brothers were thriving, but in reality they were hamstrung by the terms of their father's will. He had decided to split his yard four ways – between Jarvis, Francis, Benjamin and his daughter Hannah – but none of the siblings was to inherit until the death of their mother, Mercy Coates. What might have been intended as an even-handed gesture turned out to be an aggravating one. By 1743 the younger Jarvis was bankrupt, unable to fund his expansion plans. Benjamin and Francis continued in business throughout the 1740s, but none of them would live to inherit. By the time Mercy Coates died in 1759, all her sons had predeceased her. Within twenty years of Jarvis Coates's death in 1739, the family's wealth and influence had dispersed.[15]

The Coates's misfortunes provided opportunity for others. While Mercy retained ownership of the yards in the 1740s and 1750s, the sites were occupied by aspiring shipbuilders who had the requisite capital and drive. By 1748 – the year Charlton arrived in Whitby – the new yard built by Jarvis Jr was being 'occupied' by a shrewd thirty-year-old, Thomas Fishburn. Tradition has it that Thomas had begun his working life as an apprentice to the Coates family, but little else is known of the man who, in the 1760s, was poised to set out on one of the great careers in English shipbuilding. Fishburn, like his peers, did not consider himself a shipwright – that was considered a demeaning term ('the proper Business of a Shipwright is counted a very vulgar Imploy, and which a Man of very indifferent Qualifications may be Master of'[16], one complained) – instead he styled himself as a 'Master Builder.' He was already referring to himself as one in 1750 in his son's baptismal papers. By then he was busy with commissions, one of which was *Liberty and Property*. The vessel would bear all Fishburn's hallmarks. It was a tough, durable Whitby collier that would still be sailing the North Sea trading routes 102 years after its launch in 1752 – a vessel launched before Johnson's *Dictionary* was published, still afloat during the Crimean War.

One measure of Fishburn's ambition was his efforts to build a dry dock. Dry docks allowed for year-round work, recaulking battered seams, replanking enfeebled hulls and amending designs during the fallow winter months. It had been a proud moment for the town when a conglomerate calling itself the Dock Company had success-fully opened Whitby's first stone-lined dry dock in 1734. The event had been announced with fanfare in the *Newcastle Courant*:

> This is to give notice, *To all masters of Ships*, That at Whitby in Yorkshire are lately made two extraordinary Dry Docks ... The Ship Whitby of Whitby about 350 Tons, Mr John Linskill, Owner, is now repairing in the said Dock, where any others may be served in their Turns, at reasonable Rates.[17]

The word 'extraordinary' was hardly overplaying it. There were precious few dry docks outside of London, and for most merchantmen this meant anything more than running repairs required a wait in the Thames, for a slot at the Globe Stairs in Rotherhithe or at St Saviour's Docklands opposite the Tower. The Whitby dry dock offered an

alternative on the busy coastal route. Whether Fishburn's young eyes
had passed over this advertisement or not, an ambition for his own
dry dock became a defining objective of his early career.

Fishburn was ten years at Jarvis Jr's yard before he raised the
capital to begin his project. There is no certain evidence on the
location for Fishburn's first attempt, though it seems likely he tried
to build in front of the Coates yard. 'When nearly completed', one
local later recalled, 'it sunk down in one night, the ground below
being quite a bog.' This episode must have been financially painful
for Fishburn, but by 1757 he had found a location upstream. This lay
at the unpromising-sounding Water Stand Lane, at the even more
unpromisingly titled hamlet of Boghall. This second attempt proved
successful. A hint of the great inconvenience and expense that
Fishburn had been put to was captured by his own advert, which
he must have submitted with pride to the *Public Advertiser* in London
in December 1758:

> THOMAS FISHBURN, Ship-builder, at Whitby, having at a great
> Expense erected a Dry Dock, fit for the Reception of Ships of
> any Burden, begs Leave to acquaint Owners and Commanders
> of Ships, who will please to favour him with their Commands,
> that they may be assured of having their Business done on the
> most reasonable Terms.[18]

Fishburn's advert ran for three consecutive days. Surrounded by
news from the Marine Society and notices from patent-medicine manufacturers, it stands out as a brave statement from a provincial
tradesman, hoping to catch merchants' eyes in the capital. Fishburn's
fortunes were turning. Soon after Mercy Coates died in 1759, he took
complete ownership of the yard. He was now overseeing a substantial
business on the western banks of the Esk. Trade was brisk. 'Hence it
comes to pass', one resident wrote, 'that our docks are oft filled with
ships from distant parts of the coast.' Owners, 'being convinced they
nowhere else can be so well served', would 'apply to the master-
builders at Whitby, and frequently agree for a turn on our stocks a
year or two before their work can be done'.[19] Rising to the summit
of the flourishing trade was Fishburn. Married to Alice and with three
growing children, in the years to come Fishburn would build Esk
House as a symbol of his status in the town. It was a trim and handsome

Georgian design, replete with spacious gardens that backed down to his dockyard. Of all the shipbuilders' houses, Fishburn's, it was later commented, was 'the most elegant'.[20]

Later in life Fishburn would be described by one of Whitby's scholarly set as 'a gentleman of considerable professional reputation, and highly meritorious for his unimpeached integrity, and benevolent disposition'.[21] This appears an even-handed appraisal, free from literary snobbishness towards a practical man. More hints come in Fishburn's designs, any creation bearing some trace of its maker. They were robust, dependable, economically productive and wholly traditional sailing vessels. No verified portraits of Fishburn are known to survive, though something of his physical appearance can be guessed at through a portrayal of his son – a high forehead, mutton-chop whiskers, flushed cheeks – an elegantly turned out Yorkshire gent, sat on a moorland rock holding a gun and with the hills stretching out behind him. Flanked by his hounds, the Fishburns' son emerges not unlike one of Gainsborough's Tory squires, proud of their patch of England and with a side of beef and a glass of Madeira waiting on the table at home.

Fishburn's focus in the spring of 1764 was seeing through the construction of a new vessel, ordered by one of Whitby's master mariners for work in the Newcastle coal trade. At some point, most probably in the course of the preceding year or two, a Whitby man called Thomas Milner had approached Fishburn with plans for this. New commissions were usually agreed upon with a list of critical dimensions: the length of the keel, the extreme breadth, the depth of the hold, the height between the decks and the waist. All Fishburn needed was at hand. The yards maintained a steady supply of essentials like oak, elm for keels or stern posts, Baltic pine for spars, deal, tallow, brimstone, pitch and varnish. Anything else could be purchased at the raff yards at Baxtergate or Spital Bridge or Thomas Boulby's rope yard across the river. But it is unlikely Fishburn wanted for anything. The order was not unusual. It was for a coastal vessel, broad and rugged, about 360 tons. The kind he knew best.

Fishburn's rise in Whitby would have been watched by Lionel Charlton, whose arrival in the town in 1748, coincided with the date of Fishburn's occupation of Jarvis Jr's yard. Though the two men were divided by class, occupation and the breadth of the River Esk, there was much for Charlton to admire in the ships Fishburn built, in their proportionality, strength and geometric simplicity. Charlton's passion was for mathematics. He was variously described as an 'ingenious mathematician' and 'a man of considerable mathematical knowledge'. Born at the time of Newton's great celebrity in 1720, Charlton had grown up when thinkers like Bernoulli and Euler were unpicking Nature's secrets with numbers. When Charlton set up his school at the Toll-booth he advertised himself as a 'Teacher of Mathematics at Whitby', an indication to prospective customers that algebra, fluxions, geometry, trigonometry, physics, mechanics, astronomy and gunnery were to form the backbone of his classes.

The appetite for mathematics was not confined to schoolrooms or the universities. A striking example of its general popularity was *The Ladies Diary*, an almanac that went on sale in 1704. Capitalising on the coronation of Queen Anne, the editor of *The Ladies Diary*, a Coventry schoolmaster named John Tipper, had designed a publication to appeal to 'the fair sex' with a specially prepared collection to 'suit all conditions, qualities and humours'. 'Nothing shall be inserted that is mean and trifling; nothing to raise a Blush, or intimate an evil Thought. To conclude, nothing shall here be, but (what all Women ought to be) innocent, modest, instructive, and agreeable.'[22] The mainstay of Tipper's almanac was intended to be recipes, stories and advice to young ladies on manners and deportment. So it had continued until a chance, rhyming 'arithmetical' question, posed by a male reader in 1707, proved so popular that Tipper decided to replace the recipes with 'enigmas' or knotty mathematical puzzles.

Tipper's *Ladies Diary* soon developed a mixed readership who joined in an ongoing contest, setting and solving teasing arithmetical riddles. Women and men vied over algebraic or trigonometric solutions, an unusual and entertaining intermingling of the sexes in an intellectual pursuit. One North Yorkshire lady, Jane Squire, caught up in this numerical culture, would write of her love for mathematics, 'I do not remember any Play-thing, that does not appear to me a mathematical Instrument; nor any mathematical Instrument, that does not appear to me a Play-thing: I see not, therefore, why I should confine myself to Needles, Cards, and Dice.'[23] In time the *Ladies Diary*'s enigmas developed their own suggestive narratives, going further than the mere solving of sums. They teased, often playfully, often suggestively:

I WISH I could such a fair Charmer disclose,
I'd gladly another Equation propose,
Which the best Algebraist should never untye,
Tho' he puzzled for ever with v, x and y.[24]

This was the type of intellectual puzzle Charlton relished. In the 1760s the name 'Mr Lionel Charlton, of Whitby', appeared in *The Ladies Diary*, which by then had changed its name to *The Woman's Almanack*.[25] With an annual run of 30,000 copies, the almanac had become a prominent and popular place for an intellectual challenge. Charlton's participations in these pages were well remembered in Whitby, and it tempers somewhat the image of him as a haughty or a proud man; rather it reveals another, zealous in his use of numbers yet keen to join in the collective spirit of intellectual enquiry.

Almanacs like *The Woman's Almanack* might have provided a forum for theoretical competition, but they also encouraged the practical application of the art too. They would advise readers how best to measure eclipses and other celestial events. In the much-anticipated run-up to the Transit of Venus in 1761 – when 'the most brilliant planet Venus will pass over the glorious body of the Sun'[26] – *The Gentleman's Diary, Or Maths Repository*, spent several pages explaining the unusual significance of the event to its readers. Venus was the brightest star in the night sky, but she was poised to make a daytime appearance, too. Earlier in the century Edmond Halley, the British astronomer, had predicted that twice during the 1760s Venus's orbit would see her cross the face of the sun. An unusual event – transits happened in eight-year pairs, then not again for more than a century – the transits of the 1760s yielded a rare opportunity to science. If observations were gathered from various, dispersed places, 'the Parallax of the Sun may be ascertained; and by that Means the Distances of the Earth, and Planets from the Sun.' All that required was to apply Johannes Kepler's mathematical formula and a solution to 'this noble Problem, one of the highest in Nature'[27] would be revealed: a numerical appreciation of the dimensions of the solar system. It was all to be unlocked by observation and mathematics.

No question could be greater than that. It showed how far mathematics had come since the century before, when the Savilian Professor of Geometry, John Wallis, had written 'Mathematicks ... were scarce looked upon as accademical studies, but rather mechanical: as the business of traders, merchants, seamen, carpenters, surveyors of the lands, or the like.'[28] And in his own way, Thomas Fishburn was just as advanced in his mathematics as Charlton was in his. By the 1760s the craft of building wooden sailing ships had progressed to a state of high sophistication and elegance. From Elizabethan times mathematical curves had been absorbed into the design of hulls, leaving them sleek yet sturdy. Shipbuilders had long accepted Archimedes' theory that displaced water produces an upwards force on a vessel. Into the eighteenth century, shipwrights had increasingly studied the shapes of mackerels, dolphins and ducks, rendering them in eloquent, curving lines, in a bid to streamline the hulls. It was common for them to be fitted with a 'cod's head and mackerel's tail', meaning the hull was at its broadest towards the head and that it tapered inward as it ran to the stern. They knew that while a ship sustained an infinite number of stresses, the two key motions it underwent were pitching (rocking back and forth on its length) and rolling (rocking side to side). A hull could withstand rolling far better than it could pitching, so moderating its pitch became a task as tangled as one of Charlton's enigmas. All these stresses were played out against the sea, a constantly shifting base. What every shipbuilder and every sailor sought, as the Australian writer Ray Parkin has argued, was harmony:

> Many sailors over many hundreds of years, without ever arguing it, have known this simple fact: that the sea, the ship and the wind are not in conflict but are merely trying to live together under common circumstance. This is not to argue a fine philosophical point; it is choosing between sanity and megalomania. The sea smashing against the ship is as much smashed against by the ship; the wind howling through the rigging is powerless to do otherwise, and may just as well be howling in anguish as in anger. The sea, the air, and the ship are only seeking equilibrium.[29]

To make the whole coherent, master builders like Fishburn had come to look at hulls dispassionately, narrowly, rationally. 'Our master-builders', Charlton wrote, 'understand their business extremely well, and know the exact geometrical proportion all the parts of a ship ought to have with regard to each other.'[30] Once derided as mere 'tradesmen', shipbuilders would come to be appreciated in a fast-industrialising society. John Ruskin, the aesthete and art critic of the

Victorian age, gazed wondrously back at the practical genius of the Georgian shipbuilders, a talent that found ultimate expression in the ships of the line he saw in J. M. W. Turner's paintings. 'Take it all in all, a ship of the line is the most honourable thing that man, as a gregarious animal, has ever produced ... Into that he has put as much of his human patience, common sense, forethought, experimental philosophy, self-control, habits of order, and obedience, thoroughly wrought hard work, defiance of brute elements, and calm expectation of the judgment of God, as can well be put into a space of three hundred feet long by eighty broad.'[31]

The British waters of the 1760s were filled with sailing crafts of many types and sizes, each built to suit a specific purpose. The various classes of fighting ships of the Royal Navy were most usually seen in the Solent Sea and the anchorage of Spithead off Portsmouth. They were either designed for sheer power – as in the case of the ships of the line – with enough stability to mount heavy guns and balance an even firing platform, or for speed and dexterity with svelte underwater bodies as in the case of the new class of frigates. Vessels carrying the treasures of the East India Company – known as East Indiamen – combined spacious holds with sufficient firepower to make them formidable opponents should any privateer be tempted to prey upon them. Other merchant sailors, whose work was limited to British or European waters, required none of the East Indiaman's defensive capacities. Instead they were built expressly for economy. In many cases their design could be reduced to a simple proposition: how to transport the maximum bulk of cargo with the fewest number of sailors. The merchant fleets of modern Europe had evolved to meet this challenge, filling the northern seas with stout vessels like hagboats, flyboats, pinks, cats and barks.

Distinguishing one of these types from another required more than a landsman's eye. In the eighteenth century, that great era of classification, vessels were divided from one another based on the length and shape of their hulls. These were at once very simple and highly complex, and to understand them required an artful and specialised vocabulary that emphasised their subtleties. Catching sight of an inward-bound merchantman, Fishburn might run through a mental checklist that considered the length, stem (foremost piece of the bow), stern (the back or after part of a ship), the midship section, burthen (the number of tons it will carry at proper sea trim) and the draught (the depth of water a ship displaces). A frigate would be instantly noticeable with a figurehead on its bows and its square-stern. But few of those needed to call at Whitby. Far more familiar were the two-masted brigs and snows; or the larger lumbering cats, with their tapering, overhanging sterns and their deep waists at the waterline; or the barks, the plainer, rugged sibling of the cat, with its flush-deck and broad stern – quite different to the cat, without the swagger of the projecting stern.

The brigs, snows, cats and barks defined Whitby's profile: a practical place, not flaunting. Often difficult to taxonomise, to avoid dispute it was easier to fall back on the catch-all term 'colliers', which referred to any vessel carrying coals, a staple cargo. And in reality Whitby-built vessels were not built to fit a perfect type – they might blend different attributes, depending on the materials available in the yards at a particular time – but they were built to serve a purpose. For Whitby's coasting vessels, that meant transporting the maximum quantities of coals, as safely, and with as little labour, as possible. It was with this in mind that an onlooker had to analyse any of Coates's or Fishburn's vessels. The hulls were broad and uncluttered with interior decks. The bottoms were flat, giving them a shallow draft and the threefold advantage that they could be sailed close to shore or up shallow estuaries to take on cargo, that they could stand upright on dry land at low tide – making them both easy to unload and scrub clean – and that their hold was free of the awkward spaces formed by a sleek underwater body. The flat-bottomed, open holds were encased in a reinforced oak shell, equal to the task of heaving the hundreds of chaldrons of coal while meanwhile shouldering the thrashing waves and wicked winds of the open sea. The reinforced hulls were not glamorous. Colliers were known for their bluff, rounded bows that did not even display a figurehead. But they were designed to last rather than to dazzle. They might stay out for months at a stretch, having their hulls 'grieved' (to have the filth burnt from the bottom) or 'careened' (tilted to one side as the other is trimmed and caulked) at low tide, but otherwise living in the coastal roads for years at a stretch without ever having to visit port.

To stand at Whitby's favourite lookout post, on the east cliff, in the 1760s, was to gaze over a dynamic scene of trade and transport. The maritime highway to London ran straight by the port before it swung to the south. On any given day it would be filled with Scottish smacks ferrying passengers towards the city, brigs or snows serving the alum works, brigantines or schooners, the maids of all work, skimming over the waves with every stitch of canvas set. Between them all, lumbering like the elephants in Hannibal's army would sail the colliers. They were a typical enough sight but looking out from the east cliff on a brisk spring day with the wind in the east, even they exuded an aesthetic appeal: the interplay between their glossy, varnished hulls and their coarse matt sails, the pleasing curve of the wind pressing into the canvas. Benjamin Franklin would write about the appeal of this form. 'A ship under sail and a big-bellied Woman, are the handsomest two things that can be seen common.'[32]

Frail as colliers might appear at a distance, seen close up in Whitby's harbour or out in the roads outside the piers, their strength and rigidity was plain. But such was the productivity of Whitby's shipbuilders by the early 1760s that these hulls did not take long to assemble. In the space of a handful of months, with properly seasoned timber, Fishburn's yard would run through a well-worn process. First an elm keel – elm used for its ability to stand constant submersion – would be laid the length of the yard. This formed the backbone of the collier. In 1764 the keel was ninety-one feet long and one foot broad, dimensions dictated as much by the shape of Fishburn's yard and the availability of materials as the fancy of the buyer. Once the keel was in situ two other great pieces of structural timber would be scarfed into it: the stem at the front, and stern post at the back. Held in position on the blocks, the frame of the collier was then built from the ground upward. From the front the carcass of the collier resembled a U shape: a keelson reinforced the keel from above; floor pieces were driven in and fastened to futtocks – the ribs of the ship – that curved around and upward in three sections. To them were added the top timbers. The keel excepted, all these structural pieces were of oak, and after several weeks of hauling, hammering, fastening and locking, the whole would be girdled into a rigid frame with a series of knees – angle brackets shaped from compass timber – and wales that ran the length of the hull.

The surviving plans of the vessel Fishburn created during the spring of 1764 fit mostly with the profile of a bark, with its broad stern, bluff bows and broad body, though a Deptford Yard officer in London would soon generate several centuries of confusion by describing her, in an inverted tangle, as a 'Cat-built Bark'.*[33] This nebulous line – as confusing to Fishburn as a 'goat-shaped sheep' might be to a farmer – would wrong-foot many in years to come, but for Fishburn in 1764, the precise classification of his collier was probably not foremost in his mind. More materially, his efforts would have been directed into making her as strong and seaworthy as he could with the materials available to him. At this point in the building process the collier's naked hull resembled nothing so much as a giant ribcage. To unknowing eyes, it might have seemed as if some new antediluvian creature had been dug out of the sands. For Whitby people, though, this sight was as familiar as a sedan chair might be to strollers in Pall Mall. Charlton later produced a map of Whitby, which as well as the geography and buildings of the town also depicted Bell Island crowded with the outlines of ships in frame on the stocks. Within the space of 300 yards seven hulls are in various stages of construction. Most are stripped carcasses, but two at least seem to be near completion, with the frames planked back and forth, or in the sailors' language, fore and aft. These would be fastened onto the frame with trennels or tree nails, oak dowels an inch and a half thick and three and a half feet long that were scattered about the hull haphazardly so as not to create lines of weakness.

The transformation of the oak timbers into a coherent body was a task that spanned, at the very least, several weeks with the workers in the shipyard from 'five in the morning till seven every evening'. The changing appearance of the collier, slowly rising out from the sands, contributed to this sense of Whitby as a place of transformation. Whitby stood not only at the boundary between the land and the sea, it also had its monastery as a gatepost between the divine and temporal worlds. Where before there had been the chapter house and seminaries, it now had its shipyards and schools, symbols of the new enlightening world that was replacing the old spiritual one. They made the raw materials of nature transform into something neat, useful, even beautiful, in a process of ordering, assigning, measuring, sawing and fastening.

---

*   The German model-maker and historian of naval architecture Karl Heinz Marquardt has identified three crucial differences between the hulls of barks and cats. Firstly, a bark's wing transom was nearly always straight while a cat's was rounded. This meant that, secondly, a bark's stern was broad and a cat's was narrow. Thirdly, cats were known for their deep waists and built-up forecastles and quarterdecks. Barks were commonly flush-decked in comparison. 'None of the cat features applies to the *Earl of Pembroke*', Marquardt writes, 'which clearly shows a bark's hull form.'

While undergoing this process at the yard, the timbers underwent a second, gendered, change. Alive in the countryside, trees were regarded as a symbol of male strength. In *Sylva*, Evelyn habitually referred to living trees under the masculine pronoun – 'Chuse a *Tree* as big as your *thigh*, remove the earth from about him', runs a typical passage.[34] The outline of a tree in the landscape fitted with contemporary notions of masculinity: stoic, weathered, constant. Artists knew this too. Squires would pose before favourite trees on their estates, a fashion epitomised by Gainsborough's *Mr and Mrs Andrews* or Reynolds' *Master Thomas Lister*. But at the dockyard, as the raw materials were shaped, they were reassigned. As a living tree, *he* stood in the landscape. As timber, *it* lay at the yard. Preparing on the stocks, *she* was being built, a graceful figure, made eloquent out of the products of the earth.

There were more transformations at Whitby. There was Bell Island itself, emerging and vanishing twice a day with the tides. And then there was the meeting of distinct communities. There were the landsmen and the sea folk, or the lubbers and the jolly sailors as each derided the other. To a visiting merchant from York or Pickering, the language and nomenclature was alienating. Muddling a brig for a snow, they might be politely corrected or be silently condemned a fool. More obviously out of their context were the sailors, portrayed as off kilter on terra firma without their rigid routines, and betrayed by their profanities. In cities like London the sailors lived in their own quarters, places like Broad Street or the Old Gravel Road in Wapping. These were towns within towns, liminal zones that ticked at a higher tempo, offering a profligacy and danger not to be found elsewhere. It became an easy, favourite Georgian pastime, to ridicule these 'lusty young fellows' adrift on dry land mistaking cues, unsettled by a draught in a tavern or starting up at the sound of a pipe. Tobias Smollett did this most outrageously in *Roderick Random* (1748), assigning Roderick – the novel's bungling hero – a buccaneering uncle who 'had been long abroad, lieutenant of a man-of-war'. The uncle was an extravagant caricature. A hanger was slung from his belt, curses flew from his lips. 'Damn you, you saucy son of a bitch, I'll teach you to talk so to your officer', he bellowed at one antagonist. Eyeing a pretty girl, he leapt up as if he'd spied land. 'Odds bobs, Rory! here's a notable prize indeed, finely built and gloriously rigged.'[35]

In Whitby there was always an echo, however faint, of this in the streets and taverns, and most of all by the piers. Sailors with their striped flannel jackets, canvas trousers, rusty blue great coats and pointed hats, belonged almost to another world. To pass from dry ground into a ship was to cross a barrier where time was even counted differently, with ship's time running twelve hours in advance of the civil clock.

Whitby was a place of beginnings and endings, of changes and boundaries. Snakes were turned into stones, bodies were turned into souls, timber was turned into ships. The truth did not escape the Irish author Bram Stoker who visited a century later. Struck by Whitby's atmosphere, he decided to use it as a backdrop for a Gothic novel. Stoker's tale told how a single schooner, flying fast before the wind, appeared out of a North Sea storm, with sails set and straining. The schooner made like a dart between the piers. The town's folk, watching, could not make out a single sailor on deck. There was just the corpse of the helmsman, lashed to his wheel.

> There was ... a considerable concussion as the vessel drove up on the sand heap. Every spar, rope, and stay was strained, and some of the 'top-hammer' came crashing down. But, strangest of all, the very instant the shore was touched, an immense dog sprang up on deck from below, as if shot up by the concussion, and running forward, jumped from the bow on the sand.[36]

This dog, of course, was not a dog at all. Safely arrived in this town of transformations, Dracula would soon reveal himself.

The worst North Sea storms were called 'Widow Makers'. One of these had struck Whitby on the night of 1 December 1763. It was 'a most violent storm of wind and rain' that continued into the next day.[37] Its effects were felt across England. Houses were blown down in London. At Wells in Norfolk, residents woke to find the quay and neighbouring streets strewn with cables, boats and ships 'some in halves'. More than 1,500 sheep were said to have perished in the Norfolk countryside as the saturated marshland had flooded. Twenty miles from Whitby, at Scarborough, a 'most dreadful hurricane' had blown all night.[38] Twelve ships were wrenched from their moorings, driven against the foreshore then consumed by the pounding waves. Bodies had been cast up in the bay. 'The coast between this town and Flamborough is lined with wrecks', a Scarborough resident had

written, 'and castaway sailors throng here in great abundance, half
naked.' The anguished letter, which was published by the *Caledonian
Mercury*, continued:

> The whole town being so alarmed, the people sat up all night,
> many of them expecting every minute to be their last. It was
> dismal to hear the many cries that were poured forth in the dead
> of the night (through speaking trumpets) by persons going down
> to the deep and no relief could be had.[39]

It was reckoned the worst storm since November 1740, and Whitby
was not spared. 'The wind raged so furiously', ran a report in the
Scots Magazine, 'and the land floods rushed down so rapidly, that almost
all the houses near the river were either driven away or damaged.'[40]
Many of the ships in the harbour were damaged, and even those in
the dry docks were dislodged. More saddening still was the damage
to Whitby's abbey. Its whole western wing, which for centuries had
been supported by 'twenty strong Gothic pillars and arches', was
blown to the ground. One to survey the wreckage was Lionel Charlton.
Little was left of the original structure, except the north wall of the
cloisters and part of the west end wall. 'But it will not continue so
for many ages', Charlton predicted, 'the whole being in so ruinous a
condition that in another hundred years it must be entirely reduced
to a heap of rubbish.'[41]

If the abbey was to be levelled as Charlton envisaged, it would
mean the severance of a last bond with that ancient Christian community. And it was this dread of impending loss that inspired him to
begin work on what would become his life's project, the first modern,
comprehensive history of Whitby. From Hilda and Cædmon in the
Saxon monastery, to the shipbuilders of the modern day, Charlton's
History of Whitby would be an ambitious effort to both rescue the
past and to capture the present. 'All will readily own that it would be
a great pity to have so many noble remains of antiquity moulder away
into dust', he wrote, 'without being communicated to the world, and
preserved for the benefit and satisfaction of future generations.'[42]

Charlton's interests were not confined to the distant past. He was
aware, too, that something unusual had happened to the community
over the past century. When Henry VIII had plundered the monastery in the 1540s, Whitby had contained no more than 'thirty or

forty' cottages, home to perhaps a few hundred souls. By the 1650s
this number had risen to about 2,500, most of whom subsisted off
the local herring trade with their twenty clinker-built cobles. Much
of the third part of Charlton's *History* dealt with the century of
progress that followed the Restoration in 1660. That same year,
Charlton recorded, Whitby was 'ornamented' with a 'large new
pendulum clock' that was installed at the Toll-booth in the market
square where he would later establish his day school.[43] In Charlton's
narrative, the arrival of the clock heralds a brave new era in Whitby's
history. It meant precision, science, progress. And the pages of the
History filled with accounts from 1660 onwards, of new streets, better
piers, bigger ships, grander churches and neater gardens. In 1725 the
first sash windows were installed in houses and they were regarded
with amazement. The town swelled in these years to one of ten
thousand. Twenty boats rose to almost 200 ships. The anonymous
fishing village at the far side of the moors, fed by the tiny river,
began its upward trajectory as a shipbuilding centre, soon to outdo
Liverpool, Glasgow and Bristol.

Whitby's rise coincided with a time the writer Daniel Defoe would
term the Age of Projects. Spanning some forty years, from 1680–1720,
England (later, after the Act of Union, Britain) was, Defoe argued,
overcome by the 'Humour of Invention'.[44] Defoe proposed his idea
in a publication called *An Essay Upon Projects*. The country of Defoe's
youth had been filled with bold inventions and schemes. There had
been engines for quenching fires, the London Penny Post, pioneering
types of metal, 'Floating Machines ... wrought with Horses for the
Towing of Great Ships both against the Wind and Tide.' Then there
had been the designs for 'Planting of Foreign Collonies, as *William
Pen*, the Lord *Shaftsbury*, Dr *Cox*, and others, in *Pennsylvania*, *Carolina*,
East and *West Jersey*, and the like places.'[45] In *An Essay Upon Projects*,
Defoe put the rise of the 'projecting spirit' down to inventive minds,
attempting to right their personal losses after the Nine Years War
(1688–97). 'These, prompted by Necessity, rack their Wits for new
Contrivances, New Inventions, New Trades, Stocks, Projects, and any
thing to retrieve the desperate Credit of their Fortunes.' Equally
motivating was the story of William Phips, 'whose strange Performance
set a great many Heads on work to contrive something for themselves'.
Phips had been born the son of a shepherd in the Massachusetts Bay
Colony in about 1650. Naturally ambitious, Phips had first set up as a

shipbuilder but soon he had started hunting for treasure along the American coast in the 1680s. Defoe wrote:

> witness Sir *William Phips*'s Voyage to the Wreck; 'twas a mere Project, a Lottery of a Hundred thousand to One odds; a hazard, which if it had fail'd, every body wou'd have been asham'd to have own'd themselves concern'd in; a Voyage that wou'd have been as much ridicul'd as *Don Quixote's Adventure upon the Windmill*: Bless us! that Folks should go Three thousand Miles to Angle in the open Sea for Pieces of Eight! why, they wou'd have made Ballads of it, and the Merchants wou'd have said of every unlikely Adventure, 'Twas like *Phips* his Wreck-Voyage.[46]

No one was sure quite how much money Phips had salvaged, and Defoe settled on a high-flown figure, 'near 200,000l. *sterling*, in Pieces of Eight, fish'd up out of the open Sea remote from any shore, from an old *Spanish* ship which had been sunk above Forty Years'. The whole was carried off with such éclat, Defoe suggested, a thousand imitators appeared overnight.

In the years that followed Phips's find, 'the projector' became a recognisable and much derided type, the confidence tricksters of the day. From the start it was a derogatory term, 'The Despicable Title of a Projector', Defoe called it. For novelists, projectors were a gift, ludicrous, bombastic, swelled up and prattling with self-regard. Jonathan Swift savaged them in *Gulliver's Travels*. The Academy of Lagado became a nest of projectors trying to extract sunbeams from cucumbers. The projectors' infamy only worsened after the collapse of the South Sea Bubble in 1720. And yet, in his *Essay Upon Projects*, Defoe sought to curb prejudices against them. The existence of projectors, he argued, was merely a consequence of a society marching forwards. While some contrived to hoodwink the vulnerable, 'Others yet urg'd by the same necessity, turn their thoughts to Honest Invention, founded on the Platform of Ingenuity and Integrity ... new Discoveries in Trade, in Arts and Mysteries, of Manufacturing Goods, or Improvement of Land, are without question of as great benefit, as any Discoveries made in the Works of Nature by all the *Academies* and *Royal Societies* in the world.'[47]

This was the backdrop against which the progress at Whitby happened. Jarvis Coates may well have been called the projector of his shipyard, or Fishburn the projector of his dry dock. But Whitby enjoyed several advantages over the scheming alleys of London, where the mass of projectors were to be found. The population was fixed rather than transient, meaning people had a local character to uphold, and there was the secondary advantage of a fixed community to invest in new enterprises. The culture of the town, too, was distinct. Many of Whitby's trading families were Quakers, a nonconformist strand of Protestantism that valued clean-living, hard work and good book-keeping. A generation before Charlton, a Quaker school had provided an early education for both boys and girls, who were both taught the maxim that industriousness and godliness went hand in hand. The school could only help to enfranchise Whitby's women who – like Mercy Coates and her daughter Hannah – would not only have finan-cial control of some shipyards, but they would also be significant shareholders in Whitby merchant ships. Shares were often split into sixty-four parts, so the ownership of a single collier was diverse. For those on the make, opportunities appeared weekly in the *Newcastle Courant*:

One 64th Part of the Hopewell of Whitby, William Biggins Master
One 32nd Part of the Henry and Mary of Whitby, Henry Atkinson Master
One 64th Part of the Walker of Whitby, William Walker Master

The arrangement made for a complex scale of ownership. Speculators could pick their favourite ship and master, or spread their money to lessen the risk. The sea was a market open to everyone and the bigger players would rise to own entire ships themselves. Once funded, Whitby's vessels tended to operate in two distinct markets. There was the coal trade between Newcastle and London, and there were Baltic voyages, where coals were carried to ports like Lubec or Riga and cargoes of timber and tar were brought home. The coal trade was most dependable. Between 1700 and 1750, London's demand for the fuel rose from 800,000 tons each year to 1.5 million tons, meaning there was almost always a buyer to be found at Wapping or Shadwell on the Thames's north bank. Baltic voyages involved greater risk but attracted higher potential profits. They could last for months at a stretch, the Whitby colliers sagging low in the water, sailing east among the ice drifts, under the circling ospreys, past Moon Island, right to the banks of the Russian Empire. In the coal market, in particular, Whitby ships did well. By 1751 one in five ships entering the Port of London from the Baltic were Whitby-owned. In 1755 Whitby-owned ships were making more than 600 trips to the staithes at Newcastle each year, about a quarter of the total. And by the 1790s Whitby's shipbuilding would have expanded to such a degree that, by total tonnage, it ranked as the third biggest in Britain.

This story of progress was the one Charlton would distil into the third part of his *History of Whitby*. From an anonymous fishing town Whitby had risen to become a vibrant mercantile hub. 'From Holland we import flax, wainscot-boards, tarras, brandy, geneva, and canvas', Charlton wrote, 'From France we have brandy, and part of our wine. From the East Country we have hemp, flax, iron, timber, masts, deals, oak-plank, capravens, pipe-staves, lath-wood, battens, tar, spruce-beer, and several other articles. From America we import rice, pitch, tar, turpentine, pine boards.' By 1750 the town's population had climbed to about 5,000. In 1764 a theatre was opened, bringing metropolitan sophistication and art to the provincial town. The maritime boom had created a paradox. While Whitby remained geographically isolated from York and Pickering, the main towns in its terrestrial hinterland, it was increasingly bound to faraway ports. From the Baltic to Baltimore, a merchant might encounter a Whitby ship. Charlton under-scored this theme:

> that so long as a spirit of industry and temperance prevails among us, our trade will flourish, and we shall be a rich, opulent, and happy people; but if ever we suffer ourselves to be enervated, and become a prey to idleness, luxury, and intemperance, our riches will vanish, our trade will leave us, and we shall insensibly dwindle away into obscurity.[48]

When published in 1779, Charlton's book stretched on for 362 densely packed, trenchant pages, each one bristling with facts and dates and names and figures. Accompanied by a plan of the town and full of much original antiquarian information, it attracted more than regional interest. Five hundred and thirteen people subscribed 551 copies of the book on publication, among them Dr Samuel Johnson, Sir Joshua Reynolds, and the lawyer and antiquary Sir Daines Barrington. In these years Charlton also came into correspondence with Thomas Pennant, the naturalist and antiquarian, who sat at the heart of a wide network of philosophically minded figures, including Gilbert White in Selborne and Joseph Banks in Soho Square. For them all, Charlton would become the Whitby correspondent for the Enlightenment network of philomaths, transmitting news of strange fossils, petrified oaks, singing monks and trading ships.

Endeavour was not mentioned in Charlton's book. This is a strange omission but perhaps no historical clarity had yet settled on Fishburn's bark that, in 1764, had begun life yards from Charlton's school. There survives a picture of Bell Island showing the final stages in the building of a collier. Teams of caulkers would have crawled over the frame, driving oakum into the seams and then 'paying' them by pouring over a compound of burning pitch and Stockholm tar. There was no interior deck running the length of this collier. Instead there was a foremost fall in the bows – a cramped, low space for sailors to sleep and stores to be kept – and the afterfall or steerage in the stern, a space reserved for the master and his mates. In the days to come she would be fitted with three masts – a fore, a main and a mizzen – that ran the length of the deck. Below the waterline a viscous mix, 'black stuff' – a compound of goat or cow hair, tar, brimstone and pitch – would be payed or *cleamed* outside the hull as a protection from sea water. All this would mingle with the salt air, the stench of tar and tang of paint to create that distinct aura that clung to the yard. The rest of the deck furniture would have been shipped too: a capstan for heaving heavy objects, the bowsprit, the catheads on which the anchors hung clear of the hull, the windlass and the knightheads.

These words seem exotic to us today, but they come from a language as precise and rich to sailors, as Latin was to scholars. 'Giving a wide berth', 'hard to fathom', 'mainstay', 'knowing the ropes', 'to be on an even keel', 'taken aback', 'to the bitter end'; some sailing terms had cross-pollinated into landsmen's speak. Other phrases would remain enigmatic. Knightheads and catheads had variously ascribed origins. One explanation for 'catheads' told that shipwrights had formerly been in the habit of carving a cat's face into these timbers. Fishburn did not do this. His ships would not be known for decorations. But there was a carving on this specific vessel. It was the face of a wise old seaman that stared across the deck from the windlass. Sailors who looked over this ship would notice other things about her too. One was a confused overlapping of decks around the main mast. Another was that the bark was versatile. Fishburn had cut five ports in her side through which coal could be shovelled from the keels or loading crafts, and there was a slot in her bows through which timber could be posted.

As Fishburn's new bark had progressed on the stocks, the cold northern winds of winter had subsided. In his *Rural Economy of Yorkshire*, William Marshall had plotted the march of the season: 'The sallow in full blow,—5 April. One swallow, near water,— 12 April. White-thorn foliated,— 18 April. Swallows about houses,—27 April. Cuckow first heard,—6 May. Swifts,—12 May. Oak foliated,—29 May. Hawthorn blowed, 10 June. Ash foliated,— 11 June.'[49] The ship rose along with the season. Tracing *Endeavour*'s earliest life is always a process of working backwards from the first recorded mention. And by doing this we know that sometime in June 1764, perhaps not long after King George III's birthday on 4 June, she was completed for her owner, Thomas Milner. By now she would have been fitted out with her iron anchors and a stove, all three masts would have been rigged with halliards and braces, her hull would have been cleaned and tallowed, ready for loading with sails, stores, ropes, enough ballast to make her seaworthy, and, ultimately, men. Twelve were engaged to sail under Milner's command on this maiden voyage. He would be joined by a mate called John Brown, a cook called Robert Cuthbertson, six sailors and four servants.[50]

Just one thing was wanting: a name for the new vessel. In the navy the name of a ship often suggested its size – the *Badger* of fourteen guns seems appropriate, as does the *Dorsetshire* of seventy guns – or its intended purpose: the first-rate 104-gun *Victory* was being readied in 1764, the fast frigate *Greyhound* was already at sea, the fireships *Blast*, *Blaze* and *Etna* had been active in the Seven Years War and the *Elephant* would be an appropriately named transport in a war to come. Not every name was as dashing as these. Hugh Palliser, a Yorkshire officer, had made his name cruising on French privateers in the sloop HMS *Weazel*. In the merchant fleet there was a greater diversity of names. Whitby's Quaker roots ensured an abundance of *Brotherly Loves* and *Friendships*. Wives, daughters, sweethearts and names of gods or classical heroes supplied other inspirations, populating the harbour with *Marys*, *Janes*, *Nymphs* and *Neptunes*. Often a name revealed something, an allegiance, a friendship or an aspiration. Sometimes they were deployed artfully as, no doubt, Milner's chosen name was intended. He decided to tap into a patriotic strain still alive in Britain after the victories of the Seven Years War. The newspapers in April had carried reports that Henry Herbert, the Earl of Pembroke, had been elevated 'to the command of the 1st regiment of dragoons', a prominent army posting.[51] The news must have caught Milner's attention, for he selected *Earl of Pembroke* as his ship's name.

With so many ships emerging from the Whitby yards, it's unlikely the departure of the *Earl of Pembroke* merited any attention at all. She was merely the latest off a busy production line, being sent to work in the coal industry as scores had been before her. There are later reports of Whitby's shipwrights gathering on the piers to mark maiden voyages, throwing hats into the sky as a vessel passed. Coleridge's ancient mariner would describe the view from the deck: 'The ship was cheered, the harbour cleared, / Merrily did we drop / Below the kirk, below the hill, / Below the lighthouse top.'[52]

Crossing the bar and catching a breath of sea air, the hull beneath Milner's feet was at last in motion, the waves slapping her side. Before him a great vista would have opened up: a summer sun glinting off a sea that stretched for leagues and leagues in front of the bark's rounded bows, until at some point in the very distance it met the sky.

3

Cross Currents

A seascape only ever tells a partial story. The atmosphere above is visible, but no one knows quite what exists beneath the water. It makes for a half-empirical, half-imagined reality upon which a ship is suspended, like a reader midway through a novel: knowing much, imagining more. '*In mari multa latent*' – In the ocean many things are hidden, wrote the Danish author Erich Pontoppidan in *The Natural History of Norway* (1755).[1] 'In the hot Summer days', like those when the *Earl of Pembroke* sailed, what was hidden sometimes revealed itself. Pushing a score of miles off the coast, Norwegian fishermen would be sounding the seabed when the depth sharply rose from a hundred fathoms to thirty. They knew this was not natural geography. These were not shoals, rising like the contours of a hill. Rather the fishermen believed, Pontoppidan wrote, their lead had struck the body of a kraken, a round, flat creature, 'full of arms or branches'. 'At these places they generally find the greatest plenty of Fish', especially cod and ling tempted from the sea floor. Fishermen were glad to fish above a kraken. But they had to beware. Keeping to their lead lines, they sometimes noticed the depth growing shallower – from thirty to twenty to ten fathoms. 'They find that the Kraken is raising himself nearer the surface, and then it is not time for them to stay any longer; they immediately leave off fishing, take to their oars, and get away as fast as they can.'[2]

Telling stories about kraken or Leviathan, as much as showing his apprentice sailors how to heave a rope or to bend a sail, was part of everyday life for veteran masters like Thomas Milner, the first owner-master of the *Earl of Pembroke*. They were the keepers of knowledge and lore as much as wielders of authority. They knew a spirit of play or an hour's storytelling was as adhesive for a crew as strict discipline. For Milner these truths would have been learned over many years.

Born in Whitby in 1709, at fifty-five he was one of the older mariners in the town in 1764. His career had run in time to the rise of Whitby, her fleet and shipyards. He would have been a young boy when the Coates yard had gathered momentum at Bell Island, and he would have been established as a sailing master by the time Fishburn outflanked them.

Now in the open sea – the anchor dripping on the cathead, the red ensign flying above – in July 1764 Milner had his first chance to assess the qualities of his new collier, to hear the creaks she made, to feel her agility, the way she rolled and pitched or gathered way. In an age before standardisation, every ship was different. The mass of the wood, the curves of the hull, the height of the masts: subtle distinctions in any of these generated the peculiarities that made character. Sailors sometimes spoke of a ship 'talking'. More often they discussed a ship's trim – her set on the water, whether by the head or stern or on an even keel. The best of ships were pronounced *weatherly*, as the *Earl of Pembroke* certainly was. It was later reckoned that the *Earl of Pembroke*'s best trim was 'Three or four Inches by the Stern'.

> Her best sailing is with the Wind a point or two abaft the beam she will then run 7 or 8 Knots and carry a weather Helm ... No Sea can hurt her laying Too under a Main Sail or Mizon ballanc'd ... She is a good Roader and Careens easy and without the least danger ... She behaves as well under her courses as most ships ... (In a Top Gallant Gale) [She] Steers well and runs about 5 Knots.[3]

Feeling the first tug of wind in the sails, Milner was at least sailing in tranquil waters again. It was now more than a year since the Treaty of Paris had brought a formal end to the war between Britain and France. Since then the old seaways between the Baltic and Newcastle had filled up. Intended for the coastal trade, surviving records show that the *Earl of Pembroke*'s maiden voyage was to call for coal at Newcastle before doubling south to London. It meant the collier's first run would be for ten or eleven leagues north-west – an easy stretch on a summer's day – until they reached the mouth of the River Tyne.

Now in motion, Milner's skills were both instinctive and reactive. He was, in that fine phrase of Robert Middlekauff's, 'a mechanic of the sea'.[4] His task was catching the elemental energy, harnessing it, using it to his best advantage. The rasp of the breeze on his cheeks; a creak from the mizzen; a furtive flutter of a topgallant; the undertow of an eddy: all were hints to be decoded. Like the flinch of a card player or the darting eyes of a Fleet Street thief, the surest signs may be the subtlest. His game was to anticipate, to out-think nature before she played her hand.

There were other stories to tell on the *Earl of Pembroke*. The English had always considered themselves the masters of the seas. As far back as the reign of Edward III coins had borne devices celebrating the prowess of English ships. In 1764 there were more glorious victories to reflect upon. No story glimmered like that of Admiral Edward Hawke's 1759 victory at Quiberon Bay. Then, with Britain threatened by France, the most powerful and prosperous European nation, the only obstacle that had stood between Admiral Marshal Conflans and invasion was the navy's Western Squadron commanded by Hawke. After months of panic at home and cat-and-mouse off France's Atlantic coast, a storm had blown Hawke away from his station. It had presented Conflans with a chance to escape from the French ports, where he had previously been penned in, to join the French land and sea forces at Quiberon Bay and sail towards Britain.

Blown into port at Torbay in foul weather, Hawke had seemed helpless. A French fleet of twenty-one line-of-battle ships had sailed from Brest on 14 November with the news reaching Britain two days later. A race over the gale-lashed Atlantic had ensued. Conflans had been given a 200-mile head start as he hurried towards Quiberon Bay. But Hawke's seamanship had been exceptional. By 19 November Hawke's twenty-three battleships were bearing down on the French fleet. Conflans had no idea Hawke was so close. But even when the British were sighted, Conflans retained his cool. Quiberon Bay lay ahead as a sanctuary into which no enemy could sail. An Admiralty memo of 1756 had advised commanders that Quiberon Bay was a place 'we dare not follow them'.

Nevertheless on 20 November 1759 Hawke, riding a fierce November gale, chased Conflans among the half-tide rocks and shoals of the bay. Hawke risked everything. 'We crowded after him with every sail our ships could carry', he wrote. 'Probably no British admiral has ever risked battle in such dangerous circumstances', one historian wrote, 'no one who saw the "gallant and swift-winged Hawke" go into action ... ever forgot that day'.[5] Stories of what had happened had been told and retold on quarterdecks and forecastles ever since. There were the forty-knot winds, the French disinclination to fight, HMS *Magnanime* engaging the warship *Héros*, killing 400 of her crew before she struck, and Hawke's *Royal George* confronting Conflans' flagship *Soleil Royal*, getting off broadside after broadside before the marshal's flagship ran aground and was burnt. The Battle of Quiberon Bay had gone down as one of the most audacious and thrilling victories in British history. Having lost just two of his vessels, Hawke had destroyed the French fleet and killed thousands of its men. It would take the French navy years to recover.

The Whitby merchant fleet had an extra reason to take pride in Hawke's achievement. In the months before the battle he had adopted an innovative strategy, keeping the Western Squadron victualled at sea. The usual custom had been to relay to port to resupply exhausted stores. But instead merchant vessels had sailed out to provision Hawke in the Atlantic. Among these vessels were a number from Whitby. Hawke's policy had been successful. Not only had he been able to pen the French in at Brest, but his men had remained unusually healthy. On the day of battle just twenty sailors in the squadron had been listed sick, an astounding figure. The French, meanwhile, had been beset with typhus and dysentery.

Taking naval contracts like those to victual the Western Squadron at sea were part of a new wave of opportunities presented to Whitby's master mariners. The Seven Years War (1756–63) was unlike the wars of old. It wasn't centred on a single battlefield, a specific point of water, or even on a particular geographic territory. Considered by many as the first world war, in reality it was a matrix of interconnected conflicts, in India, Europe and North America, where it was called the French and Indian War. As much as a contest of battlefield tactics, the war was a challenge of logistics. Ferrying weapons, transporting troops, maintaining supply lines; these wartime perennials became acute from 1756 onwards. In London it had not taken the Admiralty long to realise Whitby's merchant fleet offered a solution. With their massive storage capacities and ability to probe into rivers and coastal shallows, the masters and owners of Whitby colliers were being courted by the Admiralty with generous contracts. Milner was among those to profit. In 1759 he was supplying Plymouth dockyard with masts and spars. The next year he was crossing to France. In

1762 he was carrying troops home from the port at Williamstadt. For the willing, there was money to be made. Milner, it seems, was among those to prosper.

If the conflict generated opportunity for the town's sailors, for those back on the Yorkshire coast it had been a disquieting time. Not long after war was declared against France on 8 July 1756, a letter had appeared in the *Caledonian Mercury* reporting that a 'very small Vessel. Foreign built', had been sighted off the Whitby coast one dawn. On board were seven hands, sounding the approaches to the harbour. They 'continued so doing until they came close to the Pier Head; and when the People upon the Pier expected that she would have entered the Harbour, she suddenly tacked about and drove along the Shore'.[6]

Within a year the northern ports of Whitby, Scarborough, Sunderland, Hartlepool and Tynemouth Castle had agreed on a series of flag signals to be hoisted on the sighting of similar suspicious vessels. It wasn't long before they were needed. In 1758 French privateers captured two Scarborough ships near the coast at Whitby. In February 1760 another privateer began harrying the coastal trade on the east coast, making prizes of two brigantines, plundering their stores, before ransoming them for £300. In January 1761 a twenty-gun vessel was sighted off Whitby. In May the same year, the *Otter*, a transport, was chased into the harbour by two Frenchmen, who, missing their original target, seized another.[7]

Milner had sailed in these sanguine waters. After the Capture of Belle-Île off the Brittany coast in 1761 – a brilliant amphibious assault devised by William Pitt, the political hero of the war – Milner was among the transports supplying the troops with cargoes of sheep and bullocks from Cork. The return passage across the Celtic Sea was a dangerous one. On a recent crossing a Whitby-owned vessel called *Lion* had been separated 'by a gale of wind' from the others. The *Lion*'s captain wrote a letter home, relaying subsequent events. It was post-dated 6 November 1760:

In our passage from Quiberon bay to Corke, being parted from our convoy, by a gale of wind, I was attacked by the St Teresa privateer of St Malo's, capt Noel Tromythe, of 240 tons, 16 guns, eight swivels and 68 men, but fought seven guns on one side. After a smart engagement for three hours, and monsieur's boarding me twice, he thought proper to make off, leaving in our ship two of his men killed, and the third captain wounded, who thinks their first captain and a great number of their men were killed. I, together with five of my people, were wounded, and two balls went through my hat. Most of our masts and rigging were quite shattered, all our sails full of shot holes, and our larboard side is very full of musket and cannon balls. His Majesty's ship the Speedwell has assisted us with twelve men to refit our ship. I had only six guns and twenty people, at most, men and boys.[8]

The letter not only captures the hostility of the European seas during the early 1760s, it also conveys the depth of patriotic duty sailors felt. The war had changed them. Already competent, the conflict had disrupted their normal rhythms, taking them far from the familiar sea routes. Their outlook had been recalibrated too. Everyone knew about the execution of Admiral John Byng for negligence in March 1757. The circumstances – that Byng had failed to satisfactorily engage a French opponent off Minorca – had been much debated in the coffee houses. On the quarterdecks of men-of-war the lesson had been digested rather more readily. It reinforced an existing hardness in British sailors, encouraging what would ripen into a celebrated blend of qualities: a determination to seize the initiative, a disregard for personal safety, an ironic-detachment from events. Sailors would learn to react to stimuli with opposites. They would respond to danger with indifference, to tragedy with humour, victory with magnanimity. While zigzagging through the perilous shoals, sandbanks, and incisor-like rocks in the St Lawrence River in the celebrated manoeuvre that set the stage for Wolfe's victory at the Battle of the Plains of Abraham, 'old Killick', master of a transport *Goodwill*, was said to have called to his mate, with laudable sangfroid, 'D— me, if there are not a thousand places in the Thames fifty times more hazardous than this; I am ashamed that Englishmen should make such a rout about it.'[9]

Beyond pure honour, for merchantmen there was an economic motive too. Into the 1760s, few colliers were insured, a fact that meant the loss of a cargo often resulted in the ruin of a career or the fortunes of a family. Those like Milner who doubled as owners and sailing masters had all the more reason to take care of their ships. They 'generally had such a high sense of honor', wrote one of his peers, 'that no hardships or danger appeared to them so formidable, as an imputation on their conduct as seamen. Had they lost a ship, and it was supposed to be owing either to ignorance, or carelessness, it was long before they were intrusted with the charge of another.'[10]

We know almost nothing about Milner. We don't know his height, whether he was dark or fair, round or lithe, loquacious or gloomy. He exists, historically, only in hazy hologram form. Equally, all we need to know is documented in statistics. For if sailing colliers and bringing them safely home was a test of character, it was one Milner passed time and again. The decades from the 1720s to the 1750s brim with accounts of lost transports, vessels striking against Whitby Rock or bilged on the Black Middens off Shields. Yet Milner's name does not appear once. We know he was given command of a vessel called *Mary Ann* when he was nineteen. From then, in 1728, throughout his career, there is no documented case of Milner being involved in an accident. It is a reminder that the finest of Whitby's sailors were those who left the scarcest of traces. All to be found is a laconic record of commands: the *Triton* in the 1740s, *Friends Glory* not long after, *Neptune* in the 1750s and the *Earl of Pembroke*.[11]

Milner had a spartan approach to the running of his ships. One way to calculate the workload on the Georgian seas is to compare the ratio of enlisted sailors to registered tonnage. A man-of-war commonly had a ratio of three tons per man. On an East or West Indiaman it was fifteen tons a man. But labour was hardest of all in coasting merchantmen like Whitby colliers, with the sailor-to-tonnage ratio rising to as much as thirty tons per man. In real terms this meant more effort was demanded from each sailor. Managing the ship when she was underway was only the beginning of it. In addition to this, sailors on lightly manned colliers were faced with an endless and exhausting list of duties: hauling anchors, spinning yarn, patching sails, caulking seams, shifting ballast, swabbing timbers.

On occasion masters drove their men too hard. In 1758 a merchant had arrived in the Isles of Scilly, 'which had been out so long that her bottom was quite green and her rigging and sails bleached white. The crew were so emaciated with continual fatigue and their strength so much exhausted that they could scarcely hold themselves on the yards, and one of them was so weak that he fell from the mainyard as the ship came into the Sound.'[12] Nothing like this was ever said against Milner but the facts reveal a picture. On his maiden voyage in the *Earl of Pembroke*, the ratio stood at twenty-eight tons a man. This tells us several things: Milner was parsimonious, or he had a calculating shrewdness at any rate; he was willing to run his men hard; and he was confident in his ability to pull through in a crisis. Milner's path to riches was neither paved nor straight. His wealth had been amassed through incrementalism, the gathering together of little profits from long voyages on the northern seas.

The one tangible trace of Milner's physical presence is retained in a bill of receipt from December 1748. The scrap of paper contains no compelling information at first glance. It only tells us that it was signed at Scarborough and that Milner acknowledged a debt of £1 15s, owed to a John Richardson. At the bottom of the receipt is an intriguing detail. The signature 'Thos. Milner' is not signed but written. And within the signature is a half-florid, half-timorous letter 'M'. The 'M' starts confidently with an extravagant loop. But within a fraction of a second the writer loses their confidence. What begins as a deft shape ends with a rushed downward stroke. Perhaps Milner had been resting on a moving surface – there were no shortages of these in his life – but the 'M' is more evocative than that. Printed beneath the 'M' is the word 'Mark', conclusive proof that Milner was illiterate.[13]

This frail detail opens up Milner's wider biography. There were many divisions in Georgian society, between titled and common people, men and women, masters and servants. One of the sharpest distinctions was between those able to read and those 'whose culture was still essentially oral'.[14] Milner was of this latter class. His knowledge was practical and instinctive rather than cerebral and learned. For Milner, even the basic practice of dead reckoning – measuring speed in knots with a chip-log and plotting progress on a chart – would have been fraught. That he thrived for so long with this disadvantage speaks of his vigilance. 'The best navigator is the best looker-outer', as Pepys said. Whitby sailors knew this only too well. The unusual geography of the town left them naturally cautious. To the east of the piers a treacherous shale shelf, known as Whitby Rock, lay concealed below the waterline. At some point, a channel had been cut across the rock. Known as the Sled or Sledway, it was just wide and deep enough to allow a vessel to pass at high tide. To Whitby's captains, running the Sled, as the practice was known, became a matter of pride as much as practicality. The channel was entered from the harbour by aligning the rose window of the north transept of the abbey with a starboard bow, and letting 'it roll along the cliff top' as a vessel made east.[15]

This was a typical piece of traditional wisdom, one invested with local meaning that could be handed down from the masters to mates, from servants to apprentices, one generation to the next. To make details memorable, directions were often smoothed into verse: 'First the Dudgeon, then the Spurn, Flamborough Head is next in turn, Filey Brigg is drawing nigh, Scarboro' Castle stands on high', ran the doggerel that pointed the sea path from London to Newcastle, 'Whitby Rock lies out to sea, So steer two points more northerly':

> Hartlepool lies in the bight,
> Seaham Harbour is now in sight.
> The 'Old Man' says: 'If the weather's right,
> We'll be in the Tyne this very night.'[16]

These mantras, allied with observation, moon-lore and the North Star, Polaris, accompanied Milner wherever he went. Unable to write, he could not commit to the record an eyewitness account of his spell as master of the *Earl of Pembroke*. But as he sailed out of Whitby, one of his contemporaries was not far away. Unlike Milner, Henry Taylor could write and he captured the life of a Whitby master-mariner in a memoir. 'I have not been very solicitous about the choice of language, but have endeavoured to write the whole in that plain stile I am accustomed to use in common conversation', Taylor wrote, 'and to represent facts as they really were.'[17]

'The genius of the inhabitants of Whitby has a most surprising turn for the sea', Charlton had written in his *History*. 'Children as soon as they are capable of action, endeavour to get upon the water, to handle the oar, to manage the sails of a boat, and to steer. Hence it comes to pass, that when they are sent to sea, at the age of thirteen or fourteen years, they are already more than half sailors, and understand every thing belonging to a ship.'[18]

Henry Taylor had been one such apprentice during Charlton's early years in Whitby. Raised by a lone parent, there had not been enough funds to send him to school. But even had there been, there was little chance he would have gone. 'I always had a strong inclination [of a seafaring life]', he later wrote, 'and notwithstanding the entreaties of a tender parent, to choose a less dangerous employment, I could not be prevailed on.'[19]

In 1750, at the age of thirteen, Taylor was bound into a six-year apprenticeship. These were years of drudgery in the coal trade, scarping and dubbing decks, mending sails, caulking the hull with oakum; heaving the ballast, sleeping in doghole hatches before the mast, and subsisting on a diet of beer, Stockton or Suffolk cheese, salted beef, oatmeal and the occasional ox's head. Meditating on his apprenticeship years later, Taylor decided it was the making of him. The secret, he reckoned, lay in order and routine. Obedience bred discipline. Everything ran to a strict hierarchy: master, mate, carpenter, sailors, apprentices. This chain was further shaded by age and experience. 'Each one', wrote Taylor, 'had some part of the ship's stores under his particular care, which he was bound to have in readiness whenever called for.' The sailors were rarely beaten. Instead of blows or abusive language, 'mates contrived to substitute shame and degradation'. Little challenges were set: the first to turn out of a morning, the best at shining the deck, the strongest at the windlass palls. These 'were objects contended for by men and boys as points of honor'.[20]

The surface of the ship was separated into three sections – the forecastle, the main deck and the quarterdeck – all of which were places of different work, that admitted different people, and had different rules. Time was divided into moons, days, tides, watches, the hour it took for grains of sand to empty from one side of a glass to another. Days and nights would merge and vanish in an endless round of heaving anchors, shifting berths, manning braces, bending sails, rummaging the hold and fishing masts. Apprentices 'never durst go on shore without leave of the mate', recalled Taylor, and leave was rarely given more than once a week. Instead these boys were to be the energy of the ship, their movements the whim of the captain. This was Taylor's life for six years. Only on three occasions in that time did his master choose to leave the safety of the coasting trade for something else: deep-water voyages, once to Norway and twice to Stockholm.

Taylor wrote a memoir of these years that committed to history a picture of the Newcastle coal trade. He emerges as an able, industrious hard-headed young man. Having been released from his apprenticeship, he left the coal trade, finding work on a Hull-owned ship bound for the Baltic. Taylor thought the management of this vessel slack from the outset. The master was a lazy fellow, 'proud and supercilious', and his mate, 'though he knew his duty', was a drunken sop. Sailing before the mast with a set of inexperienced sailors, Taylor watched as disharmony ripened into frequent quarrels. The ship loaded coals at Newcastle and then crossed to Lübeck. It was a well-known but challenging route, weaving between Denmark, Sweden and the splintered islands that guarded the entrance to the Baltic Sea. Each night the master slipped beneath to his cabin to sleep, while the mate drank himself senseless. Alone on deck the young apprentices were abandoned to chart whatever course they wished. Twice they almost foundered.

On returning from Riga, and turning through between the Dwall Grounds, and the main, with a press of wind, the master was so inconsiderate as to go to sleep. It was night, standing in for the land at the rate of five or six knots; the mate, standing on the windlass-end, fell asleep; a young man at the helm, who had often been at Riga, said to me, 'We are running too far in'; I immediately snatched up the lead, and finding little more than three fathoms, cried out, 'Hard-a-lee, Tom.' The helm was immediately put down, the sea being smooth, the ship came quickly about; but so stupidly drunk and asleep was the mate, that we were hauling the head yards about before he awoke.[21]

This willingness to seize control marked Taylor out. By the next year, at the age of twenty-one, he was offered command of a collier. He was nearly the same age that Milner had been when he had been appointed a master. But Taylor turned down this opportunity, believing himself inexperienced. After another season as a mate, Taylor was again offered command. This time he accepted. It was now the late-1750s, the Seven Years War was in contest. Taylor spent these years sailing the same transport routes as Milner, carrying horses to the River Weser in Germany, armaments to Belle-Île off Brittany, and bullocks and sheep from Cork to the French coast.

Still in his early twenties, Taylor took the lessons of his apprenticeship and moulded them into his own distinctive leadership style. He was firm, frank, sometimes belligerent. At Belle-Île he provoked a diplomatic squabble with the bilious captain of a sloop-of-war whom Taylor accused of rash seamanship. No accusation was as venomous to a naval officer. The incident ended up with the captain boarding Taylor's collier, catching him by the collar, then making off with his mate. Taylor, obstinate as ever, still refused to desist. He believed a level of inflexibility was vital in the management of a ship. 'Whenever I got any new men, I took an early opportunity to inform them', he explained, 'that I admitted no cursing, swearing, or the like, in my ship; that I would as long as they sailed with me treat them with tenderness and humanity; but unless they governed themselves by the rules which I had prescribed, I would take the first opportunity of discharging them.'

'The power of emulation, united with sobriety and an ardent application', Taylor believed, would deliver a sailor from both temptation and an early death on the seas. 'It has always been my maxim', Taylor elaborated, 'To love all men, and fear none.' And along with his memoir, Taylor may have left behind a tattered cash book belonging to one of the town's coal colliers which was unearthed among the archives of Barclays Bank in Whitby in the mid-twentieth century. Half-destroyed, the book was once owned by a master called 'Blash' Taylor, who had sailed in the 1750s. 'Blash', a nickname, was obscure. But Henry was the only Taylor known to have been working in the coasting trade in these years.

The cash book contains the history of a lost trade, a history conveyed by numbers. It shows Taylor's ship made thirty-four voyages from Newcastle to London during a five-year period, an average of just under seven trips a year. The total cost of the ship when it was purchased was £1,887 9s 7½d, which was divided into the usual sixty-four shares of £29 9s 10d, of which Taylor was the owner of one.[22]

The book charts the items sourced in fitting out the vessel. There were spars, oars, a topgallant mast, elm board, junk or old rope, 'coyles' of twine, hundredweights of rope, 'skeins' of Murlin wool. The food for the voyages is tallied too. Suffolk cheese was twelve or thirteen shillings a hundredweight. Salt beef was a staple and was bought for eighteen shillings per hundredweight. Sometimes there would be a bushel of peas (sixteen shillings), a hundredweight of potatoes (eighteen shillings), or a similar measure of raisins (eleven shillings) and several firkins of flour (£1 6s 8d), enough to bake a raisin pudding. To all of this was added a steady flow of alcohol, mostly beer at seven shillings a barrel but sometimes a mixture of brandy and sugar too, to toast special occasions.

But most revealing is the book's record of interactions at Newcastle. It was there, at Shields, that the Whitby mariners would conduct their business with a representative from the collieries, men known informally as 'crimps'. The cash book reads:

Brandy and sugar for delivery	10s 0d
Master's bill and lightermen	2s 0d
Ballast heaving	17s 6d
Crimp's bill and labour	£130 6s 6d
Crimp's man	2s 6d

Contained in this list is the whole interaction at Shields. It marks the meeting between master and crimp; the master treating his contact to brandy. There's another bill for the lightermen – those who sculled the coal up the Tyne in keels – the bluff-bowed sailing craft, forty foot long and twenty foot wide, steered with a great oar. Next the ballast is heaved over the side of the collier and exchanged for the coal, freshly mined from the pits around Durham and Sunderland. Once loaded, the crimp issues his bill. A tip is laid aside for his man. Then the collier is ready for the tide and the wind.

J. M. W. Turner depicted this moment of exchange in his landscape *Shields on the River Tyne* (1823). Although painted two generations after Milner and Taylor, the scene would have hardly changed. The painting is a dreamy nocturne. A huge, lambent moon shines in the east, its iridescence casting a dazzling blue light that gleams across the black water. The coolness is offset by a flaming fire that burns between two brigs that are being loaded from keels. The coal is heaped high on the crafts. On top of one pile stands a tall figure, throwing a spadeful through one of the ports. Two sailors lean over the starboard rail, idling, risking the ire of the master. In the foreground there is the outline of a lady in conversation with one of the sailors: carrying food, maybe, or enquiring after a ship. The night seems the ideal setting to portray this obscure, mostly forgotten history. The tides have lifted the keels level with the colliers, the crimp has struck his bargain, and the hopes for a profit are at their peak.

This is the scene Milner and the *Earl of Pembroke* sailed into in July 1764 on their maiden voyage. Loading would take several hours with the rattle of coal clattering against the oak floors: carbon rubbing against wood, the crackle and leap of a fire outside, the shriek of gulls and the cool breeze of a summer's night.

*

By the beginning of August 1764 the *Earl of Pembroke* was doubling back to the south. This was the peak of the sailing season and she was not alone. Making the passage from Newcastle to London alongside her was John Bernard in *Amity's Encrease*, William Russell in *Neptune*, Trews Dobson in *George and Mary*, Edward Robson in *Henry*, William Bain in *Duke of Cumberland*, Theodorus Ambrose in *Rockwood*, and a dozen others who for the next ten days would become a band of brothers cruising along the coastal route to London.

Colliers travelled in convoys like flocks of birds for protection and navigation. Although this was a passage every master in the coal trade had made dozens of times, it carried an element of danger. While the wars had concluded, there lingered the possibility a rogue privateer might be preying on commerce somewhere in the sea. Then there were the navigational advantages of being one among many. The collier fleets rarely, if ever, stopped at a port. Taylor reckoned some of them 'have gone seven years, eight or ten voyages each year, and never in all that time put into harbour by the way.' Almost always afloat, the fleet would progress from one roadstead to the next, mewed up close, their masters keeping them fast at single anchor. 'I have known upwards of one hundred sail lie wind-bound in Yarmouth-roads', Taylor wrote, 'two or three weeks in perfect safety.'[23]

Once the *Earl of Pembroke* had passed Whitby's piers and the broad, rocky expanse of Robin Hood's Bay, a series of landmarks would pass the starboard bow. There would be Scarborough, where the idea of seaside was beginning, with its castle high on the prow of the cliff and its bathing machines in the shallows. Next would be Filey with its rocky brig darting into the sea, so some fancied, like a dragon's spine. From there the golden sands of its pancake-flat beach, one of the finest in England, curved in a graceful arc to the chalk cliffs at Flamborough, where gannets nested in crevices and the sea wore hollows in the cliff bottoms. After this was the harbour of refuge at Bridlington, then Spurn Head, before the thickening of the coastal traffic as the colliers passed Hull and the Humber Estuary.

On a summer's day this would have been fair sailing, in thirty-five even fathoms. But beyond Hull the waters became treacherous. *A Chart of the Sea Coast from London to Flamborough Head* (1743) by G. Woodhouse marks the collier's path with a pricked line. After Hull, the comfortable thirty-five fathoms narrows to an undulating ten or twelve, shallows well capable of throwing up a short, boisterous sea. Where before there had been open water, there were now sandbanks off the Lincolnshire and Norfolk coasts: Burnham Flatts, the Dudgeon Shoal, Hasborough Sand, Orrey, the Lemon. By the opening days of August the collier fleet had passed Yarmouth, rounded the headland at Orford and entered the Thames Estuary. The northern seas were now behind them. Mingling in this, England's most famous artery, were the seventy-four-gun three-deckers of the Royal Navy with their lines of gun ports and towering masts; the suave, fast-sailing sloops, East Indiamen, and traders from far-flung oceans. Not many days before, a thirty-two-gun frigate, *Dolphin*, commanded by John Byron had passed through these waters, beginning a voyage of circumnavigation that, ludicrous as it would have seemed to Milner, one day his collier would follow.

All of these cast the *Earl of Pembroke*, in prime condition on her maiden voyage, into anonymity. But for the customary glance of a naval officer, to check that she had struck her topsails as she was required on passing one of the king's ships, no one would have noticed the Whitby collier, crouching low in the water with her belly full of coal. In the lower reaches of the Thames, Milner and his mate, John Brown, needed all of their experience. Sea room was narrow. Beating upriver into the westerlies without running foul of a ship was always a challenge. Colliers often ghosted in on the flood tide, a natural conveyance that lifted ships, carrying them past Tilbury, Graves, Dagenham and the horseshoe bends in the Thames at Barking and Greenwich and, finally, to the wharves and Customs House at Wapping. Hundreds of colliers clustered up the narrowing river on a single tide at the height of the season with London, dark, powerful, teeming, unfurling around them.

Opening the *Public Advertiser* on Tuesday 7 August 1764, and running their eyes down the column headed 'SHIP NEWS', a London merchant might have just noticed the earliest recorded trace of Milner's new collier. At the foot of a subsection titled 'COLLIERS *from Newcastle*', she emerges from obscurity in five neat words: '*Earl of Pembroke*, Thomas Milner.'[24]

To stroll along the Strand in 1764, London's chief commercial thoroughfare, was to see the world in miniature. Here almost every one of the elegant four- or five-storey town houses that lined the route had a shop on its ground floor. Glass-fronted, neatly ordered and brightly lit, nowhere on earth showcased such a variety of goods. There was tea from China, coffee from Arabia, cocoa and sugar from Jamaica, cottons and silks from Madras, tobacco from the plantations in Virginia and the Carolinas, furs from New York, and ladies' stays made from the bones of whales hunted in the bleak northern oceans.

It was this cosmopolitanism that had prompted Joseph Addison, fifty years before, to dub London 'a kind of Emporium for the whole Earth'.[25] Having outpaced Paris at the start of the century, London's population had climbed to about 750,000 by the 1760s. It now stood poised to become the first European capital since ancient Rome to reach a million inhabitants. 'The city is now what ancient Rome was', the *London Guide* had proclaimed. From the Strand to the opulent streets of Mayfair, the wealthy could peek into windows, hunt out exotic items and indulge in an early incarnation of the modern concept of 'shopping'. 'There was never from the earliest ages', Samuel Johnson wrote, 'a time in which trade so much engaged the attention of mankind, or commercial gain was sought with such general emulation.'[26] The papers did their best to advertise any merchandise as it became available. And on 11 December 1764, four months after Milner sailed up the Thames, they carried news of a different arrival. 'On Monday evening last', the *London Chronicle* announced, 'the ingenious and much-esteemed Dr Benjamin Franklin, arrived here from Philadelphia.'[27]

At fifty-eight, Franklin was recognised as a writer of great eloquence and wit, talents displayed in his wildly popular *Poor Richard's Almanac*. But his celebrity came most of all from his fearless electrical experiments, when he had astonished the world by taming lightning with a conducting rod. Celebrated across America and Europe as an intrepid 'electrician', Franklin had received honorary doctorates from the universities of St Andrews and Oxford, as well as the Royal Society's Copley Medal. He was now back in London, a city he knew and loved. His earliest visit had come four decades earlier when, as a hearty lad of twenty, he had made himself conspicuous in the capital, swimming gracefully up and down the Thames – skills pioneered in Boston harbour. Now a stout sage, there would be no swimming on this, his third visit to London. It had taken him just a month to cross the Atlantic on a turbulent passage from Philadelphia to the Channel. On

9 December he had reached Portsmouth and a night more had seen him to his old lodgings off the Strand at Craven Street, where Mrs Stevenson the housekeeper had been 'a good deal surpriz'd to find me in her Parlour'.[28]

Franklin was happy to be back. A year before he had written to the Stevenson family from Philadelphia:

> Of all the enviable Things England has, I envy it most its People. Why should that petty Island, which compar'd to America is but like a stepping Stone in a Brook, scarce enough of it above Water to keep one's Shoes dry; why, I say, should that little Island, enjoy in almost every Neighbourhood, more sensible, virtuous and elegant Minds, than we can collect in ranging 100 Leagues of our vast Forests.[29]

In his merry way, Franklin was reflecting on one of the geographical truths of the Georgian world. It was increasingly vast, yet it remained tiny at its core. A one-mile radius from Mrs Stevenson's parlour, Franklin knew, took in the homes of so many of the age's leading lights. The artist Joshua Reynolds lived at 47 Leicester Fields. The actor David Garrick lived at 27 Southampton Street. A short distance from there was Covent Garden, home to the composer Thomas Arne, and the elocutionist Thomas Sheridan. Closer still to Craven Street, at the far side of Hungerford Market, were the York Buildings where the maker of scientific instruments, John Bird, worked on his much-desired brass telescopes, quadrants and sextants. Near to Bird was Beaufort Street, where Tobias Smollett had written *Roderick Random* in 1748. A minute's walk more would take Franklin away from the lusty commercialism of the Strand into the earthy practicality of Fleet Street and its adjoining maze of courts and alleys – Flying House Court, Hanging Sword Alley, Red Lion Court – home to journalists, pamphleteers, poets and writers, among them Oliver Goldsmith and Samuel Johnson.

The proximity of the writers of Fleet Street, the actors of Covent Garden, the politicians of Soho or Westminster and the aristocrats of Mayfair made it all the easier for them to cluster into their own intellectual tribes. 'Man is a sociable being', Franklin had once written, a pithy distillation of his conviction that 'there is a sociable affinity based on the natural instinct of benevolence among fellow humans'.[30] Back in the heart of the hive, from December 1764 onwards Franklin would merge into the genial environment that he found so stimulating. London was filled with clubs, debating societies and coffee shops, where friends could gather to chew over the political happenings of the day, debate philosophical schemes or propose projects that may be of benefit to themselves or wider society.

The 'clubbable' culture – as Johnson termed it – was in many ways the realisation of an ambition declared by Addison in the *Spectator* in 1711, of bringing 'Philosophy out of Closets and Libraries, Schools and Colleges', and allowing it 'to dwell in Clubs and Assemblies, at Tea-tables, and in Coffee houses'.[31] There existed clubs of all political stamps and social backgrounds, but often their outlook was pragmatic and humanistic, with emphasis on the Enlightenment virtue of 'improvement'. Johnson's 'Club' – including Edmund Burke and Joshua Reynolds – met on Monday nights at the Turk's Head in Greek Street, Soho. Franklin preferred the company of practical men of science. He was a member of the Royal Society Club, styled 'The Royal Philosophers', who congregated weekly at the Mitre on Fleet Street, where they blended philosophical conversation with a pint of wine and a formidable menu of fowls and exotic fruits. Franklin would attend whenever he could. 'I find I love Company, Chat, a Laugh, a Glass and even a Song, as well as ever; and at the same Time relish, better than I used to do, the grave Observations and wise Sentences of Old Men's Conversation', he wrote.[32]

This was 'Old Men's' conversation in the main. But many things had happened in the interval between the end of Franklin's last visit, in 1762, and the beginning of this new one. Among them was the unexpected appearance of an erudite, intriguing female voice, 'The Celebrated Mrs Macaulay'. Virtually unknown, in 1763 Catharine Macaulay had delighted the literary world with the publication of the *History of England from the Accession of James I to that of the Brunswick Line*. 'The History of England by a Lady seems such an extraordinary phenomenon, that every one eagerly asks the reasons of its appearance', ran a review in the *London Chronicle*.[33] Macaulay was in her early thirties. She was recently married and lived in fashionable St James's Place, near the palace, an address that belied her political opinions. She was no timid historian. Instead her *History* of seventeenth-century England was really a long meditation on the question of 'liberty' and it emphasised the abuses of political power by a tyrannical ruling elite. Macaulay was not finished yet. She would continue publishing more volumes of her history, along with the odd political tract. In one, *Loose Remarks* (1767), Macaulay would articulate her preference for democracy, 'the only form of government which is capable of preserving dominion and freedom to the people'.[34]

Macaulay's emergence came at a time when Britons were once again questioning the role of the government in their lives. The last century had seen a development in the apparatus and reach of the state and Franklin, as much as anyone, would have been able to appreciate the massive reach of Britain's growing empire. The same Union Jacks that fluttered everywhere over London's skyline had taken on new symbolism in the last few years. It depicted Britannia reborn: boisterous, vast, brawling, brave, glorious, striving, undaunted, favoured, free. This same Union Jack, with its jet blues and fiery reds, flew not only over London and Franklin's Philadelphia, but ever since the Treaty of Paris had been signed on 10 February 1763 it was aloft in places incomprehensibly distant. In the 'scratch of a pen', as Francis Parkman would put it, France had ceded to Britain all its possessions in Quebec, the Great Lakes Region and everything to the east of the Mississippi. While Spain had taken Louisiana in the geopolitical horse-trading, Britain had swapped Florida for Havana. William Pitt had observed that Britain had 'over-run more world' in the war than the Romans had conquered in a century.

Franklin approved of Britain's expansion. As a precocious boy in Boston he had got hold of a copy of Defoe's *An Essay Upon Projects*. He had lived to see the brisk, mercantile society Defoe had envisaged take shape. Everywhere London was being improved, by glittering lights, neater pavements and elegant squares. New Westminster Bridge had opened in 1750, costing £389,500. Another bridge had opened at Kew and one at Blackfriars would follow. Land was being turned to profit. A 'small piece of ground in Piccadilly', ran a report in 1764, had been sold for £2,500 having been bought a generation before for a mere £30. Charles Dingley, known as the projector of roads, had built the New Road that ran from Edgware to the Angel at Islington, giving London a new outer boundary and plenty of room for expansion. By 1764 Dingley was nurturing ideas for a 'wind-powered' sawmill that would eventually open in Limehouse in 1767, winning him a gold medal from the Society for the Encouragement of Arts, Manufactures and Commerce. 'The folly of projection is very seldom the folly of a fool', Johnson had reminded his readers in the *Adventurer*, 'it is commonly the ebullition of a capacious mind, crowded with variety of knowledge, and heated with intenseness of thought'.[35]

To enhance the feeling of a nation on the rise was the still-recent accession of George III in October 1760. If Britain was the new Rome, George could hardly be said to be a Sulla or a Caesar – he was known to enjoy gardening too much for either of those comparisons to stick – but he was young, sober and dedicated to his role as sovereign. 'Born and educated in this country, I glory in the name of Britain', he had flattered his audience in his accession speech to Parliament. With thriving trade, a new king, a young optimistic population and a release of pent-up energy after years of conflict, the outlook could hardly have seemed rosier. Already the newspapers were trotting out the cliché 'a time of profound peace' to describe the political environment in 1764, as the *Earl of Pembroke* entered the Thames. But by the time Milner came alongside and made for the Customs House to pay the duty of five shillings a ton on his load of coal, the first signs that this was not going to be a golden age of peace and prosperity were already present. It was well known that the war had been financially ruinous. On 5 January 1763 – a month before the Treaty of Paris was signed – the British national debt stood at the quivering figure of £122,603,336, a sum which generated an annual interest of £4,409,797.[36]

Concerns about the debt had already influenced British politics. In 1761 Pitt had resigned, having failed to convince his colleagues to declare war on Spain. In May 1762 his long-time colleague and the government's figurehead, the Duke of Newcastle, had followed Pitt, having fallen out with the king. On 29 May 1762, John Stuart, third Earl of Bute, had become First Commissioner of the Treasury. Bute was a problematic character. Just shy of fifty, capable and charming in conversation, Bute had virtues. But many considered him toxic. Since 1755 he had tutored the young prince – now king – George, and there was a general feeling that he had a dangerous ascendancy over him. There were rumours the king could not operate without Bute's counsel and that a full-length portrait of him hung in the monarch's private closet. Bute's pungency was intensified by the fact that he was a Scot at a time when the Jacobite Rebellion of 1745 – supported by Highland clans – remained fresh in memory. Unfortunate for Bute, too, was his surname 'Stuart', a named loathed by the English. That a Stuart had supplanted a Pitt as Britain's premier decision-maker was hard to stomach. When it became known that Bute was an advocate for peace – again in contrast to Pitt – many felt that he was acting too hastily, ending a war that was progressing in Britain's favour. After Bute ascended to power, the dash towards peace had intensified. Following the peace of 1763, the general feeling was that France had been treated too timidly. Rather than ending years of conflict, the peace set a new series of events in motion.

This was the world the *Earl of Pembroke* entered on her first voyage to London. By 1764 it was possible to glimpse the powerful forces that would shape her life in the years ahead. Resentment towards Bute was one of these. The profound dislike for him as the king's favourite had been engendered by the most polarising political figure for decades. In 1762 John Wilkes had been in his mid-thirties. As the MP for Aylesbury he had sat on a few committees and supported the Pitt faction, but he had never risen to high office and if he was known for anything at all it was for his scandalous personal life. Famously ugly, with a projecting bottom jaw, uneven teeth and wandering eyes, in a peacock society these disadvantages may have kept Wilkes far out of fashionable circles at home in the shires. But with his sparkling wit, Wilkes had turned his physical appearance into a part of his peculiar, rakish allure. He boasted that he could explain away his face to a woman in thirty minutes. Horace Walpole declared him 'Abominable in private life, dull in Parliament, but, they say, very entertaining in a room.'[37]

In 1762 Wilkes had embarked on one of the most outrageous episodes in British political history. As a writer he was a master of devious satire and fiery invective. Loathing Bute and aiming to have Pitt reinstalled, Wilkes had devised a subversive publication he called the *North Briton*. Conceived in reaction to a pro-government title called the *Briton*, Wilkes was the chief writer and editor of the *North Briton*, which he wrote in the voice of a gleeful, smug, provocative Scotsman. For a year Wilkes had used the *North Briton* as a way of abusing Bute and undermining his political authority. In an early edition Wilkes had his 'North Briton' 'heartily congratulate my dear countrymen on our having at length accomplished the great, long sought and universally national object of all our wishes, the planting of a *Scotsman* at the head of the *English* Treasury'.[38] Tapping into popular dislike and mistrust of the Scots, Wilkes had invented a spoof publication, *The Future Chronicle*. Set at some point in the not so distant future, it contained the following news items:

> Yesterday morning the two new-raised regiments of Highland guards were reviewed in Hyde Park by his grace the duke of *Inverness*, who was pleased to say, 'They kenn'd their business right weel, and went through their exercise very connily.' ... Some time since died Mr John Bull, a very worthy, plain, honest old gentleman, of Saxon descent. He was choked by inadvertently swallowing a *thistle*, which he had placed by way of ornament on the top of his sallad. For many years before he had enjoyed a remarkable state of good health.[39]

For ten months the *North Briton* had progressed in a cocktail of jibes, flouts and jeers at Bute, or as Wilkes put it, 'good combustible material' that was served up to its rowdy readership. Although the government soon found out the paper was chiefly produced by Wilkes, they could not prosecute him for libel as he cloaked his authorship in anonymity. As his paper became infamous Wilkes grew ever more intrepid, accusing Bute of 'incapacity or villainy' over his handling of the finances. By the time of Franklin's return in 1764 the *North Briton* was defunct. Wilkes had finally overreached himself in the infamous edition No. 45, when he had accused the king of lying to Parliament. Months of legal wrangling had followed, but eventually Wilkes was chased into exile and declared an outlaw. 'This compleated the ruin of that unfortunate gentleman, who engaged for some time so great a part of the public attention, and whose wit, spirit, and good humour, if not carried to such unwarrantable excess, merited, and would, probably, have met with, a very different fortune', concluded the *Annual Register*.[40]

Wilkes had gone, but he had toppled Bute before he left. Replacing the king's favourite was a new ministry led by George Grenville, Pitt's assertive brother-in-law. Still aiming to resolve the debt problem, Grenville had continued Bute's policies. As well as persevering with the Cider Act he looked across the Atlantic for additional sources of income. At the time of the Treaty of Paris the relationship between Britain and her American colonies had seemed robust. 'Never did England make a Peace more truly and substantially advantageous to herself', Franklin had written to a friend, 'for here in America she has laid a broad and strong Foundation on which to erect the most beneficial and certain Commerce, with the Greatness and Stability of her Empire. The Glory of Britain was never higher than at present, and I think you never had a better Prince.'[41]

But over the months following Franklin's return to Craven Street, he saw the harmony between the British government and the American colonies erode. Derided as 'the grand financier' by Burke, Grenville was firmly of the mind that the colonies should contribute towards the cost of their defence. The colonies, he knew, paid far less in taxes than their British equivalents and the general feeling was that they had benefited enormously from British protection during the Seven Years War. Grenville had immediately started tinkering with the system. He introduced a levy of £7 a ton on the fine Madeira wine that sold so well in the colonies. At the same time he commanded the royal customs officials to do a more rigorous job of collecting existing taxes. On top of this he implemented a new duty on Caribbean molasses, a vital ingredient in American rum.

These measures had been passing through Parliament in 1764 as Fishburn was at work on the *Earl of Pembroke*. Known collectively as the Sugar Act, one governor reported that the new legislation 'caused greater alarm in this country than the taking of Fort William Henry did in 1757'.[42] A constitutional principle was at stake: the right of Parliament to tax the American colonies without their consent. The tax coincided with a post-war slump in the colonial economy, aggravating its reception. But worse would soon follow in 1765 as the Stamp Act became law. This would levy duties on all stamped documentation including letters, legal papers, college degrees, liquor licences, mortgages and newspapers. Franklin did not anticipate the venomous reaction. But he soon heard about it. Reports reached London of an explosive release of aggression, with raucous mobs in Virginia and Massachusetts. In the tiny Rhode Island colony the invective was as sharp as anywhere. Having seen himself burnt in effigy, one 'Tory' supporter of the British government, Dr Thomas Moffat, was outed as one of 'these infamous Traitors at the first Glance'. 'I think no Man ought to be hanged for his Looks', seethed one resident in Newport, Rhode Island, 'but I am thankfull to Providence, that the Dispositions of some Men are so strongly express'd in their Countenances that they only need to be seen to be despised.'[43]

The fury found coherence in Boston with a band of dissidents calling themselves the 'Sons of Liberty'. Colonial buildings were torched and the distributors for stamps were harassed and attacked. One was nearly buried alive. For Franklin himself, who followed reports from the heart of imperial London, the Stamp Act signalled the beginning of his transformation from loyal subject of the king, to revolutionary Patriot warrior.

These cross currents of politics and economics would soon lead to an equally complete transformation for the *Earl of Pembroke*, which, between 1764–7, lived the most settled years of her life. Milner's movements, plying the coastal trade, were captured in notices in *Lloyds Evening Post* and the *Public Advertiser*. She was in the Pool of London in August 1764. On 20 September she had arrived again from Newcastle. On 19 December she was back on a late-season dash. She returned on 21 March 1765 as the Stamp Act was being passed in Parliament, and then again in June and in October. In 1766 there are gaps – signs possibly of a Baltic cruise or a trip to the Royal Dockyards. Or perhaps the *Earl of Pembroke* was caught up in the gale of January 1767, a storm as cruel as any Henry Taylor ever saw. Both the *Earl of Pembroke* and Milner appear again in July 1767. She makes her final appearance in the newspapers on 25 August 1767.

By that time Franklin had met the figure who was to have a more direct influence on the *Earl of Pembroke*'s life. Franklin was always attracted to ambitious thinkers. In the mid-1760s he had come to know one of the brightest of these, an adventurous young projector who had a specialist knowledge of the East and eloquent insights into Pacific geography. A prickly, clever Scotsman, Alexander Dalrymple was twenty-eight and was already being spoken of as 'a more romantic person than our modern cold times have produced'. 'Bred a merchant on dry land', his brother had written, 'he has become an able navigator, and if he lives will be an author voluminous and vast.'[44]

For years Dalrymple had been nurturing ideas about how British trade could be expanded in the east. Most of all, though, he was armed with fresh intelligence about an ancient geographic riddle: the presence of an undiscovered southern continent. Arriving in London in 1765, Dalrymple began to gather friends in support of his scheme. Franklin was one convert; the political theorist Adam Smith was another. In February 1767 the Earl of Shelburne, the Secretary of State for the Southern Department, received a letter written by Smith on Dalrymple's behalf. Smith informed Shelburne that Dalrymple was finishing a manu-script 'of all the discoveries that have yet been made in the South Seas'. Whether a southern continent existed, Smith acknowledged, 'may perhaps be uncertain; but supposing it does exist, I am very certain you will never find a man fitter for discovering it, or more determined to hazard everything in order to discover it … The ship properest for such an expedition, he says, would be an old fifty-gun ship without her guns. He does not, however, insist upon this as a *sine qua non*, but will go in any ship with a hundred to a thousand tons.'[45]

At intervals Lionel Charlton may have glimpsed Fishburn's collier as she passed Whitby's piers. As much a lubber as anyone, even he must have been able to distinguish a Whitby ship. Milner may have brought the *Earl of Pembroke* home at times, for winter stretches of rest with his wife, in search of crew or supplies or stores. But by the beginning of 1768, now fifty-nine, he was on his familiar passage south again. A seascape by Thomas Luny frames the scene, *The Bark 'Earl of Pembroke', Later 'Endeavour', Leaving Whitby Harbour in 1768*. It is a bucolic image: calm, soothing. The *Earl of Pembroke* glides into a flat, settled sea. A warm light shines overhead. A few stray sailors stand on deck – it is satisfying to think of Milner among them – while on the foreshore two knots of people chat disregarding the bark that ghosts out into the sea behind them.

If the execution of the picture is unremarkable, the choice of moment is inspired. This seascape has a potent narrative force. Events are primed, yet everyone is ignorant. This would be the last the *Earl of Pembroke* ever saw of her home port. As she slid into the German Ocean events were in flux. In London, Dalrymple's plans were developing. In Paris, John Wilkes was plotting a sensational return to Britain. And then, high above the ship, high above the clouds, into the heavens and towards the firmament of fixed stars, the planet Venus was travelling on its orbit, soon to intersect the space between the earth and the sun.

4

Mr Birds Ways

On 7 January 1768, the Royal Society Club met for their weekly dinner in Fleet Street. Usually only twelve formed the evening's party, as they had the week before when Franklin had attended. But on this, the opening dinner of the new year, there was an exceptional turnout. In all thirty-three dined, and the Mitre had prepared for them a menu of delicious variety, 'salmon, soles, haddocks, achbone of beef, ham & veal pye, neck of mutton roast, plumb-pudding, 2 Lasterlings, turkey, 2 apple pyes, 2 dishes lobsters, a crab, 2 dishes of Tripe, sweetbreads fricasied, capon, beef steaks, butter and cheese'.[1]

At the head of the table sat the Earl of Morton, president of the Society. Also there was Daines Barrington, the lawyer, antiquarian and friend of Thomas Pennant; the Astronomer Royal Nevil Maskelyne; and Lord Charles Cavendish, the inventor of a self-registering thermometer and scion of the Devonshire family. On a dark January evening, between the dim light and high spirits, the crab and claret, this is where acquaintances were made and decisions were shaped. In Georgian Britain, circles of power remained relatively small, and were difficult to penetrate. For newcomers to town, cards or letters of introduction were vital passports into spheres of influence. But they would only ever admit an aspirant to the first step of a slippery staircase. To reach the places where intimacies with the great could be made and true influence could be exerted, remained an impossibility for most. 'No Strangers be admitted to dine here for the future except introduced by the President', affirmed one of the club's by-laws. To be admitted a guest was both an opportunity and a challenge. And that January night, making his debut at the dinner as the guest of the medical doctor Alexander Russell, was Alexander Dalrymple.

It was more than two years since Dalrymple had returned from the east. He had spent much of that time compiling his catalogue of

historical voyages through the South Seas – the period term for the
Pacific Ocean. Though most would have known something of Abel
Tasman, Jacob Le Maire or the Spanish adventurer Juan Fernández's
voyages, Dalrymple had gone much further. He had delved into archaic
manuscripts, uncovered and translated old letters and journals to
compile details of bewitching islands, 'all planted, sown and till'd',
richly wooded and full of fruits, overseen by native peoples who were
sometimes 'general brown like Spaniards', sometimes black, sometimes
white, 'and others of which the complexion is reddish as if burnt by
the sun.'[2] Trained by the East India Company, Dalrymple's eye was
alive to the commercial opportunity. One of the passages to have caught
his attention spoke of an island 'furnished with fine trees', cocoa-nuts,
herbs 'extremely beneficial to the sick; plenty of mussels, of *nacres*,
mother of pearl, and pearl oysters … so that there is great prospect
of an advantageous pearl fishery'.[3]

The club's meeting afforded Dalrymple a chance to describe these
worlds intimately, face to face; to elaborate, and allure those who were
sure to be interested. Along with their new taxes the government was
known to be meditating a 'blue water' policy, an expansion of British
trade across the world's nations. The hope was that new trade would
provide more debt-servicing revenue. With the contest at an end in
North America, the government's attention had turned to old, adven-
turing schemes. There were still many parts of the earth's surface
about which little was known. In an age of reason it seemed ludicrous
that few had sailed south of the fiftieth parallel in the Indian or Atlantic
oceans or that no one had properly mapped the Spice Islands of the
East. The East India Company's charter approved the commercial
exploration of these islands – whatever the Dutch protests might be –
yet in the early 1760s the British had no presence east of Sumatra,
'and scarce any intercourse or commerce in that quarter but at Canton
in China'.[4]

This was the region that Dalrymple knew, a place of glittering seas
and thriving woodlands that must have felt impossibly distant to the
wintry London outside the Mitre. A hard frost had set in before
Christmas. It had not abated as the old year turned into the new. By
9 January the cold was being spoken of as remarkable. At Bath a
temperature of 8°F had been recorded, estimated to be one of the
coldest of the century. In London the blast had laced the streets with
ice. Not far away the Thames was no longer a river of water but a

stiffening mass. 'This morning the river below the bridge carried all the appearance of a general wreck; ships, boats, and small craft, lying in a very confused manner, some on shore, and others sunk or overset.' At Deptford, a fishing boat was found choked in the ice. Inside, the hands were frozen and dead, 'the youngest of them, a youth about seventeen, was found sitting as erect almost as if alive'.[5]

What had happened at Deptford was repeated in neighbourhoods across London and out into the countryside. 'The severe frost ... has continued with remarkable, rigour, to the great calamity of the lower part of the people, who were already severely distressed by the exorbitant price of provisions', one writer judged.[6] With the Thames frozen to Westminster, the lower river had become clogged with inward-bound East Indiamen and colliers, their running ropes stiff in the blocks, their sails struck and stowed beneath. Meanwhile in the Port of London the coal heavers, lightermen and jobbing sailors were left without work. It was a relief for everyone when, on 14 January, the frost broke and a general thaw set in. After weeks of inaction, the river broke open. Within the space of a day the snow vanished, 'as if by enchantment'. Soon East Indiamen were once again coming along-side at the East India Docks.

It was on a vessel like these that Dalrymple had travelled home from Madras. He had stepped ashore from the *Nottingham* Indiaman in 1765, a cultivated traveller of twenty-eight. After thirteen years away, he had a dash of the East about him. Travelling home to his family's seat at Newhailes House, East Lothian, Scotland, he had sat for a portrait in the Chinese sitting room. The figure captured in this work by John Thomas Seton has all the slender elegance of one of Gainsborough's country squires. He is sitting with an arm draped languidly over a curved chair wearing the midnight-blue frock coat and breeches, white knee-length stockings and gold-buckled shoes of the East India Company. He seems relaxed, assured, romantic. His left arm stretches out, leading the viewer's eye to a terrestrial globe. A tricorn hat and a chart lie on the table. Most striking of all in the portrait is the quality of light. It is not the drab, diffused light of the Scottish Lowlands, but rather it has a champagne brightness to it. It is as if Dalrymple has somehow gathered the radiance of the East up and carried it to Scotland with him. Here is the geographical scholar and the prosperous merchant in one, the visual manifestation of Enlightenment.

Dalrymple was born in this Scottish country house in 1737 to Sir James Dalrymple, the auditor of the Exchequer, and Lady Christian. It was an affluent beginning. His elder brother David was the first of the siblings to rise to prominence, appointed as one of the Lords of Session under the title Lord Halles. Another became a lieutenant colonel in the army and one more Lord Provost of Edinburgh. But from an early age, Alexander had been drawn in a different direction. Stories were later told of how he was tutored in geography by his father, 'who enlivened his lessons by narratives of his own travels in Europe'. But even then, Alexander's horizons stretched far beyond Venetian canals or Parisian houses. 'The Author looking up to Columbus, to Magellan', he wrote in a third-person reflection, 'and to those immortal heroes who have display'd new worlds to our view, and extended the European name and influence amongst distant nations, was inflamed with the ambition to do *something* to promote the general benefit of mankind, at the same time that it should add to the glory and interest of his country.'[7]

Dalrymple settled on the East India Company. By the mid-eighteenth century the company was Britain's prime trading arm, with a monopoly of the trade in the eastern islands. For a boy like Dalrymple, there was no finer place. After some bursts of tuition, and with the influence of his father, he had left Scotland as a boy of fifteen. In December 1752, Dalrymple had embarked from Gravesend on an East Indiaman called *Suffolk* bound for Madras. India would be Alexander's home for the next thirteen years. Despite his pedigree and contacts, he endured a difficult beginning. Arriving at the port he found his letters of introduction worthless – all his contacts were either away from town, dead or had taken to the bottle – and worse still, his handwriting was declared so abominable he was not permitted to take up the anticipated post as a writer. Instead he was banished to toil in the storehouse, 'where nothing was to be learned worth learning'.[8] He had recovered from this inauspicious beginning. Graced with intelligence to match his ambition, at length he had won the trust of Lord Pigot, governor of Madras, and then afterwards an influential administrator called Mr Orme, who gave him 'free access' to his library, 'an advantage doubly estimable from the rarity of books, and the excellence of Mr Orme's selection'.[9]

Here on the eastern outpost of the British Empire, Dalrymple was at liberty to learn, socialise and plot among the grandees of the company. Increasingly he was sought for his opinion on efficient routes as he turned his knowledge to practical advantage. Earmarked as the company's next secretary in Madras, his future seemed secure. But the same predilection for travel that had enticed him across the globe had not yet subsided. 'In this station', an account in the *Naval Chronicle* later ran, 'we see the zeal of Mr Dalrymple verging upon ambition; for it appears, that while examining the old records, to qualify himself, by a knowledge of them, to fill the office of secretary, he found the commerce of the Eastern Islands was an object of great consideration with the Company, and the attainment of it became the immediate object of his aspiration.'[10]

Over the years 1759–63, as the Western and Eastern worlds were consumed by conflict, Dalrymple persuaded Pigot to allow him to explore the untapped islands of the East. Initially he travelled as a guest on East Indiamen which were passing Madras on voyages to China. Later Dalrymple was able to secure command of his own vessel, and he was given the freedom to explore like few others before him – combining the roles of merchant and navigator in ways not dissimilar to Milner on the British coast. Dalrymple entered into alliances, struck treaties, navigated shoals, rocks and reefs, visiting the islands of Sooloo (Sulu) and Balambangan, all the while exercising 'a nice judgment and dextrous management'.

This was the pedigree Dalrymple carried to Britain with him in 1765. Sitting for his portrait in his family's Lothian home, the world might well have lain at the end of his outstretched arms. He had made promises of discoveries that would invigorate trade, and he had delivered on them. Not only this but he had commanded his own vessel and had interacted with island populations successfully, gaining an uncommon regard for them and their ways. Now residing at the town house of his patron, Lord Pigot, in bustling Soho Square, with the transvestite spy Chevalier d'Eon, twice lord mayor William Beckford and General Henry Conway for neighbours, Dalrymple had been able to turn his attention to the greatest prize of all – one that had absorbed his imagination since boyhood: the southern continent.

For time out of mind there had been talk of an undefined land mass at the far side of the world. Eratosthenes, the chief librarian of the celebrated library of Alexandria in the third century BC – a man famous for calculating the earth's circumference – is among the candidates for sowing the seed in ancient times. The seed would germinate. By the sixteenth and seventeenth centuries, the notion of a lost austral world had become a feature on early modern maps. Called by various names – to the Spanish it was the Great South Land of the Holy Spirit, to others it was 'Beach', 'Antipodes', 'Terra Australis' – as the age of exploration wore on rumours concerning its discovery were intermittently whispered. At the end of the earth was a beguiling land inhabited by winged horses and flying fish. A beckoning land mass filled with gold, silver, minerals, rare spices.

That a continent existed in total isolation, progressing in a never-converging parallel with civilisation in the north, seemed to most 'a chimera, a thing in the clouds'.[11] They suspected the process at work. A ship, sailing without precision instruments in the South Seas, would spy an island or disembark on a coast. An anecdote would be carried home to Europe. A line would be plotted on a chart. The line would converge with something else and a fantasy would flourish until another explorer exploded it and the process started again. 'To say the truth', one writer conceded, 'all notions built upon conjectures only, however beautifully ranged in a system, serve only to puzzle and mislead.'[12] Another English writer, John Callendar, elaborated:

It is very certain that the discovery of Terra Australis Incognita is considered by many wise and knowing people, as a kind of philosopher's stone, perpetual motion, or, in plain English, as a chimera, fit only to take up the empty brains of wild projectors. Yet there seems to be no sufficient reason, why such as are competent judges of the matter in dispute, should decide peremptorily that there is no such country; or if there be that it is not worth the finding. These sort of hasty conclusions are extremely fatal to science in general and to the art of navigation in particular.[13]

As Callendar implies, the idea of a southern continent had never completely lost its appeal. And with Britain's maritime trade developing fast, the idea that an entire new land mass was yet to be explored excited many. As the global map had been filled in, less and less room remained for this land mass. Its most likely location lay right in the centre of the South Seas, at a high latitude not dissimilar to Britain's – a place perfectly suited for trading the same clothes, the same food-stuffs, the same minerals.

Not to enquire after such a land mass seemed lunacy. After all, even if there were no firm discoveries, then there were strong hints. Geographers had long marshalled evidence of a secret land betrayed by the movements of winds and currents, patterns of bird migrations and the suggestive presence of driftwood or, most telling of all, the density of ice in the sea beyond Cape Horn.* To Arthur Young it would be 'astonishing' that such proof was not lure enough for the maritime powers of Europe. Do they not have, he asked, the:

> curiosity to become acquainted with the ideas, the manners, the customs, and the knowledge of so considerable a part of the globe, all which are at present as unknown as those of the inhabitants of the moon? What a wonderful idea is it to think of the arts, the sciences, and the species of human learning which may reside among these unknown people, and wait only for the active curiosity of some European to extend them in a million of beneficial shapes to the rest of mankind![14]

These were ideals Dalrymple shared. In a book manuscript he started preparing in 1766, Dalrymple called the southern continent his 'first and most striking object of research'.[15] At the library at Madras he had sifted clues from the voyage accounts written long ago by the Spanish. 'An active mind, long employed on any subject', he reflected, 'will acquire ideas from very faint lines.'[16] He believed the southern continent had been sighted on its western edge by the Dutchman Abel Tasman in 1642 and on its east by the Spaniard Juan Fernández half a century before. There were more accounts, too, contained within the latitudes, from 64°S to 40°S, each quite possibly a tantalising peek of an enormous whole.

Dalrymple had not only relied on anecdote. Following the thinking of the French scholar Charles de Broses and his *Historie des Navigationes aux Terres Australes* (1756), he couched his theory in mathematical terms. De Broses advocated a theory of 'equipoisure', the idea that

---

*   Eighteenth-century science held that ice could not form in the open sea. Therefore ice of any description must have originated on land. So the more ice that was sighted in a particular place, the better the evidence that land was not far off.

for the globe to be kept in regular motion an exact, or similar amount of land *had* to exist to the south of the equator. This 'equipoisure' was an idea fashioned to appeal to rational minds, and its implications infected Dalrymple's outlook. He carefully tallied up all the known land masses. He found that between the equator and the tropics a similar proportion of land existed in both hemispheres. The harmony was only disturbed in the higher latitudes, the north having seven-eighths more land above the Tropic of Cancer than had been discovered beneath the Tropic of Capricorn. Extrapolating out, Dalrymple made the 'strong presumption, that there are in the southern hemisphere, hitherto totally undiscovered, valuable and extensive countries'. As Abel Tasman had proved no land existed east of the Cape of Good Hope, Dalrymple concluded that in the South Seas 'from the Tropick to 50° South latitude there are extensive countries'. He reckoned that another of Tasman's discoveries, New Zealand, to the extreme west, was likely to form the eastern edge of this continent. As for the endless stretch to the east, for Dalrymple's sums to tally, it 'must be nearly all land'.[17]

Dalrymple's conjectures were designed to appeal to the eighteenth-century mindset. Posed mathematically, his counterpoise theory aligned with the idea that there was a secret inner harmony in the earth's movements. This is precisely what Newton had shown with the tides. Ever since the Renaissance, European civilisation had admired the presence of proportion, from Florentine architecture to Leonardo da Vinci's *Vitruvian Man*. That neat proportions might exist inside the human body or the cloisters at Santa Croce was one thing; it would be the ultimate Enlightenment discovery to find that the earth – the base for everything – had its own terrestrial balance.

But how to test Dalrymple's hypothesis? If a southern continent did exist, then it was concealed from European eyes by its very remoteness. It took a minimum of six months' sailing for a British ship to even enter the South Seas. Before they got there they were forced to pass the brutal, wind-tossed barriers of Cape Horn or the Strait of Magellan and thereafter they were condemned to be 'continual wanderers' in the South Seas. Twenty-five years before, British naval administrators had looked into remedying this by founding a naval base in the south Atlantic to act as a launch pad into the Pacific, as well as providing a haven for the ships where they could replenish and repair after the arduous Atlantic passage.

A few potential sites in particular – the Falkland Islands and the elusive Pepys Island – had aroused interest. In the late 1740s the British Admiralty, under the innovative leadership of the young First Lord, John Montagu, Lord Sandwich, had begun preparations for an exploratory voyage to the region. This was a dangerous policy. Ever since the Treaty of Tordesillas, signed between Spain and Portugal in 1494, the Spanish had considered this ocean their private property.* Although the British commenced their plan in secret, the Spanish soon got wind of their ambitions. They 'so vehemently opposed it, and so strongly maintained the right of the Spaniards to the exclusive dominion of the South Sea', as well as the 'Magellanic region' in which the islands lay, that Sandwich had been obliged to abandon his plans.[18]

Fifteen years later, however, after the Treaty of Paris, British attentions had again drifted south. They were not alone. Still aggrieved at the loss of their Canadian territories, the French had 'conceived the design of indemnifying' themselves 'by a discovery of the southern continent, and of those large islands, which lie in the way to it'.[19] These aspirations had been spearheaded by a figure of European reputation, the nobleman, diplomat and former chief of staff to Montcalm in Quebec, Louis Antoine de Bougainville. He had read of the Falklands in British travel books and had recognised their strategic importance at once. Whoever controlled these islands would govern the sea paths to the Pacific.

Stealing a march on the British, de Bougainville had sailed from Saint-Malo in September 1763, and by April 1764 had arrived at the Falklands. Following close behind in the thirty-two-gun frigate *Dolphin* was Commodore John Byron. Leaving in the summer of 1764, Byron was instructed to take possession of both Pepys and the Falkland Islands. Byron failed to find Pepys Island, which turned out to be a geographic phantom, but in January 1765, nine months after de

---

*   The Treaty of Tordesillas was signed between Portugal and the crown of Castile in June 1494. It was designed to settle territorial disputes in the New World between the two powers. It did so by establishing a line across the Atlantic Ocean, 370 leagues to the west of the Cape Verde Islands. All the territories to the east of the line were to be Portugal's while all to the west were to be Castile's. The treaty was generally respected and had a lasting impact.

Bougainville, Byron sailed into a 'fine convenient bay' in the Falklands that he named Port Egmont. After a short residence of nine days, Byron claimed the islands for Great Britain. It was a 'very merry' occasion, one of his officers wrote, 'a large bowl of arrack punch being carried on shore, out of which they drank, among several loyal toasts, success to the discovery of so fine a harbour'.[20]

De Bougainville's and Byron's visits left the Falklands split. The French had landed on the east of the islands while the British had planted their flag on the west. With the situation further aggravated by Spain's insistence that the islands fell within their sphere, an uneasy geopolitical situation had developed. It would not last. The scramble for the Falklands in 1763–5 marked the beginning of a transnational rivalry between Britain and France. (Spain, a waning force but one that could not be entirely ignored, remained a jealous onlooker.) 'What continuance of happiness', Samuel Johnson pondered from Fleet Street, 'can be expected, when the whole system of European empire can be in danger of a new concussion, by a contention for a few spots of earth, which, in the deserts of the ocean, had almost escaped human notice, and which, if they had not happened to make a sea mark, had perhaps never had a name?'[21]

In the mid-1760s neither the British nor the French were of the mood to be discouraged by such moralising or by the terms of ancient treaties. After his call at the Falklands in 1765, Byron headed through the Strait of Magellan into the South Seas. Soon after, de Bougainville followed. Having encircled the world, Byron was back in London by late spring 1766 and the *Dolphin* was immediately recommissioned for another foray into the South Seas. On her second circumnavigation she sailed under the command of a Cornishman, Samuel Wallis, accompanied by Lieutenant Philip Carteret in a consort, HMS *Swallow*, and a transport for provisions. Wallis's secret instructions – to sail into the South Seas looking for Terra Australis – were so closely guarded to protect them from European spies that none of the sailors were told of their destination.

This was how matters stood in the mid-1760s as Dalrymple appeared with his new charts in London. With both the Falkland Islands and the southern continent objects of considerable interest, he was guaranteed at least the ear of the powerful. And with Adam Smith's support and a privately printed run of his *Account of the Discoveries Made in the South Pacifick Ocean Previous to 1764* – one copy was presented to the Earl of Shelburne, the Secretary of State for the Southern Department

– his prospects began to look rosy. Dalrymple wanted a ship to take
him to the South Seas. And, as luck would have it, the grandees at the
Royal Society – for reasons of their own – were inclined to help him
get there.

The Royal Society's Dining Club had a different motive for being
interested in the South Seas. On 3 June 1769, as everyone well knew,
the planet Venus would be visible not as a glimmering star in the
night sky, but as a perfect black circle that, over certain sections of
the earth's surface, would slide across the face of the sun. This 'Transit
of Venus' was a cosmic encounter not to be repeated in the lifetime
of anyone living. Transits happened in pairs every 105–122 years, and
the 1769 transit was to form the second half of this major eighteenth-
century astronomical event. The first act of the drama had been
played out on 6 June 1761. Roused by a zealous Frenchman, Joseph-
Nicolas Delisle, France, Sweden, Russia and Britain had hurriedly
dispatched teams of astronomical observers to different locations
within the transit zone, which spanned the continents of Asia and
Europe. The ambition was to gather observational data about the
transit from highly dispersed areas across both hemispheres. This
would provide mathematicians with the raw data they needed to
compute a fascinating equation: the distance between the earth and
the sun. Hopes had been high, but the results had been mixed. With
the world in conflict, the astronomers' ships had been chased, locations had been inaccessible, native populations had proved hostile
and the weather had often been unkind. On top of these issues, more
problems with the instruments had come during the observations
themselves.

Looking forward to 1769, the learned scientific societies of Europe
and America intended to rectify the past mistakes. But this time there
was a new obstacle. Only the very beginning of the transit would be
visible in Britain and western Europe. For it to be traced in its entirety,
the astronomers calculated, observers needed to travel either north
into the everlasting light of the northern summer, or west to America.
One perfect location would be the South Seas, but no one knew the
exact location of any likely island – and terra firma was absolutely
necessary, as precise observation was impossible on the rocking deck
of a ship. To this riddle, Dalrymple with his charts and experience
presented an attractive solution.

The organisation of the British transit observations was being overseen by the Royal Society. As far back as 5 June 1766 they had 'resolvd to send astronomers to several parts of the World'. More detailed discussions had begun in November 1767, when a list of possible places and people was discussed at a council meeting. Among potential sites were Fort Churchill in Hudson's Bay and Newfoundland, and it was thought to be 'proper to Send two Observers to the South Sea', though no one was quite sure where. 'Mr Dalrymple' was named among the appropriate candidates for making the observation.[22]

Over the next weeks the society's plans began to fall into place. Nevil Maskelyne, the Astronomer Royal who himself had been one of the travelling astronomers in 1761, oversaw the appointments. William Wales, a mathematician, was selected for the North American observation, and Jeremiah Dixon was favoured for a trip to Norway. Meanwhile Dalrymple's candidature for the South Seas leg was gathering momentum. It had no doubt struck the organisers that, by appointing him, they were not only selecting a navigator who might carry some certified astronomer to a charted island, but they might also probe unknown regions for the southern continent.

By December 1767 Dalrymple was receiving letters from the Earl of Morton, president of the society, that provided signals 'of the favourable intentions of the Council'. The central remaining question related to Dalrymple's status aboard ship. On occasion civilian experts, not naval officers, had been appointed to captain ships. Three times Edmond Halley had commanded HMS *Paramour* at the turn of the century as he investigated questions relating to the magnetic variation of the compass. More recently in France, de Bougainville had been given a ship, though he had no naval rank. This was the arrangement Dalrymple wanted to replicate. As he had suggested before, this was a vital matter to him. He believed that a split command – between a sea officer and philosophic gentleman – would invariably cause trouble. Sensing a decision had already been taken, Dalrymple took the chance to press his case. On 7 December 1767, he wrote to Charles Morton, secretary of the society. He knew their focus remained on the transit, and Dalrymple assured them, 'Wherever I am in June 1769, I shall most certainly not let slip an opportunity of making an Observation so important to Science.' Unabashed, he rounded off:

However it may be necessary to observe that I can have no thought of undertaking the Voyage as a Passenger going out to make the observation or on any other footing than that of having the management of the Ship intended for the service.[23]

*

Britain in the 1760s was a country riven by contradictions. For all the glittering excess, there were thousands who subsisted on short-term contracts, rarely with much more than a handful of pennies in their pocket. This was life. But it was precarious life. The frost at the start of 1768 had made their situations acute. The loss of a month's income had driven many to the edge of starvation and made the accounts of society glitz in London and opulence in the West End, reports of a 'brilliant Court' at St James's and wild bets by the county gentry, all the harder to bear. No ministry had managed to remedy the inequalities. After Grenville's administration had fallen in 1765, it was replaced by a short-lived one led by the Marquis of Rockingham, which was then replaced by a 'chequered and speckled' coalition headed by William Pitt, although he – as Earl of Chatham – was largely a symbolic figure and often away from Westminster with illness. Fed up with years of ineffective leadership, in 1766 the *Annual Register* had printed a 'Humorous Proposal for a Female Administration', which advocated a new type of government, composed entirely of women. For each political post, a society lady was proposed. If readers were tickled by the absurd idea, the author advised, then perhaps they should compare those nominated – Catharine Macaulay was allotted the position of Royal Historiographer – 'with the *Males* who at present enjoy those places'.[24]

There would be no women, of course, just more taxes. And many were starting to wonder where the drive for dominion would end. 'Power is like Fire; it warms, scorches, or destroys, according as it is watched, provoked, or increased', the English Commonwealthman John Trenchard had written.[25] Meanwhile, in the first months of 1768, the price of bread in the capital rose by a quarter to twopence a pound, disturbing the economic equilibrium in a way no one yet comprehended. As plans for Dalrymple's voyage were developing in February 1768, just one thing was wanting: a dynamic element to bring grievances to a head. And the element that soon appeared proved so combustible that it threw all London into confusion. Aside from everything else, the disorder it brought to the Thames would

almost ruin the Royal Society's South Seas expedition before it had
even begun.

Ever since John Wilkes was chased into exile in 1763, the government had been haunted by the prospect of his return. Having him
publically declared an outlaw, they had conferred on him something
of a Robin Hood status. Everyone knew the election offered him his
best chance of a return and the *Newcastle Courant* relayed his movements in veiled snatches. In the opening issue of the year, on 2 January,
came news: 'They write from the Hague, of the 16th, that "The famous
Mr Wilkes is actually here."' A month later the story had developed.
To ward Wilkes off, the government was attempting to bribe him
with the governorship of the Bahamas. The counter-rumour was that
Wilkes was preparing to join dissident forces abroad, at Boston in
Massachusetts, perhaps. But everyone knew his most explosive move
would be to hazard all and return to London. No one – not Charlton
in his Whitby classroom, not Fishburn in his shipyard, or Milner on
the *Earl of Pembroke* – would have missed the significance of the
Courant's report on 27 February: 'We hear that a celebrated Outlaw
is at the Moment actually in the Kingdom.'

In any other year, this might have been as far as the story got. But
as Milner brought the *Earl of Pembroke* into the Thames for the last
time, the Wilkes story was about to catch fire. On 11 March, to the
astonishment of everyone, Wilkes broke out into public, offering
himself as a candidate in the forthcoming election. Convicted in the
courts of law, Wilkes had chosen instead to stand trial in the court of
public opinion. 'It is said to be really true', ran a disbelieving item in
the *Chronicle* of 19 March, 'the Parliamentary Rolls furnish a Precedent
that an Outlaw may be chosen a Representative without a revoking
of the Outlawry.' This was a level of brinkmanship no one had
witnessed before. Lionised by the public and loathed by the establishment, 'this was a push', wrote one onlooker, 'which required all the
art and power of the ministry to parry'.[26]

A contagion ripped through London. Wilkes had targeted the City
of London constituency and the citizens clamoured for the latest
developments. After his speech was published on 11 March, he made
a subsequent address at the Guildhall hustings on 16 March:

> I stand here, gentlemen, a private man, unconnected with the
> great, and unsupported by any party. I have no support but you:

I wish no other support: I can have none more certain, none more honourable.[27]

The polls opened directly. Georgian general elections had a different rhythm to those of today. Instead of a long run-up to a single polling day, the campaigns were shorter, while the process of voting continued for days. The Guildhall poll opened on 16 March and as days passed voters came in increasing numbers. And it was during these days, around 21 March 1768, that an official from the Navy Board approached Thomas Milner with a request to examine his ship.

This meeting of Milner and the faceless official is one of those significant moments in history that hides in a half-light. All we know is that it probably happened near to a wharf called Mr Birds Ways. This was the sailors' quarters. On the river's north bank at Wapping sprawled a neighbourhood of narrow, densely populated streets. Radcliffe Highway, the road from Smithfield to Essex, ran through this area. Branching off the Highway as it crossed Wapping was Old Gravel Lane, a place of linen drapers, taverns and chophouses that grew insalubrious as it reached the riverside. This was a transient area populated by sailors, coal heavers, prostitutes and petty criminals, a voluble mass who lived most of their lives out of doors: hauling home their sea chests, or hawking for business. Bird Street was just seconds from Old Gravel Lane, closer to the river next to Wapping Old Stairs and a minute along from Execution Dock where pirates, smugglers and mutineers were hanged. Somewhere here on the riverside, at Mr Birds Ways, the *Earl of Pembroke* lay at anchor.

Across London in Westminster, the last month had been one of tumult at the Royal Society. As Benjamin Franklin wrote to Jean-Baptise LeRoy in France, 'Our Society are about to send three Setts of Astronomers abroad, to observe the next Transit of Venus; the Places, Hudson's Bay, the North Cape, and somewhere South of the Line.' But while they had been 'attentive to what is to pass in the Heavens', they had neglected terrestrial affairs. Their 'Clerk and Collector, has unobserv'd run away with our Money upon Earth, to the amount of near 1500 Pounds, which makes it necessary for us in the Affair to apply for Royal Assistance'.[28]

This sorry affair, stinging for the society's finances, would have yet greater consequences. Franklin had put his name to the memorial 'To the King's most excellent Majesty' which had been drawn up explaining the 'passage of the Planet Venus over the Disc of the Sun ... That the like appearance after the 3rd of June 1769 will not happen for more than 100 years.'[29] The 'Memorialists' bolstered their case with an appeal not just to patriotism, but also to the king's sense of his regal legacy. They reminded him that a hundred years before, the society had been established to fulfil the very task with which they were currently concerned. The memorial was sent in February and it took only a few weeks for the king to approve the request and forward £4,000, 'to defray the expense of conveying such persons as it shall be thought proper to send'. The finances were secured. But with the king's money came a loss of independence. No longer were the society to act unilaterally. On 29 February 1768 the Admiralty were brought into the planning of the voyage, being told that the king had decided 'a suitable vessel should be provided by the Royal Navy'.[30]

At once the administrative cogs had begun to turn. The search for an exploration vessel was underway by the start of March. Details of the hunt are committed to history in a succession of letters between Whitehall, Wapping and Deptford. The Admiralty's secretary wrote to the Navy Board on 5 March asking for a proposal for 'a proper vessel to be fitted for this service'.[31] Three days later the board replied that a sloop, *Tryal*, 'would be suitable'. She was being refitted in Deptford dock but it would be the end of May before she could be got ready 'and there is no vessel at home to be depended upon for so long a voyage, that can be sooner fitted'. The Admiralty replied within two days, suggesting a ship called the *Rose*, reminding the board 'it is necessary the ship should sail this spring'. Eleven days passed before the board replied with a verdict. It had looked into the *Rose* but found that she 'may be unable to stow the quantity of provisions required'. But although the *Rose* was unsuitable, they had another suggestion: 'The Board suggests a cat-built vessel, which would be roomy enough for the purpose. One of about 350 tons can be purchased in the River Thames.'[32]

This was, on the face of it, a left-field suggestion. A collier had no elegance to merit such a glamorous commission. She had no figurehead, no guns to protect her, no great cabin for the officers to entertain in style. There existed a prejudice against merchant ships among naval men. The very idea of the tawdry bows of a collier in the sparkling waters of the Pacific must have seemed horrifyingly incongruous – like a debutante arriving to a Piccadilly ball in arm with a Limehouse costermonger. And yet this was a suggestion borne of experience. In the Seven Years War colliers had often been used to carry cargoes and men. Moreover, after the winter there was a plentiful supply in the Thames: strong-built, with massive hold capacities. The idea appealed. The Admiralty replied to the board the very same day, 21 March. There was an urgency in the letter, as if a presentable solution, or at least a tolerable one, had at last been struck upon. 'The recommendation of a cat-built vessel is approved, and the purchase is to be effected at once.' Two days later the Admiralty were discussing the vices and virtues of two colliers at their daily meeting. One was called the *Valentine*, the other, *Earl of Pembroke*.

The precise nature of what happened over the next few days is uncertain and contested. The letters suggest responsibility for assessing the ships had devolved from the Navy Board to the Deptford Yard officers, those who worked with vessels each day and understood them best. Perhaps it was they who preferred Milner's ship, but others later claimed to have swung the decision. One of them was Dalrymple himself. Twice in public Dalrymple asserted that he chose Fishburn's collier over the others. Once he maintained that he had travelled to Mr Birds Ways, in company with the surveyor of the navy, to view the two vessels. 'The one he approved was accordingly purchased.'[33] Dalrymple only made this assertion in 1802, but he made a similar statement in 1773, arguing he had preferred the *Earl of Pembroke* 'to the other ship which was smaller', because it was 'able to carry *another anchor* and *cable*', features which he felt 'might be of the utmost consequence'.[34]

There is nothing in the official documents to support Dalrymple's claim. Different traditions state that the *Earl of Pembroke* was selected by a naval captain, Hugh Palliser, or even by James Cook – a fact which is a chronological impossibility. In the retelling of the history, Dalrymple's assertion has come to be viewed as exaggeration or bombast, but there remains something persuasive in his account. Dalrymple was later derided as many things: intemperate, volatile, grudging – he certainly had some magma at his core – but no one ever suggested he was a liar. And taking the maxim that one certain lie is suggestive of many more, Dalrymple would have been foolish to persist with a claim so easily countered had he known it to be false.

Who really instigated the transaction between Milner and the Navy Board is unknowable. All that can be said for sure is that the *Earl of Pembroke* emerged in the last week of March as the best of all the options. It took a week for the surveys to be completed. Three colliers were inspected: the *Valentine*, *Earl of Pembroke* and *Ann & Elizabeth*.

The decision, in the end, seems to have rested on availability, utility and condition, after which the *Earl of Pembroke* was judged best. Along with the question of who made this choice, a second puzzle for posterity has its origins in this time. The Navy Board's original order had been for a 'cat-built vessel', something that, strictly speaking – with her wide stern and flush deck – the *Earl of Pembroke* was not. Perhaps the Deptford Yard officer could not judge the subtle differences, or perhaps he sought to conceal the fact to speed along the process with a fudged description of a 'Cat-built Bark'. Either way, the sentence would distort interpretations of Fishburn's collier for centuries to come.

The attributes of the *Earl of Pembroke* are captured in a letter of 27 March from the Deptford Yard officers to the Navy Board. Her tonnage was 368.71/94. The value of her hull was £2,212 15s 6d, and of her masts and yards £94 10s. For Milner, it was the luckiest of all encounters. His collier, a trim and steady sailor, three years and nine months old, was valued at £2,307 5s 6d. The Navy Board offered £2,840 10s 11d. It was a deal that would take his ship but leave him rich. On 29 March, the Navy Board reported to the Admiralty:

> A Cat-built Bark in Burthen 368 Tons, 3 years 9 months old, has been purchased. Requests permission to proceed with fitting her for the voyage. It may be necessary to sheath and fill her bottom and prepare her for carrying six or eight carriage guns of four pounders and eight swivel, as was proposed for the *Tyral*. In what name is she to be registered?[35]

The Admiralty mulled this question for a week. But for the moment one important thing at least was assured. Whether or not Dalrymple had been involved or not, the more material fact was that he had his ship.

A note from the Deptford Yard officers to the Navy Board on 31 March suggests the decision to purchase the *Earl of Pembroke* was authorised in a warrant issued three days earlier, on the 28th. It means there is a chronological convergence. In one city, on one date, in one year, two monumental events occurred: the acquisition by the Royal Navy of the *Earl of Pembroke* and the re-election to Parliament of John Wilkes.

Taken alone, Wilkes's 1762–3 subversion campaign against Bute and his ministry stands as an extraordinary event in British politics. But his actions in the early spring of 1768 outdid even this. Hundreds crammed into the Guildhall on 16 March to hear him speak at the hustings. 'So great was the Curiosity of the People to see Mr Wilkes', the *Newcastle Courant* explained, the streets outside the Guildhall were twice as full. When hands were shown – the simplest and most common method of electing candidates – Wilkes seemed to have scraped in third. But an official poll was demanded and, over a week, faction had its way. On 23 March the results were announced, with Wilkes finishing a distant last. But then came the twist. Mounting the platform he turned what many anticipated as a concession speech into a launch announcement for a new campaign. 'And now, gentlemen, permit me to address you as friends to liberty', Wilkes said, 'and freeholders of the county of Middlesex; declaring my intention of appearing as a candidate to represent you in parliament.'[36]

The day for the Middlesex poll was set for 28 March. It was to take place at Brentford, west London. After five days' electioneering, the Wilkes campaign was in jovial spirits. Wilkes set out on 27 March and the following morning he was the first candidate on the hustings. It was one o'clock before any opponents arrived. Sir William Beauchamp Proctor came on horseback, while George Cooke arrived in a coach and six.

The results were announced the following morning, Tuesday 29 March, at nine o'clock.

Mr Wilkes	1292
Mr Cooke	827
Sir William Beauchamp Proctor	807[37]

Thereafter it was euphoria. A mob formed in Brentford that would not let any coach pass without 'Wilkes and Liberty' daubed on its sides. Flags were hoisted with the jeering maxim: *'More Meat, and fewer Cooks'*, much to the chagrin of George Cooke. As night fell on 29 March, lighted candles – symbols of liberty – stood in every window.

Wilkes's election thrilled and disgusted in equal measure. Ballads were roared on every street, mobs required 'gentlemen and ladies of all ranks as they passed in their carriages to shout for Wilkes and liberty'. What had begun on the banks of the Thames was soon being repeated in other parts of the country. On his way to Winchester, Benjamin Franklin 'observed that for fifteen miles out of town, there was scarce a door or window shutter next the road' not daubed with

Wilkite slogans, 'this continued here and there quite to Winchester, which is 64 miles.'[38] Meanwhile Milner, north-bound to Whitby with money enough to retire, would have arrived as disturbances were starting in Newcastle. They began in the first week of April. Five hundred sailors gathered in protest at the staithes in North Shields. They marched from there to Sunderland where they read a list of grievances and demanded 'immediate redress'. After this they boarded colliers and struck their yards. Their numbers swelled. They spent the day parading through the streets, beating drums, colours flying. 'In the afternoon', a report later emerged in the *Annual Register*, 'they separated, and the former returned again to Shields, where they committed great outrages, particularly on the butchers and bakers, who suffered the loss of all that lay in their way.'[39]

By the end of March it must have seemed to the Earl of Morton and the council of the Royal Society that, after so much dissembling, their plans had at last slotted into place. They had their commander, they had a vessel and they had the financing from the king to subsidise it all. But just as the political order had disintegrated in Middlesex, their plans had parted at the seams.

The problem was Dalrymple himself. If he was known for his industry and intelligence, he was also known for his independent mind. Dalrymple had long cultivated this vision of himself as free-thinker. 'Errors may lead to the truth', he had once written, 'but when all men's notions are ground in one mill, they serve no purpose of investigation or discovery.'[40] His attitude had been fixed in his many years of contemplation. The voyage was to be *his* voyage, a fact he had made plain from the outset in both his application to the Earl of Sherburne through Adam Smith, and latterly in his letter to the Royal Society in December. The long process of diplomacy – finding and cultivating contacts, writing letters, advancing his case – had occupied him for years. For the most part Dalrymple had been successful. Ranged behind him now were the council of the Royal Society. But a change of circumstances in February had rendered all this interest useless. Having set down a list of ambitions for the voyage, tailoring its scope and helping source a vessel, Dalrymple's role in his long cherished project was about to end.

His problems had begun with the Royal Society's memorial to King George in February. Along with the king's financial assistance came the involvement of the Admiralty. The voyage was no longer to be a private undertaking, instead it was to be a joint venture between the Royal Society and the navy. The Royal Society would take responsibility for the observations while the navy would supply the vessel and the nautical expertise. This was not how Dalrymple had envisaged affairs. No longer were Morton, Franklin, Cavendish and Maskelyne in control. Instead a set of new names had materialised: Admiral Hawke, the old hero of Quiberon Bay and now First Lord of the Admiralty; Sir Charles Saunders, Hawke's predecessor; Hugh Palliser, the returning governor of Newfoundland; and Philip Stephens, the influential secretary to the Admiralty. Once the *Earl of Pembroke* had been bought and plans were underway for her fitting out and the appointment of her officers, these were the people that mattered. And with them, Dalrymple held no sway.

In Dalrymple's later account he hinted of an immediate antagonism on the part of the navy. When he was viewing the colliers, Dalrymple wrote, he had favoured the *Earl of Pembroke* over the other because of her storage capacity, 'being able to carry *another anchor* and *cable*'. But having mentioned this to the Admiralty official – whom he refused to name – Dalrymple wrote 'A *navy Oracle* told me I was much mistaken if I thought I should have just what stores I pleased, that there was an *Establishment*, altho' I *might* be allowed an anchor and cable extraordinary on such a voyage.'[41]

If this exchange did happen, it must have occurred at the end of March, as the purchase of the *Earl of Pembroke* was underway. It was a harbinger of what would happen the following week when the Royal Society gathered for a council meeting on 3 April 1768. Dalrymple was invited to attend as a guest, presumably eager to hear that everything was ready to begin the complicated process of fitting out. But on 3 April he learned that was not so. The Earl of Morton announced he had recommended Dalrymple to the Lords of the Admiralty for the command, 'but was told that such appointment was totaly repugnant to the rules of the navy'. The idea a civilian should take command of a king's ship subverted the entire hierarchical system that had been established for a century. Dalrymple's response is captured in an exchange, recorded briefly enough. 'Mr Dalrymple attending the Council declind the Employment of Observer unless he could Command so it was resolvd to Consider of a proper person in his place.'[42]

The 'worthy' Hawke, Dalrymple later wrote, 'was wrought upon by insinuations that he would be exposed to a parliamentary impeachment if he employed any but a Navy Officer'. Caught in an impossible situation, Dalrymple explained, Hawke had no choice but to halt his commission. Dalrymple did not blame Hawke, as many in later years supposed, instead he felt betrayed by others who had deliberately frustrated his plans. 'Although offers were made to Alexander Dalrymple', he wrote in his third-person account of the episode, 'that the instructions of the voyage should be entrusted to him, and the Officer commanding the vessel be positively ordered to follow his opinion, on the compliance with which his promotion was to depend, yet Alexander Dalrymple, sensible, from experience ... that a divided command was incompatible with the public service in such voyages, declined going out on that footing.'[43]

There are two ways to interpret Dalrymple's behaviour. His refusal to join may have been the entitled outburst of a man determined to have it all his own way. Dalrymple certainly had an ungovernable temper. Later in his life he would act petulantly. But equally it may have been, as he claims, a selfless decision made in the knowledge – and in this he surely would have been right – that trouble would ensue from a split command. In either case, during a single Royal Society meeting, perhaps an hour or two in length, Dalrymple's dream ended. He was to be denied the greatest opportunity of his life. Meanwhile the Royal Society had been tossed from the horns of one dilemma to another. A week before, they had had a commander and no ship. Now they had their ship, but no one to sail it.

5

Land of Liberty

The *Earl of Pembroke* made her last journey under her old identity on 2 April 1768. That Saturday she sailed through the turbid waters of Thames to the single dock at Deptford. Here all her merchant coarseness was to be smoothed into the neat regularity of a ship of His Majesty's Navy.

Deptford nestles on the western bank of the Thames as the river darts south towards Greenwich. In 1768 the yard dominated the town. Dry and wet docks were cut into the riverbank, and cascading back from the shoreline were warehouses, victualling offices, rope yards, sail lofts and buildings occupied by the yard's officials. Out in the river lay the ships the yard existed to maintain. There would be the great men-of-war, the iconic seventy-fours like HMS *Bellona* or the older sixty-gun fourth-rates like HMS *Anson*, both with complements of several hundred. Some would be paid off in ordinary. Newer arrivals would be anchored further out, the sixth-rate frigates or sloops with thirty-two or twenty-four guns, the store ships, hospital ships and yachts, then the yard boats plying between them all. Other vessels would be fitting out at the quayside or being attended on the stocks. For all this variety, these vessels would in some ways conform to a type. Many would be painted with a blue stripe along their hull's upper body, a dash of vivacity sometimes offset with bursts of canary yellow across the stern. Their pennants reflected the ranks of the commissioned officers, and the adherence to order continued in the yard itself with its teams of shipwrights, storekeepers, clerks, ropers and victuallers, all of whom were subservient to the most prominent figure: the master shipwright, Adam Hayes.

It was into Hayes's care that the *Earl of Pembroke* was now passed. Three days after her arrival, on 5 April, he received his instructions. The vessel was to be 'sheathed, filled and fitted' to convey 'to the

Southward the persons intended to be sent thither to observe the Transit of Venus over the Sun's Disk'. The board had settled on a second, administrative, point too. She was 'to be registered on the List of the Navy as a Bark by the name of the *Endeavour*'.[1]

The decision to call the exploration ship *Endeavour* was almost certainly confirmed at the Board of Admiralty on 5 April – the day the note to Deptford was sent. The First Lord and leading voice of the 1768 Commission was Admiral Hawke. It is appealing to think of Hawke proposing the name, *Endeavour*, eager to imbue the forthcoming voyage with a quality many had associated with him since Quiberon Bay. By doing so he would not only instil a daring identity onto the ship but, as he well knew, it would be a signal for the crew: an inner quality of temperament for them to aspire towards.

Perhaps the better question is not *who* suggested the name but why it was a likely choice in April 1768. The Admiralty meeting took place exactly a week after Wilkes's election victory at Middlesex. All London remained in thrall to his audacity. 'I will endeavour through life', Wilkes had proclaimed, 'to merit the continuation of your approbation ... I intreat you to accept of my best endeavours to express the joy which inspires me on so interesting, so affecting, an occasion.'[2] 'Best Endeavours' was the resonant term of the moment. On 16 April Franklin wrote to one of his Pennsylvanian correspondents, 'While I stay, I shall use my best Endeavours in the Service of the Province.'[3] It seems that something of the brave, resolute atmosphere of April 1768 rubbed off on Fishburn's bark. It was no longer to be the starchy *Earl of Pembroke*. Instead it was the lucent, probing *Endeavour*.

Though the name conferred a fresh sense of identity, it would hardly have been among Adam Hayes's chief concerns. Hayes was a veteran of his trade. Over the past decade he had specialised in the pioneering class of seventy-four-gun third-rate ships of the line, dashing warships with swaggering names – *Magnificent, Albion, Superb, Dragon* – all elegant lines and brute firepower. Occasionally he was obliged to take a different type of vessel in hand, a fourteen-gun sloop, a cutter or a yacht like the *William and Mary*. But in his career Hayes had never had to superintend the conversion of a Whitby collier. Nothing of her type had ever been formally purchased into the navy before.

Hayes was in his twelfth year as Deptford's master shipwright, a position of considerable status. Now land-bound, Hayes nonetheless had as much an understanding of the sea as anyone. As a young boy in the 1730s he had begun his career as a ship's carpenter. Soon after he was taken on board HMS *Centurion*, starting an association with the most celebrated voyage of the age. The *Centurion* had sailed from Spithead in September 1740, a ship of sixty guns with a complement of 400, under the command of Commodore George Anson. She embarked in convoy with the *Gloucester* (fifty guns), the *Severn* (fifty guns), the *Pearl* (forty guns), *Wager* (twenty-four guns), the *Tryal* (eight guns), and a set of merchant vessels – including a Whitby collier – that carried supplies for the total 1,900 men. At the beginning of a war with Spain, Anson had been instructed to disrupt the Spanish trade across the South Seas.

Almost everyone in Britain knew something of Anson's voyage. There were the tremendous hardships the squadron had encountered off Cape Horn. There was the subsequent outbreak of scurvy and other sicknesses which killed nearly 1,400 of the original crew. Then there was the majestic triumph when Anson's *Centurion* sighted the fabled treasure galleon, *Nuestra Señora de Covadonga*, on its passage between Manila and Acapulco in 1743. Called the Prize of all the Oceans, Anson bore down on the galleon and in an action of less than two hours had taken her. Not since the age of Sir Francis Drake had there been such plunder. The galleon was carrying 1,313,843 pieces of eight, and 35,682 ounces of virgin silver, enough to transform Anson, once the prize money had been calculated, into one of England's richest men. The whole expedition was immortalised in *A Voyage Around the World by George Anson*, which became the dramatic travel narrative of the age, with the fight against the *Nuestra Señora de Covadonga* its central breathless scene. The *Centurion*'s voyage had come to epitomise the glory of adventure and was told and retold in thousands of tavern tales and street-corner ballads.

Even now, more than twenty years on, those who had fought on the *Centurion* had their reputations illuminated by a radiant afterglow. Some of the officers – John Campbell and Augustus Keppel among them – had since risen to prominence in the navy. Whether Hayes, like Keppel, still bore the scars of that voyage in missing teeth or shrapnel gashes is unknown, but he had been there on 20 June 1743 when Anson engaged the galleon. Thereafter, too, it seems that he had become one of Anson's protégés. Soon after the *Centurion*'s return, in 1746, Hayes had been appointed master shipwright of the Gibraltar shipyard. From there he progressed to Plymouth to work under the influential Benjamin Slade. Among Britain's leading shipbuilders, there were few better mentors. Slade seems to have introduced Hayes to his nephew, Thomas Slade, an innovative young shipbuilder who designed many of the iconic warships of the time, including the revolutionary class of seventy-fours, as well as massive warships like HMS *Victory*.

Hayes followed Thomas Slade through a series of appointments in the 1750s: as master shipwright at Sheerness, then master shipwright at Woolwich, then at Chatham. Hayes was not only competent, he was popular too. When his promotion to the Deptford Yard came through in 1755, the *Whitehall Evening Post* reported how he had set out from Chatham 'attended by a great number of Officers and others from the Dock Yard, who (to show their true Regard for so worthy and so good a Man) intend to accompany him as far as Deptford. It is remarkable that his kind and affable Behaviour had gained him a universal Love and Esteem.'[4]

Hayes knew that ships were fundamentally strong objects. Were they to be attacked with axes or hammers, it would take some effort to split them apart. But theirs was not robust strength. As soon as a ship was sailing in the open sea it began to degrade. The hempen ropes shrank, frayed or chafed. Sails tore. Yards and masts might spring and the caulked seams that kept a ship watertight were worn down by salt water. In the coastal service this was not a problem. Relays between London and Shields took no longer than a month and at any time a collier could be beached. Any Whitby master knew how to perform basic sea-side maintenance. A collier might be *breamed*, burning the grass, ooze and weeds from her bottom, then rubbing her with a mixture of sulphur and tallow. A similar procedure was called *boot-topping*, when a ship was scraped at the waterline. The favoured method of the diligent was *careening*, which meant ballasting the ship to one side so she could be scraped right under.

But once on a long, deep sea passage, all this routine maintenance became difficult. Weeds or periwinkles or other sea creatures might accumulate on the bottom. The officers of the warship *Champion* paused one day to have her hull inspected in the Firth of Fife, finding 'to their amazement, large clusters of shell-fish, almost as large as sugar loaves' stuck to the bottom. The *Champion*'s enterprising captain had these pulled off and used them to 'scrub and cleanse' her bottom, but in the midst of an ocean this sort of thing was not possible. A ragged hull would disrupt sailing and make fraught the simplest of manoeuvres. An even worse pest lurked in the South Seas. This was the teredo worm, a bivalve mollusc. 'The worm' had been the source of much destruction since the age of exploration began. Thriving in temperatures between 60–80°F, in its larval stage the worm burrowed into the submerged timbers of a ship, infesting it, hollowing it out, with inevitable consequences.

That such a meek invertebrate could destroy a massive ship seemed the stuff of Greek myth, but as the era of exploration advanced the challenge had become acute. For centuries shipwrights had sought a remedy for the worm, smearing ships' bottoms with tar, ox or goat hair, and covering them with brass or, lately, copper. Several experimental 'coppered' ships had come out of Deptford Yard recently, but with time short and no settled opinion yet reached on the process, the Admiralty had decided it best for *Endeavour* simply to be 'filled'. This meant that Fishburn's oak floor pieces were to be smeared with tar and matted hair. Onto this viscous surface, more oak boards were fitted before the whole of the bottom portion of the hull was covered with broad-headed iron nails, a process called 'hob-nailing'.

Once this preparatory step was done, Hayes was able to concentrate on the interior. The *Earl of Pembroke* had been selected for her broad voluminous hull. Every inch of this was to be turned to use. By mid-April, plans had been drawn up. An entire new deck was to run through her middle, seven feet below the main deck, giving room for the expanded crew to sleep and eat. The two existing decks – the foremost fall and the after fall – were to be retained but integrated within this design, which generated some odd spaces. Beneath the forecastle and quarterdeck the interior deck would be just four feet high, hopeless for standing in and awkward for everything else. At least it left a generous space in the stern for the commissioned officers: a great cabin, a lobby, cabins and a pantry lit by a skylight, all accessible by a ladder from the quarterdeck. More cabins were inserted into the bows, just behind the eyes, spaces for her warrant officers to mess. Beneath this, in the depths, there were to be more partitions, places for the stores needed on a long voyage.

Everything was detailed in letters between Deptford and Whitehall. On 7 April the order for the sheathing was given. On 12 April a longboat, a pinnace and a yawl were added to the list of requirements. Progress, at long, satisfying last, was coming at a pace. On 19 April, the initials AH – almost certainly those of Adam Hayes – appear on a note to the Navy Board, proposing certain tasks be outsourced to joiners: that a run of steps be added to the side, that lockers and cott cabins be fitted, new bulkheads and compartments installed. *Endeavour* was becoming something new. Where there had been space, there was now shape. Hatches led down into an interior unmistakeably that of a naval ship. On 25 April the yard officers were able to report to Stephens, the Admiralty secretary, 'The officers of HM Yard at Deptford say the *Endeavour* Bark will be ready to receive men next week.'[5]

In the heated aftermath of Wilkes's election victory a cantankerous letter from a 'Mr John Trott' appeared in the *Public Advertiser*. 'The rage for carriages is so great at present', it began, 'and the town and its avenues so full of them, that some speedy method should be taken to stop them.' Trott, aptly named and certainly a pseudonym for one of the city's wits, complained that 'every man who pretends to the smallest share of taste, has almost forgot how to use his legs'.[6]

As so often with the Georgian press, the letter used wry comedy to make a serious point. The rising mercantile classes, Trott asserted, had exchanged freedom for luxury. '[I] sincerely beseech them, as they love liberty, to stand upon their own feet, nor any longer suffer them-selves to be run away with by any headstrong brute or brutes, to whose caprice, the moment they step into a carriage, they submit their persons.'

All the nations we read of, that from a state of freedom have fallen into slavery, have bought that disgrace upon themselves by luxury. That carriages are strong symptoms of luxury, is not to be disputed; and I think I know some men yet who look upon them but as stately prisons. The freest people are certainly those who never knew the use of them, and are most likely to *stand their ground*. We have a late instance in our own country, where the only few who seem to be possessed of the genuine and *uncontroulable* spirit of freedom, I mean the voters for Mr Wilkes, almost to a man, walked on foot to Brentford, to poll for that honest gentleman; and many of them, I dare say, dread the thought of being *conveyed in a carriage* as much, nay more, than they would the pillory.[7]

Trott's letter is a sample of the conversations happening in London after the Middlesex election. The focus was 'liberty', which today means 'freedom' in a general sense but which in the eighteenth century was a word loaded with political significance. As the nation state had strengthened and expanded, with its national bank, standing army, judiciary and taxes, individuals had increasingly felt its force pressing in upon them. 'Man was born free, and he is everywhere in chains', Jean-Jacques Rousseau had famously written in *The Social Contract* (1762).[8] By 1768 the extent of a person's subjection to the state was foremost in their minds. At one of the capital's 'great speaking or disputing clubs', the question was proposed: 'If happiness be in our power, in what state of life is it most easily acquired?' One answer came back, 'What is it that we pant after in this country: – Liberty. What is the favourite wish and solace of our hearts? – Liberty. What is the surest road to fame in this country, – to signalize one's self in the cause of liberty.'[9]

Watching on, Catharine Macaulay wrote of 'the peculiar spirit' loose in the city's streets. Wilkes had stirred something fervent, something latent. 'Wilkes and Liberty!' rang the slogan. For Macaulay, whose convictions about liberty were every bit as (and perhaps much more) deeply held as Wilkes's, the Middlesex episode had been a confusing one. She was thrilled at the humbling of the ministerial faction at the ballot box, but equally she felt consternation that 'a man guilty of so many excesses and inconsistencies' as Wilkes had become a popular hero.[10] High on his success, Wilkes had soared to altitudes of grandiloquence in his victory speech to the Middlesex voters:

Let them call their PUSILLANIMITY prudence, while they igno-miniously kiss the rod of power, and tamely stoop to the yoke, which artful ministers insidiously prepare, and arbitrarily impose. You, Gentlemen, have shewn, that you are neither to be deceived nor enslaved.[11]

Swelling Wilkes's vanity to a pitch was a letter from Denis Diderot in Paris, written days after his election. 'I am the first to felicitate you on the occasion, and to join my congratulations to those of all the friends of the human race, which was certainly never intended to wear fetters. The august senate of Great-Britain will still count a Wilkes among its most illustrious members.'[12]

Or would it? No one was yet sure how the government would react. 'The ferment is not yet over', Benjamin Franklin conceded in a letter to his son in mid-April, 'he has promised to surrender himself to the Court next Wednesday, and another tumult is then expected; and what the upshot will be no one can yet foresee.' The showdown to which Franklin alluded was set for 20 April. Then the British legal system would have its say on Wilkes's status as an outlaw. With typical brio, Wilkes had let it be known that he would present himself voluntarily to the Court of the King's Bench at Westminster and act in perfect obedience with its wishes. He also let it be known that he expected to be acquitted to take up his seat in the Commons and resume his former status as an MP.

Wednesday 20 April came and Wilkes kept his word, surrendering to the court. The streets all around the Palace of Westminster were thronged with expectant crowds. Wilkes later complained that 'an idle tale was artfully and industriously propagated' by 'the spies and runners' of the government, warning that 'great riots and tumults would certainly happen.'[13] In consequence all Westminster's constables had been put on patrol, two battalions of guards were on standby in St James's Park while more troops were posted in St George's Fields, the Savoy and the Tower. This, many reckoned, was Bute's doing. It was said that the troops 'were furnished with sixteen rounds of ammunition'.

The day turned out anticlimactic. There were legal problems that prevented Wilkes's case from going ahead. It was postponed for a week, during which time tensions simmered. On 27 April, at noon, Wilkes came to court again. This time the charges were admitted and a future date appointed for the case to go ahead. In the meantime, Wilkes was refused bail. Until his case could be tried he was to be committed to the King's Bench Prison, in St George's Fields. Now a prisoner, Wilkes was taken into a private room by the marshal of the prison and from there was escorted out by two tipstaffs who ushered him into a hackney coach. This scene was inevitably played out in front of the crowds that now followed Wilkes everywhere – Horace Walpole had taken to calling them 'the third house of parliament' – and the sight of their hero being arrested provided them with just the provocation they needed.

The hackney carriage only progressed as far as Westminster Bridge before it was halted by the mob. Wilkes appealed for calm, but within a minute the officials were overpowered. 'I tell you, Master Wilkes', one cried out, 'horses often draw asses, but as you are a man, you shall be drawn by men.'[14] The horses were then unhitched, and Wilkes, sensing the trouble, bid the tipstaffs to flee while they could. Then, in brazen violation of the court's order, the crowd bore Wilkes in triumph through London's streets. The procession ended up far to the east at the Three Tuns tavern, Spitalfields. There boisterous celebrations commenced. Having first been the prisoner of the Crown then the prisoner of the people, only as night fell in Spitalfields was Wilkes able to make his getaway. He slipped out of the tavern in disguise and made his way to St George's Fields, surrendering to the turnkey. 'Many persons have fled disguised out of a *Prison*', wondered the *Courant* in astonishment, 'but Mr Wilkes is perhaps the first who ever stole disguised *into one*.'[15]

These were unsettling days for the ministry. The people had demonstrated a disturbing fact: that, together, they could face down the might of the government and win. This was the terror of democracy – a word that still carried disturbing connotations of its original Greek, 'mob rule'. At St George's Fields, to the south of the Thames, Wilkes understood how tense the situation had become. Remembering the incident on Westminster Bridge, he wrote to a friend, 'I have saved three lives last Wednesday, which I hold to be the most glorious day of my life. Such a rescue, such a triumphant entry from Westminster to Spitalfields. I am king of this great people, and will reign for their good.'[16]

As April brightened into May, St George's Fields was established as Wilkes's new headquarters. His every appearance at the gaol window was deemed newsworthy, and the disruption he had seeded continued to intensify. Outraged at the government's treatment of their hero, tradesmen and apprentices took the opportunity to vent their own grievances. The King's Yard at Deptford was not spared. After the vigorous weeks of work on *Endeavour* in early April, all momentum stalled. The yard was dependent on manual labour, but like the milliners, the hatters and the coal-heavers further upriver, the carpenters laid down their tools – seizing the chance to petition for higher wages.

On 1 May, traditionally a day of fairs, dancing and merriment, 'a very numerous body of sailors' began to congregate on the shores of the Thames at Wapping. They detained all the outward-bound ships. On 2 May they massed 'to the amount of many thousands' in Stepney

Fields, where their demands were gathered into a petition. This done, the sailors paraded towards the Royal Exchange, joining all the way 'in repeated huzzas'.[17] Only as they reached the City were they persuaded to disband. Some of the sailors acquiesced and went home but others joined the steady stream of malcontents who were making their way to St George's Fields. For now, at least, Wilkes was their king and the King's Bench Prison his palace.

Desperate to contain the situation, Lord North, Chancellor of the Exchequer, hosted a meeting of the king's party in Whitehall. It was agreed that Wilkes must not be permitted to take his seat in the Commons. When the king heard this, he approved. Excluding Wilkes, wrote George III, would act to 'curb that levelling principle that has been of late years gaining ground and restore that due obedience to law and government which this constitution has so wisely formed as the sole means of preventing liberty from degenerating into licentiousness'.[18]

It was too late for high-mindedness. For the first ten days of May London's streets were filled with marching protestors, 'colours flying, drums beating, and fifes playing', carrying petitions to their nervous masters. Wilkes later maintained that everything would have calmed down but for the unfortunate arrival of a Scottish detachment of troops. 'Afterwards they raised a disturbance by the rough manner of treating the people, by their abuse, their menaces, and the actually pushing at and wounding them with their bayonets.'[19] As ever in these situations, accounts differ on the specifics of what happened next. The government would laud the troops' alacrity, their 'zeal and good behaviour'. Others would say they panicked. One story, at least, is clear. Provoked by a man wearing a red coat, a small band of Scottish troops pursued him to a 'cow house'. There they cornered him and shot him dead. This had barely happened before they realised they had hit the wrong man. The innocent victim, William Allen, was the son of an innkeeper. A spectator, not knowing what was happening, 'on seeing some persons run, he ran also, but was unhappily mistaken'.[20]

As news of Allen's murder was relayed through the streets, the situation caught fire. Stones and bricks were thrown. A party of horse grenadiers was called, as was a justice of the peace who read the riot act. 'Damn the king, damn the Parliament, damn the justices!', chanted the mob. Within minutes the soldiers were told to fire. But again they were clumsy rather than clinical. Aiming over the crowd's heads, the soldiers inadvertently struck bystanders further off. One was sat in a hay cart. Another was selling oranges. A third was innocently walking down the road. The mob, seething, surging, began to move. Horses were rushing at full speed, galloping 'backwards and forwards'. 'Such a day has not been in England since the accession of the mild house of Brunswick'[21], one of Wilkes's publications later asserted. The mob progressed to London Bridge then crossed into the City, carrying Allen's body on a slab, telling everyone of the outrages. The news flew. The English had been mown down 'like flocks of sparrows, in absolute wantonness'. There had 'not been such a massacre of the English by Scotsmen since *Prestonpans* and *Falkirk.*'[22] Riots and violence spilled through London for days. This was the moment for everyone to voice their own latent grievances. In Limehouse and Shadwell, some 5,000 to 15,000 sailors – the number was variously estimated – marched all the way to the Palace of Westminster to see their petition accepted.

The mob came to Deptford too. 'A great body of sailors assembled' jubilant around the docks, went a report. They 'forcibly went on board several ships, unreefed their top-sails, and vowed no ships should sail out of the Thames till the merchants had consented to raise their wages.'[23] In Deptford, where precious weeks had slipped away without a day's work being completed on *Endeavour*, the collier could hardly have escaped the attentions of the mob, being the easiest of all targets in the single dock.

Out of this multitude, one sailor emerged from Assembly Row, Mile End Old Town. He was not setting out to march or to riot. James Cook – tall, purposeful, calm, deliberate – late master of HMS *Grenville*, was not the rioting type. Nor did this man have reason to complain. Unlike his peers at Stepney Fields, the spring of 1768 had been kind to Cook. It had provided him with an excellent opportunity, and the most unusual of jobs.

On 13 May, as the disorder was at its height, Cook took and passed his lieutenant's examination. The event is captured in the usual terse language of official documents. 'We have examined Mr James Cook, who by Certificate appears to be more than 39 Years of Age, and find he has gone to Sea more than 11 Years in the Ships and Qualities undermentioned.' There follows a list of names and dates: the *Eagle* (able seaman then master's mate), the *Solebay* (master), the *Pembroke* (master), the *Northumberland* (master), the *Grenville Schooner* (master). 'He produceth Journals kept by himself in the *Eagle* & *Northumberland* and Certificates from Captains Craig, Palliser, & Bateman of his Diligence & he can Splice, Knot, Reef a Sail, &c and is qualified to do the duty of an Able Seaman and Midshipman – 13 May, 1768.'[24]

This was a deft, administrative review of what already had been an impressive career for the 'strong-faced, tall, well set-up, healthy' man that presented himself at the Admiralty that day.[25] With riots outside, it was an appropriate context for them to meet Cook. Throughout his service, whether on the quarterdeck of a man-of-war under fire or mazing through coastal shoals in a boat, Cook was known to retain an even temperament. He was not docile or wooden, but Cook had a seemingly natural ability to absorb the manifold happenings of life and counter them with cool rationalism. Some might have appreciated Cook's talents already, but few knew just how good he was.

Like Thomas Milner and Henry Taylor, Cook had begun his professional sailing career in Whitby, in ships like those Fishburn built. Born the son of a farm labourer in Marton, a moorside village, Cook had ventured over the hills to Whitby as a lad of seventeen in 1746. His master, John Walker, was one of the leading Quaker shipowners in the town, and he took a special interest in his new boy. Cook learned the art of loading, hauling and splicing, eventually progressing to the art of ship management and elementary mathematics. In late 1747, aged eighteen or nineteen, Cook had first gone to sea on the 318-ton collier *Freelove*, a collier built by the Coates family.[26]

Cook had stayed in Whitby until 1755, overlapping with a young Henry Taylor. The two of them shared traits. Cook had Taylor's caution, the same knack for building camaraderie among his crews, the same levels of diligence and love of duty. But Cook also had traits Taylor did not. Chief among these was ambition. Having completed his training and risen to the point of being offered his own command, Cook abruptly left Walker, Whitby and the coal trade for greater things. What prompted him to go has been much debated. A difficult man to know well, reticent, not given to outward reflection, Cook wrote of his desire 'to take future fortune'. This may have been wanderlust. But equally it feels more calculated than that. All that can be said for certain is that in June 1755, Cook volunteered for the Royal Navy at Wapping. A relatively old and unusually skilled recruit, Cook had signed up for a hard life in the lowest strata of the navy while his old friends in the north grew rich working contracts during the Seven Years War.

But if adventure was the lure, then Cook certainly found it. Within a month of volunteering he had earned a promotion to master's mate on HMS *Eagle*. From there he had risen to become the sailing master – 'the chief professional on board though not the highest ranking one' – of the seventy-gun *Northumberland*, with her complement of 500. Cook had seen action in the Bay of Biscay, commanding a prize into Plymouth. He had crossed the Atlantic to Virginia and New York and he had been involved in the Canadian campaign, helping to usher the fleet up the St Lawrence River in the superb prelude to the Battle of the Plains of Abraham.

Throughout these years Cook had thrived. He demonstrated himself as diligent, capable and having some usual inner force of character. As his biographer J. C. Beaglehole observed:

> The genius of Cook was not, in the ordinary sense, creative. Nor was it precocious. There was nothing aesthetic, nothing of early brilliance, about him. He would have been startled at the idea that anything he did might touch the emotions. His energy of mind was of that mature kind that is, on the intellectual side, critical, a sort of analytical and detective energy; on the practical, the constructive side, it was an energy of planning, of adminis-tration and foresight. It came to fruition almost by accident.[27]

The 'analytical and detective energy' Beaglehole writes of could be seen most of all in Cook's surveying work. It is intriguing to wonder whether he got his earliest taste of precise measurement watching Charlton plotting out the Esk-side farms in the 1750s. Perhaps Cook did see the schoolmaster with his flags and theodolites, demon-strating techniques Cook was to perfect during his spare hours as a young warrant officer. Then, Cook, thirsty for knowledge, learned to draw with clarity and precision. He mastered scientific instruments. By the time the Seven Years War had finished, Cook's skills had been noticed by one of his old captains, a fellow Yorkshireman, Hugh Palliser, who had him appointed to the Newfoundland Survey. Retaining his rank as master, Cook had been given a twelve-gun schooner, HMS *Grenville*.

Taken in the broad context of events in the colonies, the *Grenville* was no glorious command. But for Cook she had served admirably. Impelled by a preternatural desire to master his environment, to freeze the wild coasts within the confines of a chart of an inch to a league, he had sailed over hundreds of miles of foggy coastline in Newfoundland. He had probed into bays, inlets and creeks, planted flags, triangulated points, computed angles and sounded depths, in the estimation of Nicholas Thomas, 'working magic on rugged and intricate coastlines, reducing a shoreline as torn as an awful wound to points and lines on paper'.[28] Approaching forty, Cook had become something different to the keen-eyed, dutiful Whitby sailor Taylor epitomised. He was a naval asset, one of a few hydrographically trained experts. For some years he had been noticed by the grandees at the Admiralty who had acknowledged his 'Genius and Capacity'. Now these skills and connections had brought him an unexpected opportunity.

Cook had established a routine during his time on the Newfoundland Survey. He sailed in early spring and returned in autumn, spending the winters with his wife Elizabeth and their family – James and Nathaniel, their two young boys, and Elizabeth their infant daughter – at their home in Mile End, drawing and perfecting his charts, corresponding with the Admiralty, sourcing books and preparing for the next year's season. It was shortly before the *Grenville*'s intended departure in April 1768 that the first indication came that something else was intended for him. On 12 April, nine days after Dalrymple's appearance at the Royal Society Council meeting, the Admiralty minutes signalled 'Mr Cook who is master of the *Grenville* schooner, is to be employed elsewhere.'[29] Opaque as it was, the plan may already have been in motion. The Lords of the Admiralty and organisers of the Venus expedition at the Royal Society knew that time was running short. A voyage to the far side of the world, to an as yet unspecified location, could take as long as a year. By April 1768 just fourteen months remained to them.

To those like Franklin or Nevil Maskelyne at the Royal Society, it must have seemed that this was history repeating itself. During the transit expeditions of 1761 voyagers had set off too late, alternative locations had had to be substituted and attempts had been abandoned. Desperate not to fail again, having lost Dalrymple and with London abandoned to rioting and disorder, it seems the responsibility for finding a replacement commander was passed to the navy. Cook's nomination rested on his relationship with Hugh Palliser, the outgoing governor of Newfoundland and an influential figure. Palliser liked Cook; he had seen him as both a sailing master and a hydrographical surveyor and he had faith in his abilities.

Cook heard of the South Seas voyage during the first ten days of April. If he was surprised at the news of such an unusual commission, the first shock must have been followed by a second. Cook had first gone to sea in a Whitby collier. Twenty-one years later, having travelled across the Atlantic to find his fortune, it transpired that this fortune was to be precisely the type of ship he had first learned to sail. Events had conspired strangely but auspiciously. Like any Whitby apprentice, Cook had an instinctive understanding of what Whitby colliers could do, how they might behave in a given scenario, how far they might be driven and when they needed care.

But before Cook could take command his lieutenant's examinations were a necessary step. Passing the test must have been a moment of pride for Cook. He could now count himself among the sons of gentlemen as part of the Royal Navy's officer class. As first lieutenant of HM Bark *Endeavour*, he had the undisputed privilege of the quarterdeck, a servant of his own and a distinct uniform of a blue wool coat with white facings, white waistcoat, cuffs and breeches. There would be money too. On 5 May Cook attended a Royal Society meeting with the Earl of Morton, Franklin, Maskelyne and the rest of the council who had all been 'informd that Mr Js Cook ... was a proper person to be one of the Observers' of the Transit of Venus. In a society where class boundaries were often impenetrable, Cook must have felt off kilter standing in front of peers and philosophers, receiving the news he was to be paid '£120 a year for victualling himself'. The upturn in his fortunes was crowned on 19 May at a further meeting when Cook 'accepted the sum of one hundred Guineas as a Gratuity for his trouble as one of the Observers'.[30]

The die was now cast. Both the Admiralty and Royal Society were content. Lieutenant Cook was to lead a voyage to the South Seas in *Endeavour* to observe the Transit of Venus. This clarity coincided with easing tensions in London. Never again after mid-May was the threat of riot so extreme. On 18 May news reached the Navy Board from Deptford: 'We have undocked the *Endeavour* from the single dock and put her into the Bason in order to finish the painting &c'. A week

later the Admiralty minutes signalled it was 'Resolved that the
Endeavour Bark be fitted out at Deptford for Foreign Service, manned
with 70 men and victualled for 12 months.'[31]

It is enchanting to think of Cook first clapping eyes on *Endeavour*,
a Whitby collier, lifted up on the stocks of the dry dock as if she
was a fighting frigate. Cook had seen scores of cats and barks aloft
in such a state at the Coates and Fishburn yards. But to encounter
one at the King's Yard must have been completely novel – like visiting
an old house to find the rooms repainted and the favourite furniture
replaced. This was a Fishburn bark, there was no doubt about that.
But it had been subjected to a surprising transformation. The
Endeavour had a complete internal deck running through its middle
where the coals used to be heaped high. There were cot cabins for
the warrant officers, fitted with miniature pantry doors. There were
the even rows of hooks for the hammocks, long benches for meal-
times, sail rooms, a magazine and the officer quarters further back.
Gone was the spartan emptiness Milner had presided over. There
was more to *Endeavour* yet. Down below this interior deck was space
for provisions, which would soon be heaped high with bags of flour,
barrels of beers, casks of spirits. There would be bags of bread
(21,226 pounds), 4,000 pieces of salt beef, 6,000 pieces of salt pork
and 800 pounds of suet, 120 bushels of wheat, 10 bushels of oatmeal,
2,500 pounds of raisins, 120 gallons of oil, 1,500 pounds of sugar,
500 gallons of vinegar, 160 pounds of mustard seeds.[32]

Endeavour's transformation gathered pace as spring turned to
summer. With the major structural changes complete, the insides of
the ship acquired a different feel. A regulator clock was brought aboard,
part of the apparatus for the Venus observation. It was a precision
instrument that suggested *Endeavour*'s purpose. She was no longer to
be governed by traditional chants, rules of thumb and good lookouts;
she was to be an instrument of scientific exactitude. Along with the
regulator clock came more quantifying devices: globes, sextants, telescopes, azimuth compasses, dipping needles, thermometers, and then
there were technical books on navigation, medicine and histories of
South Seas voyages by explorers like Anson and Abel Tasman that
were slotted into bookcases in the great cabin.

As Cook went about sourcing his philosophical instruments and
books in Fleet Street, the first members of crew began to enlist.
Assigned to the newly fitted cabins was the second lieutenant, a

twenty-nine-year-old Londoner called Zachary Hicks. Also with his own quarters was the surgeon William Monkhouse. Further forward, two other warrant officers were allotted cabins: the boatswain John Gathrey – 'of good testimony' – whose berth was to the larboard side beneath the forecastle, and the carpenter, whose cabin lay opposite on the starboard side. Cook did not have much of a following of his own to bring with him from the *Grenville*, just four dependable seamen, one of whom, Peter Flowers, had served with him in Newfoundland for five years. But he did exploit his position to draft in a few of his own picks, including a young cousin of his wife's called Isaac Smith, who had some aptitude as a draughtsman.

Scores of other, faceless recruits would join this inner core. The names of all of these survive, though in most cases little else. But even so it becomes less necessary to imagine. As the *Earl of Pembroke* vanishes and the *Endeavour* supplants her, so details emerge into faith-fully recorded history. On Friday 10 June, for instance, we know 'a proper quantity of Sour Krout' was hauled on board as a remedy for scurvy.[33] The same day *Endeavour* was 'supplied with a machine for sweetening foul water'. On 30 June Cook requested a 'Green Baize Floor Cloth' for the great cabin, and on Wednesday 20 July the Admiralty confirmed that 'twenty cork jackets' had been purchased and sent aboard. These are snippets plucked from the scores of letters that flew from Whitehall to Deptford, their contents relating to every deck, every mast, every yard, every cabin and every boat – there were to be three: a long boat, a pinnace and a yawl. The sight of all this would have been a delight to Fishburn, who by now would have heard the news of the voyage from Milner. Moreover he would have loved to have looked over the plans Hayes signed off in July. They froze *Endeavour* in profile, a ship unlike any other. She had metamorphosed into a hybrid, a blend of a transport and a sloop. Even for those sages on the river she must have posed a problem of classification. Whatever she was, Cook was doing his best to get a feel of her. Running her through her paces in the Thames, he scribbled notes to the Navy Board that she 'swims too much by the head' and needed more ballasting to fix her trim.

There was little time for such meddling. It was now weeks since the Admiralty secretary had fired off his impatient note, sanctioning the purchase of the *Earl of Pembroke* 'to save time'. Months later, Cook had still to depart. It was now much less than a year before the expedition was required to be in the South Seas and, as far as planetary orbits went, they may as well be a decade late as a day. But the delay had yielded an unexpected advantage. On 19 May, HMS *Dolphin*, under the command of Samuel Wallis, had anchored in the Downs after a circumnavigation of the globe that had taken them across the Pacific. Wallis had been sent as Byron had before him, to search for Terra Australis. The continent, if it existed, had eluded him, but he had made one tantalising discovery. It was a tropical island, 'large, fertile and extremely populous', where Wallis had stayed six weeks. 'From the behaviour of the inhabitants', ran an account that was syndicated in newspapers across Britain, 'they had reason to believe she was the first and only ship they had ever seen.'[34]

Wallis had taken possession of this land for Britain, calling it King George's Island, and from the stories that were soon circulating it was an extraordinary place. The island was governed by a queen, 'to whom the natives seemed to pay the utmost reverence, as they obeyed not only her words, but even her looks and gestures'. This 'Queen of the Island' had loaded the *Dolphin* with presents and she had breakfasted with Wallis in the great cabin on tea, bread and butter. Along with her chief minister she had made a tour of the frigate. 'She took very particular notice of everything she saw, and seemd highly pleasd.' The *Dolphin* had returned her gifts in the form of looking glasses, wine glasses, buttons and earrings, 'but what she seemd most fond of was Linnen Cloath', revealed one of the crew. 'I therefor gave her a very Good Ruffeld Shirt, and showd her how to put it on, this trifeling present gaind her heart.'[35]

With their own country mired in confusion, this faraway, untainted island was bound to appeal. That it was ruled by a beneficent queen reminded the English, too, of their own golden days. Two hundred thousand people were said to live on the island, a significant size, and after some skirmishes, the islanders who were 'in general taller and stouter made than our people, and are mostly of a copper colour, with black hair', had proved friendly and eager to trade. 'It abounds with all the choicest productions of the earth', went the report, and these were exchanged for such trivialities as nails, buttons, beads and trinkets. Wallis, ill in the *Dolphin*, had forbidden his men from exploring much beyond 'a small part of the Bay where the Ship Lay'. But one of the officers had struck five miles up a river where he had discovered 'cotton, Ginger, Indigo and many oyther things growing, that we knowed nothing of before'. In Wallis's absence, too, an amity had sprung up between the *Dolphin* and the inhabitants that had quickly ripened. The women were said to be beautiful, nubile and with no trace of modesty or chastity, being happy to consort with the sailors. They wore garlands about their necks and danced seductive dances in the warm evenings as the Pacific sun sank behind the ocean waves.

All this was a welcome contrast to the reports of rioting and hardship at home. The news from America was no better. The repeal of the Stamp Act in March 1766 had briefly brought the colonial relationship back onto a happy footing. But the cordiality had not lasted long. In the summer of 1767 Charles Townshend, Chancellor of the Exchequer, 'a dazzling orator and an amusing but unreliable man', had introduced a new series of taxes.[36] The 'Townshend Acts' established levies on tea, paper, glass, lead and painter's colours. They were designed, like the Stamp Act before, to raise a proportion of the revenue required for maintaining an army in America directly from the colonies.

Townshend died suddenly in September 1767 so did not live to witness the furious response his legislation elicited. In colonial America it was treated as the second coming of the Stamp Act. Talk was again of non-compliance and of the non-importation of British goods. 'Save your money, and you save your country', the *Boston Gazette*'s slogan ran. The British press, meanwhile, had begun to growl back at 'the Americans', as 'diggers of pits for this country', 'lunaticks', 'sworn enemies', 'false', 'ungrateful', 'cut-throats', slurs to which Franklin had objected, 'as a treatment of customers that I doubt is not like to bring them back to our shop'.[37]

News of George's Island, a sweet, zephyr land, sparkled in comparison with this. Accounts lengthened with the days. It was being spoken of as an Elysium, a fairy land of innocence, play and plenty.

It was not just the British who were animated by the news. Ever since the end of the Seven Years War, the French minister Choiseul had kept a close watch on Britain's overseas activities. By 1768 he had spies in the Navy Board as well as the dockyards. As fascinated by reports as the British, soon a French syndicate was preparing an expedition to the island. The Spanish were alerted too. Their ambassador in London succeeded in purchasing a copy of the *Dolphin*'s secret accounts, which included bearings for the island. Guessing that enterprises of these sorts would be underway, the government had leaked the wrong latitude to the press. In the meantime Wallis had Anglicised the area as much as he was able, not just naming King George's Island, but also scattering a variety of other titles on islets and atolls: Charlotte Island, Gloucester Island, Boscawen Island, Keppel Island and Duke of York Island.

The government did not yet know what advantages George's Island would bring in the future as a trading post. But for the Royal Society it presented a perfect solution to a nagging problem. Its South Seas location fell right within the area Maskelyne had marked as suitable for the transit observation. On 9 June, soon after Wallis's arrival in British waters, the Royal Society informed the Admiralty of their decision 'to have their Observers conveyed to Port Royal in Georges Land Lately discovered by Mr Wallace in the *Dolphin*'. There was more news too. The society had appointed Charles Green to accompany Cook and act as one of the official observers. Green, thirty-three years old, was a trained astronomer who had worked at Greenwich under Maskelyne. His appointment brought a weight of formal education to the *Endeavour* crew that Cook, on his own, lacked.

Another benefit of the *Dolphin*'s return was that Cook was able to enlist several members of her crew. The most useful addition was a Virginian-born officer called John Gore. A superb sailor, Gore had twice sailed round the world in the *Dolphin*, first with Byron then with Wallis, both times as master's mate. His duties on the last voyage had been considerably inflated because an illness had kept Wallis in his cabin for much of the time. In Wallis's absence Gore had proved himself a figure of strength among the ship's company, 'imperturbably and absolutely reliable'. Another of the mates, Robert Molyneux, a Lancastrian, was appointed sailing master, while an eighteen-year-old Yorkshireman called Richard Pickersgill, a gifted draughtsman, was to serve as one of his mates. Joining them all was Charles Clerke, who had sailed on the *Dolphin*'s first circumnavigation with Byron. To protect them all from attack, *Endeavour* was to be fitted with ten carriage guns and twelve swivels.[38]

The disorder of spring behind, London returned to normality over the summer. The government tried to assert itself over American affairs, with a new Cabinet post, Secretary of State for the American Colonies, being established. Wilkes remained in St George's Fields.

There he would receive a letter of encouragement from New England. The letter – it came along with a gift of another turtle for Wilkes to roast – ran:

> That the British constitution still exists is our glory; feeble and infirm as it is, we cannot, we will not despair of it. To a Wilkes much is already due for his strenuous efforts to preserve it ... Your perseverance in the good old cause may still prevent the great system from dashing to pieces.[39]

Among the signatures were names Wilkes would not have recognised, but ones that would be immortalised by history: John Adams, Samuel Adams, James Otis Jr, John Hancock, Richard Dana, Joseph Warren, Benjamin Kent, Thomas Young, Josiah Quincy II and Benjamin Church. Wilkes had replied, high-spirited and thrilled with the turtle, 'I hope freedom will ever flourish under your hemisphere as well as ours.'

Despite the resolves not to import any English goods, Wilkes's speeches and papers would continue to find an outlet across the Atlantic, as would Catharine Macaulay's *History of England*. The work was given a 'free sale', revealed the *Kentish Gazette*. The 'Ladies of America' were said to read her with a 'great avidity, and speak of her with the greatest applause'.[40]

Ships carrying Macaulay's books and Wilkes's speeches mingled in the Thames along with East Indiamen with their spices and teas, West Indiamen with their sugar and cocoa, and the Whitby colliers that brought even more coal to fuel the growing, seething, tempestuous capital. Among all these, on 30 July, *Endeavour* had left her last London anchorage and begun her slow progress downstream. At a glance she would still seem like the other northern merchants congregated in the Thames, but a closer look would reveal something more. There was the sweeping blue stripe beneath her gunwale, the red ensign over her stern signalling she was a commissioned ship of the navy on detached duties; there was her lowness in the water beneath the strain of the provisions, drawing something like fourteen feet fore and aft. Then more than anything else, there was the sheer number of sailors: men teeming everywhere, cross-legged on the forecastle and the main deck, hanging from the shrouds, leaning over the bows, high in the tops.

Earlier that day Cook had been given his orders. They came in two sealed packets: 'The Instructions', which ordered him to sail to 'Port Royal Harbour in King Georges Island' to observe the transit, and the 'Additional Instructions' – not to be pursued until he had complied with his initial orders. Soon, having bid farewell to his wife Elizabeth, Cook joined the *Endeavour* at the Downs to take formal command. In the Channel he had the chance to a get a feel for the ship, as Milner had with the *Earl of Pembroke*. She no doubt felt altered by all her adjustments – heavier, more solid, but brighter, neater, attentive to her helm: a taut ship. 'A better ship for such a Service I never would wish for', Cook later said.[41]

Once on board, naval custom saw that Lieutenant Cook was addressed instead as 'Captain'. George's Island might have been his ultimate destination, but first he was compelled to 'make the best of your way to Plymouth Sound', where the crew were to be paid two months' wages in advance, some last-minute changes were to be completed, extra supplies of beef, water, powder and cordage were to be taken aboard, as were a sergeant, corporal, drummer and nine private marines. All this left *Endeavour* with just about room for its most curious and colourful cargo of all. This was a 'suite' or group of supernumeraries belonging to the 'remarkable' botanist and intrepid man of science, Joseph Banks.

PART THREE

Exploration

6

'Take a Trip in disguise'

On 7 October 1768 HM Bark *Endeavour* was sailing south over a warm sea. At some unmarked moment over the last day the tenth parallel had passed beneath her hull. Somewhere, they knew, about 600 miles beyond the eastern horizon rim, lay Guinea and the smouldering coast of Africa. Cook had turned the north-east trade to good purpose over the last fortnight. The officers, mustering on the quarterdeck for the midday observations, had often found that they had travelled more than a hundred miles in a day. But as they neared the equator the robust wind of the mid-latitudes had faded into a 'steady breeze and pleasant weather'.[1] Now *Endeavour* cruised over a glassy ocean and behind her – presumably lashed to her stern by a rope – trailed Joseph Banks in his collecting boat.

If the prospect of a Whitby collier far outside her natural habitat was surprising to any passing vessels, the impression would have been reinforced by the sight of a tall, youthful English gentleman: dark-haired, lithe, bobbing about in his lighterman's skiff, swotting at insects and scooping at weeds. Perhaps it would have been possible to discern the brightness in Banks's face, the urgency of his movements or even to catch the sparkle of his conversation. Except for the fact that he was surrounded by miles and miles of empty sea, he might for all the world have been a squire at home on his trout lake.

But Banks had foresworn the comforts of home for the lure of adventure. The Atlantic was an enticing habitat to explore and still better places awaited. Six weeks into the voyage, Banks had settled into his maritime existence. He rose early each morning to survey the surrounding seas for signs of life. He had spotted crabs, swallows and dolphins, catching some and missing others. He had been thrilled above all by the flying fish, 'whose bea[u]ty especialy when seen from the cabbin windows is beyond imagination, their sides shining like burnishd silver'. To Banks's delight, one of these had actually 'flown into Mr Green the Astronomer's Cabbin'. 'I suppose chasd by some other fish', Banks had speculated, 'or maybe merely because he did not see the ship.'[2]

With the trade winds slackening, there were more chances for Banks to explore the environment. On 7 October, collecting in his boat, he was to have his most rewarding session yet. By midday he had returned to the great cabin with a haul of marine invertebrates. One, a Siphonophorae, 'what is calld by the Seaman a Portuguese man of war', charmed Banks with its intricate form and colour. It was 'one of the most bea[u]tifull sights I have ever seen'. Dissecting it with his philosophical friend, the Swedish botanist Daniel Solander, they divided the 'small bladder' of its body from 'a number of strings of bright blue and red' that dangled beneath like silks from a festooned roof. Some of these strings were three or four feet long and Banks found that if touched, they stung 'in the same manner as nettles, only much stronger'.[3]

Less hazardous to handle were a quantity of marine snails. Again Banks and Solander analysed them. Conspicuous by their bobbing at the surface, Banks reckoned that they owed this buoyancy to a 'small cluster of Bubbles' he found inside the shells, which acted like modern lifejackets. Squeezing the snails, Banks noticed that 'a teaspoonfull of Liquid' was discharged, of 'a most beautifull red purple colour' that 'easily dies linen clothes'. It may be worth enquiry, Banks wrote a reminder to himself in his journal, whether these snails were the source of the distinctive red 'purpora' shade known and used in ancient Rome, 'as the shell is certainly found in the Mediterranean'.[4]

Once analysed, the specimens were assigned scientific names by Banks and Solander. The Portuguese Man of War was entered as *Holothuria physalis* and the marine snails as *Helix janthina*. Both of these were then forwarded to the artists Sydney Parkinson and Alexander Buchan to be sketched in outline or painted in watercolours. The process ran brisk and fluent. It needed to. Above Banks's scientific enclave in the great cabin, on the quarterdeck, Cook was adjusting the ship's trim for a shift in the weather. Finely tuned to atmospheric fluctuations, Cook had noticed the morning's calm was poised to break. Soon there would be 'Thunder and Lightning all round the compass'.[5] Cook made no mention of Banks that day in his journal of 'Remarkable Occurrences'. But not one to miss much, the captain had doubtless cast an intrigued eye in his direction. Banks was an outsider in his naval world. It was only two months since Banks had been attending the opera in Covent Garden where he had met the Genevan physicist Horace-Bénédict de Saussure. Sauntering through the London streets, Saussure and Banks had fallen into conversation. In a letter written after the encounter, Saussure had declared himself 'charmed' to 'have seen before his departure a remarkable man'.[6]

According to a story he later told, Banks's attitude towards nature was established very early on under the influence of his mother. Sarah Banks, a lady 'void of all imaginary fear', had taught him that nature did not exist merely to be admired, as the poets admired it, or avoided, as the timorous avoided it. Rather it existed to be interacted with: touched, tasted, sniffed. Banks gave the toad as an example of his attitude. Toads were treated warily in Georgian England for the toxic ooze they were said to secrete, a prejudice bolstered by frequent newspaper stories of accidental poisonings. Through the teaching of his mother, Banks learned early to disdain the superstition. He made it a 'constant habit' when he spied toads to pick them up, 'applying them to my nose and face as it may happen'. Once, a party of Banks's friends were travelling through Yorkshire with him when he spotted one. Jumping out of his carriage and pouncing on the creature, Banks had held it up in his hand 'to convince' them there was 'nothing poisonous' about it.[7] Hoping that it would perform a somersault to crown the occasion, the amphibian had disobliged Banks and amused his friends by leaping into his mouth instead.

This was exactly the sort of event which might have driven a Georgian to their sickbed, but with his mother's attitude imprinted in him, it was not much of an inconvenience for Banks. Similar things, and perhaps some worse, must have happened to him during his childhood, scampering around the family's Lincolnshire estate with his younger sister, Sarah Sophia, to whom he always remained close. He was born in February 1743, the first son of a family of no great status but one of considerable wealth. The Banks family owned lands in Derbyshire, Sussex, Staffordshire and Lincolnshire that, in time, supplied Joseph with £6,000 per annum. For all his mother's influence on his personality, it was Joseph's father, William, who had held the reins during his childhood. A member of the politicking gentry with a Cornish seat in Parliament, William had otherwise ploughed his energy into decorating the family seat at Revesby Abbey in Lincolnshire. Left a chair-bound paraplegic by a mysterious malady when he was twenty-six, the family's hopes were transferred from William to his high-spirited son, who was dispatched first to Harrow and then to Eton.

Joseph had not thrived in the strict rote of the classroom. News had come back to Revesby Abbey from his form master that Joseph was a cheerful enough boy, but one hindered by a lack of interest in the curriculum. That Banks was not a diligent student of the rules of language is suggested to anyone today who reads over his letters or journals. His prose flows like a dashing brook without trace of punctuation. Sometimes there are capitalisations and sometimes not, according to his fancy. Some words – 'friend' is one – he never quite learned to spell. This haphazardness may be a symptom of a neurological imbalance or, equally, might have been produced by his innate restlessness. Banks was a boy who needed action, and he made it when he could not find it. In 1757 a report had arrived in Lincolnshire from Eton, speaking of 'a great Inattention' in Master Banks, 'and an immoderate Love of Play', vices to be countered as 'a constant Obstacle to his Improvement.'[8]

By the time Banks left Eton he had found a subject that would awake his interest in learning. There are various accounts of what originally brought Banks to botany. One story, supposedly told by Banks in his later years, depicts him alone in a lane near Eton one summer afternoon, powerfully overwhelmed by the majesty of the flowers around him. 'It is surely more natural that I should be taught to know all these productions of Nature, in preference to Greek or Latin.'[9] A less Damascene account has him as a boy of fourteen, home for the holidays, discovering the Elizabethan classic, *The Herball or Generall Historie of Plantes* by John Gerrard (1597) in his mother's dressing room. He was soon turning his love of the outdoors to purpose, on hands and knees, pressing plants and trapping insects in Lincolnshire, and then in the lanes near Eton where it was said he would reward the women who ran the local apothecaries with sixpence for each gem of traditional wisdom.

The seventeen-year-old Banks – blithe, cheerful, on the make – had gone up to Oxford in 1760 to continue his studies, matriculating as a gentleman commoner at Christ Church. These were not innovative years for the university. As the printing boom brought more books

Oak trees were a timeless feature of the English countryside. This landscape shows how they were adapted to play social roles in a parish: an oak tree doubles as the Man in the Moon Inn. The timber used in *Endeavour*'s hull came from much younger oaks, cut when they were about a hundred years old.

Whitby in the eighteenth century was a potent mixture of old and new, tradition and innovation. The road in this picture rises up from the busy shipyards while Whitby Abbey stands on the east cliff behind.

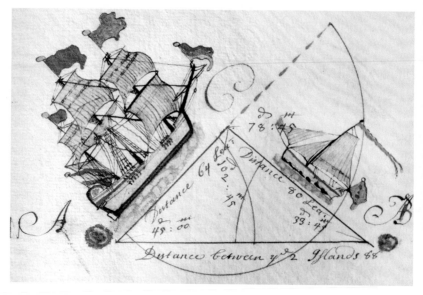

This fusion of the mathematical and maritime worlds is taken from the workbook of a Whitby apprentice, Henry Simpson, in the early 1700s. Simpson's half-serious, half-merry sketches calculate the distance between two islands.

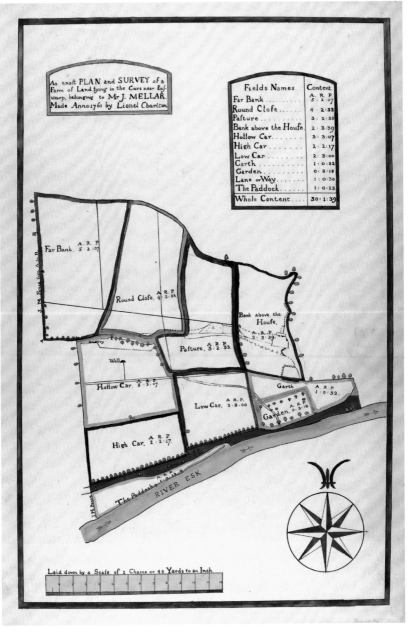

An exact PLAN and SURVEY of a
Farm of Land lying in the Cars near Ruſ-
warp, belonging to Mr J. MELLAR.
Made Anno 1761 by Lionel Charlton

Fields Names	Content
	A. R. P.
Far Bank	5 · 2 · 07
Round Cloſe	4 · 2 · 33
Paſture	3 · 2 · 33
Bank above the Houſe	2 · 3 · 39
Hollow Car	3 · 3 · 07
High Car	2 · 2 · 17
Low Car	2 · 3 · 00
Garth	1 · 0 · 32
Garden	0 · 3 · 18
Lane or Way	1 · 0 · 30
The Paddock	1 · 0 · 23
Whole Content	30 · 1 · 39

Far Bank. A. R. P. 5 · 2 · 07

Round Cloſe. A. R. P. 4 · 2 · 33

Bank above the Houſe. A. R. P. 2 · 3 · 39

Paſture, A. R. P. 3 · 2 · 33

Well

Hollow Car. A. R. P. 3 · 3 · 07

Low Car, A. R. P. 2 · 3 · 00

Garth A. R. P. 1 · 0 · 32

Garden, 0 · 3 · 18

High Car, A. R. P. 2 · 2 · 17

The Paddock A. R. P. 1 · 0 · 23   RIVER ESK

Laid down by a Scale of 2 Chains or 44 Yards to an Inch.

In 1748 the 'philomath' or 'lover of learning' Lionel Charlton arrived in Whitby. He established a school in the heart of the town and completed a series of pioneering land surveys, bringing the Enlightenment ideals of rationalism and precision to Whitby.

Top: In 1764 the coal collier *Earl of Pembroke* sailed on her maiden voyage. Those watching her from the coast would have witnessed a scene much like *Shields, on the River Tyne* by J. M. W. Turner.

Bottom: The *Earl of Pembroke* leaves Whitby for the last time, soon to be purchased by the Royal Navy and renamed *Endeavour*. A new life was set to begin.

Top left: The poised 'projector'. A young and
ambitious Alexander Dalrymple on his return
from the East, 1765.

Top right: John Wilkes: unmatched political agita-
tor and satirist. Voltaire wrote that Wilkes set him 'in
flames' with his courage and charmed him with his wit.

Bottom left: 'The Celebrated Mrs Catharine
Macaulay', bestselling historian, pamphleteer
and champion of liberty.

Bottom right: Benjamin Franklin arrived for his
third stay in London in 1764, soon to become
deeply embroiled in the quarrel between the British
government and the American colonies.

Top: *Endeavour* is shown off the coast of Tierra del Fuego in this seascape by Alexander Buchan. Sydney Parkinson described the 'barren rocks and tremendous precipices, covered with snow…which human nature can scare behold without shuddering'.

Bottom: Originally hired as a botanical draughtsman, Parkinson's range of subjects widened as *Endeavour*'s voyage progressed. By the time they reached Tahiti he was routinely sketching landscapes, like this view over Matavai Bay.

Right: Observations of the Transit of Venus at Tahiti were impeded by the 'Black Drop Effect'. In these sketches, James Cook depicts the sun appearing to stretch out and embrace Venus, a recurring difficulty he experienced during the transit.

Bottom: *A Scene in Tahiti* is one of a series of watercolours made by Tupaia from May 1769 onwards. The action in the foreground may represent his experience of the inter-island conflict in Tōtaiete mā.

Here Parkinson captures the hue and succulence of the breadfruit tree or *uru*, a plant that played a prominent role in Tahitian life. As the voyage went on Parkinson worked with increasing skill and speed. Off New Holland, Joseph Banks noted that Parkinson had made '94 sketch drawings' in just fourteen days, 'so quick a hand has he acquird by use'.

into circulation, the ancient form of oral instruction still prevailed in most colleges. Far from a place of light, liberty and learning, many of the best students like Edward Gibbon had arrived in Oxford to find they knew more than their lecturers. Gibbon's verdict of his tutor, Dr Winchester – who 'well remembered that he had a salary to receive, and only forgot that he had a duty to perform'[10] – could also have stood for the professor of botany, Humphrey Sidthorp, who is said to have delivered only one lecture in thirty-six years. Frustrated at Sidthorp's absence, Banks was characteristically proactive. He gathered the necessary letters of introduction, set off for Cambridge, fetching back Israel Lyons, a botanist and astronomer, who he engaged for a course of private tuition.

Banks's interest was nothing out of the ordinary. 'The Study of Botany is of late Years become a very general Amusement', wrote the nurseryman James Lee in 1760.[11] And that this branch of the sciences was seen as exciting, daring and revolutionary was due mostly to one man. To some, Carl Linnaeus was a vain and carping Swede, the man who according to one Oxford don, had 'thrown all botany into confusion'.[12] To a growing set of others, though, Linnaeus – Knight of the Polar Star, first physician to the King of Sweden, professor of botany at the University of Uppsala and honoured fellow of learned societies across Europe – was a genius. 'You have led your Readers', wrote Lee, 'by an *Ariadne's* Clue, through the Turnings and Labyrinths of the three Kingdoms of Nature and, by a scientific and perspicuous Method, explained her Laws, in a Manner superior to all that have gone before you.'[13]

Lee was referring to Linnaeus's revolutionary classification system. There had always been problems ordering plants. When John Evelyn wrote *Sylva*, he had even encountered problems finding the proper name for oak. Sometimes people picked a bit of old Latin. Sometimes people relied on colours or even scents to find some natural unity between flowers. But for Linnaeus this was wrong-headed pettifoggery. A plant's smell, he argued, was not in the least 'to be depended on'. Colour was worse. It was 'below the Notice of the true Botanist', and he cautioned his peers from 'catching the Infection of such idle Amusement.'[14]

Earlier in the century the British had relied on the methods of John Ray, established over the previous century. Ray's system was comprehensive. It centred on the comparison of various botanical characteristics – seeds, shapes, habitats. But Linnaeus had again considered this complexity too much. It took years of practice to master Ray's and other competing methods, and Linnaeus had set out to simplify the botanist's task by focussing narrowly on a plant's reproductive organs, the workings of which modern science was beginning to grasp. The stamens or 'husbands' comprised the male part of the plant and the pistils or 'wives' the female. Though Linnaeus admitted this was an artificial rather than a natural system, he nonetheless argued that all plants could be classified into one of twenty-four classes by simply counting the number, proportion and situation of their sexual organs.

When Linnaeus had originally proposed his 'sexual system' in *Systema naturae* in the 1730s it had alarmed many fellow botanists. For some it rendered useless years of work they had ploughed into the previous taxonomies, essentially demanding they start afresh. Others were scandalised by the sexual nature of his proposition. Johann Georg Siegesbeck, who worked at the botanic garden in St Petersburg, roundly derided it as 'loathsome harlotry', an affront Linnaeus would not forget. But when compared with Ray's messy esotericism, Linnaeus's system – so simple it could be attempted by anyone who could see and count – fitted with the period's fanaticism for order. This was the age of the price tag, the signpost and Johnson's *Dictionary*. A clear, concise, quantitative system for plants fitted this wider culture. 'God created and Linnaeus organised', declared one acolyte. The magic of Linnaeus's 'Language of Flowers' lay in its simplicity.

But simplicity was only the start of it. Finding the plant and counting its sexual organs would begin a process that would progressively reveal a class, an order, a genera, a species and, possibly, even a variety. So the method that began with numerical simplicity extended into high complexity. The student Banks and Israel Lyons doubtless ran through Linnaeus's system countless times at Oxford, seeing how 'Thyme' might be attributed to the class 'Didynamia', for example, because it had 'four stamens disposed in pairs of unequal length', that it belonged to the order 'Gymnosperms' as it produced exposed seeds, and the genus '*Thymus*'. This process could be repeated over and over, combining empirical observation with Linnaeus's publications which, throughout the 1750s, increasingly became the key to making sense of nature.

The most important of these books was Linnaeus's 1753 *Systema plantarum*, published as the young Banks went to school. It not only

included the results of twenty years' classification work by Linnaeus
in Uppsala, it brought an even greater degree of order by allocating
a two-word name to every plant species. It countered the old trend
for serpentine Latin names that described a plant's appearance. The
tomato, for instance, had become *Solanum caule inermi herbaceo, foliis
pinnatis incisis*. Linnaeus's two-word name was like allocating, as
Andrea Wulf explains it, a Christian name and a surname to each
species. 'The "surname" was the genus, such as *Magnolia or Collinsonia*,
which often commemorated a friend [of Linnaeus's] or the genus's
discoverer. To this he added a second word (like a Christian name)
such as *grandiflora* or *canadensis* to signify individual species.'[15] With
this so-called binomial nomenclature, the tomato became the *Solanum
lycopersicum*. Within years this innovation was expanded from the
vegetable kingdom into the mineral and the animal kingdoms too,
ushering in names like *Homo sapiens* for humans. Linnaeus's achievements thrilled. James Lee praised his 'Doctrines' that not only made
'Men wiser, by teaching them the Knowledge of Things' but made
them 'better and happier, in admiring the Creator in his wonderful
Creation.'[16]

As Banks passed through Oxford, some in the British intellectual
and horticultural establishment continued to resist Linnaeus's ideas.
But Banks, young and eager, had no reservations. The new system
washed away the old, staid framework of the last century and presented
him with opportunities as part of Linnaeus's new generation of botanists. Perhaps the system's taint of scandal appealed to Banks, too,
who by this time had grown tall, effervescent and attractive. Not only
did the new taxonomy offer potential immortality to those intrepid
or virtuous souls who supported it – Linnaeus rewarded his teacher
Olof Rudbeck by naming the strikingly beautiful *Rudbeckia* in his
honour – but it could be applied, in an ongoing game of 'Find and
Classify', to the steady flow of unknown plants arriving from America,
India and Africa. All this brought botany into high vogue. King George
was an enthusiast, as was the Earl of Bute. Augusta, Dowager Princess
of Wales, let it be known that she intended to sow a garden at Kew
near the Thames that contained 'all the plants known on Earth'.[17]

As Banks was leaving Oxford, James Lee's book on Linnaeus was
bringing to an English-speaking audience the clarity of a new approach,
to assist the botanist with 'his Endeavours'.[18] Some spirit was needed
because 'the Palm', as one of Banks's friends had referred to botanical

pre-eminence, had transferred 'from us to Sweden'.[19] One of Banks's ambitions was to get it back. In 1761 William Banks died, and on his twenty-first birthday in 1764 Joseph became fabulously wealthy. This might have been the moment Banks turned away from the sciences, replacing botany with the usual recreations of a young blade in town. But this did not happen. If Banks's passion burnt fiercely, it did not burn out. After coming of age, Banks was still just as likely to be found among exotics as they were unpacked at the Chelsea Physic Garden or the Vineyard Nursery in Hammersmith.

During the four years after Banks's move to London he became an increasingly visible presence in the capital's scientific community. On 3 August 1764, as the *Earl of Pembroke* entered the Thames on her maiden voyage, Banks was applying for a reader's ticket at the British Museum. Eighteen months later, in February 1766 he was elected a fellow of the Society of Antiquaries. Three months later he received the prestigious accolade of a fellowship of the Royal Society. Banks's company or correspondence was increasingly sought. In 1766 the Reverend John Lightfoot was overjoyed to receive a letter from him. He wrote in animated reply, 'When Pythagoras discovered his golden Proposition he is said to have run about the streets like a Madman, crying out ... I had like to have done the same, when I open'd your Letter & saw *Banks* at the Bottom of it.'[20]

Lightfoot was among the scores of friends that Banks was forging like the naturalists Thomas Pennant and John Ellis, or the nurseryman James Lee. But among the new connections, two stand out. One was the Swedish botanist Daniel Solander. Solander was a popular figure in London, known and admired as Linnaeus's protégé. Having attended the University of Uppsala, Solander had demonstrated uncommon ability as a young botanist, with Linnaeus's regard for him ripening into a genuine fondness. 'I looked after him like a son, under my own roof', he later wrote. Groomed as Linnaeus's successor, Solander had turned down various academic posts and instead had settled in London, finding a job organising the sprawling collections at the British Museum. It was here, presumably, that Solander ran into Banks. A decade Banks's senior, the two nonetheless soon forged an amity that would endure, both of them united by their love of science and convivial conversation.

The second of Banks's great contacts was a stranger one. John Montagu, the fourth Earl of Sandwich, was already approaching fifty by the time Banks moved to London. Sandwich was a gangling aristocrat with the ruddy face of a fox-chasing squire. A strong man both intellectually and physically – on seeing him for the first time the novelist Fanny Burney declared him as *'weather-proof* as any sailor in the navy'[21] – Sandwich had a poor public reputation and was often subject to the jeers of the press for his infamously abandoned private life. The abuse did not seem to trouble him unduly. Horace Walpole observed, 'No man had so many public enemies who had so few private.'[22] For years Sandwich had operated at the top of politics and had served twice as First Lord of the Admiralty as well as a Secretary of State. An Old Etonian with lands in Lincolnshire, he and Banks had overlapping interests. Striking up an accord, the elder statesman and the ebullient youth 'passed whole days, and sometimes whole nights' on the Thames, enjoying their 'favourite amusements as botanists and fishers'.[23] The 'peregrinations' undertaken in a 'large and comfortable punt' were long and fondly remembered.[24]

In Sandwich, Banks had gained an influential friend. Banks offered Sandwich a constant fund of enthusiasm. Banks was a young man on the make, gregarious, brave, decided. As Sandwich would one day discover, Banks was susceptible to flashes of arrogance that could manifest themselves in insensitive ways. But this was the exception rather than the rule. Most knew him for his lively wit, gift for storytelling, relish for the natural world and magpie mind. As one of his earliest biographers wrote of Banks's early, infectious energy, 'His ardent ambition to distinguish himself as an active promoter of his favourite pursuit, soon began to manifest itself ... he nobly resolved to forego the parade of courts, the glitter of fashion, and the pleasure of a town life, for the investigation of Nature in her wildest haunts, and in her most inclement regions.'[25]

This was the man who now occupied the finest quarters on *Endeavour*, a space eight feet square, branching off the great cabin. In a disquieting rearrangement of internal geography, Banks's arrival had relegated Cook to quarters further forward on the larboard side, a berth usually occupied by a subservient lieutenant. This was the sort of muddling power dynamic Dalrymple had tried to avoid. Indeed, Banks's role aboard was not entirely understood by some of his friends. One had informed another that the expedition was to 'proceed under the direction of Mr Banks, by order of the Lords of the Admiralty', a sentence that, had Cook spotted it, would no doubt have made his toes curl. But Cook was a new captain and if he took any offence at Banks's appearance, there is no surviving evidence of it.

Although neither figure appeared much in the other's journals during the opening weeks of the voyage, both Cook and Banks must have tacitly acknowledged that they were the two leading figures aboard. The differences between them were stark. Banks was warm and animated, Cook was aloof. Banks brought with him an education from Harrow, Eton and Christ Church, Oxford – a more prestigious one it is difficult to imagine – while Cook had a practical Whitby apprenticeship. Banks's world was West London – Pall Mall and Grosvenor Square, the pleasure gardens of Vauxhall and Ranelagh and the theatres of Covent Garden and Drury Lane. Cook's world was East London: the jostling streets and quays of Wapping, the chart depot at the Tower of London. Their minds ticked in different ways, to different rhythms. Cook was rushing to reach George's Island for the transit observation. Banks, determined not to miss a thing, had already noted in his journal that he could 'well dispence with a much slower pace'.[26] Ameliorating and resolving the differences in their personalities and situations would be one of the great unspoken challenges of the voyage.

This was not Banks's first time at sea. In 1766 he had joined the crew of HMS *Niger* and crossed to Newfoundland. During this voyage – presumably made possible by Sandwich – Banks might have briefly met Cook the surveyor. Whether they did or not, Banks had a much better opportunity to watch Cook assert himself on the quarterdeck. There is no evidence that Banks had ever had a close relationship such as the one he was about to embark on with Cook. Sailors were considered hard men, grown strange and knotty like compass timber. A gentleman's status was usually so far above that of a sailing master they would hardly ever communicate when on terra firma. But while Banks was on *Endeavour*, Cook was his superior. And though Banks did not state it bluntly, during the opening six weeks of the Atlantic passage Cook appeared to rise in Banks's estimation in that imperceptible manner – more sensed than written – in which his reputation always seemed to rise. Perhaps Banks watched the diligence with which he turned and trimmed the ship to the wind. Perhaps it was how Cook managed the gale that engulfed *Endeavour* in the Bay of Biscay.

Most of those under Cook's command lived not in the stern cabins with Banks's 'suite', but in the main interior deck. This was a gloomier space. Here the sunlight did not shine softly through glass windows, instead it came honeycombing down, square tunnels of anaemic light, poking through the grating. This, at least, gave a glow to an atmosphere thickened by fumes from the galley stove. If a ship was a wooden world, then to leave the comforts of the great cabin and travel through the gun room to the lower deck was like crossing from the fashionable shops of the Strand into the rookeries of St Giles. Here bodies were packed tight, the hempen hammocks swinging from their clews in rhythm with the waves, each bulging with the body of a sailor.

This was Cook's dominion. Doubtless he had spent these early days committing names to memory: Gray, Magra, Sutherland, Wolfe, though he would have done well to master more than half of the ninety-four in all. His task was not to befriend these sailors, it was something greater than that: to earn their respect while simultaneously rendering them productive and efficient. As master of the *Grenville*, Cook had commanded a crew of twenty. Now as many bodies were crammed into *Endeavour* as might be found in a small English parish. This is how the ship was to be, a managed human unit. But if it resembled a parish in size, then it was quite different in character. Everyone aboard was male. Most of them were younger than thirty, the sailmaker John Ravenhill the oldest at forty-nine. To most of the crew Cook, now nearly forty would have seemed a grizzled veteran.

Whatever their opinions there was no hope of sharing them in private. Where the Whitby colliermen might have been able to steal away beneath the forecastle, or the masters – like Henry Taylor's drunken captain – might have been able to dive into the steerage to amuse themselves with a bottle, for the sailors on *Endeavour* there was no escape. Every nook on board had been turned to some purpose. Life for the sixty or so sailors who comprised the ship's larboard or starboard watches was to be lived in a public sphere. This intensified life. Those who liked one another clustered into cliques, while those who did not had no choice but to seethe or stew. On voyages like this grievances could fester. One day Cook heard the charge of one shipmate against another, that he 'hatched like a basilisk in the damp and noisome cabbins'.[27]

In exchange for the lack of privacy, at least, *Endeavour*'s crew enjoyed a lighter workload than their forebears had on the *Earl of Pembroke*. Thirteen had sailed with Milner on that maiden voyage, a ratio of twenty-eight tons each. On *Endeavour* this was reduced to about four tons per man, making for an easier life, if not a quieter one. Their existence was to be ordered, replete with divisions and boundaries, penalties and rewards. Already the men had been allocated ratings. One of Cook's first actions was to assign them to a watch, larboard or starboard. That gave shape to their days, dictating when they should be on deck, hauling, reefing, splicing, or asleep in their hammocks. To begin with it was the regulation four-hour watches, with the two shorter dog watches from four o'clock until six and six o'clock until eight in the evening. Because *Endeavour* was so small, so well manned and so easily handled, Cook was able to ease this, switching to a three-watch system that allowed the sailors an eight-hour sleep. The subdividing continued, watches being split between masts, top men who climbed the shrouds and waisters who remained on deck. Everything they ate was measured. Sailors who smoked tobacco were obliged to do so on the forecastle. They were compelled to eat specific meals at appointed times on particular days before they retired into numbered hammocks, each one of which was slung in regulation lines fourteen inches apart.

It had been a bright beginning. By 22 October Banks was openly deferring to 'the Captain' in his journal. They had called at Madeira for provisions. The visit had given Banks and Solander a chance to comb the land near Funchal for specimens. Impatient to study as much of its flora as possible, they had been exasperated to be detained by a sociable governor who with 'that unsought honour lost us very near the whole day'. Madeira brought a meeting, too, between the old spiritual world and the new enlightening one, when the naturalists visited a religious house. Presumably having heard rumours of Franklin's electrical experiments, Solander described that when 'the Nuns heard that we belonged to the R. Society, they immediately concluded that we must be Conjurers, and wanted us to tell the Signs of Thunder and Tempests, to find out a place in their Garden where they might dig for Water, &c'.[28]

Back at sea, Banks was getting used to *Endeavour*. He had suffered seasickness before on his trip across to Newfoundland and he had been afflicted again on *Endeavour*. The deep roll of the heavily laden collier had played cruelly with his stomach as they had left the Channel. He had 'found the ship to be but a heavy sailer', a verdict committed to his journal. 'indeed we could not Expect her to be any other from her built, so are obliged to set down with this Inconvenience, as a necessary consequence of her form; which is much more calculated for stowage, than for sailing'.[29] But Banks had no reason to complain of *Endeavour*'s bulk. It was owing to this that he had been able to bring so much equipment. As John Ellis, a fellow of the Royal Society, had gossiped in a letter to Linnaeus:

> No people ever went to sea better fitted out for the purpose of Natural History, nor more elegantly. They have got a fine library of Natural History; they have all sorts of machines for catching and preserving insects; all kinds of nets, trawls, drags and hooks for coral fishing; they have even a curious contrivance of a tele-scope, by which, put into the water, you can see the bottom to a great depth, where it is clear. They have many cases of bottles with ground stoppers, of several sizes, to preserve animals in spirits. They have the several sorts of salts to surround the seeds; and wax, both beeswax and that of the *Myrica*; besides there are many people whose sole business it is to attend them for this very purpose. They have two painters and draughtsmen, several volunteers who have a tolerable notion of Natural History; in short Solander assured me this expedition would cost Mr Banks ten thousand pounds.[30]

Ellis's is a thorough account, but he does not mention everything. He does not mention the twenty wooden chests for storing dried flowers; the bell tent for George's Island, the three-foot achromatic telescopes and the microscopes; the razors, knives and chemicals and spirits for working on specimens. He does not list all the pistols and guns – some mounted with bayonets – Banks had brought for hunting. All this, plus the books on historical voyages and a pre-publication copy of Dalrymple's *Voyages to the Southern Pacific Ocean*, had been crammed into *Endeavour* in the days before she had sailed from Plymouth.

Banks's preparations for the voyage had begun in the spring. As with anyone connected to the Royal Society, Banks had been aware

of the transit voyage to the South Seas for some time. But at the start
of the year he had no notion of being involved and instead had been
planning a visit to Linnaeus at Uppsala. On two other points he had
also resolved himself. Thoroughly disinterested in politics, he had
promised friends that he would never follow his father into the
Commons. Secondly he had vowed not to 'consider marriage as an
experiment with his own happiness until driven to it by the extent of
his own misery'.[31] For many this would have been disheartening intelligence, particularly for one. Banks had embarked on an impetuous
affair with a Miss Harriet Blosset – remember the name – soon after,
who he had met at the Vineyard Nursery at Hammersmith, deeming
her the 'fairest among the flowers'.[32]

Records from the Royal Society Club show him dining with them
as early as February as their memorial to King George about the
transit expedition was being sent. Whether the possibility of him
joining the voyage was mooted then is uncertain. But by 14 April,
when Banks dined with the Club again, plans were in motion. Pennant
was writing with advice that he take a pair of umbrellas, 'both the
fine silk kind and the strong oilskin kind'. The news that Banks was
to tour the world spread fast. It soon reached Linnaeus in Uppsala
and naturalists in St Petersburg.

'Upon considering the Plan of this Scheme', Banks wrote, 'it immediately occurd to me that it would be a most desirable one for me to
Engage in. The Whole tract of the South Seas, &, I may say, all South
America is Intirely unknown to a Naturalist.'[33] It was an irresistible
prospect. Now Linnaeus's system was being accepted, it needed to be
extended. Linnaeus himself had pioneered the concept of collecting
expeditions, touring the neighbourhood of Uppsala with his band of
fellow collectors. Since those early adventures the scope of collection
tours had become more and more ambitious as they sought an
increasing quantity of animal, vegetable and mineral specimens that
could be embraced within the Linnaean system. Now Banks had been
presented with the chance of all chances, far beyond the easy charms
of a continental grand tour. 'Every blockhead does that', Banks had
pronounced; 'my Grand Tour shall be one round the whole globe'.[34]

Banks had not only brought a slew of equipment with him, but a
full philosophic 'suite'. The most notable member of this team was
Daniel Solander. By 1768 Banks and Solander had been acquainted for
as many as four years and a vivid story tells how Solander had sprung

to his feet, midway through a dinner party, to announce his intention
of joining the voyage. The British Museum had formally released him
from his duties at the end of June, and Solander's enlistment added
intellectual heft to Banks's effervescence. Augmenting their number
further were four specialist collectors. Twenty-six-year-old Peter
Briscoe was a faithful attendant of Banks's who had followed him to
Newfoundland. Briscoe was joined by sixteen-year-old James Roberts,
and two black servants, Thomas Richmond and George Dorlton. The
First Lord of the Admiralty, Edward Hawke, had been against such a
large addition, but with his usual chicanery Banks had navigated the
obstacle by avoiding Hawke. 'I have not been near Sir E:H', he had
written to a friend, 'but made Every application to the Secretary who
has done Everything we wanted with as much alacrity & spirit as
could be wishd.'

The process was to run as smooth as the tides. The mornings, from
eight o'clock till past midday, would be given over to collecting with
Briscoe, Roberts, Richmond and Dorlton or, if the weather was
inclement, study. Once 'whatever natural productions ... worth taking
notice of' had been secured they would be analysed by Banks and
Solander, assisted by Herman Spöring, Banks's Finnish clerk. Any
discoveries thought noteworthy were then to be passed on to the final
members of Banks's suite: his draughtsmen. One of these was called
Sydney Parkinson, a Scottish Quaker aged about twenty-two. Parkinson
was to concentrate on natural-history specimens. The other artist,
Alexander Buchan, was to focus on landscapes and 'scenes' – the
transient ephemera of the societies they would encounter.

The arrival of Banks's suite had altered the nature of *Endeavour*, a
ship that had already mutated far beyond the designs of her maker.
Sailing down the Atlantic she had become a scientific probe. Catching
nets trawled the waters, gathering the contents of the ocean, drawing
them into the ship where they could be subjected to Linnaean rigour
and digested for the benefit of science in notebooks and journals. No
one had ever done this on so systematic a footing before. It must have
seemed a distant time since natural philosophers were confined to
universities, publishing their findings in Latin. Over the previous
decades scientific work had been happening in increasingly diverse
spaces, from farms to coffee houses to palaces. Now Banks was
bringing popular science into the great cabin of a Royal Navy ship. It
capped an extraordinary refashioning of space. Six months before, the

spot where Banks and Solander sat, working on the very borderlines of human knowledge, had been home to Milner, an illiterate sailing master. The *Earl of Pembroke* had been a machine for making money. *Endeavour* had become a machine for making knowledge.

Ever since they left Plymouth Banks had detailed the day's events in his journal. This journal, a plain-leaved, leather-bound quarto that Banks filled with entries in a fluent, expressive hand, was to be his primary record of the voyage. Though he did not know it, he was beginning one of the most significant eyewitness accounts of the Enlightenment, a perceptive, entertaining chronicle of his travels. From the off Banks displays talent as a diarist. Although he had an abundance of leisure hours and the advantage of sharpening his observations in conversation with Solander, who was by all accounts a delightful companion, Banks does not abuse his journal, setting out in a blaze before losing focus. Instead he limits his accounts, or 'lucubrations' to significant events, and is happy to concede, as he does on 19 September, 'Light Breezes all day, without any event worth talking about.'

Banks is rarely less than entertaining as an observer and writes with a poetic turn. Passing the Pike of Tenerife as the sun sets he writes of 'the rays of the Sun' lingering on the heights as the rest of the landscape grew 'quite Black', 'giving it a warmth of colour not to be express'd by painting'. He describes the experience of witnessing a lunar rainbow, 'very faint and almost without colour, so that it could be traced by little More than an appearance which lookd like shade on cloud'. This keen eye for natural phenomena is always there. Banks knew any given moment might supply a prize or a puzzle. One September day he had watched as the ocean's surface was covered by a small species of crab, 'floating upon the surface of the water, and moving themselves with tolerable agility, as if the surface of the water and not the bottom was their Proper station'. When a new species of wagtail was blown onto *Endeavour*'s rigging, perhaps carried by a storm from the Spanish coast, Banks teasingly declares that they 'must be sailors who would venture themselves aboard a ship which is going round the world'.[35]

Read today, Banks's journal shows a man who sets to his collecting every morning with the cheer and spring of a parson on Easter Sunday. It has a Pepysian honesty too. Banks's entries are so firmly fixed in the present that one doesn't get the impression he is worrying what future generations will make of him. Events happen, actions happen. They are to be decoded, not to be dwelt upon. That Banks's eye is always fixed outwards makes his journal the antithesis of a twenty-first-century introspective memoir. Reflections do come in the 'Manners & Customs' of a particular island or 'Flora & Wildlife' of a given shore, but Banks is not given to self-analysis. He does not scrutinise his emotional response to a stimuli. His reflections exist to a purpose. Of his own emotional health, his separation from friends and British society, and his inner life or spiritual anxieties, he remains almost always silent.

At eight in the morning on 25 October, *Endeavour* crossed from the northern into the southern hemisphere. Cook characteristically double-checked the reckoning with the midday latitude observation, after which 'it was no longer doubted that we were to the southward of the Line'. Exactly two months had passed since they left Plymouth. These were two months of order and regulation, but the order was now to be temporarily suspended as 'the Ceremony ... practised by all Nations' was put in motion.

Tradition as much as discipline was the essence of the sailor's life, and for them the equator had more than a geographical significance. 'That Line marked entry into a topsy-turvy world', wrote Greg Dening, the Australian historian; the sailors were passing into 'an antipodes, a place of mirror opposites, where seasons were reversed, where even the unchanging heavens were different'. The act of crossing from a familiar world into a subverted one demanded recognition. It had come to be marked in the form of a 'grotesque satire on institutions and roles of power'.[36] Just as the stars and seasons altered in nature, so too must the shipboard hierarchies of human society. Powers vested in the captain and his officers would transfer temporarily to the veterans who had already crossed the line.

The former *Dolphin* crew members who had sailed with Byron or Wallis – Gore, Clerke, Pickersgill and Molyneux – were among these. The afternoon was spent in preparation. At dinner time a list of every person aboard 'in which the dogs and catts were not forgot', was delivered to the quarterdeck, 'sign'd "the ships company"'. Everyone was then summoned and interviewed by Gore, 'he markd every name either to be duckd or let off according as their qualification directed'. Uncomfortably for Banks, he found himself on the 'Black list', along with Cook, Solander and all his suite, including his two dogs, a grey-hound called 'Lady' and a spaniel. Banks paid off the charges with a bribe of brandy 'for which they willingly excusd us the ceremony'. Cook presumably bought himself out too.

Many of the Men however chose to be duckd rather than give up 4 days allowance of wine which was the price fixd upon, and as for the boys they are always duckd of course; so that about 21 underwent the ceremony which was performd thus:

A block was made fast to the end of the Main Yard and a long line reved through it, to which three Cross peices of wood were fastned, one of which was put between the leggs of the man who was to be duckd and to this he was tyed very fast, another was for him to hold in his hands and the third was over his head least the rope should be hoisted too near the block and by that means the man be hurt. When he was fas[t]ned upon this machine the Boatswain gave the command by his whistle and the man was hoisted up as high as the cross peice over his head would allow, when another signal was made and immediately the rope was let go and his own weight carried him down, he was then immediately hoisted up again and three times served in this manner which was every mans allowance. Thus ended the diversion of the day, for the ducking lasted till almost night, and sufficiently diverting it certainly was to see the different faces that were made on this occasion, some grinning and exulting in their hardiness whilst others were almost suffocated and came up ready enough to have compounded after the first or second duck, had such proceeding been allowable.[37]

This whole scene was a parody of a moment at Plymouth, on 19 August 1768, when Cook had mustered the ship's company reading them the Articles of War and the Act of Parliament. However enjoyable it was, it must have also reminded the officers that the ship was a stage in which the balance of power was always in flux. The proportion of common hands to commissioned officers on the *Endeavour* was great. It was useful for Cook that he had Gore, the third lieutenant, to lead the court rather than a lower-deck man who might have some fantasy of power aroused. Even Gore's elevation was potentially ominous. It would not be many years afterwards that Fletcher Christian burst into William Bligh's cabin, instigating a mutiny on HMS *Bounty*. There were many similarities between Cook and Bligh, in their backgrounds, their drive and ability. But in one important way they differed: Cook understood the vital paradox that some disorder, dispensed at the right time in the right context, enforced rather than undermined discipline.

The crew content, Cook had turned his thoughts to his ship. Their long Atlantic passage was now halfway through, and to inspect the hull and gather fresh provisions, at the start of November he made towards the Brazilian coast. Rio de Janeiro offered a superb deep-water harbour, the finest in South America. Rio was a familiar place to the British, recalled by its 'remarkable peak, in the form of a Sugar-Loaf', which towered over the harbour, the mountains behind cradling round the bay as if it were an enormous amphitheatre with the scores of merchant ships as dolls in the jet-blue water below. Cook was not so much enticed by the setting as the facilities. Rio had a large, convenient yard, big enough to heave down any vessel. Byron had visited in 1764 and had received every care from the Portuguese viceroy who had 'shewed him all the respect that a stranger of his distinction could possibly claim'. There was an attraction for Banks and Solander too. Rio's neighbourhood was said to abound in trees, 'fit for any use many of them unknown in Europe'. There was sugar cane, indigo and cotton. Gold was said to twinkle in the river bottoms and beyond the unstudied plants were racoons, armadillos, flying squirrels, guanos, opossums, sloths, snakes and birds, 'remarkable for the beauty of their plumage'.[38]

While Cook was engaged with the overhaul, Banks and Solander would be free for a week at least of botanising in a place seldom visited by naturalists. On 13 November the harbour was two leagues off, and Banks was already examining a sea 'inconceivably full of small vermes [invertebrates] which we took without the least difficulty'. Coming up the river, Banks was greeted by palm trees, something he had never seen before, 'and from which as well as every thing else which we saw we promis'd ourselves the highest satisfaction'. Solander was equally sanguine, 'we rejoiced to see Land', he wrote home, 'and flattered our selves with the hope of Pleasures unknown to them that are not enthusiastically curious. Every prospect promised us entertainment. We passed by Hills and Shores that we coud see were covered with Palms and fine Trees unknown to us; so were we impatient to get into the harbour.'[39]

Finding no official boat had come to meet them, Cook hove to and sent the second lieutenant Hicks to find a pilot. Nothing materialising, at length Cook 'made Sail up the river' and came to anchor beside the shore. Now midday, Banks and Solander were already on deck and impatient to land when a ten-oared boat with twelve or fourteen soldiers pushed off from the shore. It approached *Endeavour* and 'rowed round us without taking any notice of us or saying a word'. Another boat drew alongside. The officials inside boarded, asking Cook about his intentions. It was the earliest sign of the trouble to come. Cook was told that Hicks had been kept ashore by the Rio authorities. Cook notes in his journal the nice distinction the Rio officials made: '[he] had not been confin'd but allow'd that he had been detain'd' – as it was the 'Constant Custom to detain any one who came ashore from a Ship'.

Ports were places of order. Guns marked the watches. Colours delineated the ships. British ports took pride in their regularity. In the navy, flag officers saluted their admirals with fifteen guns. Captains were required to give an admiral seventeen guns. Were a flag officer to visit one of the king's ships in harbour, he could expect to be received with a guard under arms and with drums beating in his honour. When in foreign waters the British could not expect the customs of home to be practised with quite so much rigidity, but some degree of protocol was anticipated. A naval ship, for example, anchoring in a foreign port, might 'salute the Place with such a Number of Guns as hath been customary, on good Assurance of having the like Number returned, but not otherwise'.[40]

The principle in question was the 'peculiar and sovereign authority' Britons felt 'upon the Ocean'. But when *Endeavour* arrived at Rio, they received nothing. No deference, no warmth. Detaining a lieutenant was hardly standard practice. In short order, Banks and Solander were told they would not be permitted to come ashore, while Cook sought an interview with the new viceroy, the Conde de Azambuja. The meeting between the two went badly. Cook asked for the use of Rio's facilities and for the freedom for his sailors to collect provisions and water. He instead gained his own personal guard who insisted on accompanying him into his boat, 'an insult which I am well convinced was never before borne by any Commander of a Ship of War'. Cook explained to the viceroy they were on a voyage 'to the Southward to Observe the transit of Venus'. It was clear the viceroy did not believe a word of it, 'but look'd upon it only as an invented story to cover some other design we must be upon', Cook despaired, 'for he could form no other Idea of that Phenomenon (after I had explained it to him) than the North Star passing thro the South Pole (these were his own words)'.[41]

Disquieted by *Endeavour*'s appearance, the viceroy resolved to guard her as if she was a prison hulk. He decreed, too, that Banks and Solander were not to be permitted ashore and that all Cook's transactions were to be made through an intermediary. Outraged at the affront, Banks declared his intention to meet the viceroy himself. The day after their arrival he ordered a boat to row him ashore. Banks, however, was 'stopd by the Guard boat whose officer told us that he had particular orders, which he could not transgress, to Lett no officer or passenger except the Captain pass the boat'.

Riled, Cook considered quitting Rio at once. But when he reflected on the time already lost, all to no avail, and how they were in dear need of provisions before they progressed southward, he decided to make the best of it. Yet even in the everyday matters of ship maintenance, the viceroy proved maddeningly pig-headed. He forbid Cook a stage for tallowing the ship's bottom, informing him he would not be permitted one unless one of his own carpenters first inspected *Endeavour* and reported it necessary. 'This I would not permit', Cook protested. All the time Banks and Solander were kept prisoners aboard. Solander bemoaned the physical discomforts they suffered, 'in this land-lock't harbour, where we sometimes have hardly had a breath of air', being tilted to and fro, on 'days when our Ship was heeled down for cleaning; during which time we hardly coud walk'.[42]

Believing they had been subservient long enough, Cook and Banks conspired to fire a diplomatic volley of their own. They each wrote to the Conde de Azambuja. 'Three days have I remain'd in this Situation the same indignities & Affronts being Daily repeated', ran Cook's letter, 'notwithstanding I have every Day waited on Your Excellency & remonstrated against them in Person'.[43] Cook showed something of his own personality, making frequent references to the affronted dignity of His Brittanick Majesty. Banks took a different tack:

Disagreeable as it is for any man to declare his own rank and consequence my situation makes it necessary: I am a gentleman,

and one of fortune sufficient to have (at my own expence) fitted
out that part of this expedition under my direction; which is
intended to examine the natural history of the Countries where
we shall touch, for the execution of this undertaking I have with
me proper people who as well as myself, have made that science
their particular study.[44]

Having asserted his right as a gentleman, Banks went on to demand
he be allowed ashore. Rather than being penned like a wild animal,
he should be able to take 'with me proper people who may assist me
in Collecting, and examining, such trees, shrubs, Plants, Birds, beasts,
fishes, and insects, as I may meet with the Collection and examination
of such things, being the sole business I have undertaken in this voyage
this is the only indulgence which I ask'.

But no insect in the world would move the Conde de Azambuja.
As Gore revealed in his journal, 'We learn that one suspicion of us
among many Others is that our Ship is a Trading Spy and That Mr
Banks and the Doctor are both Supercargoes and Engineers and not
naturalists for the Business of such being so very abstruse and unprof-
itable That They cannot believe Gentlemen would come so far as
Brazil on that Account only. Our going into the south sea to observe
the Transit of Venus They Cannot believe by any means. Say They:
"That Ship Donn't look like an English man of war nor have her
officers the same dress."'[45]

At last understanding the cause, Cook offered his commission as
proof that 'my Ship realy belongs to His Brittanick Majesty'. But the
impasse was too far gone. On 22 November the viceroy replied, 'His
Brittanick Majesty's Ships of War that have come to this Port of
themselves manifested what they were. Yours of its self alone does
not discover that she is His Brittanick Majesty's.' For Cook this was a
nonsense. He knew there was nothing to be gained from further
diplomacy. He responded on 24 November, 'It is admitted that this
Ship hath not that Warlike appearance ... [but] it seems strange & is
a new thing to me that the Built, make, or Shape of a Ship should
prove whether she belongs to the King or Subject.' Of the viceroy's
suspicion of his commission, too, he added:

If my Commission should be counterfeited it follows of course
that every other Officers Commissions & Warrants are Counter-

feits, that all other Papers in the Ship tending to the same end are Counterfeits. that the Officers and Marines Uniforms are Counterfeited, and lastly the Letters of Credit I brought with me from Madeira are Counterfeits, Was this true, Your Excellency must agree with me in declaring it to be the most Strange, the most daring, & the most Publick peice of Forgery that was ever committed in the Whole world.[46]

The scene in Rio harbour had become a satire fit for Voltaire. The impasse would persist for another week yet, during which time Banks's exasperated collecting team would take the lieutenant John Gore's advice: 'Those That like it may Take a Trip in disguise.' On 22 November Banks sent one of his servants on a surreptitious mission ashore, who 'brought off many plants and insects'. On the 24th the servant was dispatched again. The next day Solander stole into Rio, dressed as the ship's surgeon. On 26 November Banks recorded triumphantly in his journal, 'I went ashore myself this morn before day break and stayd till dark night.'

These yielded some specimens, among them a hummingbird nest. But the authorities got wind of the subterfuge and both Banks and Solander brought a halt to the clandestine visits. The remaining days in Rio were a trial for the naturalists. 'Your lordship Can more easily imagine our situation than I can describe it all that we so ardently wishd to examine was in our sight we could almost but not quite touch', Banks wrote home to the Earl of Morton. He and Solander likened their situation to that of Tantalus, the mythological Greek figure who was forced to stand upright in a pool of water beneath the boughs of a tree, whose fruit receded when he tried to eat, and water receded when he tried to drink.

On 2 December Cook sailed without ceremony. The viceroy, at last growing nervous that he might have initiated a diplomatic quarrel, sent a note reminding Cook, 'I never said that your Ship was not belonging to the Crown, but only that I Have not seen Proofs sufficient to Convince me and on the Contrario have Observe some Circumstances which makes me Suspicious.' Cook had no time for the viceroy's prevarications. All that remained was for them to quietly leave. But the Rio authorities did not even allow them this, with the fort of Santa Cruz mistakenly firing two shots over *Endeavour*'s mast; 'such extraordinary behavior', seethed Banks.[47]

This affair had been Cook's first test as captain of *Endeavour*. And during the last weeks he had performed professionally, even impressively, as his crew watched on. He had never failed to press the claims of a Royal Navy officer, had used all possible means to better their situation, had avoided any violence and at the same time had managed to repair and provision the ship, which were his initial objectives. A hotter head – one shudders at what action Dalrymple might have considered appropriate – may have provoked something more, and time, precious tides, hours or days, might have been lost.

The Rio incident had a second consequence too. It demanded Banks and Cook act in unity. Up to this point there had been a lingering ambiguity over command. Even in his memorial to the viceroy on 17 November, Banks was writing of 'that part of this expedition under my direction'. In the Conde de Azambuja, Banks and Cook had found that most useful of things: a common foe.

Endeavour left Rio in fine physical shape. And in a social sense she had become more cohesive, as if in the explaining of their expedition to others the officers had come to understand it better themselves. The days fell back into their old routine. Cook's journal looked once again to the winds and the sea, while Banks turned his eye back to the natural world. On 5 December, while waiting for the land breeze off Rio, he savoured the spectacle of the air 'crowded in an uncommon manner with Butterflies'. Two days later, they finally shook off the guard boat, 'so we were left our own masters'. In defiance they 'immediately resolved to go ashore on one of the Islands in the mouth of the harbour'. Banks wrote:

> we gatherd many species of Plants and some insects ... we stayd
> till about 4 oClock and then came aboard the ship heartily tired,
> for the desire of doing as much as we could in a short time had
> made us all exert ourselves in a particular manner tho exposd
> to the hottest rays of the sun just at noonday.[48]

They were now sailing south towards Rio de la Plata. After that it was to be the blasted flatlands of Patagonia, the frozen limits of Tierra del Fuego and then Cape Horn itself. As 1769 began, the topical warmth receded. Beyond the gunwales an icy blue appeared in the curl of the waves. Seals were seen leaping from the water with such elegance many of the crew mistook them for fish. 'All hands bend their Magellan

Jackets', wrote Banks on 6 January, 'and myself put on a flannel Jacket and waistcoat and thick trousers.'[49]

Cook had hoped to call at the Falklands, islands that were still causing trouble in Europe. After de Bougainville's and Byron's initial visits in 1764 and 1765, the Spanish had been so 'offended' that the French had ceded their presence on the east of the islands. The British had, in the meantime, begun to build up a settlement in the west. An irritation in Europe, in reality the settlement only consisted of a small blockhouse and a dreary vegetable garden. A tiny garrison had been stationed among the penguins, snipes and wild geese, dependent on the annual supply ship from London. Imagining the extreme isolation of a place where 'the cold continued long, and the ocean was seldom at rest', back in Fleet Street Samuel Johnson reasoned that tolerating such privations was a triumph of human will. 'There is nothing which human courage will not undertake, and little that human patience not endure. The garrison lived upon Falkland's island, shrinking from the blast, and shuddering at the billows.'[50]

Endeavour missed the Falklands, though they found the blast and the billows. On 6 January a gale bore down on the ship. *Endeavour* was so jolted by the combination of waves and wind that Banks's bureau was overset, 'and most of the books were about the Cabbin floor'. Amid the groan of the oak timber, the straining of the sailcloth and the jerking of the cots, 'we spent a very disagreeable night.' But *Endeavour* stood the assault. 'The ship during this gale has shewn her excellence in laying too remarkably well, shipping scarce any water tho it blew at times vastly strong; the seamen in general say they never knew the ship lay too as well this does, so lively and at the same time so easy.'[51]

Over the coming days, as albatrosses appeared in the sky, the crew began to notice further improvements in *Endeavour*'s sailing qualities. She seemed smoother, easier in her shouldering of the water and gentler in her roll. 'The seamen say it is a general observation that ships go better for being what they call Loosnen in the Joints,' Banks wrote, 'so much so that in chase it is often customary to knock down Stantions &c. and make the ship as loose as possible.' A few months before Banks had been maligning 'a heavy sailer'; he was now amending his opinion, anthropomorphising her, likening her to an athlete warming up for the marathon ahead.

Endeavour was now passing a second boundary. Unlike the equator this one was not marked. The Western civilisation they knew, the world of banks and commerce, theatres and courts, churches and monarchs, was being put astern. All traces of this would disappear henceforth, making a paradox of *Endeavour* herself. The further she sailed from Britain, the more British she became. On 12 January, Alexander Buchan painted a scene of the ship off Tierra del Fuego. It is a spare, seductive composition. *Endeavour* is in silhouette; chilly blue water stretches behind, to the faded greens and browns of the coast. The sun shines with a feeble light, suggesting either a morning or evening setting. Buchan's piece emits a feeling of loneliness, but even more so of space. Here is Fishburn's tiny bark in the limitless world: frail, vulnerable and preparing for the rigours of Cape Horn. She slides purposefully across the seascape, those she carries apprehensive about what awaits, but sustained by dreams of brighter places.

7

Airy Dreams

As *Endeavour* moved forward across space, some of her crew looked backwards into the past. They looked into history so they could better anticipate what they were to confront. As they neared Cape Horn there was no more relevant book than *A Voyage Around the World* (1748), compiled from Lord Anson's papers and recollections. As Anson's ships had approached the hooked tip of South America, his crew had seen Staten Island. Situated twenty miles into the ocean, they described a place 'entirely composed of inaccessible rocks', terminating in 'ragged points, which spire up to a prodigious height, and are all of them covered with everlasting snow':

> the points themselves are on every side surrounded with frightful precipices, and often overhang in a most astonishing manner; and the hills which bear them, are generally separated from each other by narrow clefts, which appear as if the country had been rent by earthquakes; for these chasms are nearly perpendicular, and extend through the substance of the main rocks, almost to their very bottoms: So that nothing can be imagined more savage and gloomy, than the whole aspect of this coast. But to proceed.[1]

A copy of Anson's book was on *Endeavour*. It may already have influenced Alexander Buchan, whose seascape is reminiscent of a woodcut of Anson's squadron, passing the Patagonian coast. Banks had picked up the book, too. 'Staten land is much more craggy than Terra del Fuego', he decided, 'tho the view of it in Ld Ansons Voyage is exaggerated.'[2] Sydney Parkinson, one of Banks's draughtsmen, seems to have been the third to consult the work. An echo in his journal entry betrays him:

The land on both sides, particularly Staten-land, affords most dismal prospect, being made up chiefly of barren rocks and tremendous precipices, covered with snow and uninhabited, forming one of those natural views which human nature can scare behold without shuddering ... But to proceed.[3]

If Parkinson sounded tremulous, then he had good reason. For readers of Anson, the Cape was a region of elemental terrors. What Anson's men – among them Adam Hayes – had experienced in the surrounding seas went beyond language. In 1741 they had arrived late in the season as the equinoctial gales were rising. The wind had blown so strongly it had left sailors crawling along the decks, cowering in the lee of the gunwales, breathing as much water as air. It had been hellish energy: black nights, white snow, sails wrenched from hands or yards disappearing noiselessly in the screaming wind. Ships had disintegrated. Masts had sprung. Brittle sails had torn like paper. An unforgettable episode had distilled their manifold sufferings into a single tragedy:

one of our ablest seamen was canted over-board; and notwith-standing the prodigious agitation of the waves, we perceived that he swam very strong, and it was with the utmost concern that we found ourselves incapable of assisting him; and we were the more grieved at his unhappy fate, since we lost sight of him struggling with the waves, and conceived from the manner in which he swam, that he might continue sensible for a considerable time longer, of the horror attending his irretriev-able situation.[4]

It was the carpenters like Hayes who had seen Anson's squadron through these evil weeks, working up new yards and fixing damaged ones. Sometimes they had been ferried between ships like emergency mechanics. On 21 January, Parkinson and *Endeavour* were on the cusp of these waters. The prospect struck Parkinson with foreboding:

How amazingly diversified are the works of the Deity within the narrow limits of this globe we inhabit, which, compared with the vast aggregate of systems that compose the universe, appears but a dark speck in the creation! A curiosity, perhaps, equal to Solomon's, though accompanied with less wisdom than was possessed by the Royal Philosopher, induced some of us to quit our native land, to investigate the heavenly bodies minutely in distant regions, as well as to trace the signature of the Supreme Power and Intelligence throughout several species of animals, and different genera of plant in the vegetable system, 'from the cedar that is in Lebanon, even unto the hyssop that springeth out of the wall'; and the more we investigate, the more we ought to admire the power, wisdom, and goodness, of the Great Superintendent of the universe; which attributes are amply displayed throughout all his works; the smallest object, seen through the microscope, declares its origin to be divine, as well as those larger ones which the unassisted eye is capable of contemplating.[5]

Parkinson exists today in the shadow of Cook, Banks and Solander. But in several ways his perspective is the most revealing of them all. Younger than Cook and Banks, his character was correspondingly less formed. Here he grappled with a central question: *why* he exchanged the comforts of home for the dangers of the sea. His answer was a mix of Enlightenment impulse – 'to trace' the 'genera of plant in the vegetable system' – and something more theologically profound.

Like so many of Whitby's sailing families, Parkinson was a Quaker. His was a faith that placed less store in preachers, scriptures and dogmas than conformists, instead promoting a more meaningful and pure relationship with God. The divine was not to be found in a church but rather by standing 'in the light'. Ever since George Fox, the founder of Quakerism, had experienced 'the Light' while walking through a dew-filled field, their worship had focussed more on the natural world than the supernatural one. A spire of rock, a wheeling albatross, a climbing vine or a frail insect, all these equally contained 'the signature of the Supreme Power', nourishment for Parkinson's inner Light. And however much he was daunted by the world, this passage in his journal shows him as determined to experience it.

Parkinson can also be forgiven his trepidation. In stark statistics, travelling on *Endeavour* was as dangerous as entering a battlefield. Two out of three of those to sail with Anson had perished. Were *Endeavour* to return without any fatalities it would have been thought astonishing. Reconciled to the inevitable, the only uncertainty was how much death there would be. Already the count had begun. First to die had been a Mr Ware, one of the mates, at Madeira. Parkinson had regarded him 'a very honest worthy man'. Ware had been wretchedly tangled in an anchor and dragged to the bottom. Second had been Cook's old companion, Peter Flowers, who had fallen from the shrouds at Rio. Banks had not considered either of these incidents important enough to note in his journal. Parkinson, though, had marked them in entries shaded with self-reproach. Flowers 'was drowned before we could reach him'.[6]

Death had crept nearer still. Perhaps overzealous after missing out at Rio, Banks had led one of his collecting rambles ashore in mid-January. Straying too far into the hills, the party – which included all of Banks's suite except Parkinson – had lost their way. There had been no sign of them for a whole, freezing night. Only the next morning, 'to our great joy', had Banks, Solander, Buchan, the artist, and several servants appeared, shivering on the beach. Relief was tempered by the discovery that Richmond and Dorlton, 'having made too free with the brandy-bottle', had become separated and had perished in the cold. Faced with being the sole survivor of Banks's enterprise, Parkinson had been left to grieve the death of two companions, but to be thankful at the deliverance of the rest.

Now worse might await. The gap between Staten Island and Tierra del Fuego marked the entrance to the Strait of le Maire: gateway to Cape Horn. This was exactly the route Anson had taken. In *A Voyage Around the World* the strait had formed an ominous prelude to the ghastly events that followed. Running through on the tide, 'we presumed we had nothing now before us but an open sea'. Anson's men indulged their 'imaginations in those romantick schemes, which the fancied possession of the *Chilian* gold and *Peruvian* silver might be conceived to inspire'.[7]

The infamous Chapter VIII of *A Voyage Around the World* documented the misery that followed: storms upon howling storms, sailors canted into the sea, others with their necks dislocated, their collar bones broken and thighs smashed in two. Ever since Anson's time the Royal Navy had avoided Cape Horn, favouring the Strait of Magellan instead. The conditions there, though, had turned out equally foul. It had taken Wallis a whole southern summer to fight through the strait on the *Dolphin*'s last voyage. With time short the Admiralty had decided to attempt the Cape again. *Endeavour* neared the Strait of le Maire at a similar month to Anson. Yet all nerves were quickly soothed. *Endeavour* sailed through with an eerie tranquillity. There were no storms, only a steady undertow that checked their way. On 25 January, Parkinson, relaxing, was looking at the Cape, five leagues away, 'which, contrary to our expectations, we doubled with as little danger as the North Foreland on the Kentish coast; the heavens were fair, the wind temperate, the weather pleasant'.[8]

From here Cook plied south-west, the best he could do with the contrary winds. It took them into a region of dank mists, surging winds and squalling showers of rain and hail. Increasingly south of the Cape, *Endeavour* and the royal albatrosses overhead were left as the only punctuating signs of life. Each must have looked odd to the other. By 30 January 1769 they had progressed to 60° 4'S. Few had ventured so far into the high southern latitudes. The next day the wind backed from west to east. For Cook this was a golden chance. He spread all the sail he could. Not satisfied with that, he had the lower yards extended so they stretched beyond the breadth of the deck. He then let his studding sails fly. In the most dangerous waters on the planet, Cook opened *Endeavour*'s wings as if she were a swan.

It was the start of the dash into the South Seas that everyone had anticipated. Cook would make good use of these studding sails in the next month as they raced towards the location they had been given for George's Island. 'There is not anything', John Ruskin wrote, 'in nature so absolutely notable, bewitching and, according to its means and measure, heart-occupying as a well-handled ship under sail on a stormy day'.[9] He would have relished the sight of *Endeavour* in February 1769. Cook had his studding sails set again on 24 February, much to the approval of Banks. 'At 12 last night the wind settled at NE; this morn found studding Sails set and the ship going at the rate of 7 knotts', he cheered, 'no very usual thing with Mrs Endeavour'.[10]

Later in life Banks was to earn a reputation as a talent-spotter, elevating the work of clever amateurs and allowing them to operate on higher stages. In time he would have a long list of protégés, encompassing all the branches of the sciences. But his first find would forever remain one of his very best: Sydney Parkinson, his botanical draughtsman.

Banks met Parkinson in about 1767 through James Lee, a mutual acquaintance. Lee, a Scotsman and a Quaker, was a prominent figure in London's horticultural community. He ran the Hammersmith

Vineyard Nursery, which was known for the quality of its blooms and the diversity of its exotics. Lee was also a devotee and a populariser of Linnaeus, having translated *Philosophia botanica* into English as *Introduction to Botany*. All this made Lee an obvious connection for Banks. And it was through Lee that Banks met the bright and aspiring young friend, Parkinson.

Parkinson was still relatively new in London. He had moved south from his home town of Edinburgh with his mother and two siblings after the death of their father, a brewer, Joel Parkinson. For the Parkinsons, the move had been a fresh beginning. Sydney was perhaps their best hope. He was inquisitive and able and had, it seems, already received some tuition in draughtsmanship. In London this had been sharpened into a professional trade. His elder brother, Stansfield, related that Sydney took a 'particular delight in drawing flowers, fruits, and other objects of natural history'.[11] With Linnaean botany all the rage, soon Sydney was exhibiting at the Free Society and working as a private tutor to Lee.

An oil on canvas of Sydney Parkinson – possibly a self-portrait – survives from this time. It shows a slight figure with flushed cheeks, stretched to the maximum of his height in an immaculately tailored jacket. His face is caught between an eagerness to please and daunted apprehension, the sort of terror that accompanies a first day at school. This was the figure Banks met in 1767. Seeing something in the boy, he commissioned Parkinson to complete some zoological paintings from his Newfoundland expedition. More commissions followed. After several hard years for the family, Sydney's career could not have taken a more auspicious turn. By 1768 Parkinson had Banks and Lee as wealthy, ambitious clients, both of them with connections to Linnaeus himself. Then came the *Endeavour* voyage.

It was entirely natural that Banks should approach Parkinson. Banks never displayed any aptitude for painting himself but it was important that someone should sketch as they went. Few of Linnaeus's publications were illustrated, and with artists he would be able to bring life to the visually dull fare of botanical books – mostly endless pages of Latin names and tables. And for a voyage artist, Banks needed someone with special qualities: a sharp eye, a talent for working quickly, enough skill to bring a specimen to life, but not too much imagination to mar its authenticity. He required someone with enough learning to understand the tenets of natural history but no one so grandly educated they would not tolerate the hardships of life aboard. Parkinson seemed an obvious choice. He was young, 'of unblemished character, and strict veracity'.[12] Banks offered him £80 per annum and the chance to see the world. The proposal meant that Parkinson would have to leave his family, a possible sweetheart – a cousin, Jane Gomeldon – and his prospects in London. But he made his will and within a few months he was gone.

From the start Parkinson had been a paragon of an employee. He had reported aboard three weeks early at Deptford and as soon as *Endeavour* sailed, his diligence began to show. He struck up a friendship with Molyneux, helping *Endeavour*'s sailing master out with sketches for his journal. Another shipmate noticed his assiduity, commenting that 'he frequently sat up all night, drawing for himself or writing his journal'.[13] Banks admired Parkinson's 'unbounded industry'. He was soon producing tender watercolours, of date plums with their golden orbs of fruit, or of enticing evergreen trees like the Myrsinaceae from Madeira. Beauty was one thing, but Parkinson knew it was far more important to represent the anatomical features of a specimen – its buds, edges, tips, margins, sub lateral and lateral veins – so it might be properly appreciated and classified. A knack for form is evident in his watercolour of a climber, *Convolvulus serpens*, collected in one of the surreptitious forays at Rio. There is a dynamism to the painting, a boldness in the inviting greens of the leaves, offset by delicate splashes of rose-purple in the flowers.

The relationship between Banks and Parkinson was a formal one. It was 'Mr Parkinson' as much as it was 'Mr Banks'. But there was also levity, as when a roguish Atlantic wave sent 'Mr Parkinson and his potts going to leeward, which diverted us more than it hurt him'.[14] The vision of Parkinson in motion is apt. He was required to paint fast to fix the shade or texture of a specimen before it faded. Banks wanted the bright vivacity of a leaf, the gleam of a bird's eye, the iridescence of a fish's scales. The young Quaker did his best to please. By the time they reached Rio he had already, according to a letter to his brother, finished '100 drawings on various subjects, and taken sketches of many more'.

While taking pride in his duty, the voyage also presented Parkinson with chances for the occasional transgression. He went ashore on Banks's clandestine visits to the Rio countryside. He described how they stole out of one of *Endeavour*'s cabins and lowered themselves

to a boat with a rope. They had then pulled, silently, to an 'unfre-
quented part of the shore, when we landed, and made excursions up
into the country, though not so far as we could have wished to have
done'.[15]

There is a delight in Parkinson's telling of this story. He revels in
the subterfuge, explaining how the following morning he had 'feasted'
on a collection of 'many very curious plants'. One can't help thinking
the specimens were all the more alive, because they were forbidden.
It is a testament to Banks's character that a bashful soul like Parkinson
should find himself on covert collecting missions on the far side of
the Atlantic. Writing up his journal after the escapade, the thrill of
their enterprise, simply 'to gratify our curiosity', still reverberated.

By the time *Endeavour* rounded the Cape, Parkinson and his fellow
artist Buchan had grown accustomed to seafaring life. The draughtsmen,
Banks wrote, 'are now so used to the sea that it must blow a gale of
wind before they let off'. Parkinson spent his leisure hours working
at his journal and reading. His 'Memoranda of Books etc' from his
sketchbook gives a flavour of his tastes. He had poetry, Virgil, Chaucer,
Pope, Dryden and Spenser. He had the plays of Shakespeare and *Don
Quixote* as well as Homer's *Iliad* and the *Odyssey*. Then there were
more instructive works like Hogarth's *Anatomy of Beauty*, and
monographs on portraiture and architecture.[16] Along with his journal,
these books depict a young man with a hungry mind, a desire for
self-improvement and something of a voyaging soul.

By now *Endeavour* had crossed from the Atlantic into the South Seas.
This ocean, called 'Mar Pacifico' by Magellan, spanned a third of the
globe's surface, yet little was known of it. To look at charts before
the 1760s was to see a void, a territory the Spanish claimed, but a
place in reality they knew almost as little about as anyone else. In an
increasingly mapped world the South Seas stood at a forbidding
remove, like a locked room in a manor house. Into this void people
could transpose desires of undiscovered islands, or continents of
splendid wealth and greater beauty, lands without the taint of slave
trades or dynastic wars, free, depending on their politics, from King
Georges or John Wilkeses.

The discovery of George's Island by Wallis and the *Dolphin* had at
last given the Pacific some definite form. The *Dolphin*'s had spoken
of thundering waterfalls, enchanting beaches and, above all, the

amorous women. One sailor, Francis Wilkinson, had depicted their lustrous lures:

> The Women were far from being Coy. For when A Man Found a Girl to his Mind, which he might Easily Do Amongst so many, there was not much Ceremony on Either Side, and I believe whoever comes here after will find Evident Proofs that they are not the First Discoverys. The men are so far from having Objaction to an Intercourse of this Kind that they Brought down their Women & Recommend them to us with the Greatest Eagerness, which makes me Imagine they want a Breed of English Men Amongst them.[17]

The navigational and topographical descriptions of the islands had been lost in the torrent of such accounts. George Robertson, the *Dolphin*'s master, had elaborated. 'All the sailors swore that they never saw handsomer made women in their lives and declard that they would all to a man, live on two thirds allowance, rather than lose so fine an opportunity of getting a Girl apiece.'

Robertson, who wrote with an entertaining bluff prose, noticed the ameliorating effect these girls had on the *Dolphin*'s sick list. Sailors rose from convalescences, he noted, and 'declard they would be happy if they were permited to go ashore, at same time said a Young Girl would make an Excelent Nurse'.[18] So many ship's nails had been bartered for sex that not a sufficient number remained to sling the hammocks, or so the story went. The crew had taken to sleeping on deck or even on the island itself, a hardship they bore cheerfully enough.

Three and a half months out from Rio, with a heavily manned ship, these stories were charged with potency. But there were other reasons for wanting to see the land. For Cook and Charles Green it marked the site of their Venus observations. For Banks and Solander there was the possibility of botanical treasures. Then for them all there was the prospect of fresh food. For months they had been fed endless rounds of salt beef, salt pork, suet, peas and oatmeal, boiled to varying magnitudes by the cook, a one-armed man called John Thompson. Twenty-five years before, it had been this diet that had caused a massive outbreak of scurvy on Anson's voyage. It was perhaps the worst instance of the disease in maritime history. The ghastly list of symptoms – the 'low unequal Pulse, lixivial Urine, a pale-brown or livid Complexion, a

Weakness and Swelling or sometimes Wasting of the Legs, a Difficulty in walking, acute transient Pains, frequent Bleeding at the Nose, stinking Breath, putrid Gums, loose Teeth, ill-condition'd Ulcers, and rotten Bones'[19] – had cascaded through his ships.

To some, scurvy was a toxin that rose up from the sea or fell down out of the atmosphere, seeping into the timbers of a ship then infecting the bodies of the sailors, suffocating, dry-drowning them. To others it was a dietary complaint, although they could not tell what. In an effort to check the disease, sailors were aggressively physicked. Anson's crew were compelled to swallow elixir of vitriol, a mix of sulphuric acid, spice and alcohol. Mustard was tried, as were thimbles of vinegar or rations of pickled cabbage. The last of these were served out when it struck the *Dolphin*, as was wort – a liquid yielded in the brewing process. The ideas of James Lind, who in the 1750s had demonstrated experimentally that citrus juices had a favourable effect, were generally lost in the babble of competing theories.

On *Endeavour* Cook trailed a selection of remedies with an eagerness that would bring him the reputation of an innovator, something, in the navy, that could be a slur as much as a compliment. Cook was later lampooned for his 'experimental beef', his 'experimental beer', his 'experimental water' distilled from the sea. But it was in his character to seek out better ways of doing things. From the start he kept a careful eye on the men's diets, making sure they ate their sauerkraut. 'Every man that had the least symptoms of Scurvy upon him', Cook later wrote, was treated with a quick dose of malt.[20]

It would be the 1920s before the discovery of vitamin C and the earliest understandings of its role in human biology. Vitamin C depletion inhibits the body's production of collagen – 'the glue of the cell and the scaffold of the body' – provoking the familiar symptoms. There is a second consequence of vitamin C deficiency, not so well known. As well as stimulating the production of collagen, it regulates the stable operation of the nervous system, in particular the production of dopamine and serotonin. The resulting cognitive disturbances are now thought to have left sufferers emotionally vulnerable: elated, lonely, dejected, and frequently suspended between ebullience, euphoria, despair.

Such emotions may well have been on the loose as *Endeavour* entered the Pacific. We know Banks was experiencing the early physical signs of the disease – swollen gums and pimples in his mouth – symptoms he successfully treated with lemon juice. That Banks, with all the perks of the officers' table, was inflicted suggests that less fortunate others may have been stricken too. It is with this in mind that one has to interpret the events of 25 March, when one of the marines, William Greenslade, threw himself overboard.

It was a strange affair. Greenslade had been standing sentry at a cabin door when one of his shipmates had given him a piece of seal-skin to look after, which was to be cut into small pieces so that it could be used for tobacco pouches. Greenslade, as Cook and Banks later found out, had taken it into his head that he was to be excluded when the skin was divided up. So while he had his opportunity he had stolen a piece of the skin 'and was of course found out immediately.'

The misdemeanour, such as it was, happened at midday. During the afternoon Greenslade had been taunted by his fellow marines, who represented 'his crime in the blackest coulours as a breach of trust of the worst consequence'. His sergeant had decided to bring Greenslade before Cook. But on the way Greenslade had slipped free and, as Cook wrote, 'was seen go upon the Fore Castle, and from that time was seen no more'. That a marine would prefer death to being reprimanded was seen as a peculiar thing. 'He was a very quiet young man scarce 21 years of age, remarkably quiet and industrious', wrote Banks, 'and to make his exit the more melancholy was drove to the rash resolution by an accident so trifling that it must appear incredible to every body who is not well acquainted with the power-full effects that shame can work upon young minds.'[21]

It is a story that bears at least a trace of a scurvied mind. And if scurvy plays with the emotions, it also toys with perceptions. The scholar Jonathan Lamb has written of the malfunctioning senses of a scurvy sufferer:

> When these sensory modulators fail to work, the ear will hear too much, the palate taste, and the nose smell, more than can possibly be pleasant, and the eye become inordinately sensitive to light and color. These uninhibited sensations are commonly called 'sensory phantoms', the offspring of unregulated excita-tions in the cranial nerves, but actually they are intensifiers, carrying more information from the senses to the brain than it can handle, so that fragrance becomes disgusting, light blinding, and music deafening.[22]

Literature from the age of exploration is filled with curious, warped accounts, of blood-red oceans, towering precipices, booming waterfalls and sailors shrieking at the smell of flowers. Even the equanimous Cook would one day fall into a trance at the beguiling twinkle of ice on the rigging. To read of scurvy's effects on perception in the voyaging age is like first learning of unreliable narrators in fiction. But this was not wilful deception. These were worlds constructed inside sailors as much as they were realities existing outside them. As their bodies declined, their senses soared. And it was with scurvied eyes the sailors on the *Dolphin* had glimpsed George's Island in 1767. Robertson, the master, had written:

> the countrey hade the most Beautiful appearance its posable to Imagin, from the shore side one two and three miles Back there is a fine Leavel country that appears to be all laid out in planta-tions ... the Interior part of this country is very Mountainous ... from that to the very topes of the Mountains is all full of tall Trees, but what sort they are I know not but the whole was Green.[23]

This was the island *Endeavour* approached in early April 1769. From 4 April when Banks's lad Peter Briscoe sighted land, they passed atolls and little islands. Parkinson was among those to crowd the decks so he could savour the sight. He saw semicircular bays, reefs and lagoons with the water 'as smooth as a mill-pond', abounding in flying fish. The islands spired up from unimaginable depths, because 'to our surprise, we could not reach the bottom with 130 fathom of line' not a mile from the shore.

After emptiness, there was luminosity, a vibrancy so different to the washed skies and silvery seas of Britain. Gazing around, the ocean was divided up into zones of colour like an artist's palette with lapis blue or indigo for the deep sea, turquoise for the lagoons, vitreous teals making the shallows and, here and there, a broken white line tracing the surf over hidden reefs. Out on the bowsprit netting, the sailors could listen to the thump of the hull, see the splash of the water as it ran under the bows, feeling the rhythmic lift and fall of the hundreds of tons of oak behind them. *Endeavour*, built by Fishburn for the dreary northern seas, was thriving in the sparkling tropical ocean.

The morning sun warming their faces, on 13 April 1769, Cook brought *Endeavour* into Port Royal Harbour, George's Island. Beyond the black sand of the palm-fringed beaches, Parkinson gazed across this place they had all longed to see. It was as 'uneven as a piece of crumpled paper, being divided irregularly into hills and valleys; but a beautiful verdure covered both, even to the tops of the highest peaks', he wrote.[24] After months of solitude the ship was instantly a focal point for the scores of canoes that pushed off from the shore. Coming to anchor, boats were hoisted out for Cook, Banks 'and the other gentlemen with a party of Men under arms' who intended to venture ashore to establish relations.

It was perhaps a hint of Parkinson's Quakerism that he never joined the initial shore-going parties. His religion demanded pacifism and these opening encounters provided the greatest potential for violence. But this did not stop him from seeing the 'Georgians' who approached the ship with an eagerness to trade. Parkinson spent the 'forenoon' in 'trucking'. Coconuts, breadfruit, bananas, apples and small fish were all offered for nails and beads. In these earliest exchanges Parkinson managed to acquire some bark cloth. He would also get something else that it would take his shipmates weeks to discover. This place, famous in Britain as 'George's Island', had, of course, a name of its own. It was the island of 'Otaheite'.*

Fond of numerical precision, Cook must have been satisfied to note that exactly a year divided the Admiralty's earliest correspondence with him about the voyage and *Endeavour*'s arrival in Tahiti. In that time Cook had followed his orders to the letter. Each of his navigational instructions – 'to stand well to the Southward in your Passage round the Cape', to 'fall into the parallel' of the island well in advance and to 'arrive there at least a month or six Weeks before the 3rd day of June next' – had been complied with. He might have been allotted a lumbering collier, but it had not much mattered. They had arrived with seven weeks to spare.

Something like 10,000 miles separated the site where *Endeavour* now lay at anchor from Deptford Dockyard. This was isolation. It was

---

*   It would take another voyage yet for the British to grasp that the 'O' in Otaheite was an article rather than a true component of the word. 'Otaheite' is therefore 'Tahiti' and, going for cultural accuracy over historical veracity, I have used 'Tahiti' from this point onwards, even when the sailors did not.

isolation in some ways beyond even that which the astronauts of *Apollo 11* experienced in 1969 as they stood on the moon, exactly two centuries on. The *Endeavour*'s crew were nine months from Europe, five from Rio. They were not only isolated geographically, but were also disconnected from the increasingly intense blare of news in Europe. Johnson had pondered in the *Idler*, 'it is difficult to conceive how man can subsist without a news-paper, or to what entertainments companies can assemble, in those wide regions of the earth that have neither Chronicles nor Magazines, neither Gazettes nor Advertisers, neither Journals nor Evening Posts'.[25]

Endeavour had sailed well into these regions and inevitably questions must have nagged. What of Wilkes? For Gore what of the disturbances in America? For Cook there was his wife Elizabeth to think about in Mile End and the fate of their baby – unborn when he had left the previous summer. But the futility of speculation was something every sea officer knew. To quell a wandering mind Cook had a date to concentrate on. What happened on 3 June would shape the fate of the voyage more than anything else. Should they succeed in their observations then they must surely return home triumphant. Should they not, all Cook's early promise would count for nothing.

One of Cook's shipmates now became more significant than the rest. Charles Green was the Royal Society-appointed astronomer. He had trained at Greenwich under Maskelyne, a man whose zest for precision was legendary. If Maskelyne couldn't be with Cook himself, then Green was the next best thing. Green was already a veteran of scientific voyaging – he had joined the trials for John Harrison's marine timepieces in a crossing to Barbados – and his presence had been felt on *Endeavour*'s outward passage when he joined in with the daily observations. Just as Solander's erudition outstripped Banks's, Green's outdid Cook's. Cook had meddled in astronomy before – he had recorded an eclipse of the sun while in Newfoundland – though he had never received any formal training. But as Banks and Solander had turned the great cabin into a botanist's workshop, Green had converted the quarterdeck into something of an astronomy school. Adept and avuncular, Green had tutored Cook and the 'young gentlemen' in the art of taking lunars – a method for establishing longitude at sea by tracking the position of the moon. It took a lot to impress Cook, but Green – proclaimed an 'indefatigable observer' – had done so.

Whatever precision Cook and Green had achieved at sea, much more was expected now. Their first task had been securing an observation site on the island. Cook settled on the north-east point of the bay:

> I went a Shore with a party of men accompanie'd by Mr Banks, Dr Solander and Mr Green. We took along with us one of Mr Banks Tents, and after we had fix'd upon a place fit for our purpose we set up the Tent and Mark'd out the ground we intended to occupy. By this time a great number of the Natives had got collected together about us, seemingly only to look on as not one of them had any weapon either offensive or defensive. I would suffer none to come within the lines I had marked out excepting one who appear'd to be a Chief and old Owhaa, to these two men we endeavour'd to explain as well as we could that we wanted that ground to sleep upon such a number of nights and then we should go away.[26]

So goes the earliest account of British colonial presence in the Pacific. Cook explained that he selected this site not so much for topographical reasons, but rather because it lay far away from 'any of their habitations'. On 18 April Cook had 'as many people out of the Ship as could possibly be spar'd and set around Erecting a Fort'. The sailors dug trenches and chopped wood to make pickets. 'The natives were so far from hindering us that several of them assisted in bring[ing] the Pickets and Faccines out of the woods'. This exceeded Cook's hopes. The transit expeditions of 1761 had been hindered by diplomatic misunderstandings. One Frenchman, Jean-Baptiste Chappe, had caused consternation when he arrived with his telescope, clock and quadrants in Siberia where the local population had declared him a magician, and a protective guard had been required to guarantee his safety.

But there was an extra dynamic at play in Tahiti. Two years earlier the *Dolphin* had been warmly greeted. The intrigue at the strange arrival had soon, however, turned to something else. On the morning of 24 June – Midsummer Day in Old England – the *Dolphin* had been, as ever, surrounded by trading canoes. Robertson, the master, estimated there were 300 of them, 'and at a Moderate Computation there was near four thousand men'. The whole bay, he added, 'was all lined round with men women and children, to see the Onset which was now near at hand'.

A double canoe had drawn from the beach, 'and was observed to hoist some signal'. 'In a few secants of time all our Decks was full of Great and small stones', with the sailors left cradling bleeding heads. As more stones rattled aboard, rifles had echoed in reply. Wallis had ordered the guns run out: twelve on each side of her gun deck, four more either side of the quarterdeck. The *Dolphin*, roused, let fly. It 'struck such terror amongs the poor unhapy croad that it would require the pen of Milton to describe', Robertson conceded, 'therefor too mutch for mine'.[27]

In Britain accounts of the 'battle' had gained wide circulation, with people transfixed by what was perceived as the futile bravery of the islanders. Less thought was given to the question of whether the 'Georgians' were within their rights to defend their land. The story told in Britain – a woodcut of the battle was made, and a patriotic poem by one of the *Dolphin*'s sailors was circulated widely in publications like the *Gentleman's Magazine* – glossed over other facts too: that the Tahitians had continued to fight long after the discharge of the *Dolphin*'s guns, and that the day had ended in impasse rather than neat triumph.

Cook may have guessed there was more to the story. But he also grasped *Endeavour*'s use as a defensive weapon. On 16 April he warped the ship in, 'and moor'd her in such a Manner as to command all the Shore of the NE part of the Bay, but more particularly the place where we intended to Erect a Fort'.[28]

This site soon acquired a name 'Fort Venus'. By 10 May the encampment was complete. The section of the beach had been encircled by trenches and a wooden palisade, a barrier further defended by swivel guns. Inside stood a cluster of tents, a forge and several sheep pens. Two tents housed the scientific instruments. In one ticked the Royal Society's astronomical clock. Cook had it 'fixed firm and as low in the ground as the door' allowed, adding an extra protective framing around it 'to prevent its being disturbed by any accident'. This gave Fort Venus – a place of science – its calm, beating heart. Twelve feet away was the observatory. This consisted of a smaller, conical tent, with gaps in its roof through which telescopes could be pointed. Here Cook erected a second clock and stood an astronomical quadrant – used for measuring the altitude of celestial objects – on a large cask, which was weighed down with 'wett heavy sand'.

Cook and Green were left to fret about the transit throughout the rest of May. The degree of their dependence on fragile instruments was displayed when an astronomical quadrant was briefly stolen. Another, more persistent worry was the weather. The strongest telescope and sharpest eye in Britain would be rendered helpless by an awkward cloud or some other interference in the atmosphere. On 22 May, Fort Venus was beset by a rainstorm, 'accompanied with thunder and lightning', Parkinson wrote, 'more terrible than any I had ever heard, or seen, before'. Water came racing through Banks's tent 'and wetted everything in it'. So intense was the downpour that Parkinson feared for the ship, which 'providentially escaped'.[29]

Should anything like that happen on 3 June, it would be disastrous. To circumvent the threat Cook decided to dispatch supplementary teams to other regions of the island, 'for fear we should fail here'. On 1 June John Gore, Monkhouse the surgeon and Banks's personal secretary, Herman Spöring, were sent to neighbouring 'York Island'. The next day Zachary Hicks, Charles Clerke and several sailors were dispatched in the opposite direction, to the eastern coast. Solander was also incorporated into the observing team, though Banks, revealingly, was not given any responsibility – perhaps an indication Cook deemed him too much of a maverick to be trusted with the delicate task of exact measurement.

As the sun set on 2 June 1769, Fort Venus was tense with anticipation. Banks, who had travelled with Gore and Monkhouse, wrote: 'Before night our observatory was in order, telescopes all set up and tried &c. and we went to rest anxious for the events of tomorrow; the evening having been very fine gave us however great hopes of success.'[30]

The eighteenth-century world was a localised one. It was still decades before the first semaphore telegraphs, and news concertinaed across space at a stagger. It took a day for a letter to travel between New York and Philadelphia. The same letter might rattle over the turnpikes between London to Edinburgh in three days, or cross from London to Paris in a week, but a minimum of a month was needed for it to pass between Boston and Portsmouth.

In a globe parcelled up in parishes and towns, provinces and colonies, the Transit of Venus is a rare instance of simultaneous experience, of people undertaking the simple action of pausing,

looking and counting across dispersed space. As Cook and Green
sat at their chairs in Fort Venus, another of the Royal Society's
observers, Jeremiah Dixon, was gazing upwards from Hammerfest
Island in the Arctic Circle, and William Wales was peering through
a telescope at Hudson's Bay. In Newport, Rhode Island, Reverend
Ezra Stiles braced himself for the observation. Nearby in Cambridge,
New England, John Winthrop, professor of mathematics at Harvard,
looked through smoked glass at the sun, as did Maskelyne at
Greenwich, London.

But not everyone who looked was a trained professional. Hundreds
of amateurs followed instructions laid down by the press. At Whitby
in Yorkshire several enthusiasts crowded into a darkened room to see
what they could in the fading light of a summer's evening. An unsigned
report from Whitby made the newspapers (might these be the words
of Lionel Charlton?):

> Intervening Clouds hindered us from observing the exact Time
> of the Transit's beginning; and too much Company prevented
> our taking the nearest central Distance, though Venus did not
> appear to us to be above one Thirty-second of the whole
> Diameter within the Sun's Disk.[31]

As they watched the black speck melt into the night, perhaps the
Whitby conversation dwelt, for a proud moment, on Milner's old ship
and Walker's old apprentice, who had travelled halfway around the
world to observe the very same thing.

'Various were the Changes observd in the weather during the course
of last night', Banks wrote in his journal on 3 June, 'some one or
other of us was up every half hour who constantly informd the rest
that it was either clear or Hazey. at day break we rose and soon after
had the satisfaction of seeing the sun rise as clear and bright as we
could wish him.' Pickersgill, one of the mates, added, rather unsym-
pathetically, that 'if the Observation is not well made it is intirely
owing to the Observers'.[32]

Cook was equally sanguine: 'not a Clowd was to be seen the whole
day and the Air was perfectly clear', he wrote, 'so that we had every
advantage we could desire in Observing the whole of the passage of
the Planet Venus over the Suns disk'. The observation was split into

four sections. The first was the external ingress, when Venus's outer rim touched the edge of the sun. The internal ingress followed this, when Venus's entire body passed in front of the sun's face. Then the pattern was repeated with an internal egress, when Venus's disc first began to slip outside the sun, and finally an external egress when Venus had gone, her transit at an end. With a clock ticking beside them, each observer was to record these four crucial steps.

At 09:21:45 Green saw something first: a slight blackened blemish like a shadow on the sun's limb. Presumably he said nothing, keeping silent to avoid interfering with Cook's observation. Green was five seconds ahead of Cook, who jotted down 09:21:50. But, then again, it was 09:22:00 before Green was 'Certain'. Eleven seconds later and not far away, Solander jotted down his initial contact, though he conceded a 'wavering haze' seconds before.

A little more than quarter of an hour passed before, at 09:39:20, both Cook and Green recorded the internal contact, as the black dot slid completely within the sun. Thereafter they waited. For five hours they sat at their stations in the sweltering heat, watching the black dot drift across the sun's surface. Perhaps it was the longest stretch of physical inactivity Cook had for the entire voyage. Only after three o'clock in the afternoon were he and Green called into action. At 15:10:15 Cook saw Venus break through the far edge of the sun. Again Green was ten seconds ahead, but for the final milestone, Venus's exit, Cook was fourteen seconds in advance of Green, setting down the time 15:28:04.

They had the numbers they had travelled halfway around the world to collect. The relief at gathering them was tempered with frustration. They had been warned about an interfering haze that had clung to Venus during the 1761 observations. Sure enough it had come again. Cook reasoned it was 'only the penumbra' – the shaded outer region of an opaque object – and not Venus herself. Later this phenomena would become known as the 'black drop effect', when the sun appeared to stretch out to embrace Venus as she neared. In 1769 the reasons for this were not yet comprehended, but the beguiling fuzz had made difficult what should have been straightforward. It made the determinations of the entry and exit points so fraught that Cook felt it necessary to depict the problem in a series of sketches. That two observers with identical equipment in the same location should differ to such a degree was confounding. Perhaps Cook could hear Maskelyne's voice

in his head as he jotted the final word beside his last observation:
'dubious'.[33]

Sydney Parkinson also watched Venus cross the sun. It seems he
exploited the occasion to elicit some words for his growing 'Vocabulary
of the Language of Otaheite':

Manaha	The Sun
Taowruah	The Planet Venus
Eparai	The horizon
Tota, also Eeno	A looking glass[34]

It was now almost two months since Parkinson had stepped ashore
on Tahiti. That afternoon, 14 April, he had joined 'a small party' on
'an excursion into the country'. Parkinson had found the walk from
the beach into the shaded canopy of the woodland exhilarating. 'The
first experience can never be repeated', another Scot, Robert Louis
Stevenson, described the sensation a century on. 'The first love, the
first sunrise, the first South Sea island are memories apart and touched
by a virginity of sense.'[35] In April 1769 Parkinson felt this intensity of
experience. Growing weary, his party had 'sat down under the shade
of some lofty trees':

> the undulation of whose leaves rendered it very cool and pleasant.
> The high cocoas, and the low branching fruit trees, formed an
> agreeable contrast; while the cloud-topt hills, appearing between
> them, added to the natural grandeur of the prospect ... We feasted
> on the cocoa nut milk, which afforded us a pleasing repast.[36]

This was the kind of undiluted nature that Parkinson had sacrificed
his London life to see. For three months after this he engaged in a
heartfelt relationship with the island. He worked, as ever, at an outdoor
table at Fort Venus, depicting spiky green herbs and fleshy-leaved
shrubs, striking orchids, and fiery red hibiscus as Banks or Solander
brought them to him. In all he painted about a hundred specimens
in his time in Tahiti, at a rate of about one a day. But painting was
not everything. Leaving Hammersmith, James Lee had cautioned him
that he was 'to minute everything he saw and trust nothing to his
memory'.[37]

One of his shipmates recalled Parkinson's assiduity 'in collecting accounts of the languages, customs, and, manners of the people', as he drew up 'a very fair journal, which was looked upon, by the ship's company, to be the best that was kept', particularly in relation to Tahiti.[38] The 'fair copy' of Parkinson's journal is the great lost document of the *Endeavour* voyage. For reasons that will later emerge (though will never entirely be reconciled), it would never be published. What did go into print is the 'foul copy', of drafts, snatched observations, inchoate reflections and insights. These were subject to the interfering hand of a London editor, but enough survives to intrigue. Reading over it today, there is a rawness to Parkinson's writing. As might be expected of a draft, there's no literary polish but there's a lucidity and a sense of striving for truth. The whole of Parkinson's journal stretches for 200 pages, but it is the section on Tahiti – spanning fifty pages, about a quarter of the total – which feels most alive.

Cook and Banks also compiled surveys of Tahiti, and both of them had talents as observers. Cook had the finely tuned surveyor's eye. Banks had an abundance of enthusiasm, his vigorous prose and a journalistic knack for unearthing stories. Parkinson's stance was different. Rather than being the star of a scene, like Banks, or burdened with the status of the 'leader', as Cook was, Parkinson was a far less obtrusive figure. In his observations, he often exists on the periphery of scenes, quietly watching, recording and absorbing the meaning of actions as they happen. This makes for something that feels more authentically ethnographic than produced by Cook or Banks. Of everyone on *Endeavour*, the historian Bernard Smith has written, it was Parkinson who developed 'the most sympathetic relationships with but also the greatest sympathy for the peoples of the Pacific'.[39]

Parkinson began his study in even steps. He recorded the Tahitians' appearance as 'pale, tawny', and with 'long black hair' which they cut with a shark's tooth. The men, he observed, were physically impressive, standing at more than six feet tall while the ladies were much shorter. Although they had mastered the art of dyeing fabrics, they seldom wore more than a few clothes around their middles. This made it all the easier for them to bathe in the rivers, he noted, something they did 'three times a day', a striking preference for cleanliness, as was the habit of washing 'hands and teeth after every meal.' Most of them, he noticed, carried a strong scent of cocoa oil.[40]

In contrast to *Endeavour*'s crew, many of whom could not swim, the Tahitians thrived in the water. He watched the boys playing in the surf and fishing, dragging the bottom with a net made of convolvulus leaves, or ingeniously hooking fishes with an oyster shell. He noticed more subtle behaviours. When Tahitians beckoned at a distance they did so with their fingers pointing downwards, something 'contrary to our mode'. Another contrast was their manner of greeting friends, especially those who had been separated for some time. Parkinson explained 'they affect to cry for joy', but judged, cynically, that 'it seems to be entirely ceremonial'.

Parkinson was brave enough to venture out alone in the evenings after his work at Fort Venus was completed. Although many of his shipmates did the same, it is worth recalling that almost all his peers carried firearms or weapons for protection, but Parkinson, a Quaker, would not have done so. Unarmed he wandered along beaches and through glades, being 'almost stunned with the noise of the grasshoppers'. All the while Parkinson passed the steady string of huts, 'built at a considerable distance from each other; so that the island looks like one continued village'. On one occasion he was delighted to be invited inside one. To welcome his visitor a father sent his son 'up a tall cocoa-tree to gather nuts'. Parkinson watched as the boy 'climbed it very dextrously ... tying his feet together' and then 'vaulting up very swiftly'.[41]

On one of his evening strolls Parkinson stumbled across a breadfruit market, where islanders were gathered at a long open house, dividing the breadfruit into baskets. This was a culture far more authentic than that at Fort Venus, where Cook had set up *Endeavour*'s trading hub under Banks's and Solander's command. Banks had thrived as a 'market man' – one morning 'trafficking' 350 coconuts by half past six – but here Parkinson watched something very different. It was the social mechanics of Tahiti as they really existed. He listened to the boys playing their nose flutes. He watched little knots of girls 'divert themselves' in the evening, dividing 'into two parties, one standing opposite to the other, one party throws apples, which the other endeavours to catch'.[42]

This was a society so different to the dank Edinburgh of Parkinson's youth or the glitz and grime of London. To help him understand it

Parkinson looked to the writings of the Genevan social philosopher Jean-Jacques Rousseau. Rousseau had risen to prominence in 1750 with his prize-winning essay, *Discourse on the Moral Effects of the Arts and Sciences*. Ever since, he had remained a combative voice in a restless European world. In 1766 the *Scots Magazine* had printed a generous profile of 'an extraordinary man' with the 'paradoxical turn of thinking'.[43] Rousseau, everyone realised, was the counterpoint. He lived and wrote in opposition to everything the enlightening, endeavouring classes were striving to achieve.

For Rousseau civilisation was not an achievement, it was a curse. Immersing humanity within it, as far as he was concerned, was like smothering a body in clothes until it was so swaddled that it could neither move nor breathe. Rousseau had cast his imagination back through time, envisioning humanity in its original 'state of nature'. Comparing his 'natural man' with 'man-made man', Rousseau wrote, he had 'discovered that his supposed improvement had generated all his miseries'.[44] Civilisation was a wasting force. Look, for instance, at the sickly, stressed Europeans, and then picture a natural man, at one with his body, 'the only Instrument that savage Man is acquainted with':

> Had he a Hatchet, would his Hand so easily snap off from an Oak so stout a Branch? Had he a Sling, would it dart a Stone to so great a Distance? Had he a Ladder, would he run so nimbly up a Tree? Had he a Horse, would he with such Swiftness shoot along the Plain?[45]

Rousseau's ideas were not new. Arguments about primitivism – that truer versions of human nature were to be found in less-developed places – had existed for years. But the force of his prose as well as his platform as one of the French *philosophes* had made them notorious. All the intellectuals on *Endeavour* would have known about Rousseau, but they held a particular appeal for Parkinson who was part of the generation to come of age as Rousseau's arguments about the state of nature, the lost joys of savage existence and the corrupting force of civilisation, had their greatest appeal. Cook plotting the perimeter of Fort Venus was oddly reminiscent of one of the central passages from Rousseau's 'greatest and best performance', *Discourse on the Origin and Basis of Inequality Among Men* (1755):

The first Man, who, after enclosing a Piece of Ground, took it into his Head to say, *This is mine,* and found People simple enough to believe him, was the true Founder of civil Society. How many Crimes, how many Wars, how many Murders, how many Misfortunes and Horrors, would that Man have saved the Human Species, who pulling up the Stakes or filling up the Ditches should have cried to his Fellows: Be sure not to listen to this Imposter; you are lost, if you forget that the Fruits of the Earth belong equally to us all, and the Earth itself to nobody![46]

It is tempting to make the connection between this and the scene at Matavai Bay in April 1769. But to do so would be to distort well-known facts. Even before *Endeavour* had reached 'George's Island' there was an understanding that it was a place of some complexity. There was talk of a queen, which implied a social hierarchy. Trade with the *Dolphin*'s crew – despite the thieving – had otherwise carried on regularly enough. George's Island was 'pretty much civilized', explained the earliest reports of Wallis's discovery in the newspapers. No one expected to find a state of nature, but a devotee of Rousseau's ideas might encounter what he had termed 'nascent society'. This was Rousseau's *'juste milieu'* or happy medium: a stage in human development suspended between the 'stupidity of brutes and the disastrous enlightenment of civil man'.[47]

These were the ideas Parkinson brought to Tahiti with him. There is a feeling of him evaluating what he sees in his journal. He wonders whether the abundance of 'cocoa, bread-fruit, and apple-trees, the fruit of which drops, as it were, into their mouths' resulted in them being 'an indolent people'. But he counters this. The people seem 'contented', he writes, 'with what is spontaneously produced, as if they had attained to the ne plus ultra, and are therefore happier than Europeans generally are, whose desires are unbounded.'[48]

In a few short weeks Parkinson was grasping at a better understanding of Tahiti than the crew of the *Dolphin* ever had. They had merely depicted a permissive paradise of culinary and sexual plenty. The subsequent invention, 'George's Island', Parkinson recognises, was a nonsense. The icy winters and entrenched inequality, political upheavals and relentless wars of Europe made it all the easier for people to conjure up an island they would love to exist. That Parkinson never used the label 'George's Island' is suggestive. But Rousseau's theories did attract him. Although the Tahitians continued to be great thieves, he pondered, 'They must be very honest amongst themselves, as every house is without any fastening. Locks, bolts and bars are peculiar to civilized countries, where their moral theory is the best, and their moral practices too generally of the worst'. This:

> might induce a celebrated writer to conclude, though errone-ously, that mankind, upon the whole, are necessarily rendered worse, and less happy, by civilization, and the cultivation of the arts and sciences. Nature's wants, it is true, are but few, and the uncivilized part of mankind, in general, seem contented if they can acquire those few. Ambition, and the love of luxurious banquets, and other superfluities, are but little known in the barbarous nations: they have, in general, less anxious thought for the morrow, than civilized; and therefore feel more enjoyment while they partake of heaven's bounty in the present day.[49]

Whether swayed by Rousseau or not, visiting Tahiti allowed Parkinson and his shipmates to cast off their fetters temporarily. 'Most of our ship's company procured temporary wives amongst the natives', Parkinson conceded. Attempting to justify the transgres-sion, Parkinson wrote 'even many reputed virtuous Europeans allow themselves, in uncivilized parts of the world, [to act] with impunity; as if a change of place altered the moral turpitude of fornication; and what is a sin in Europe, is only a simple innocent gratification in America'.[50]

In Britain, Parkinson's reference to the 'many reputed virtuous Europeans' would no doubt be interpreted as code for Banks and Solander, both of whom conducted amorous relationships on Tahiti. But perhaps that was not all. One day, as Solander reported it, when Banks was returning with a female companion, he revealed that 'the first thing he saw was Shyboots Parkinson in bed with the girl's sister'.

Three days after *Endeavour* had arrived in April, Parkinson's fellow draughtsman, Buchan, had suffered an epileptic fit. He 'remained insensible' for some hours, then died. Parkinson, Solander, Spöring and several of the officers had rowed out to the offing and slid him into the sea. 'I sincerely regret him as an ingenious and good young man', Banks had written:

but his Loss to me is irretrevable, my airy dreams of entertaining my friends in England with the scenes that I am to see here are vanishd. No account of the figures and dresses of men can be satisfactory unless illustrated with figures: had providence spard him a month longer what an advantage would it have been to my undertaking but I must submit.[51]

Buchan's death doubled Parkinson's workload. Originally he had been engaged solely as a natural-history painter, but from this moment onwards he worked more diversely across subjects. One day Parkinson climbed One Tree Hill, an iconic eminence that commanded the view over the bay. The 'one tree', a massive, wizened specimen, dominates the view. Several figures mill nearby, caught in the business of life. Then, almost easy to overlook, is the slight form of an artist in the foreground, sat sketching on the grass. In the shade of the tree he gazes over Matavai Bay where *Endeavour* lies at anchor. His presence transforms the picture into a self-portrait. Here is Parkinson, as far from Edinburgh as can be, gazing over the Great South Seas.

Parkinson continued to work, too, on his 'Vocabulary'. As Banks picked flowers, Parkinson gathered words:

Eahoo	The nose
Ohaa te manoo	A bird's nest
Earoc	The swell of the sea or the surf
Anooa nooa	The rainbow

Reading these translations today you are left with the impression of distant conversations: Parkinson – pointing, mimicking, nodding, smiling, eking out phonetic sounds, jotting them down. His list would graduate from single words to complex phrases, some of which bring island life in 1769 echoing down the ages. *Tai poe etee noow* (pray give me a little bead), *eeyaha* (get you gone), *ara mai* (follow me or come hither). Just one word would complete the journey from Tahitian to English: 'tatau', the name given to the ceremonial process of imprinting a person's skin with artistic markings. Intrigued, Parkinson would 'undergo the operation' himself, anticipating an age to come by commemorating a significant moment in his life with a tattoo.

*

By the end of *Endeavour*'s stay in Tahiti in July, Parkinson had recorded 403 words, a list of popular names, numbers from one to twenty and the transcription of an Otaheitian song. This was an impressive achievement, but one that he could only ever take so far. He might be able to point to a nose or a foot, but it was much harder to confirm or comprehend the intricacies of this different belief system he was encountering.

Tahiti was a far more complex place than anyone had grasped. Far from romanticised ideas about equality, Cook found that every fruiting tree on the island was the property of some person or other. The beauty of the landscape, too, seemed to conceal darker truths. Skeletons were sighted and Banks came across a number of jawbones, hanging as trophies. Other things were inexplicable. One day Parkinson watched as a lady mutilated herself with a shark's tooth in public.

Then there was a perplexing scene one morning at Fort Venus. Banks had been presiding over the market as usual when a double canoe rounded the point of the bay and glided to the shallows. A man and two women alighted and beckoned to him. In a fluid movement, a lane was made, running between the visitors and Banks. The man approached with 'a small bunch of parrot's feathers'.[52] Six times he passed to and fro, bringing gifts. Cloth was then spread over the sand. The scene now prepared, one of the women walked towards Banks. She wore 'a great many clothes upon her', wrote Parkinson. She twice twisted around, allowing the cloth to fall to the floor 'and exposed herself quite naked'. The girl was then handed more garments, which she arranged on the floor, before she 'exposed herself as before.'

Although the meaning of the performance was lost on Banks, he was delighted at what he interpreted as a sexual invitation. He led both ladies to his tent, although he 'could not prevail upon them to stay more than an hour'. But Banks noted a second, subtle significance to the ceremony in his journal. All the while a man called Tupaia had stood beside him and 'acted as my deputy', Banks wrote, helping to receive gifts and place them in the boat. It is a telling detail. Episodes of cultural confusion usually progressed along similar lines. Two parties would be divided. There would be a moment of contact or exchange, often misunderstood, generating powerful responses: bewilderment, anger, hilarity, embarrassment. That morning the choreography was confused by Tupaia's presence.

He straddled both worlds. He participated, he understood, but he sided with Banks.

Reading back through the *Endeavour* journals today, it is difficult to get an authentic impression of the Tahitian people. Responding to a place they considered ethereal or exotic, the sailors allotted many Tahitians names from the classical world like Hercules, Lycurgus or Epicurus that served only to mask their true identities. Other people feel cartoonish. When they finally met the fabled 'Queen Oboreah', her true biography was entirely missed. 'Oboreah' was not a 'queen', but rather she was Purea, a formidable, high-born woman, embroiled in active power tussles around Matavai Bay. It was through their dealings with Purea that *Endeavour*'s crew got to know Tupaia. He celebrated King George's birthday with them. He prepared a dinner of roasted dog for the officers and gentlemen and he assumed the general role of fixer, diplomat and translator. Of everyone, Tupaia seemed to especially align himself with Banks.

Amid all the watercolours and sketches of flowers and birds, coastal and other scenes, it is surprising no portrait of Tupaia survives. Nor did anyone commit to history a physical description of him. In the beginning they only had an approximate understanding of his status within Tahitian society, as 'Oboreah's favourite' or 'a sort of high-priest of Otaheite'. Banks dubbed him a 'cheif *Tahowa* or preist of this Island, consequently skilld in the mysteries of their religion'.[53] Only in time was Banks's clumsy, catch-all definition of 'A Man of Knowledge' sharpened into something meaningful. Later it would become evident they had met one of the most inquisitive, learned and perceptive people in all of these islands. Within a decade Georg Forster, the German naturalist who sailed with Cook on a later voyage, described Tupaia as 'an extraordinary genius'.

For decades, even centuries, after the *Endeavour* voyage the story was retold within the framework of a traditional European exploration narrative. This not only emphasised the clear division between the 'civilized' visitors and the 'savage' or 'barbarian' natives, it also implied that the explorers were always the active, controlling participants in the drama of encounter while those they met played passive roles. Recent scholarship has demonstrated how wrong this assumption was. In 1769 *Endeavour* did not sail into a benign, ahistorical world. The people the sailors met had strong and distinct motivations for behaving the way they did. In no one is this truth more clearly expressed than in Tupaia.

Rather than meek generosity Tupaia's interactions with *Endeavour*'s crew, and Banks in particular, were shrewd and calculated to serve a purpose. With little direct testimony from him his motivations can never entirely be known. But it seems clear that not long after *Endeavour*'s arrival in Matavai Bay he conceived a plan to travel with the ship when she left. Towards the end of the sailors' three-month stay in Tahiti he made his request. He was persistent. On 12 July 1769, the day before *Endeavour* was due to sail, Tupaia came aboard and, as Banks put it, he 'renewd his resolves of going with us to England'.

At about ten the next morning the collier caught a breeze from the west. As *Endeavour* gathered way, Matavai Bay was dotted with canoes. Parkinson heard the woeful cry '*Awai! Awai!*', 'to go or pass away'. Some drew alongside, offering parting gifts of coconut and bananas. Looking up, they must have been startled at the familiar figure standing on the quarterdeck.

'By Tobias Directions', Pickersgill wrote, 'we stood to the Wt in Quest of some Islds which he said lay that way not far distant'. Banks watched as Tupaia shed 'a few heartfelt tears, so I judge them to have been by the Efforts I saw him make use of to hide them'.[54] The voyage in motion once again, Banks took his newest shipmate to the masthead, where they 'stood a long time waving to the Canoes as they went off'. Tahiti faded into the horizon behind them, never to be seen by Banks or Parkinson or Tupaia again.

8

Perfect Strangers

'Tōtaiete mā' is one phrase Parkinson did not record. It is the collective Tahitian name for the archipelago of islands, sprinkled midway across the Pacific, that Cook would name the Society Islands. Prior to the *Endeavour*'s visit in 1769, these islands – ranging over 250 miles of longitude, from Tahiti in the east to Bora Bora in the west – had yet to be reconciled into the western unit of geographical comprehension: a chart. But, as Tupaia knew, there was order here. Each island or atoll in the group was knitted together by a matrix of sea paths that ran, like the threads in a spider's web, from one to another. However hard they looked none of the *Endeavour*'s crew could see these, but Tupaia had no problems finding them. It was onto one of these paths he guided *Endeavour* as she left Matavai Bay. Banks had watched the few 'heartfelt tears' gather in Tupaia's eyes. He might have concluded, reasonably enough, that Tupaia was weeping for Tahiti. But there might have been another reason. For Tupaia was not leaving at all. He was going home.

Huahine, Ra'iātea, Bora Bora, the islands the *Endeavour*'s crew saw, shared much of Tahiti's aesthetic charm. They rose jagged and jade green out of a lapis sea. They were all ringed by the same shimmering turquoise shallows, with the same palm-skirted beaches. Unadorned with solid architecture and the smoke of forges or factories, it was easy enough for people to equate this natural beauty with Rousseau's ideas of calm innocence. But the reality was quite different. *Endeavour* was not gliding over tranquil waters. Rather in 1769 she was sailing through a contested geographical space riven by an intergenerational conflict. The source of the discontent was the island of Ra'iātea. Smaller than Tahiti in both size and population, Ra'iātea was nonetheless more revered. On its southern shores, in the district of Opua, stood the Marae Taputapuatea, the most sacred temple in Tōtaiete mā. To explain Taputapuatea's significance to an Enlightenment man like Banks would be to ask them to imagine Oxford, Rome and Uppsala blended into one and concentrated into a small collection of flattened rocks and pillars by the sea. Taputapuatea was the lodestone, the beating magnetic heart for the islands, where priests prayed, scholars chanted and human sacrifices were offered. This was the place of Creation and birthplace of the gods, like Oro, the great god of war.

The eighteenth century is often remembered as an era of colonial expansion, when belligerent European nations probed further and further into North America, the Caribbean and India. The conflicts within Tōtaiete mā hardly seem to belong to the same historical universe, but as red-coated British soldiers marched across ever wider territories, at the same time the worship of Oro was radiating outwards from Taputapuatea: to Bora Bora in about 1710 and Tahiti about a decade later. Red was Oro's colour too. His cult was carried from Ra'iātea to the outlying islands by an exclusive, priestly order named the *arioi*. The *arioi* existed beyond the normal, rigid binds of class identity. Exclusive and mostly non-hereditary – *arioi* were not permitted offspring, being limited like Catholic priests to unmarried life – only the most gifted, the most physically attractive and capable members of either sex were admitted. In an *arioi* was combined wisdom and physical prowess. Fond of travel, wherever the *arioi* went festivals of feasting, dancing, sacrifice, dark comedies and sex were held. One European visitor to the Society Islands, shortly after *Endeavour*'s time, watched as a flotilla of *arioi* approached a shore. Their canoes:

advanced towards the land, with their streamers floating in the wind, their drums and flutes sounding, and the Areois, attended by their chief, who acted as their prompter, appeared on a stage erected for the purpose, with their wild distortions of person, antic gestures, painted bodies, and vociferated songs, mingling with the sound of the drum and the flute, the dashing of the sea, and the rolling and the breaking of the surf.[1]

The *arioi* policy was of shock and awe and their principal aim during the first half of the eighteenth century was to convert the people of Tōtaiete mā to the cult of Oro. Banks, who on 13 July 1769 sat beside

Tupaia on *Endeavour*'s masthead, comprehended none of this. He was unconcerned with spiritual matters, instead confining his attention to temporal things that he could see and evaluate. What was the purpose in speculating about things that could be proved neither true or false? 'Religion has been in ages', he wrote in his survey of the South Seas islands, and 'is still in all Countreys Cloak'd in mysteries unexplicable to human understanding.' There was an additional disadvantage, he explained: 'the Language in which it is conveyd'.[2]

Endeavour's topmast head was a tiny space, a mere few feet square. Huddled together, to those who looked up at them, Banks and Tupaia must have almost blended into one. Perhaps this is how Tupaia envisioned it. It seems that midway through *Endeavour*'s visit to Tahiti he had decided to enter into a '*taio*' relationship with Banks, a type of formalised friendship, forged for mutual benefit. *Taio* meant a melding of two into one: of aims, outlooks, identities and names. Rarely can a *taio* friendship have had stranger constituent parts. On one was the Lincolnshire gentleman with £6,000 a year and his town house in Mayfair. On the other was Tupaia, a priest, a star navigator and a political refugee from Hamanimo Bay, Ra'iātea. Later, when the officers were trying to impress Tupaia with stories of Britain and brave King George and his many children, he replied that he 'thought himself much greater, because he belonged to the arreoys'.[3]

Tupaia's life had been, in equal measure, privileged and confused. Born in Ra'iātea in about 1725 he had not only come from a hallowed island, he had received oral instruction at Taputapuatea itself. Only a select few were afforded this honour. Concentrated into the minds of the chosen was the knowledge of the islands. Their skills took in practical as well as spiritual matters. Tupaia is said to have come from a family particularly talented in the art of maritime navigation. From his boyhood he would have learned to analyse *te moana*, the sea, treating it not as an indistinct mass, but rather a combination of aspects: the water's colour and its hue, the pattern of the waves, the height of a swell, the tug of a current, the loom of the land and the behaviour of migratory birds and insects. Admitted into the third order of the *arioi*, Tupaia's status must have been confirmed by the elaborate tattoos that criss-crossed his body, from the small of his back to the insides of his elbows. As a man of consequence, he had sailed across Tōtaiete mā on *arioi* missions during his young adulthood, accompanied, no doubt, by the requisite ceremony and fiery symbolism of Oro.

These early missions had run their course by the time Tupaia reached adulthood. Oro had been established on many islands and, soon, had come the backlash. The cause of the trouble, as Tupaia explained it to Parkinson, was an ill-fated decision to banish thieves from across the Society Islands to the 'almost barren and uninhabited' island called Bora Bora. Hoping to rid themselves of a problem, the move compounded it. Parkinson sketched the account: 'In process of time, their numbers so greatly increased that the island was insufficient for their subsistence. Being men of desperate fortunes, they made themselves canoes, turned pirates, and made prisoners such of the people of the islands near them as had the misfortune to fall in their way, and seized their canoes and effects.'[4]

It was during the incursions of the Bora Borans that Tupaia had been forced from his comfortable lifestyle and ancestral homeland in Ra'iātea. Years of restlessness between the Bora Borans and Ra'iāteans had led to a bloody climax off the coast of Ra'iātea in about 1763. The contest had ended in 'great slaughter'. Betrayed in the heat of battle, the Ra'iāteans had been defeated and Tupaia had nearly been killed. Engulfed in the fighting, he had been struck by a stingray barb which 'peircd quite through his body, entering at his back and coming out just under his breast'.[5] More than five years later the injury was still visible. Banks saw the scar, and thought it 'as smooth and as small as any I have seen from the cures of our best European surgeons'. Tupaia survived but his previous life was over. It was only then, it is said, that he adopted 'Tupaia' for a name, a word that signified 'beaten'. As Molyneux, *Endeavour*'s master, laconically summed up the story, he was driven 'from his Possessions & Oblig'd him to Fly to Queen Obree[a] for shelter'.[6]

Tupaia was among many Ra'iāteans to find refuge on Tahiti. He may have been wounded and shorn of his lands, wealth and previous identity, but Tupaia remained an *arioi*, a priest of Oro and a gallant survivor of the Bora Boran hostility. In Tahiti he had soon found a new powerbase, allying himself with Purea – the much-vaunted 'Queen Oboreah' – becoming her lover. Recovering physically and socially rejuvenated, Purea and Tupaia had schemed to consolidate and expand their status around Papara in the southern part of Tahiti. This was how matters had stood in the mid-1760s. So far Tupaia had experienced the ebb and flow of life. He had been elevated to a status of enormous power and reduced to an existence of homeless despair. But what came next must have been more perplexing than anything that had gone before.

Within two years of the sea battle off Ra'iātea, sightings were swapped among the islands of massive, floating objects to the north. These were provoking reports. Recent prophecies had spoken of the coming of strange canoes 'without outriggers', carrying even stranger people, or of sacred birds returning home. Many of the foundation stories in Tōtaiete mā centred on the concept of voyaging. The gods travelled the skies in marvellous winged canoes, like Tane, the god of peace and beauty, or Maui and Ru, who had traversed the world, filling it with islands. The mention of birds, too, added gravity. Banks had noticed the special status of birds among the people. Each island had its own sacred bird. At one it was a heron, for another 'a kind of kingfisher'. These were neither molested nor killed, instead they were considered the bringers of good or bad fortune. Just like the voyaging gods, the birds symbolised freedom for a geographically isolated people. The scholar Anne Salmond has described the South Seas islanders' feeling of 'cosmic loneliness'.[7] The tiny islands that were their home merely pricked the surface of a massive ocean. Lost within it, what existed over the horizon's rim was only half known. And from the eastern horizon had appeared, in short order, four great canoes. The *Dolphin*, then – though Cook did not yet know this – two French ships commanded by de Bougainville, and finally, *Endeavour*.

It is impossible to know exactly what people thought of the ships. Oral histories tell of a strange apparition, floating islands or a godlike creature. 'They were struck with astonishment at so extraordinary an appearance', wrote a descendant of one who witnessed the *Dolphin*'s arrival, they 'could not account for such an amazing phenomena, which filled them with wonder and fear'. This feeling of wonder seems to have been transient, but the fear lasted longer. Banks acknowledged 'terrour which the Dolphins guns put them into' and when he asked how many had died in the battle, 'they number names upon their fingers, some ten some twenty some thirty, and then say *worrow worow* the same word as is usd for a flock of birds or a shoal of fish'.[8]

That Tupaia should be attracted to *Endeavour* in 1769 was entirely natural. From his childhood as an *arioi*, to his relationship with Purea, he had stayed close to power. *Endeavour* was the second ship he had visited, and perhaps his idea for leaving had its origin the year before when he had toured the *Dolphin*. Furthermore, water was Tupaia's medium. He might be venerated on land, but an *arioi* was never quite so magnificent as when navigating the sea. Another clue into Tupaia's motivations is, perhaps, hidden in a compelling archival document.

We know that at some point during the summer of 1769, Tupaia started to sketch with Parkinson. Tupaia's watercolours – mostly domestic scenes of boys playing the nose flute, or of mourning ceremonies – have only recently been acknowledged as his work. At first view they look awkward and stiff. The figures are coarsely drawn, linear and flat against the paper. But when one learns these are the earliest attempts of a man from Ra'iātea who had never previously seen watercolour and had no experience or technical training in form, colour, composition or perspective, the traditional frame of reference melts away.

Among Tupaia's sketches is a particularly intriguing one, more technically complex and confident than the rest. It is known as *A Scene in Tahiti*. Outlined in pencil and partly finished with watercolours, it shows a long meeting house, overhung with palm, banana and breadfruit trees. The trees are delicately rendered – one wonders whether it is a joint composition with Parkinson – the trunks are filled with an oaky brown, the leaves with a juniper green. But it's the foreground that holds the drama. Here Tupaia depicts the scene of a sea battle, with fighting canoes. Three are shown in combat. One hurries out of the frame to the right as the others join in battle. The warriors stand on platforms, gripping clubs and lances. Unfinished pencil figures muster in the bellies of the canoes, poised to join the fray.

There are two ways of reading this picture. It may be an entire, coherent scene; but equally it may be a layered narrative, like the Bayeux Tapestry. In this reading *A Scene in Tahiti* becomes something different, turning the piece from a portrait of Tahitian life, into a pictorial autobiography. The watercolour is incomplete, as, perhaps, was Tupaia's story. From the middle of May 1769, he appears to have made it his ambition to join *Endeavour*, to forge a *taio* relationship with Banks, to guide them all to Taputapuatea and, perhaps, even to harness the power of *Endeavour*'s lethal weapons to revenge himself on the Bora Borans.

Several Tahitians had offered to sail with the British, but Tupaia had been the most insistent. He 'has appear'd always to be infinitely superiour in every Respect to any other Indian we have met with, he has conceiv'd so strong a Freindship for Mr Banks that he is Determind to Visit Britannia', Molyneux the master had observed.[9] Hearing the news, Banks had been thrilled. He had promised to provide for him when they reached Britain and admitted him as part of his suite. On 12 July 1769, Tupaia had spent his last day in Tahiti, praying and bidding farewell to friends. Before nightfall, accompanied by a boy servant Taiato, he was rowed aboard to take up 'lodgins for the first time'. 'He is certainly a most proper man, well born', Banks wrote:

> Thank heaven I have a sufficiency and I do not know why I may not keep him as a curiosity, as well as some of my neighbours do lions and tygers at a larger expence than he will probably ever put me to; the amusement I shall have in his future conversation and the benefit it will be of to this ship, as well as what he may be if another should be sent into these seas, will I think fully repay me.[10]

This is one of those passages in Banks that jars, seemingly outing him as a rapacious imperial meddler, seizing what he fancies and hauling it home for display. This verdict is not entirely fair. The scholar Nicholas Thomas has contextualised Banks's 'rightly notorious' depiction of Tupaia, pointing out in mitigation, 'his attitude was entirely unlike that of nineteenth-century imperial entrepreneurs who really did collect indigenous people, really did keep them in zoo-like conditions, and really did exhibit them in precisely the way they exhibited animals':

> Banks saw Tupaia as a collectible, but also as a companion, and he was not someone who would use the expression 'a most proper man' lightly. He goes on to make it clear that what he means is that Tupaia is a man of rank and social eminence. Banks would never have described any of the common seamen in these terms, and no doubt saw Tupaia as a fitter person to conduct a conversation with than any of them. In any case, Tupaia was not 'collected' by anyone on the *Endeavour*. He made a decision

to voyage (and he took a boy, usually described as his servant, with him).[11]

Nor was Tupaia an ornamental presence aboard. In the weeks after they left Tahiti his influence infused the ship. Within days he had brought Huahine into view. Lying behind a reef, Tupaia summoned islanders to dive beneath the hull to test the depth of her keel. The 'chief' of Huahine had been rowed, 'trembling', to meet them but his anxiety vanished at the sight of Tupaia who then led the officers and gentlemen ashore. There he performed a speech or prayer, stripped to his waist and made gifts of beads and handkerchiefs. Whatever confusion the Europeans felt at this display was repaid instantly by the officers, who hammered a staff into the earth, hoisted up a Union Jack, and claimed the island for King George.

By 20 July, Tupaia had navigated them across the short passage to the place he most held dear, Opua, and Taputapuatea. Here, again, ceremonies were repeated, Tupaia offering thanks, the British taking possession with a flag. They were then at liberty to explore the *marae*. Banks detected the different aura to this site than those he had experienced in Tahiti, but the gravity he sensed did not prevent him from meddling. In his most crass moment of cultural vandalism, he jammed his hand inside one of the god-houses and tore at the wrappings, 'with my fingers till I came to a covering of mat made of platted Cocoa nut fibres which it was impossible to get through so I was obligd to desist, especialy as what I had already done gave much offence to our new freinds'.[12] There was nowhere Banks's curiosity would not lead him. But one wonders how Banks would react if a South Seas islander toured Canterbury Cathedral, prised open the lid of Thomas Becket's tomb then stirred round the bones.

Endeavour was soon back at sea. Tupaia thrived in these tricksy coastal waters, where spires of coral jutted up and reefs threatened to cut into *Endeavour*'s side. Despite all the care they almost scraped against a shoal off Opua, only veering away at the last minute. They went on to circle Ra'iātea, and at the start of August, with a leak in the powder room needing attention, Tupaia led *Endeavour* into a commodious bay on Ra'iātea's western shore. 'We have now a very good opinion of Tupias pilotage', Banks confirmed in his journal.[13]

For some days they lay at anchor at Hamanimo Bay, where they were 'very agreably entertaind'. This was Tupaia's home and his return was marked with feasting and dancing. For Tupaia the last weeks must have been the most thrilling and disorientating of his life. He was an *arioi* touring Tōtaiete mā, following old sea paths, performing ceremonies, meeting and dancing and eating in familiar island settings. Only this time he was not commanding the ceremonial canoes or *pahi*, but something far bigger. During these heady weeks in 1769 *Endeavour*, now five years old, was at her most magnificent. She was a hybrid of astonishing parts. A Whitby coal collier, converted into a Royal Navy exploration vessel, was sailing in the South Seas under the direction of an *arioi* according to a lore and method alien to all of her officers.

Cook had worried about Tupaia joining the crew from the start. He had discussed the idea with Banks before they left Tahiti. Cook argued that the British government 'will never in all human probability' provide financially for Tupaia. Banks had countered Cook's argument, admitting Tupaia into his suite – Buchan's death had freed a cabin – and resolving to support him when they reached home. Mollified, Cook had retreated to his journal to rationalise the decision, Tupaia being 'a very intelligent person' who knew 'more of the Geography of the Islands situated in these seas, their produce and the religion laws and customs of the inhabitants then any one we had met with and was the likeliest person to answer our purpose'.[14]

Before *Endeavour* sailed, consideration had been given to how they should behave towards the peoples they met. Dalrymple had been resolute that no 'accession to the British Empire' be made by 'fraud or violence', and perspectives had long changed since John Cabot had sailed the first English ship to the Indies with instructions 'to attract on board all the natives of foreign lands, and to intoxicate them with beer and wine, so as to grow acquainted with the secrets of their hearts'.[15] The Earl of Morton, president of the Royal Society, had composed a series of 'hints' for 'Captain Cooke, Mr Banks, Doctor Solander, and the other Gentlemen'. It began:

> To exercise the utmost patience and forbearance with respect to the Natives of the several Lands where the Ship may touch.
>
> To check the petulance of the Sailors, and restrain the wanton use of Fire Arms.
>
> To have it still in view that sheding the blood of those people is a crime of the highest nature:– They are all human creatures,

the work of the same omnipotent Author, equally under his care with the most polished European, perhaps being less offensive, more entitled to his favor.

They are the natural, and in the strictest sense of the word, the legal possessors of the several Regions they inhabit.

No European Nation has a right to occupy any part of their country, or settle among them without their voluntary consent.[16]

It was important that thought be given to interactions with indigenous peoples as, if the voyage progressed as planned, interaction was inevitable. But how to make sense of those they met? As Rousseau had pointed out, 'The most useful and the least developed of all the science seems to me to be that of man.' He, of course, argued that humans should best be understood from their social context, which put them somewhere on a scale between civilised and savage. Then, in tune with the classifying urge of the times, there were those who sought to divide humanity into races. High on his success with the botanical world, Linnaeus had proposed four 'types' of *Homo sapiens*: the white *Europaeus albus*, the yellow *Asiaticus luridus*, the black *Afer niger* and the red *Americanus rufus*. A forerunner of the nasty racial ideas of future ages, on *Endeavour* no one took any notice of Linnaeus's crass method – not even Banks or Solander. Even then they sensed humans were more awkward to divide up than plants.

There were other ambitious ideas too. One was that the two extremes of the human condition – civilisation and barbarism – were created by contrasting climatic zones, that we 'can impute freedom and slavery to the temperature of the air, can fix the meridian of vice and virtue and tell at what degree of latitude we are to expect courage or timidity, knowledge or ignorance', lampooned a sceptical Samuel Johnson. Then, in the face of all this determinism, were the arguments of the French statesman Anne Robert Jacques Turgot who suggested 'a lucky arrangement of the fibres in the brain, a greater or lesser quickness of the blood, these are probably the only differences which nature establishes among men.'[17]

As with scurvy remedies, there was plenty of conjecture, but really those aboard were left to feel their way. After their time in Tahiti all of them were familiar with the complexities inherent in encountering 'natives' or 'Indians' for the first time. No one was going to stand still to be studied. People's attitudes were bound to change depending on whether an encounter was friendly or not. But their relationship with Tupaia changed this. With him they were forced into the close confinement of shipboard life. Traits might be concealed during a fleeting visit, but it was impossible to maintain a mask for twenty-four hours a day.

As Banks's intriguing companion, Cook must have recognised the benefits Tupaia brought. Banks and Cook completed lucid, perceptive 'Manners and Customs of S. Sea Islands', much of the information of which was gleaned from Tupaia after they had sailed. But it must have been with some unease that Cook gave Tupaia the right to the great cabin. So far this had been a place of precision. There was Cook and his charts, Banks and Solander and their specimens, or Green the astronomer with his mathematical reductions. It was an inner sanctum of rationalism in a voyage sent out to measure, classify and discover. It must have come as a shock to Cook, then, to see Tupaia praying at the stern windows. Parkinson was there. He heard him call 'with much fervor: O Tane, *ara mai, matai, ora mai matai*'; Parkinson rendered this into English: 'Tane (the God of his Morai) send to me, or come to me with a fair wind'. 'His prayer proving ineffectual', Parkinson wrote, Tupaia called out '*Wooreede waow*, I am angry.'[18]

In his journal Cook passed over the incident in silence. It would have been hard to admit to such a thing in the officers' quarters of one of the king's ships. Tupaia represented everything Cook was trying to flee: opaque methods, an over-reliance on the empirical not the mathematical, the veneration of a flaunting, mystic world of spirits, rather than one of clocks, telescopes and sextants. Prayers were encouraged on *Endeavour*, but only during allotted hours on a Sunday morning. But Cook did benefit from the expertise Tupaia brought. The care Tupaia took about the reefs was not so removed from the vigilance practised on the Yorkshire coast. And in his month observing Tupaia, Cook had come to a tentative conclusion that was later admired for its foresight.

Ever since European sailors had broken into the South Seas in the sixteenth century they had been perplexed by the dispersed human populations. Without any of the Europeans' technological advantages, here in front of their eyes were navigators who seemed equally as good as them. One of de Bougainville's officers had posed the conundrum in a burst of exasperation: 'Who the devil went and placed them on a small sandbank like this one and as far from the continent as they are?'[19] Two centuries of further study were required to begin to solve the question of how islands, islets and atolls, altogether distributed across an area larger than Africa, had been populated by people with cultural, biological and linguistic ties. In 1769 Cook proposed an answer:

> these people sail in those seas from Island to Island for several hundred Leagues, the Sun serving them for a compass by day and the Moon and Stars by night. When this comes to be prov'd we Shall be no longer at a loss to know how the Islands lying in those Seas came to be people'd, for if the inhabitants of [Ra'iātea] have been at Islands laying 2 or 300 Leagues to the westward of them it cannot be doubted but that the inhabitants of those western Islands may have been at others as far to westward of them and so we may trace them from Island to Island quite to the East Indies.[20]

This is one of the earliest Western appreciations of what the writer Lincoln Paine termed 'the oldest, most sustained, and perhaps most enigmatic effort of maritime exploration and migration in the history of the world'. The Polynesians had not floundered across in the darkness, but rather they had progressed from one island to the next in a migration that had begun in South East Asia 5,000 years before. They had travelled in great canoes fitted with sails, carrying pigs, dogs and chickens, traversing almost the entire Pacific from Hawaii to New Zealand. Though the period of long-distance voyaging had lapsed by the eighteenth century, with the various peoples confined to their specific territories, tales of epic voyages continued to live on in the collective memory. Tupaia was among the heirs to the corpus of knowledge that had made the voyages possible. The key was a simple, elegant system. All of nature's signs would be studied but, figuratively and literally, above all would shine the stars. Once an island had been found and settled it would be assimilated into the Polynesian world with its location coordinated with a star in the sky. From childhood, navigators would learn the solar chart. The trick was to know which star shone above which island on a given day in the year. Banks would record his astonishment at this feat of memory, which was something hardly to be 'beleivd by an Europaean astronomer.'[21]

Later Dalrymple heard a story from Cook: Tupaia 'could shew them at all times during the course of their voyage, to *half a point* of the compass, the direction in which Otaheite lay'.[22]

The system was at once incredibly simple and enormously complex. To know it took an unusual capacity of memory. But it was not a system for all. Rather, star navigators were a select few of the very best. This was the history Cook was beginning to recognise in August 1769. In one sense this idea was utterly at odds with his instincts for technical precision. But in another way, perhaps it wasn't so different after all. On leaving London, Green had brought a copy of Maskelyne's *Nautical Almanac* with him, an innovative navigational tool that helped mariners derive longitude by tallying observations of the moon or other celestial objects. It is striking to picture Cook and Green taking lunar readings on one of those dazzling Pacific nights. Beside them Tupaia was gazing upward too.

Cook had acquiesced to a tour of the Society Islands. The transit observations had been completed and there was no need to hurry. *Endeavour* and her crew were in tolerable health and, having fulfilled his first objectives, Cook wanted to see what Samuel Wallis had not. It was roughly two years since the *Dolphin* had left these waters. She had been in as trim a state as *Endeavour*. But for Wallis and a few lieutenants, 'all the rest of our Ships Company was mutch healthyer [than] the day we left Plymouth', wrote the *Dolphin*'s master, George Robertson. 'The Ship was light', he went on, 'Sails and Rigging all in good Order', so he was bemused at Wallis's order to steer to westward. The 'princaple Officers wanted to go post home', he explained, 'for the recovery of their health, and to receive the reward of their Merit and good Luck in finding out a Country'.[23]

Wallis's decision had irritated Robertson, who thought a southern continent stood just to the south. Cook had been told as much. On leaving Tahiti he turned to the second part of his orders:

You are to proceed to the southward in order to make discovery of the Continent above-mentioned until you arrive in the Latitude of 40°, unless you sooner fall in with it. But not having discover'd it, or any Evident signs of it in that Run, you are to proceed in search of it to the Westward between the Latitude before mentioned and the Latitude of 35° until you discover it, or fall in with the Eastern side of the Land discover'd by Tasman and now called New Zeland.[24]

Cook was about to plunge into a part of the world few had visited. Here, directly to the south of the Society Islands, midway across the South Seas, was the heart of the region Dalrymple had outlined as the space for a southern continent. Cook, in all probability, was sceptical already. Tupaia had been quizzed about 'a Continent or large track of land', but had no knowledge of one. Getting no aid from that quarter, Cook had been left to run his eye over his instructions again. They mentioned one place that Europeans knew to exist in the lower regions of the South Seas: New Zealand.

In a chart full of enigmas, New Zealand was yet another. It existed only as a single curved line adrift in the higher latitudes of the South Seas. Its coastline seemed to run broadly from north to south and it had a kink in the middle, a sign to an inquisitive mind like Cook's of a possible strait or river. These tenuous details were the fruits of Abel Tasman's well-known seventeenth-century voyage. In the 1640s Tasman was in the service of the Dutch East India Company and he was sent to probe the Indian Ocean and South Seas for signs of a continent. Sailing east from Mauritius, he skirted past one land mass he named Van Diemen's Land and, on 13 December 1642, after months on a boisterous ocean of 'huge billows and swells', his ships neared a coastline. They skimmed along it, coming to anchor in a bay. The story of what happened next was well enough known. Tasman was greeted by people who were 'rough, uncivilised, full of verve', paddling in canoes. Attempting to establish communication, some of his men were ambushed. Four sailors were clubbed to death and, within a day, Tasman hurried away, leaving behind nothing more than a name: 'Murderers Bay'. Tasman followed the coast northward until it vanished behind a cape and he rejoined the open ocean.

No Europeans had returned to this place, 'Zeelandia Nova', since, and the Dutch East India Company had suppressed Tasman's journal to conceal news of the discovery. But reports had seeped out, adding one more faint line onto the confused cartography of the South Seas. Dalrymple had interpreted New Zealand as the western coastline of the southern continent, and it remained as Cook's only sound point of reference, far to the south-west of the Society Islands. First, though,

Cook took *Endeavour* south. Soon the sea lost its lustre, the waves rode higher and a chill returned to the air.

Having dropped to the prescribed latitude of 40°S by 1 September they reached a zone of 'great seas', high handsome waves with a long, languid fetch. There was no trace of land. If their hunt for Terra Australis seemed futile to the officers, it must have seemed all the worse for Tupaia who by now had succumbed to 'a distemper' and pains in the stomach. It was not only Tupaia's body that had suffered, but also his standing aboard. One of Cook's later sailors attested that Tupaia:

> was a man of real genius, a priest of the first order, and an excellent artist; he was, however, by no means beloved by the *Endeavour*'s crew, being looked upon as proud and austere, extorting homage, which the sailors who thought themselves degraded by bending to an Indian, were very unwilling to pay, and preferring complaints against them on the most trivial occasions.[25]

Having progressed far enough to the south, Cook now took *Endeavour* westwards, tracing a line along the thirty-eighth parallel where New Zealand was said to lie. To sharpen eyes, he 'promised one gallon of rum to the man who should first discover it by day and two if he should discover it by night'. September turned into October and there was a noticeable alteration in the colour of the water. A pair of sleeping seals were spotted. Then some small birds 'which Mr Gore calls Port Egmont hens' were seen. After many weeks of sailing, these had a jollifying effect on Banks. On 3 October he sketched a merry portrait:

> Now do I wish that our freinds in England could by the assistance of some magical spying glass take a peep at our situation: Dr Solander setts at the Cabbin table describing, myself at my Bureau Journalizing, between us hangs a large bunch of sea weed, upon the table lays the wood and barnacles; they would see that notwithstanding our different occupations our lips move very often, and without being conjurors might guess that we were talking about what we should see upon the land which there is now no doubt we shall see very soon.[26]

On the afternoon of 8 October, Cook took *Endeavour* into a three-mile-wide bay that cut into the landscape in a perfect semicircle. Passing the bluff, chalky headland at the southern tip of the bay, Cook could be forgiven a fleeting memory of Flamborough Head thousands of leagues and half a turn of a globe away on the North Yorkshire coast, with its gannets and puffins, razorbills and guillemots. He could have no idea what wildlife might exist here. There had been a 'difference of opinion and many conjectures about Islands', wrote Banks, 'rivers, inlets &c, but all hands seem to agree that this is certainly the Continent we are in search of'.[27] Cook, more careful than excitable, knew that in all likelihood this was the eastern edge of New Zealand. Being in need of water and provisions, he stood in. As *Endeavour* neared shore several canoes pulled out, crossing their path. Parkinson saw more people, 'seemingly observing us'. At about four o'clock in the afternoon, *Endeavour* dropped anchor at the mouth of a small river.

Cook and his party were rowed ashore, landing on the north lip of the river. It was then Cook saw 'some of the natives', on the opposite bank. Striving to speak with them but finding the water impossible to ford, he called for the yawl – a boat with two pairs of oars – to ferry them over while the pinnace – the larger of the boats – stayed guarding the entrance. Among Cook's party was the ship's surgeon, William Monkhouse, a Cumberland man. He kept a careful account of what happened next. Seeing the yawl approach the people 'made off'. Free to examine the shoreline, Monkhouse, with Banks, Solander and Cook, pried into some reed huts 'of the wigwam construction' and sifted the contents. Inside were the remains of a fishing net, a grass dress, a pile of burnt sticks. Outside limpet and lobster shells were scattered about. Monkhouse and the others were 'thus amused' when 'we were suddenly alarmed with the firing of a musket'.[28]

They hurried back to a dismal scene. The boys left guarding the yawl had been surprised by an ambush, launched by 'four of the Natives'. Armed with lances, they had approached the boys. Noticing the attack, the coxswain had fired a musket in the air, 'which our friends paid no other reguard to than brandishing their weapons'. A second shot had then been fired. This had no effect. The coxswain had 'then levelled at the headmost of the party and shot him'. His friends had 'instantly' fallen back. A moment later they had returned and had carried his body fifty yards, but 'now finding him dead' had left him 'and retired tho' in no kind of haste'. Monkhouse examined the body. 'He was a short, but very stout bodied man – measured about 5 f 3 I', he wrote. He had three arched tattoos over his left eye and 'spirals of tattaou' on his right cheek and nose. 'The ball had passed from the sixth rib on the left side thro' the right shoulder blade. Some nails and beads were put upon the body, and we took our leave from the shore.'[29]

Back aboard, Monkhouse could hear 'a loud clamour of voices', and Cook ordered a 'strict watch to be kept all the night'. Parkinson looked out towards the beach, too, where a large 'clamorous' meeting was being held, a sight that left him uneasy.

The dead man was Te Maro of the Ngati Rakai hapu. Te Maro had lived in a bay the Māori called Tūranganui-a-Kiwa where the Tūranganui River reached the sea. This was a special place. Traditions hold that, centuries before, it was the landing place of the *Horouta waka*, one of the great ocean-going canoes of the early migrations. The *Horouta* is known for bringing dried *kūmara* (sweet potato) to Aotearoa (New Zealand) from the ancestral homelands at Hawaiki* and, in turn, it brought the first inhabitants to the east coast.

A story is told about the voyage of the *Horouta* to Tūranganui-a-Kiwa. The *waka* set out from Ahauhu (Great Mercury Island) after a dispute over the ownership of some trees. On its way along the north coast, the *Horouta* collided with a sandbar or a sunken rock and capsized. Its *haumi* or headpiece was ripped off and some of the cargo had to be retrieved from the sea floor. Unable to carry everyone, a man called Kiwa was made the commander of a skeleton crew and told to continue to the east coast. Others progressed overland. Kiwa then brought the *Horouta* to the Tūranganui River, where he decided to wait for the overland party to join them. 'To commemorate this decision, Kiwa gave the title Tūranganui-a-Kiwa (the rendezvous selected by Kiwa) to the neighbouring land, sea, streams.'[30]

---

*   'Hawaiki is the traditional Māori place of origin. The first Māori are said to have sailed to New Zealand from Hawaiki. And in Māori mythology Hawaiki is the place where Io, the supreme being, created the world and its first people. It is the place from which each person comes, and it is where each will return after death.' (*Te Ara: Encyclopedia of New Zealand*)

In October 1769, *Endeavour* approached the same landing site. Visiting the area two generations later, an English traveller called Joel Polack recorded various stories connected to *Endeavour*'s arrival. One stated that she was initially taken for a bird, 'and that many remarks passed among the people as to the beauty and the size of its wings'. Watching the long boat, yawl and the pinnace being lowered was like seeing small birds 'unfledged'. Another account described the ship as a floating island. A third suggested it was a 'houseful of divinities'. The astonishment of the people, Polack wrote:

> on seeing Cook's ship was so great that they were benumbed with fear, but presently, recollecting themselves, they felt determined to find out if the gods (as the newcomers were thought to be) were as pugnacious as themselves ... Many of the natives observed that they felt themselves taken ill by only being particularly looked upon by these atuas (gods) and it was, therefore, agreed that, as these newcomers could bewitch by a simple look, the sooner their society was dismissed the better it would be for the general welfare.[31]

In Tahiti *Endeavour*'s safety had been guaranteed by the violence of the *Dolphin*'s visit. None of that power was known here. There were no terms of reference, no traditions of friendship. They had been in the bay just two hours yet already they had contravened the first two rules the Earl of Morton had set down in his 'hints': 'To exercise the utmost patience and forbearance with respect to the Natives of the several Lands where the Ship may touch', and 'To check the petulance of the Sailors, and restrain the wanton use of Fire-Arms.'

Looking through his glass at dawn the following morning, Banks saw 'but few people' on the beach. Those he could make out were walking towards the river where they had landed the previous day, though most of them seemed unarmed, just '3 or 4 with long Pikes in their hands'. Cook disagreed, recording 'a good number' in his journal. He ordered all the boats – longboat, yawl and pinnace – to be filled with seamen and marines. They were to go and 'try to establish a communication with them'. Their task was made difficult by a short, lively sea and a high surf. They eventually weathered this and landed again at the river mouth. Banks was there, as always, and

Solander. And Cook had brought Tupaia too. 'The moment the first party landed', Monkhouse wrote, the Māori 'formed into a close body upon the bank of the river', and 'set up a war dance'. This was the first *haka* ever witnessed by a British crew. Gore described it:

> About an hundred of the Natives all Arm'd came down on the opposite side of the Salt River, drew themselves up in lines. Then with a Regular Jump from Left to Right and the Reverse, They brandish'd Their Weapons, distort'd their Mouths, Lolling out their Tongues and Turn'd up the Whites of their Eyes Accompanied with a strong hoarse song. Calculated in my opinion to Chear Each Other and Intimidate their Enemies, and may be call'd perhaps with propriety A Dancing War Song. It lasted 3 or 4 minutes.[32]

Cook attempted to shout across in 'the George Island Language'. They replied by 'flourishing their weapons over their heads and danceing'. He next ordered the marines to file up 200 yards behind so they commanded the scene. Then an entirely unanticipated thing occurred. Tupaia, so far a quiet presence, called over 'in his own language'. It was, Cook reported, 'an [a]greeable surprise to us to find that they perfectly understood him'. An extraordinary conversation followed. On one side of the river stood the Māori, on the other the British. Between them was Tupaia: a man who belonged to neither country, or knew much of either of the cultures he was trying to bridge.

Banks, who must have elicited the content of their conversations later, wrote how Tupaia 'immediately began to tell them that we wanted provisions and water for which we would give them Iron in exchange'. The Māori agreed to this, but refused to 'lay by' their arms, something Tupaia 'lookd upon as a sign of treachery and continualy told us to be upon our guard for they were not our freinds'. Cook also recorded his warning, that 'they were not our friends'. But the conversation did ease tensions. Monkhouse noticed how Tupaia 'at length prevailed on one of them to strip of his covering and swim across'.[33] This man came to a rock 'surrounded by the tide' and beckoned for the officers to approach. Cook responded. He gave away his musket 'to put himself on a footing' and managed to meet the man at the river's edge.

The brief encounter that ensued between Cook and the unknown Māori man was one of true historical significance. Not only was this the first formal greeting between the Europeans and Māori, it happened at a place infused with cultural and historical meaning. The rock was named Te Toka-a-Taiau. Oral histories later explained that it was connected with a man called Maia, one of the earliest migrants from Hawaiki. In these distant days, Maia used frequently to ford the Tūranganui River here. One day when he was crossing he encountered a young girl called Taiau. He beckoned for her to cross and meet him. Taiau obeyed Maia. But when she approached he drowned her and transformed her body into the treasured rock which bore her name. In the centuries since, Te Toka-a-Taiau had marked tribal boundaries. It had acted as a spiritual gathering place, as a favoured location for mooring *waka* and fishing. On 9 October 1769, James Cook and this unknown Māori man met at Te Toka-a-Taiau. Monkhouse watched as they 'saluted by touching noses'.

It was now the Europeans' turn to lose their terms of reference. A handshake between friends, a tip of a hat to a superior, a bow to the great and worthy; their own culture was embroidered with its own coded intricacies. But this greeting was entirely new. This *hongi* – the traditional Māori greeting when two breaths are joined into one bond of friendship – undertaken in front of such a gathering of people, is an iconic first encounter. For a fleeting moment it joined two cultures in parity and goodwill. It broke the tension. 'A few trinkets put our friend into high spirits', Monkhouse wrote, and soon he was followed by '20 or 30 more.' The first man had dropped his weapons; those who followed did not. Presents were exchanged: iron and beads, though 'they seemd to set little value upon either', Banks wrote. Instead what appealed were the swords, hatchets and firearms, which were grabbed at. 'We were upon our guard so much that their attempts faild and they were made to understand that we must kill them if they snatched any thing from us'.

Not all of the ship's company were as vigilant. In particular Monkhouse had an eye on Green, the astronomer, who was being 'much teased' by the people who 'expressed a desire' to have his hanger – or hunting sword. As Green backed away from the melee, a man seized his chance, laying hold of the sword, tearing it from his belt and immediately making away with his prize. Events now happened apace. Green, furious, 'snapt his musket' while Banks 'pronounced

aloud' his opinion 'that so daring an act should be instantly punishd'.
A roar was put up. Banks fired a volley of small shot into the man's
back. It had no effect. The man 'ceasd his cry but instead of quitting
his prize continued to wave it over his head retreating as gently as
before'. Monkhouse, even closer to the incident than Banks, then fired
a ball at the man, 'at which he dropt'.[34]

As Monkhouse wrote later, 'matters were now in great confusion'.
The Māori were flying across the river. Two stayed behind and tried
to rescue a treasured object from the body. 'Some of our party unacquainted with the true state of things', the surgeon wrote, 'begun to
fire upon them by which two or three were wounded.' The last of
the guns Banks saw fire was aimed by Tupaia, a burst of shot which
he 'clearly saw strike two men low down upon their legs'. The Māori,
wrote Monkhouse, 'now set up a most lamentable noise and retired
slowly along the beach'.

> The Shot man had a human tooth hanging at one ear and a
> girdle of Matting about four inches broad was passed twice round
> his loins & tied. He had a paddle in his hand which, tho' drawing
> his last breath, he would not part with without the greatest
> reluctance.[35]

It was a calamitous end to a fraught meeting. To add a trivial disappointment to the personal tragedies, the ship's company were not able
to collect any water from the river, finding it brackish. In exasperation,
Cook reboarded the pinnace with Banks, Solander and Tupaia, and
they pushed off, aiming to skirt the bay to the south and round the
headland in search of water. Cook also devised what Molyneux called
'a generous christianlike Plan', to surprise some of the Māori, 'take
them on board and by good treatment and presents endeavour to gain
their friendship'. Approaching the headland, Cook saw his chance. A
fishing canoe was standing in towards them. It was returning from a
trip to sea. Behind it followed a second.

Thinking this the best time to spring his plan, Cook ordered the
pinnace brought up, abreast of the canoes. He did not anticipate
trouble. As fishermen they 'probably were without arms', reasoned
Banks, and they were drawn up 'in such a manner that they could
not well escape us.' The pinnace neared the canoes. As they
approached, the first spotted them and 'made immediately for the

nearest land'. The second, though, continued as before. Almost alongside, Tupaia called over the water, to tell the fishermen they would
not be hurt. Instead of submitting, the canoe struck sail and 'began
to paddle so briskly', Banks wrote, 'that she outran our boat'. Cook
ordered a musket to be fired over the canoe. But rather than stop-
ping, the fishermen ceased paddling and all seven of them began to
strip their clothes. Banks thought they were poised to jump into the
water, to make for shore. As soon as the pinnace ran alongside, they
began to attack.

The fishermen fought desperately. They threw 'Pikes or Spears from
18 to 10 feet long', 'and Fought as long as ever they had things to
Throw', even 'a Parcel of Fish which they had in the Canoe they
flung'.[36] Those in the pinnace retaliated with gunfire. Cook estimated
in his journal that 'two or three' were killed, while Banks set the
number at four. Three other boys had leapt overboard, one swimming
'with great agility' towards the shore, 'and when taken made every
effort in his power to prevent being taken into the boat, the other two
were more easily prevaild upon'.[37]

The boys were carried to *Endeavour*, where they cowered on the
deck, anticipating death. An order was given for them to be clothed
and 'treated with all imaginable kindness', and both Cook and Banks
observed an immediate shift in their moods, they becoming 'as cheerful
and as merry as if they had been with their own friends'. They were
young boys, the eldest about twenty, the youngest ten or twelve.
Retiring to his cabin after the miseries of the day, Cook retreated to
his journal in self-reproach:

I am aware that most humane men who have not experienced
things of this nature will cencure my conduct in fireing upon
the people in this boat nor do I my self think that the reason I
had for seizing upon her will att all justify me, and had I thought
that they would have made the least resistance I would not have
come near them, but as they did I was not to stand still and
suffer either my self or those that were with me to be knocked
on the head.[38]

Banks, too, was disturbed. He was with the boys at sunset as they
continued to eat vast quantities of food, relishing the salt pork above
all else. Banks seems to have helped in the making of beds 'upon the

lockers', a rare concession to domesticity for him. Then, with angry voices audible from the shore, he retired to his cabin. There survives a coastal profile of this bay, drawn for Banks. Onto it Banks inserted a numeric key, each number relating to one of the day's incidents. He mapped out the fatal progression of events as a twenty-first-century detective might depict a crime scene. He finished the day's journal entry, 'Thus ended the most disagreeable day My life has yet seen, black be the mark for it and heaven send that such may never return to embitter future reflection.'[39]

Both Cook and Banks are betrayed by their journal entries. That Cook errs into approximation, with 'two or three' deaths, rather than Banks's unambiguous 'four' is revealing. Either he found it traumatic to reduce the calamity into precision, or by diminishing the numbers he was trying to absolve his guilt. But for a man with a mania for accuracy, the lapse is telling. Cook would not brook such an approximation for a longitude, yet at this moment he cannot bring himself to count to four. Banks's entry, meanwhile, is more precise, though one wonders whether it is entirely candid. Banks was not one to dwell. He dispelled unpleasant thoughts, as if by doing so he stops them from manifesting into melancholy. Even on this, of all days, he managed to record a snippet of natural history. But as with Cook there was a fact Banks shied away from committing to paper. As Parkinson detailed it in his journal, Banks was among those who fired. The 'black mark' he allocated to the day, therefore, perhaps, carries a personal as well as a general meaning. It stands against the date he first killed a fellow person.

As night fell, Banks heard the boys 'sighing often and loud', from their beds. 'Tupaia', though, Banks added, 'was always upon the watch to comfort them' and he 'soon made them easy'. Banks listened as they all sang a song. 'It was not without some taste, like a Psalm tune and containd many notes and semitones; they sung it in parts which gives us no indifferent Idea of their taste as well as skill in musick.'[40]

Cook sailed from the bay on 11 October, returning the boys to the shore as soon as he could. *Endeavour* had lain at anchor for two days and fourteen hours. In all that time they had failed every bit as much as Tasman had to secure provisions or forge any meaningful relationship with the people. Botanically speaking, the bay had yielded little to excite Banks and Solander, but this seemed insignificant when they dwelt on the lives lost. Cook had formed an ill view of this place, which, he ruminated, offered no fresh water and stood open to the east winds. Originally he had planned to designate it 'Endeavour Bay', a name he had jotted in his journal. But on almost instant reflection he changed his mind, blotting 'Endeavour' out and amending it to 'Poverty Bay', 'because it afforded us no one thing we wanted'.[41]

Leaving the bay, Cook exchanged fraught diplomacy for something he knew far better. For the first time on the voyage he was faced with the prospect of surveying an unknown shoreline. Now he could do what he had done so well in Newfoundland: sail, watch, measure and map until, by degrees, a frail line would develop into something more intricate. Looking at Cook's charts today they have a visual austerity. There are no embellishments, no splashes of colour or jaunty, illustrative waves. Instead all his attention was concentrated into accurately depicting the run of the coastline. Rounding the headline at the bottom of Poverty Bay, Cook followed the land as it trended south. Soon he was in another bay, this time a wider, more elegant one, ten times the dimensions of that he had just left. Skimming the shoreline with a sounding lead, he kept his eyes open for rivers, gulfs, havens, estuaries and headlands, each day the line getting a little longer.

In October 1769 Cook embarked on a survey that occupied him for the next six months. As pencil lines replaced the open sea, he began to confer an identity on the places he mapped to make them memorable. Sometimes names were taken from the transient events of daily life. 'Cape Kidnappers', a little to the south of Poverty Bay, marked a headland where Tupaia's servant Taiato was briefly abducted by a passing canoe. A little further south than this was 'Cape Turnagain', where Cook opted to halt *Endeavour*'s drive towards the south and double back towards Poverty Bay. Later there was 'Cape Runaway', named after a brief skirmish with a Māori canoe, and 'Mercury Bay', where they paused to observe a transit of the planet Mercury. Other names – Table Cape, White Island, the Bay of Islands, Dusky Bay, Gannett Isle or the Snowy Mountains – had more straightforward origins. Then there were the transplanted names from Britain. Perhaps it felt appropriate to foist an Isle of Portland, a River Thames and an Admiralty Bay onto this green and pleasant coastline they looked at, something in its geography feeling intrinsically 'British'. Spying 'a cluster of Islands & rocks' that spired out of the sea, Banks wrote playfully:

208   ENDEAVOUR

we calld [them] the Court of Aldermen in respect to that worthy
body and entertaind ourselves some time with giving names to
each of them from their resemblance, thick & squat or lank and
tall to some one or other of those respectable citizens.[42]

Perhaps the joke was also a play on the alderman's ponderous
docility, or inflexibility. Less cryptic were the slew of headlands, bays
and islands named for various worthies or members of the crew, for
Cook was able to play God over the geographical world as Linnaeus
had over the botanical one. Nicholas Young, the boy who had first
spotted land on 6 October, was rewarded with Young Nick's Head.*
Ten years after the Battle of Quiberon Bay, Admiral Hawke was
recognised in Hawke's Bay, the elegant bay south of Poverty Bay.
Others bays were named for the second and third lieutenants, Hicks
and Gore, while Cook also remembered his mentor, Hugh Palliser,
and the Admiralty secretary, Philip Stephens, with capes. This whole
process of renaming land roused Dalrymple's ire back home. He
derided the habit a 'ridiculous affectation', 'giving new names to places
before known is inexcusable, as it introduces perplexity and confusion
instead of elucidating the Geography of those parts; the custom of
giving the *native* names is highly commendable'.[43]

From October into the new year, 1770, Cook hugged the coastline.
Progressing in an anticlockwise direction he revealed an island as
sprawled and jagged and vividly coloured as one of Banks's jellyfish.
Fierce storms chased them, but when the weather broke the *Endeavour*'s
crew were treated to captivating views. Intersecting Tasman's path as
they rounded the north cape and turned south again, they saw a vast
mountain. 'How high it may be I do not take upon me to judge',
Banks wrote, 'but it is certainly the noblest hill I have ever seen.' This
– named Mount Egmont for the erstwhile First Lord – seemed a lone
giant when compared with what was to come. Having completed
their circuit of the northern island they plunged into even higher
latitudes, passing shorelines with 'a most romantick appearance from
the immence steepness of the hills', many of which were capped with
everlasting snow.[44]

---

*   Young Nick's Head is therefore often cited as the first New Zealand land
sighted from *Endeavour*. Recent research suggests that Nicholas Young
more likely glimpsed the peak of Arowhana Mountain on 6 October.

All this time Cook was achieving the geographical clarity he sought. When they had first sighted land back in October there was some hope that it might comprise some part of a southern continent. Perhaps New Zealand was an outreached arm, or something of the sort. Banks had enthusiastically adopted this viewpoint, proclaiming himself part of the 'Continent party' in opposition to Cook's saturnine 'No Continents'. Cook was proved right. As *Endeavour* rounded the cape at the bottom of the southern island, it was clear to everyone that New Zealand comprised two secluded islands. In his journal, Banks was forced to concede 'the total demolition of our aerial fabrick calld continent'.[45] A century later, the Victorian hydrographer William Wharton wrote that:

> the astonishing accuracy of his outline of New Zealand must be the admiration of all who understand the difficulties of laying down a coast; and when it is considered that this coastline is 2,400 miles in extent, the magnitude of the task will be realised by everybody. Never has a coast been so well laid down by a first explorer, and it must have required unceasing vigilance and continual observation, in fair weather and foul, to arrive at such a satisfactory conclusion; and with such a dull sailer as the *Endeavour* was, the six and a half months occupied in the work must be counted as a short interval in which to do it.[46]

Wharton's appraisal of Cook is justified, though his derision of *Endeavour* is hardly merited. Few frigates or sloops could weather what Fishburn's collier did over these months. Tough and flat-bottomed, *Endeavour* was sailing in just the environment she was designed to withstand.

If Cook's mastery of his surroundings was one exceptional thing about *Endeavour*'s circumnavigation, then Tupaia's presence was another. After the incident at Poverty Bay, he acted as *Endeavour*'s interpreter and chief diplomat. Easing relations, he made it possible for them to trade in mussels and lobsters with the coasting fishermen. He was alive to danger too. One day, when *Endeavour* was approached by war canoes, he hurried 'immediately' to the deck, 'and talkd to them a good deal, telling them what if they provokd us we should do and how easily we could in a moment destroy them all'. His cautions not being heeded, he said something that struck Banks:

Well, said Tupia, but while we are at sea you have no manner
of Business with us, the Sea is our property as much as yours.
Such reasoning from an Indian who had not had the smallest
hint from any of us surprizd me much and the more as these
were sentiments I never had before heard him give a hint about
in his own case.[47]

Wherever they went they would hear Tupaia's name called out.
Banks marvelled at this, 'we never suspected him to have had so much
influence'. As they travelled, Cook and Banks learned to respect the
qualities of the Māori they encountered. They saw an intricate society;
strong, active people who were generally honest, and zealous in
defence of their own. Only the disquieting possibility of cannibalism
– something they at length found evidence of – really troubled them.
But their interactions with the Māori would have been far less vibrant
had Tupaia not been permitted aboard. Beyond his quarterdeck diplomacy, on several occasions he drifted ashore, interacting with the
Māori, discussing the ship, their shared homeland and the purpose of
their visit. The most significant of these interactions came at Tolaga
Bay, a little distance north of Poverty Bay on the North Island.

Tolaga Bay was one of the great centres of Māori culture and
learning, a community not only renowned for its carvings but also
as a spiritual centre. Here Tupaia had 'much conversation' with one
of the priests. Banks wrote how the two 'seemd to agree very well
in their notions of religion only Tupia was much more learned than
the other and all his discourse was heard with much attention'. It is
difficult to underplay the gravity of what must have passed between
them. Memories of Tupaia's and the priest's shared ancestors were
only kept alive in song and story. But here the Polynesian heritage
was joined again, with the two of them left to reconcile the reality
of what Banks called 'This Universe and its marvelous parts.' Tupaia
'seemd to be much better vers'd in such legends', Banks observed,
'than any of them, for whenever he began to preach as we calld it
he was sure of a numerous audience who attended with most
profound silence to his doctrines'.[48]

Touring the district Banks came across 'an extraordinary natural
curiosity', a great arch or cavern that guided a walker directly to the
sea. 'It was certainly the most magnificent surprize I have ever met
with', Banks wrote. Near this arch was a cavern, in which Tupaia was

said to have slept at night. Two generations later, when Joel Polack visited this cave, he saw a painting 'evidently faded by time'. It was 'a representation of a ship and some boats, which was unanimously pointed out to me by all present as the reproductions of the faithful follower of Cook – Tupaea'.

Tupaia became a local favourite. When Cook visited again in later years, he was crowded with questioners, asking for news of Tupaia. When they heard he was not among them, they performed 'a kind of dirge-like melancholy song' in his memory.[49]

During his hydrographical tour of New Zealand, Cook found a place he liked better than any other. It lay at the very northern tip of the South Island, where the landscape fractured into scores of bays, coves and inlets that provided shelter from the winds and currents of the nearby strait. It was a green, fresh, lively place. In the morning, tunnels of gauzy light angled over the triangular tops of the surrounding hills, giving life to the shallows where shellfish abounded. Nearby were deeper channels where dolphins, porpoises and orca could be seen. Cook first visited this anchorage he called Ship's Cove in January 1770. The beauty of the view was matched by a melodious soundscape. Bellbirds, tui, kākā and kokako chattered in the beeches that lined the hills, singing their convivial songs. Banks declared it 'certainly the most melodious wild musick I have ever heard, almost imitating small bells but with the most tuneable silver sound imaginable.'[50]

It was to this region that Cook returned at the end of March with his circumnavigation complete. The inlet was a short distance from Ship's Cove and Cook named it Admiralty Bay. The name was suggestive. Cook was thinking of home again. They had so much to report back: the transit observations, the charts of the Society Islands and New Zealand, and all of Banks's treasures. Cook's 'most wished' route was to return across the South Seas in the high latitudes, to check again for the continent. Whether the masts and sails were up to such a crossing, though, was doubtful. And if they couldn't get across the Pacific at high latitudes, then they could neither sail around the Indian Ocean in the opposite direction.

There was a third option. Cook carried with him a chart of the southern hemisphere that included Tasman's discoveries. Along with New Zealand it also showed Van Diemen's Land, which seemed joined to the speculative land mass called 'New Holland'. In 1770 there remained confusion over what 'New Holland' actually was. What knowledge there was came primarily from Dutch merchants, who had sighted – and sometimes collided with – its western and northern edges as they sailed through the Indian Ocean, towards their trading hubs in the East Indies. Over the years sightings had accumulated. By the mid-eighteenth century they had come to show, in outline, a potentially huge land mass. Lying to the west rather than the east of New Zealand, it existed in quite a different place to Dalrymple's southern continent. But if Cook found Van Diemen's Land, he could sail up the unknown, eastern edge of New Holland, and then follow that northwards all the way to Batavia and the Dutch East Indies.

This was the plan that Cook constructed in the gentle surroundings of Admiralty Bay. With the hills rising up in jade-green triangles behind him, the air filled with the morning concerts of their 'musical neighbours', it must have seemed that the worst of their hardships – the Cape, the South Seas, the beating storms and wicked waves of New Zealand – were left behind them. There was no need to return to the high latitudes at all. And yet the central drama of the voyage, and of Endeavour's life, lay ahead in the place Europeans came to call Australia.

9

'That rainbow serpent place'

Cook had always sought out paths. From his boyhood on the wet slopes of Cleveland he knew the emotional tug of uncharted terrain. For Thomas Pierson, a poet of Cook's time, the moors were a 'sterile' and 'shaken' land, 'whence fall unnumbered streams'. To climb from the grassy lowlands onto the moors was to pass into the 'impervious glens', where 'weeds, wild fern, coarse brakes, black heath, and moss' carpeted the earth from the conical hill called Roseberry Topping in a 'pathless desert' all the way to Whitby.[1]

A keen eye could pick out the pony or foot tracks on a good day, but when the clouds swept over the moorlands the landscape became indistinct and perilous. Cook had many great voyages, but the earliest of them were his treks over these swelling hills, not the rolling seas. In the time of Cook's apprenticeship, the moors were an obstacle he had to master. One can imagine him – long-limbed and footloose – striking out from Ayton to Whitby in the January snows, wrapped in a borrowed greatcoat, with no one for company but the hen harriers in the skies above. Or, again, tramping home at the end of the sailing season in autumn, mazing through the bronze bracken, purple heather and burnished gorse, testing the terrain with a wary foot or tracing the contours of a hill.

Had Cook not left home he would, no doubt, have made a tolerable moorland guide. But Cook had left to encounter new geographies and establish new paths. As one of his midshipmen later observed, 'Action was life to him & repose a sort of death.'[2] For a decade and a half Cook had been finding his paths. He had guided the British fleet along the rock-strewn St Lawrence River in Canada. He had negotiated the treacherous coastlines of Newfoundland and Labrador. And now with *Endeavour* he had found his most dramatic paths yet: through the Strait of Le Maire and past Cape Horn, to Tahiti and the

Society Islands, to Tasman's New Zealand and all the way around both its land masses.

New Zealand was as far as the Admiralty's ambitions had extended. They had mentioned no new island or coast after it. To find New Zealand would have been impressive enough. They may have counted themselves lucky if such an untried commander as Cook had managed to find his way past Cape Horn and kept his crew content for long enough for them to locate George's Island and observe the Transit of Venus. They needn't have worried. Once again Cook found his way, and his curiosity was not yet sated. As those at the Admiralty came to recognise, one of Cook's best qualities was his resourcefulness. He was never one to let an opportunity slip and now he turned his attention to New Holland, a place that even those at the Admiralty had not felt fit to mention. And yet here in front of *Endeavour*, in April 1770, a new coastline rose out of the sea. It was one that had never appeared on a European chart before.

Understanding Cook's deep character has always posed a challenge for his biographers. To some he remains as fathomless as the Pacific. But it is in fleeting moments like this – catching the first glimpse of a coast – that the opacity sometimes fades and he admits 'small satisfactions'. Reading his accounts of these moments you can almost detect, if not quite see, a transient gleam in his eye or smile on his face. Perhaps it's the same emotional pang he may have felt fording a moorland river decades before, or the feeling he carried home having established a better way of traversing a dale. Now, though, his paths had taken him further than he could ever have imagined. Zealous in his cartography, Cook would have noticed that at Poverty Bay he had been almost exactly at the opposite side of the globe to Valencia in Spain. Rounding the South Cape of the South Island of New Zealand, they had been just a short distance from London's counterpoint, Mile End and his family. There were few places further to go. As Cook recorded in a rare candid statement, some years later: 'I who had Ambition not only to go farther than any one had done before, but as far as it was possible for man to go.'[3]

Reflections like these were put aside in April 1770. Before him was a new coastline to explore. As *Endeavour* cruised northwards at a steady four knots, the sun shone brightly over the landscape. Through his telescope he looked over a land 'which had a very agreeable and promising Aspect'. The land behind the line of the coast was 'diversified with hills, ridges, planes and Vallies with some few small lawns, but for the most part the whole was cover'd with wood'.[4] Cook brought *Endeavour* close to the shore. They came so near as 'to distinguish several people upon the Sea beach'. As he and all ninety or so of his shipmates stared towards them, the people on the beach looked back.

There is an intensity to *Endeavour*'s gaze: the sailors, divided into their watches, studying the skies and the sea; Green the astronomer and Tupaia, looking at the moon and stars; the botanists scanning the surrounding water for signs of life. Their watching is intensified by technologies like eye glasses or telescopes. So penetrating does their gaze seem, it's easy to think the attention travels in one direction. This overlooks a central truth. At many times during *Endeavour*'s voyage more eyes stared back at the ship than gazed out from her.

The question of what people saw had tantalised history. Fragments have travelled across the centuries. From Tahiti come accounts of a floating island or a godlike creature. From New Zealand, descriptions of 'a houseful of divinities' or a fledgling bird. A memorable description of *Endeavour*'s arrival derives from Whitianga in the Waikato Region of New Zealand:

> In the days long past ... we lived at Whitianga, and a vessel came there, and when our old men saw the ship they said it was an *atua*, a god, and the people on board were *tupua*, strange beings or 'goblins'. The ship came to anchor, and the boats pulled on shore. As our old men looked at the manner in which they came on shore, the rowers pulling with their backs to the bows of the boat, the old people said, 'Yes, it is so: these people are goblins; their eyes are at the back of their heads; they pull on shore with their backs to the land to which they are going.'[5]

Yet more stories attempt to capture the sightings of *Endeavour*'s cruise northwards along the eastern coastline of what would become modern-day Australia. A particularly vivid one comes from the Aboriginal people living in the Kamay or Botany Bay area. It tells that they saw a 'big bird' filled with something like opossums scampering 'up and down the legs and wings of the bird'.[6] Other oral traditions suggest that people thought the ship was carrying '*wawu-ngay*' or the spirits of departed ancestors.[7]

At first the vibrancy of these accounts seems to befit a moment of true historical gravity. Geographically speaking, a mile or so might have separated *Endeavour* from the shore, but that space contained – in Australia's case – something like fifty millennia of divergent human history. The instant *Endeavour*'s mainmast was sighted, represented a moment of reconnection. It feels appropriate, then, that this rejoining should be marked by a sparkling account, a historical firework to crown the momentous occasion.

In the 1750s Edmund Burke, the Irish writer, had written about the psychological process humans undergo when they encounter new objects. A human mind, he contended in his *A Philosophical Enquiry into the Origin of Our Ideas of the Sublime and Beautiful* (1757), always cleaves to the familiar. 'By making resemblances we produce new images, we unite, we create, we enlarge our stock', whereas 'in making distinctions we offer no food at all to the imagination'.[8] For Burke, perception was a three-stage process. First the senses would transmit the information to the brain. Then the imagination would scour the mind for familiar equivalents. The image produced would then be subject to a person's judgement. Accounts of birds or goblins or spirits, then, were more than delightful pictures, they were a door into a wider culture or a belief system.

But it is dangerous to over-philosophise. To look more carefully at the eyewitness accounts from the shore is to see that people soon rationalised *Endeavour*. It was not long before she became just 'a big canoe'. If the figures inside were said to be long-tailed possums, then they did not remain so for more than a passing moment. Rather the sailors were soon recognised as people 'something like themselves'.[9] This is demonstrated in Parkinson's 'Vocabulary of the Language of Otaheite' where the English word 'ship' – presumably Parkinson was pointing to *Endeavour* as he elicited – is translated as '*paee*'. The very next word in Parkinson's list is 'canoe', and back comes the same Tahitian word, '*paee*'.[10]

There are more complexities to these accounts too. They have come down to us today through storytelling traditions, not in contemporary journals or documents. Most of the accounts were originally collected in the late nineteenth century, a very different period of human history, when the imperial enterprises of the European superpowers were well underway, infecting many accounts with narratives of dispossession and conflict. As the historian Maria Nugent explains, when analysed closely many 'seemingly strange' stories about Captain Cook or *Endeavour* are not so strange after all. They are often 'an amalgam, or a montage, of incidents from different times and different spaces, which have become telescoped, condensed and conflated into a singular moment involving a singular man' – or in this case, a single ship.[11]

What is more clear is that *Endeavour* elicited three distinctive reactions in the three geographical territories she visited. Arriving in Tahiti after the *Dolphin*, she was treated with caution. The people knew what her weapons could do. In New Zealand, where there was no understanding of gunpowder, the reaction was belligerent. Cook had been prepared for such responses. But no one aboard could have anticipated what materialised when they came to Australia. Having anchored at what was soon to be named Botany Bay, the general reaction was aloofness. The people seemed unimpressed both by *Endeavour* and the trinkets and other objects the officers tried to please them with. Banks, in particular, found the attitude perplexing. The opening day of their visit he watched as:

> an old woman follow'd by three children came out of the wood; she carried several peice[s] of stick and the children also had their little burthens; when she came to the houses 3 more younger children came out of one of them to meet her. She often look'd at the ship but express'd neither surprize nor concern.[12]

As ever Banks had been reading in preparation for what he was to experience. In particular he had looked at William Dampier's racially charged description of 'the miserablest People in the World', which he admitted had left him with low expectations.[13] His prejudices seemed to be confirmed by what he viewed through his glasses, the complete nakedness – 'the women did not copy our mother Eve even in the fig leaf' – and the absence of the 'large fires' they had seen in the Society Islands and New Zealand, made 'in order to clear the ground for cultivation'. 'We thence concluded not much in favour of our future freinds.'[14]

Thereafter the people Banks saw at Botany Bay seemed to exist as an antithesis to him and his inquisitive, endeavouring peers. Parkinson described how:

The natives often reconnoitred us, but we could not prevail on them to come near us or to be social; for, as soon as we advanced, they fled nimbly as deer, excepting at one time, when they seemed determined to face us: then they came armed with spears, having their breasts painted white; but, as soon as they saw our boat go off from the ship, they retreated. Constrained by hunger, they often came into the bay to fish; but they kept in the shallows, and as near as possible to the shore. In one of their houses, at the top of the bay, we had laid some nails, pieces of cloth, and various trinkets; and though the natives had been there in our absence yet they had not taken any of them.[15]

This was a place to intrigue the European philosophers like Rousseau and Montesquieu, who contended that 'nothing is more fearful than Man in a State of Nature, that he is always in a tremble, and ready to fly at the first Motion he perceives, at the first Noise that strikes his Ears'.[16] Whatever the cause of the behaviour, Banks did not like it. He derided the Aboriginal people as 'rank cowards' in his journal. Apathy was a crime for him far greater than the violence of the Māori or the thieving of the Tahitians. It was made worse by these people's proximity to the thriving plant life of the bay. Ever since their arrival he and Solander had been galloping around like young spaniels, botanising in the sunshine.

By now their collection of plants had swelled to such enormous proportions that Banks decided to take 'some extraordinary care' of them to stop the pressed specimens spoiling in the books. Plant collecting was a challenging task on a voyage like this. Each seed had to be dried and folded up in paper and kept apart from others to prevent muddling. Books of pressed flowers needed to be carefully labelled and everything had to be stored in a part of the ship free from moisture. Banks spent a whole day bringing the pressed flowers, 'near 200 Quires of which the larger part was full', to the shore and spreading 'them upon a sail in the sun', turning them every few hours until they were in pristine condition.[17] This done, the books were carried back into Endeavour where they were filed back in their places alongside all his other collections: the Tahitian bark cloth beaters, drums and nose flutes, the feathered helmets, the cleavers and quarterstaffs, the flax cloaks and canoe paddles, all crowded into every nook.

Just as the voyage had overshot Cook's orders, it must have outshone Banks's expectations. Plants were not merely growing matter, delicate shapes, fragrant blooms, exotic tastes, captivating colours. They were power. Ever since the pharaoh Hetshepsut had imported incense trees from Punt to Egypt in the fifteenth century BC – species like myrrh and frankincense – people had understood both the economic and symbolic value of owning plants. A lust for spices like cloves, nutmeg and mace had inspired much of the exploration age. Banks might have been classifying within the Linnaean tradition, but equally he knew that with every new species he obtained, his power inflated. What he might find on these strange shores it was impossible to say. A plant as beautiful and economically valuable as the tulip? That may have been his ultimate hope.

Banks was the most charismatic figure aboard *Endeavour*. By the standards of his time he acted impressively well and generously – within the context of his social standing – to the people he met. But in him we can see the British imperial project of the next century in embryo. Impelled onwards to find, pick and preserve, he did not pause to consider that the great diversity of plant life at Botany Bay was a product of the way of life of the people who lived there. While gathering his collecting materials in London before *Endeavour*'s departure, Banks had picked up some old newspapers that he and Solander could use to press the botanical specimens they found. It is both a historical irony and darkly poignant that among these newspapers was a copy of the *Spectator*, containing a 'Critique and Notes' on John Milton's *Paradise Lost*. Some of Banks's specimens survive today in the Natural History Museum in London, pressed inside the lines:

the fruit of that forbidden tree whose mortal taste,
Brought death into the world and all our woe, with loss of Eden.

*

Endeavour sailed on 6 May. Crossing into the open ocean, Cook put the ship's head north. Having pleased himself with finding Botany Bay, Cook didn't feel the need to explore the next bay to the north, thereby missing what became Sydney Harbour. 'It is indeed rather curious, though not important, that Cook so consistently missed the best harbours in those countries he deemed of most importance', Beaglehole, his biographer, wrote.

Creeping along the coast, people continued to watch from the shore. One glistening account has been handed down in oral memory by the Badtjala people of K'gari or Fraser Island. It is the single most poignant depiction of *Endeavour*. It was recently translated into English:

Strangers are travelling with a cloud, Areeram!!
It has fire inside, must be a bad water spirit.
It's stupid maybe? It's going directly to that rainbow serpent place,
This is the truth that I bring.
It is breathing smoke rhythmically from its rear, must be song men and sorcerers.
Coming up and going back with the wind at its rear, like a sand crab.
The sea carries this ship here, why??[18]

Rainbows were shining over *Endeavour*. One day Parkinson saw 'two of the most beautiful rainbows my eyes ever beheld; the colours were strong, clear and lively; those of the inner one were so bright as to reflect its shadow on the water. They formed a complete semi-circle; and the space between them was much darker than the rest of the sky.'[19] To his mind the rainbow must have been a reminder that God's majesty was better experienced in nature than it was in a church. The rainbow may well have been uplifting for Tupaia, too. Thousands of miles away in the Society Islands rainbows were a powerful sign of Oro.

For Parkinson this was a rare escape from his cabin, where he was racing through drawings. 'In 14 days just, one draughtsman has made 94 sketch drawings, so quick a hand has he acquird by use', his admiring master wrote.[20] As Parkinson hurried through his backlog, elsewhere the ship's usual rhythms were being tailored to their changing environment. Once again the sea had grown shallow and colourful. Banks was able to peer 'distinctly' towards the seafloor 'at innumerable large fish, Sharks, Dolphins &c, and one large Turtle'. This brought challenges for Cook. The water was uncertain. The depth was sometimes thirty fathoms, sometimes ten or sometimes six. This was a danger he recognised. Just as it was for the coal colliers sailing south and passing the Humber at Hull, everything thereafter was caution. He opted to tread carefully – sounding often, sending boats ahead to find the route for the ship to follow.

At least Cook could be confident of *Endeavour*'s condition. In Rio, at Tahiti and, recently, at Queen Charlotte Sound, she had been overhauled, cleaned fore and aft and recaulked. In New Zealand, too, he had been able at long last to perfect her trim, hauling aboard stones to bring her a little more by the stern. Now, thousands of leagues from any dry dock and way off the charts that existed at the Admiralty, she was little worse than a collier on the run to Wapping. Only her rigging and sails were in a frail state. As for her hull, battered around New Zealand, it remained as sound as ever. Even Banks had been impressed with her dexterity off New Zealand: 'We turnd all day without loosing any thing, much to the credit of our old Collier, who we never fail to praise if she turns as well as this.'[21]

The relationship between Cook and Banks had turned out remarkably well. When the close confines of the ship and the confused social standing of each of them are taken into account, there was explosive potential for things to go disastrously wrong. But ever since Rio, Cook and Banks had worked efficiently and kept to their own responsibilities. Cook did his best to accommodate Banks's collecting whims and Banks respected that Cook was in ultimate command. There had only been one obvious collision between them. It had come when Cook had refused to put into a bay on the west coast of New Zealand's South Island. Cook had eyed up the entrance with its sheer cliffs and concluded that were they to go in they might wait a month to get out again. It was an astute reading of the circumstances, but Banks grieved a missed opportunity. He brooded on this, but it did not detract from his admiration for a navigator and a leader who, he well knew, was something quite outside of the ordinary.

At nine o'clock at night on 10 June, *Endeavour* was running on an east-north-east course, straying from the coast out several leagues into the open sea. A man was at the chains as ever, hauling the sounding lead. 'My intention was to stretch off all night as well as to avoid all the dangers we saw ahead', Cook later explained. They were carried along by a fine, even breeze of wind. It was a clear moonlit night. Swinging the lead, though, the sailor found something that surprised him. The depth had been deepening, from fourteen to twenty-one fathoms, but then in an instant the trend reversed. Eight fathoms were called. Cook responded by ordering everyone to their stations, ready to bring the ship round, 'and every heart felt some trepidation',

Parkinson wrote. Banks and his suite were at supper, but the shoal, or whatever it was, passed beneath, and they were left to retire to bed in 'perfect security'.

Endeavour continued on her course over the next few hours. She was travelling at about two knots, a ponderous pace over the black water. All this time she was putting the mainland further off her larboard quarter. The depth had deepened to twenty fathoms. The hush of another night, the 655th of the voyage, had settled over the deck. Then, at a few minutes to eleven o'clock, just before the lead could be heaved again, the hull clattered against something. All her forward motion was arrested in a single, jarring instant: 'the Ship Struck and stuck fast'.[22]

Banks was scarcely warm in his bed when the collision happened. In a few moments he left his cabin, passed through the great cabin and climbed the companionway onto the quarterdeck. There through the timbers, he felt the sensation of *Endeavour* 'beating very violently' against what he supposed to be submerged rocks. The realisation then succeeded that these must be coral rocks, 'the most dreadfull of all others on account of their sharp points and grinding quality which cut through a ships bottom almost immediately'. Absorbing this, the wretchedness of their situation began to settle. *Endeavour* had spent three hours running offshore. They were well into the open sea. Parkinson, now on deck, experienced the same dreadful thought. His mind raced to Britain, 'our native land', a place 'many thousand leagues' away.[23]

The officers responded quite differently. It was all 'coolness void of all hurry and confusion'. Pickersgill, one of the prime hands, was already out in one of the boats, sounding the depth right round the ship. He found that she had come to 'on the edge of a bank of coral'. Verifying what he must have suspected, Cook now set in motion a period of tremendous activity. The sails were immediately handed, the yards and the topmasts struck down; the smaller, coasting anchor was got out of the hold and loaded into a boat to see if they could use it to lever *Endeavour* clear. All of this was already done by midnight when, 'by the light of the moon', Banks spotted several timbers and boards floating beside the ship. Then another, more substantial piece appeared. 'All this time she continued to beat very much so that we could hardly keep our legs upon the Quarter deck'.[24]

To confuse their situation still further was the news that *Endeavour* had run against the coral at almost the top of high tide. For the next six hours the water would drop, bringing, minute by minute, increasing stresses to bear against the floor timbers. The noise, Banks decided, was coming from somewhere under her starboard bow, it 'kept grating her bottom making a noise very plainly to be heard in the fore store rooms'. No one doubted this would eventually bore a hole through *Endeavour*'s bottom. Only three factors remained in their favour: the sea was calm, the sky was clear, and the moonlight strong enough to illuminate the work. If the wind freshened and whipped the sea into motion, they could not possibly hope to survive long.

The sailors' unremitting work continued. As soon as the coasting anchor was out, Cook tried to heave off with 'a very great strean'. But nothing would free the ship. With the tide ebbing, the grating continuing, and hours left before low water, there was only one course available to him. The valuable guns, the terror of Tahiti, were cut loose from their breechings and heaved overboard. Anything heavy the crew could lay their hands on was jettisoned next. Part of the eight tons of iron ballast, loaded at Deptford, was thrown over, then the stones gathered from Queen Charlotte's Sound and neatly arranged to settle the trim. Hoops and staves went too, and the oil jars and firewood and then cask after cask of water. This was hours of heroic, relentless toil. The sailors, wrote Banks, 'workd with surprizing chearfullness and alacrity; no grumbling or growling was to be heard throughout the ship, no not even an oath'.[25]

This activity consumed the night and, at least, gave the crew a feeling of purpose. At about a quarter to seven on 11 June, a bright morning broke over the troubled scene. There was the warm southern sun, and calm settled sea, and *Endeavour* lodged fast in the centre of it, listing to starboard. They had survived the night and the low tide at least. But if the morning had lightened spirits, they were soon to be dampened by news from Pickersgill who had discovered a leak in the ship's floor. Of the four elm pumps on board, two were set to work, endless heaving revolutions in fifteen-minute stints, teams not just of the sailors and warrant officers, but also the commissioned officers Gore and Hicks, and the captain, and Banks himself too.

Eleven o'clock brought high tide. By now Cook had ordered all the anchors out, their flukes biting into the ocean floor to stop *Endeavour* drifting further onto the coral. The captain estimated that forty or fifty tons had been thrown over. This was the time to heave her off. But again she proved immovable, a deadweight in the fluid

ocean. With high tide went the great sustaining hope. At noon
Endeavour's listing became more noticeable, Cook estimated that she
was 'three or four Strakes heel to Starboard' – a strake being a panel
of wood. Though depressed on all other fronts, at least the weather
was holding. Again Cook had *Endeavour* braced with the anchors to
hold her as the tide fell. By one in the afternoon it had already fallen
so low that Banks, despair descending, saw the pinnace almost
touching the sea bottom. The ship's oak had now been ground by
the coral rock for fourteen hours.

Water was rising in the well now. At 5 p.m. Cook had a third pump
set to work, if not to staunch the leak, then at least to stall its progress.
The fourth of *Endeavour*'s pumps would have been got going too, had
it not been choked and useless. The turning continued, and continued,
watch and watch. At dusk there was at last some movement in the
ship as the tide rose a second time. But by now *Endeavour* was making
so much water she could barely be expected to float if she was
wrenched clear. The coral was now, strangely enough, both the cause
of her injury and the reason for her survival. As it had collided with
the hull it had, most probably, plugged the leak. To escape the coral,
therefore, was also to expose to the ocean the damage they had
sustained.

In the darkness of nine o'clock, *Endeavour* righted perceptibly. But
if this suggested any improvement, then it was misleading. Below, the
situation was desperate. 'The leak gaind upon the Pumps considerably', Cook conceded. 'This was an alarming and I may say terrible
Circumstance and threatened immidiate destruction to us as soon as
the Ship was afloat.' By now, Banks had given *Endeavour* up entirely.
In his cabin he was, 'packing up what I thought I might save', and
preparing himself for the worst.

The worst they must all have contemplated, though no one had
quite said it yet. Everyone knew that their boats could not carry all
of them ashore. Nor could Cook give cork jackets to everyone. Twenty
of them had been stowed away on *Endeavour*, but they were designed
only as a protection for 'the use of the men that it may be necessary
to employ in boats'. Whether some of these might be distributed or
not, they would have proved mostly useless. The closest land lay about
eight miles away. It would be a miracle if any of them could swim
that distance. Even for those in the boats it would be a few hours'
work. And even if they did get to the shore, what then? As for those

who might make off in boats, Banks thought a more desperate fate awaited, 'ashore without arms to defend themselves from the Indians or provide themselves with food, on a countrey where we had not the least reason to hope for subsistence'. There, stranded at the far side of the world, the ship destroyed, half of them dead, his immense collections on the sea bottom, he might be better drowned.

Cook's thoughts can only have followed a similar path. Cautious by nature, one of the qualities that made him an exceptional commander was his recognition that chances sometimes needed to be taken. 'Adversity does not build character, it reveals it', the novelist James Lane Allen wrote. And Cook's was to be exposed here, on the reef. After the ship righted at nine o'clock, he knew that he had two hours before high tide. 'I resolved', he wrote, 'to risk all and heave her off.' The time spared him was given over to setting this plan in process.

There were four possible outcomes. First, they might fail to move *Endeavour* at all, as before. Then she could hardly be expected to weather a second night and another tide. Second, they might free her, but even then any coral in her hull would work loose and in a matter of minutes she would settle, then slide to the bottom. Third, they might get her off and be able to keep pace with the leak until they reached some nearby island. Then they might be able to fashion something 'out of her materials' to get them to the East Indies. The final possibility was the one that they all wished for: *Endeavour* would float.

'The dreadfull time now approachd', Banks wrote, 'and the anziety in every bodys countenance was visible enough.' The equation was not unlike one of Charlton's mathematical enigmas. The ship, a solid object, was suspended between forces. One of these was the upward pressure of the tide. A further force was generated by Cook and the sailors heaving on anchors, the flukes of which had bit into the seabed forty or fifty yards off. Was the combination of these forces sufficient to wrest the collier from the grip of the coral? Banks framed the scene with words that would have seemed melodramatic at any other time: 'fear of Death now stard us in the face'. Just after ten o'clock, with three feet nine inches of water in the hold, Cook ordered all hands that could be spared up from the pumps to man the capstan and the windlass. With sailors rowing in the boats and everyone else heaving with all their might, at 10.20 p.m., after twenty-three hours lodged on the reef, *Endeavour* slid clear.

For an instant it seemed as if everything had gone perfectly. *Endeavour* righted and was hauled into deep water at a safe distance from the corals. 'This desirable event gave us spirits', Parkinson recorded, 'which, however, proved to be the transient gleam of sunshine, in a tempestuous day; for they were soon depressed again, by observing that the water increased in the hold, faster than we could throw it out; and we expected, every minute, that the ship would sink, or that we should be obliged to run her again upon the rocks.'[26]

Cook felt this fear too. He heard from the well that the pump was increasing fast, 'which for the first time caused fear to operate upon every man in the Ship'. But for once, a pleasant surprise awaited him. It turned out that one man relieving another had formulated a new way of calculating the depth. When the difference in methods was discovered, eighteen inches of water vanished in a second. As the news of the mistake was passed through the ship, it 'acted upon every man like a charm'.[27]

Another night was spent at the pumps. Cook noticed that the improvement in their circumstances had made the sailors more productive. By sunrise on 12 June the depth of water had lowered considerably. Rest had no longer been thought of, Banks wrote, 'but the pumps went with unwearied vigour till the water was all out which was done in a much shorter time than was expected'. By ten in the morning the yards were being hoisted back up, the sails were being retrieved and preparations were all being made to hobble the ship to the mainland so they could solve the greatest question of all and find the location of the leak.

To aid them on their passage an innovative technique was now proposed by Jonathan Monkhouse, younger relation of the surgeon, who was among the ablest of the midshipmen. He suggested they try to fother the leak. This was something he had executed once in a voyage across the Atlantic from Virginia, and involved wrapping a specially prepared sail around the bottom of the hull so that the pressure of the water would clamp it over the hole. Approving of Monkhouse's design, four or five sailors were set to accompany him, mixing together 'a large quantity of Oakum chopd fine and wool' and sticking it down on one of the studding sails. Ropes were then tied to either end of this sail. It was then threaded down under *Endeavour*'s hull, in a complicated sequence of pulling, adjusting and fastening, and it proved to be so successful the leak was almost stopped.

Although Cook detailed the preparation of the fothering sail he did not explain just how it was applied or whether any sailor was obliged to plunge beneath the waterline to help heave the ropes around. What they would have experienced if they had, beneath the surf that beat on the surface, was a marine environment of unmatched colour. It was a world of slanting light, rainbow-coloured fish being thrust to and fro like leaves on a breeze by the play of the underwater currents and the carry of the tide; of turtles and eels and pristine, glinting light, ricocheting off the corals themselves. They did not know it, but they had been suspended above a marine city, one as complex as London with all its medley of inhabitants. He would have caught sight of a small fragment of the largest living structure on the planet, that irreplaceable wonder of nature we call the Great Barrier Reef.

Ten days passed until, on the morning of 22 June, they got to examine the damage to *Endeavour*'s hull. The coral had gashed a hole in the floor heads a little forward of the starboard fore chains. It was a deep cut. In either the initial contact or the slamming that had followed it, four planks had been punched through in the most extraordinary way. This was no livid gash, no splintered mess; rather a neat hole, 'as if', Cook decided, 'it had been done by the hands of Man with a blunt edged tool'. Luckily the coral had collided with one of the strongest sections of the hull, in the internal scaffold of her rounded bows where the oak timbers were reinforced. Had this not been the case, Cook plainly saw, 'it would have been impossible to have saved the ship, and even as it was it appear'd very extraordinary that she made no more water than what she did'. Plugging the injury was a piece of dislodged coral, 'as large as a Mans fist', as well as remnants of the fothering sail. There was more destruction too. The protective sheathing had come away, the false keel had gone while the main keel – the backbone of everything – had suffered too, though not 'materialy'.[28]

Banks looked over *Endeavour*'s injuries as well, reinforcing his view that it had been a close run thing. As ever, he had quickly regained his equilibrium, beginning his botanising ashore even before the ship was safely beached. But he came away from the episode with a new-found admiration for the ship's crew. 'I beleive every man exerted his utmost for the preservation of the ship', he wrote, 'This was no doubt owing intirely to the cool and steady conduct of the officers, who

during the whole time never gave an order which did not shew them
to be perfectly composd and unmovd by the circumstances howsoever
dreadfull they might appear.'²⁹ Cook, too, had committed to his journal
some choice words, acknowledging 'In justice to the ships Company
I must say that no men ever behaved better than they had done on
this occasion animated by the behaviour of every gentleman on board,
every man seemed to have a just sense of the danger we were in and
exercised himself to the utmost.'

Endeavour – which must have felt a comfortably spacious ship after
all the jettisoning – was now careened on the steep bank of a river
on the mainland. A camp had been established on the slopes as well,
the smiths had set up a forge, a stage had been built for the carpenters
to work on, making the bank as good a dry dock as they could have
hoped to find. It had been an anxious cruise ashore. Cook had sent
Molyneux ahead with two boats to sound and look out for a suitable
location. One of the mates had returned in the pinnace with news
they had 'found just the place we wanted, in which the tide rose
sufficiently and there was every natural convenience that could be
wishd for either laying the ship ashore or heaving her down'. This
was more than any of them had expected, 'too much to be beleivd
by our most sanguine wishes', Banks admitted, their situation still
dire, 'nothing but a lock of Wool between us and destruction'.³⁰

This was far from being their only piece of good fortune. They
had not long escaped the open sea when the weather broke. The soft
breezes of the days before were replaced by rising winds, too brisk
for them to weigh and sail at all. Had this come just two days before
then it would have proved deadly. But rather than *Endeavour* being
sunk and lost in a mystery, she now cruised into a harbour that was
narrow yet shallow, with tides that rose and fell six or so feet, just the
natural levers they needed. It was not quite a Bell Island at Whitby,
but it was a place where they might moor in safety and explore the
surrounding terrain to replenish provisions. To Banks, this good
fortune, so hot on the heels of their unlikely deliverance, even drove
him towards a religious concession, being 'almost providential'.³¹

Endeavour's situation on the riverbank is portrayed in one of the best-
known visual representations of the voyage. It depicts the collier, tilted
to one side at the water's edge with all her masts bare but a pennant
still streaming above as a symbol of hope. Behind them is a dreary

landscape. Mangrove trees skirt the riverbank and the hill crests. A
few tents and some anchors stand in a clearing and a party of sailors
row in dogged solemnity towards the opposite bank. Portraying British
resourcefulness *in extremis*, the engraving emphasises the alien nature
of the New Holland landscape. It was an inhospitability that Parkinson
had already remarked upon before the accident on the reef. 'The
main-land looked very barren and dreary', he had written, 'the hills
upon it looked like a heap of rubbish, on which nothing was to be
seen, excepting a few low bushes.'[32]

This was the terrain they would have to subsist off until they could
sail again. But Parkinson found that it contained more than he anticipated. Over the next days the sailors ate cabbage palms, beans, seeding
plants 'the kernels of which, roasted, tasted like parched pease', a
sweet-tasting 'black-purple fruit', 'a small-leaved plant that smelt like
lemon and orange peel, and made an agreeable substitute for tea',
and something that reminded Parkinson of a fig tree, which tasted
'very insipid'. Parkinson's list of experimental foodstuffs is a reminder
that exploration was not just about seeing. The ship's company had
tasted their way around the world. Supplementing John Thompson's
boiled rations had been gannets, geese, albatrosses, limpets, green-
lipped mussels, oysters, clams, roast dog and rats by the dozen in
Tahiti, and stingray in Botany Bay (so big were the stingray they
encountered there, the bay had originally been called 'Stingray Bay').

In this river – Cook called it 'Endeavour River' – more wildlife
emerged by the day. Banks was pleased to find an 'Opossum', 'with
two young ones sucking at her breasts'. Parkinson saw two cockatoos,
an owl-like bird 'having the iris of its eyes gold colour', a 'very
uncommon' hawk with eyes of a 'rich scarlet colour'. There were also
ants, snakes, venomous flies and many alligators, which 'we frequently
saw ... swimming round the ship'. None of these were eaten but the
near-hundred men kept their eyes open for anything they could find.
It wasn't long before they found something that would rank as a dainty
in Britain. Turtles existed in abundance on the nearby reefs. Once
they had been chanced upon, they became the sailors' staple, and, not
long after, the cause of their conflict with the Guugu Yimithirr people.

Parkinson's journal tells us that *Endeavour* had been watched in the
days before the shipwreck. On 8 June he wrote of 'a company of the
natives' watching them from one of the inland islands. They were
'standing quite still, and beholding the ship with astonishment'.

Parkinson afterwards saw a fire being lit. It 'yielded a very grateful odour, not unlike that produced by burning the wood of gum benjamin'.[33]

The story is also told from a different perspective:

On the morning of 10 June 1770 a strange large canoe, which the coastal people had kept under observation, was seen just east of Kulki (in Koko Yalanji), which is now known as Cape Tribulation. It appeared that something was not right. Then it started moving along the coast again.

At times our Bama [Guugu Yimithirr people] lit small fires to inform other clan members regarding the whereabouts of this strange canoe. Two days later our Bama saw it drop anchor at the mouth of the 'Waalumbaal Birri', which Captain Cook later named the Endeavour River. Our Guugu Yimithirr ancestors considered that these boat people like others who came and went, would not cause problems.

After these strange beings beached their canoe our Bama decided not to make contact but to observe. They decided to do what they normally did. Bama got into their canoes, they speared fish, women and children collected wood and other things from the beach; two Bama even paddled close to the visitors' boat.

The strangers gave our Bama fish and beads. Next day four of our men went back and gave them fish in return, which is customary. Though our Bama recognised the predicament these visitors were in, they were discreet because they needed to make sure the visitors were not reincarnations of 'wawu-ngay' spirits of our ancestors. Every effort was made to be tactful. Women were not allowed to approach the strangers.

In this telling of the story it was only when the Guugu Yimithirr saw how many turtles the Europeans had taken that 'it became an offence'.

The sharing code was broken. The visitors had trespassed. They should have got permission from us as the owners or custodians. Then things got out of hand. Our Bama were so confused and angry that they set fire to the campsite. Then they heard a loud bang and saw a puff of smoke. One of the men could not believe that something invisible punctured his leg and blood started to flow. They all ran away. Before going back to their camp our Bama lit more fires to warn other clans that something had gone wrong.[34]

Marooned and short on provisions, anything might have happened next. But what did ensue was far better than Cook might have expected. A remarkable peace conference was held, with Cook and Banks on one side and a tribal elder on the other, on some rocks about a mile from the river. The Guugu Yimithirr people 'set up their lances against a tree, and advanced towards us in a friendly manner', the British account went. Cook and Banks laid down their weapons too.

The account continues:

Before leaving to board their canoes, our Bama agreed between themselves that the things the strangers gave them were to be got rid of and that no further contact was to be made and that the visitors should have freedom of movement. Then, finally, one day they watched the ship sail out of the Waalumbaal birri and away from our Guugu Yimithirr land.[35]

Although Cook would never appreciate it, he had experienced an enormous stroke of luck. *Endeavour*'s life had been lived in hallowed places. Fishburn's yard lay beneath Whitby Abbey. She had been to Taputapuatea in Opua and to Tolaga Bay in New Zealand. Now Cook had unwittingly careened her at a section of the Waalumbaal birri river known as 'Gungardie', where the Guugu Yimithirr and other tribes in the region gathered to reconcile disputes and for meditation. As one knowledge custodian, Eric Deeral, has explained, 'The law that governed this area was that no blood was ever to be shed.' He elaborated, 'My theory is that my forefathers recognised the plight that the visitors were in ... Their spiritual beliefs led them to be generous towards these strangers because they did not want them to perish in their lands and be troubled by their spirits in the future.'

These meetings with the Aboriginal and Torres Strait Islander peoples had an effect on Cook. Some weeks later he wrote what would become a surprising and much-reproduced journal entry. It is worth quoting in full:

From what I have said of the Natives of New-Holland they may appear to some to be the most wretched people upon Earth, but in reality they are far more happier than we Europeans; being wholy unacquainted not only with the superfluous but the necessary Conveniences so much sought after in Europe, they are happy in not knowing the use of them. They live in a Tranquility which is not disturb'd by the Inequality of Condition: The Earth and sea of their own accord furnishes them with all things necessary for life, they covet not Magnificent Houses, Household-stuff &c^a, they live in a warm and fine Climate and enjoy a very wholesome Air, so that they have very little need of Clothing and this they seem to be fully sencible of, for many to whome we gave Cloth &c^a to, left it carlessly upon the Sea beach and in the woods as a thing they had no manner of use for. In short they seem'd to set no Value upon any thing we gave them, nor would they ever part with any thing of their own for any one article we could offer them; this in my opinion argues that they think themselves provided with all the necessarys of Life and that they have no superfluities.[36]

Few Britons over the next 150 years would write such an open-minded appraisal. Cook's statement surprises because he, an English naval officer in trim uniform, seems to exist in opposition to all they were. Theirs was a dreamland world of spirits and traditions. Cook's was a geographical world of instruments and the Enlightenment. Some have connected Cook's sympathies to the fact that he was tutored in Whitby's Quaker environment, where a simple lifestyle was valued. Henry Taylor – who lived and learned in exactly the same culture as Cook – proclaimed in his memoir, 'O self interest! Thou art the god of this world, and almost all the world doth worship thee!', and at John Walker's in Grape Lane it was forbidden for apprentices to 'play dice, cards or bowls' or 'haunt taverns or playhouses'.[37] It seems that much of this sobriety stuck. Cook never openly consorted with Rousseau's philosophy, though some have wondered whether he passed time discussing its merits with Banks.

It should perhaps be borne in mind that Cook had just endured a near-death experience on the reef. He had seen the destructive nature of the endeavouring impulse and, if European society was racing forwards, then it was kicking up a cloud of dust and debris as it went.

Every time he had returned to London from Newfoundland in the 1760s, things must have seemed more chaotic. There was the *North Briton* in 1763, then the Cider Riots in 1764, the Stamp Act a year later, then all the upheavals he had witnessed first-hand in the spring of 1768.

This, though, was the world that the ship's company were increasingly eager to return to. It may be confused and intricate, but it was the world they knew. As Banks wrote in his journal, many of them were 'pretty far gone with the longing for home which the Physicians have gone so far as to esteem a disease under the name of Nostalgia'. Only Cook, Solander and himself were immune to such a distemper, something he put down to the thoroughly Banksian prescription of 'constant employment for our minds which I beleive to be the best if not the only remedy for it'.[38]

They would soon sail from Endeavour River, but not before they made one final discovery. As soon as they had careened the ship in June, sightings of a bizarre new creature had begun. The thing, whatever it was, had been sighted on an opposite shoreline by a party of sailors sent out to shoot pigeons. They had caught a glimpse of this beast, 'as large as a grey hound, of a mouse coulour and very swift'.[39] More reports followed. A better description was set down by Cook, who saw the creature 'a little way from the Ship'. It was, Cook reckoned, of 'a light Mouse colour and the full size of a grey hound and shaped in every respect like one, with a long tail which it carried like a grey hound, in short I should have taken it for a wild dog, but for its walking or running in which it jumped like a Hare or a dear'.[40]

For so long the *Endeavour*'s crew had instigated confusion. It is refreshing to watch the tables turn, and see them grasping for adjectives. Banks himself 'had the good fortune to see the beast so much talkd of' on 25 June, 'but imperfectly'. 'He was not only like a grey hound in size and running but had a long tail, as long as any grey hounds; what to liken him to I could not tell, nothing certainly that I have seen at all resembles him.' Parkinson had a stab at a description too:

The tail, which is carried like a grey-hound's, was almost as long as the body, and tapered gradually to the end. The chief bulk of this animal is behind; the belly being largest, and the back rising toward the posteriors. The whole body is covered with short ash-coloured hair; and the flesh of it tasted like a hare's, but has a more agreeable flavour.[41]

Banks eventually got a name from the Guugu Yimithirr people: 'kanguru'.

The sailors might have been eager to sail for home, but to leave Endeavour River was to return to a sea that was seemingly strewn with coral reefs, 'innumerable shoals, some above and some under water, and no prospect of any straight passage out'. These were Banks's words at the start of July 1770. He posed the dilemma best. 'We began to think how we should get out of this place, where so lately to get only in was our utmost ambition ... To return as we came was impossible, the trade wind blew directly in our teeth; most dangerous then our navigation must be among unknown dangers. How soon might we again be reducd to the misfortune we had so lately escapd!'[42]

To gather all the intelligence he could, while the sailors were busy rigging the ship again, Cook climbed a hill over their anchorage. 'I saw what gave me no small uneasiness', he admitted in his journal, a succession of sandbanks and shoals in a chain that extended right along the coast. Keeping between them and the land was one option. But by doing so they would be exposed to all the dangers of the coast, 'besides the risk we should run of being locke'd in within the Main reef'. Should they become trapped then they would miss the trade winds that blew from June to October and which he hoped would carry them to the East Indies. This, Cook reasoned, might 'prove the ruin of the Voyage, as we have now little more than 3 Months provisions on board and that short allowance in many Articles'.

These reflections ran through Cook's mind right through July and into August, as a sea breeze kept the ship penned in the river. Only at the beginning of August did they timorously launch into the water, but several fraught days followed with them narrowly avoiding submerged rocks and reefs. On 6 August, having analysed their surroundings from the masthead, Cook experienced an unusual sensation: doubt.

I saw that we were surrounded on every side with Shoals and no such thing as a passage to Sea but through the winding channels between them, dangerous to the highest degree in so much that I was quite at a loss which way to steer when the weather would permit us to get under sail; for to beat back to the SE the way we came as the Master would have had me done would be an endless peice of work, as the winds blow now constantly strong from that quarter without hardly any intermission – on the other hand if we do not find a passage to the north[d] we shall have to come [back] at last.[43]

At a loss, Cook decided to visit in his boat one of the high islands five leagues out to sea. They 'seemed to be of such a height that from the top of one of them I hoped to see and find a Passage'. On 11 August, accompanied by Banks, Cook set out. As soon as the boat landed, Cook 'immediately went upon the highest hill on the Island'. What he saw 'mortified' him. About two or three leagues out to sea, 'extending in a line NW and SE farther than I could see', was a 'Reef of Rocks ... on which the Sea broke very high.'

It was a sight to defeat many. For weeks Molyneux, the sailing master, had been arguing they should turn back southwards, sounding all the way with the yawl and pinnace. Anything to retreat to the open waters of May. Cook knew the folly of this, but now, high on this isolated hill in an uncharted sea, strewn with coral rocks and concealed shoals he must have entertained second thoughts. He stayed on the hill until sunset, thinking. He had confirmed the danger of the reefs. But he also came to a resolution that *if* he could navigate through them, the open sea awaited. And to the north-east of where he stood he thought he had spied a channel.

Returning to *Endeavour* he combined what he had learned on the hill with a report from Molyneux, whom he had ordered out in the pinnace. Molyneux's news was more of the same: treacherous seas and only wicked passages. 'I therefore resolved to weigh in the morning and endeavour to quit the coast altogether untill we could approach it with less danger', Cook declared. He had had enough. This meant cruising out into the sea, taking every chance.

On 13 August they sailed and stood out to the north-east, towards the place where Cook thought he had seen a channel. At around midday they approached it, an opening in the reef about half a mile broad. Cook put *Endeavour* on a tack and again sent Molyneux ahead to examine the channel. 'He soon made the Signal for the Ship to follow which we accordingly did', Cook wrote, and at about two o'clock in the afternoon they threaded through. 'We had no sooner got without the breakers than we had no ground with 150 fathom of line and found a well growen Sea rowling in from the SE.' They were finally liberated, 'free'd from fears of Shoals &c[a]', Cook wrote in a line he would soon repeat to John Walker at Whitby, 'after having been intangled among them more or less ever since the 26th of May, in which time we have saild 360 Leagues without ever having a Man out of the cheans heaving the Lead when the Ship was under way, a circumstance that I dare say never happen'd to any ship before'.[44]

In the open sea they found *Endeavour* was in worse repair than they had feared. With water seeping in, the pumps were set to work again, although this was 'looked upon as trifeling to the danger we had lately made our escape from'. A rising gale from the south-east gave them all the speed they could want and at last they were crossing more miles in an hour than they had done in as many weeks. Cook's aim was to take *Endeavour* into the lower latitudes, clear of the corals, before turning back to fall in with the coast to locate a passage that Dalrymple had marked on a chart. Dalrymple's strait, if it existed, would lead them to charted waters once again, just a few hundred leagues from Batavia and the Dutch East Indies, where they could give *Endeavour* the attention she needed. After a day of making steady progress to the north-west, crossing a whole degree of latitude, on the morning of 15 August Cook reached the thirteenth parallel and turned *Endeavour* west. He was, he reflected, 'fearfull of over shooting' the passage they so dearly needed to find.[45]

After a few hours of westing, at one o'clock on 15 August land was sighted again from the masthead, a sign they had perhaps turned too soon. Any disappointment at this was nothing to the feelings when they saw, an hour later, that dead ahead the same reef barred the water in front of them. Thinking he could see an end to the reef somewhere towards the north, Cook stood on. But what had looked like open water turned out to be nothing more than a tiny passage. Cook now hauled close reefed on an east-south-east wind, to bear back out to sea, but, this time, his luck entirely failed. The breeze shifted, so that it now blew from east by north, 'which was right upon the Reef and of Course made our clearing of it doubtfull.'

As darkness fell on 15 August the jollity of the previous days evaporated and *Endeavour* became tense once again. 'All the dangers we had escapd were little in comparison of being thrown upon this reef if that should be our lot', Banks wrote in his journal:

> A Reef such a one as I now speak of is a thing scarcely known in Europe or indeed any where but in these seas: it is a wall of Coral rock rising almost perpendicularly out of the unfathomable ocean, always overflown at high water commonly 7 or 8 feet, and generaly bare at low water; the large waves of the vast ocean meeting with so sudden a resistance make here a most terrible surf Breaking mountain high, especialy when as in our case the general trade wind blows directly upon it.[46]

With the wind offering them little assistance, a northward course that took them parallel to the coral was their best hope. Cook kept to this 'with all the Sail we could set' as long as he could. Then, 'fearing' the consequences, he turned *Endeavour* south. They had barely completed this manoeuvre before it fell quite still. Second to an east wind, this was the worst of all outcomes. They were becalmed. A sounding lead was thrown out to test the depth of the sea, but there was nothing with 120 fathoms. The time was three o'clock in the morning, 'we judgd ourselves not more than 4 or 5 l'gs from the reef', Banks wrote, 'maybe much less, and the swell of the sea which drove right in upon it carried the ship towards it fast. We tried the lead often in hopes to find ground that we might anchor but in vain.'[47]

Though no reefs like this existed in Britain, it was a scenario every Whitby master would have recognised and shuddered at in an instant. With no wind, a ship had few ways of propelling herself. However skilful a commander, however good they were at executing manoeuvres, it did not matter if they did not have wind. With little ability to steer or to move, a ship would usually go where the swell of the sea carried it. The best that could be hoped for was a sandy beach, a smooth bottom or, best of all, plenty of open water. Keeping sea room was a mantra of every collier master. But there was none to be found here. Everyone aboard, whether versed in marine dynamics or not, could absorb the simple fact that without wind a ship would go where it was taken. And they had all seen the reefs. Looking out at them from Endeavour River, they had studied their sandy tops, their uneven spires of rock that jutted this way and that in defiance to any sense of proportion or shape or form. They had seen, too, what the

coral could do to the ship's bottom on a glassy sea on a moonlit night
at a few knots. That had nearly finished them all. But to be flung,
broach to, against a reef wall with the whole weight of the South
Seas – waves that might have started their journey in Tahiti, as far as
they knew – would have the most logical of all outcomes.

By four o'clock in the morning 'the roaring of the Surf was plainly
heard and at day break the vast foaming breakers were too plainly to
be seen', Cook recorded. The waves were propelling them 'surprisingly
fast'. 'We had at this time not an air of wind and the depth of water
was unfathomable'. About now Cook ordered out the boats, in the
hope that their feeble influence in the whole equation would have
some bearing. Two sweeps were fetched up out of the hold – long
oars – that were thrust out of the portholes in the gun room. Together
with the boats these managed to pull *Endeavour*'s head 'round to the
northward which seem'd to be the only way to keep her off the reef
or at least to delay time'.

As day broke, Banks got his first view of 'the vast foaming billows',
'scarce a mile from us'. By six they had drifted alarmingly close, like
a reed approaching the top of a waterfall. Cook reckoned they stood
at a remove of 'not above 80 or 100 Yards':

> the same Sea that washed the sides of the Ship rose in a breaker
> prodigiously high the very next time it did rise so that between
> us and distruction was only a dismal Vally the breadth of one
> wave and even now no ground could be felt with 120 fathoms.
> The Pinnace by this time was patched up and hoisted out and
> sent ahead to tow; still we had hardly any hopes of saving the
> Ship and full as little our lives as we were full 10 Leagues from
> the nearest land and the boats not sufficient to carry the whole
> of us, yet in this truly terrible situation not one man ceased to
> do his utmost and that with as much calmness as if no danger
> had been near.[48]

Just now, 'at this critical juncture when all our endeavours seem'd
too little', a faint breeze 'sprung up'. Cook recorded that it was 'so
small that at any other time in a Calm we should not have observed
it', and captive to terror some might not have done. But with the faint
tug of the breeze and the help of the boats, they felt *Endeavour* 'move
off from the Reef in a slanting direction'. The wind lasted not more

than ten minutes. But it blew them about 200 yards from the breakers. 'Soon after our friendly breeze Viseted us again', he wrote, 'and lasted about as long as before.'

The wind – its strength, its direction, its timing – acted on the ship's company as nothing else could. Banks wrote: 'The fear of Death is Bitter: the prospect we now had before us of saving our lives tho at the expence of every thing we had made my heart set much lighter on its throne, and I suppose there were none but what felt the same sensations.'[49] Within minutes, an opening was discerned in the reef, a quarter of a mile away. Cook instantly sent one of the mates to examine it. 'Its breadth was not more than the length of the Ship but within was smooth water, into this place it was resolve'd to push her if possible haveing no other probable Views to save her, for we were still in the very jaws of distruction.'[50]

They managed to master the distance, but only found water 'gushing' out on the ebb, 'so that it was impossible to get in'. The audacious manoeuvre brought Cook another chance, though. The force of the ebb catapulted them a quarter of a mile into the ocean and by midday, six hours after the worst moment of their desperation, they were one and a half or perhaps two miles out to sea. From there another opening was seen and Hicks, the lieutenant, was immediately sent to survey it.

At two o'clock in the afternoon Hicks returned 'with a favourable account'. Cook instantly 'resolved to try to secure the Ship in it, narrow and dangerous as it was'. They were aided by a light breeze from the east-north-east which, with the help of the boats and the spring tide, allowed them to approach the gap in the reefs. It was about quarter of a mile broad, an irregular space filled with mottled, skittish water for the quartermaster to aim at. As the afternoon sun began to dip at the start of its downward arc, Cook pointed *Endeavour*'s head into the gap and felt her gather way. 'We soon enter'd the opening', he wrote, and were 'hurried through in a short time by a rappid tide like a Mill race'.[51] Beneath, the unfathomable ocean's bottom disappeared astern, the reef slid alongside their gunwales, the waves retreated and the glossy water of the inner lagoon opened up before them. Once again James Cook had found his path.

PART FOUR

War

10

360°

No one in Britain had heard anything of *Endeavour* for a year and a half. It had been the beginning of 1769 when the letters from Rio had reached London. Thereafter there had been silence.

On 22 September 1770 a different Royal Naval vessel anchored at Spithead. Aboard HMS *Favourite*, sloop of war, were captains George Farmer and William Maltby. They carried news of an ominous kind. Farmer and Maltby were returning to England from their station on the Falkland Islands. In a scandalous affront they had been attacked by a hostile Spanish force and evicted from their colonial base. The rest of the story was contained in a letter to Philip Stephens, the Admiralty secretary, that was hurried in secrecy at speed from Portsmouth to Whitehall.

Outraged columns were soon printed in the newspapers, telling the full story. In June a Spanish frigate had appeared off the British settlement of Port Egmont. Unnerved, Farmer hailed the ship. She replied that she needed water. For three days the frigate lay at anchor in the bay. Then, instead of sailing away replenished, four more frigates appeared. The conceit dropped, a broad Spanish pennant was hoisted. Having confirmed what they suspected, the bulk of the British forces fell back to the blockhouse while several sailors attempted to bring the *Favourite* into a defensive posture by the shore. The Spanish ships pursued her and fired two shots 'which fell at a distance'.

A few tense days ensued. The outcome, though, could not be doubted. In the blockhouse was a British force of fifty or so. Against them were 'about sixteen Hundred, with a Train of Artillery sufficient to reduce a regular Fortification'. This, along with the five frigates 'from Twenty to Thirty-two Guns', made opposition futile. A few obligatory shots were fired but, as Samuel Johnson put it, it was clear that any further resistance would have been 'only to lavish life without use or hope'.[1] A truce was called. Articles of capitulation were signed.

The annexation complete, the *Favourite* was initially detained for twenty days, during which time her rudder was removed. After this the garrison were permitted to gather their belongings and steer to the northwards. When news of what – in British eyes – was an unprovoked incursion, 'at a time of profound peace', became known, the initial shock turned to fury. The crisis was the first overseas test for the new government headed by Lord North, which had come to office at the start of 1770. The immediate consequences had not been confined to Parliament. The stock exchange fell three per cent. Within days the newspapers reported that the press gangs had been set to work in the ports, rounding up sailors for a ferocious British response.

At his home, Strawberry Hill in Twickenham, Horace Walpole was bemused at the reports as others were furious. 'England that lives in the north of Europe, and Spain that dwells in the south, are vehemently angry with one another about a morsel of rock that lies somewhere at the very bottom of America, for modern nations are too neighbourly to quarrel about anything that lies so near that as in the same quarter of the globe.' For Walpole this habit of chasing after faraway islands had gone too far: 'Spain huffs, and we arm, for one of the extremities of the southern hemisphere. It takes a twelvemonth for any one of us to arrive at our object, and almost another twelvemonth before we can learn what we have been about.' Where this was all to end Walpole had no notion. 'By next century I suppose we shall fight for the Dog Star and the Great Bear.'[2]

Many took the episode as evidence of Britain's waning power. Not ten years ago she had been peerless after the Treaty of Paris. Since then the country's standing had been undermined by a series of indecisive governments that had allowed discontent to fester in the colonies, had failed to deal with Wilkes, and had recently allowed the French to occupy Corsica, giving them an enormous strategic advantage in the Mediterranean. Adding to the dreary picture was a report in the *General Evening Post*, on 25 September 1770, which surmised:

> that one ground of the present preparations for war is, some
> secret intelligence received by the ministry, that the *Endeavour*
> man of war, which was sent into the South Sea with the

Astronomers, to make observations, and afterwards to go into a new track to make discoveries, has been sunk, with all her people, by order of a jealous Court, who has committed other hostilities against us in the Southern hemisphere.[3]

The piece was not founded on solid intelligence. But it seeded the idea that 'Mr Banks and the famous Doctor Solander', notables among the crew, 'have shared the common fate with the rest of the ship's company.' In November 1770 another report, though one swiftly disavowed, revealed *Endeavour* had been destroyed by the Spanish in an action off the Philippines. Although there was no proof of this, the newspapers were only reporting in public what was being said in private. Sarah Sophia, Banks's sister, felt obliged to counter the rumours, writing to Thomas Pennant, 'we begin to fear we shall not see them till spring, upon account of their having missed the Trade Wind, but that is a very different situation to what the papers represented'.[4]

Endeavour's fate was of little consequence in the larger context of the imminent war. Spain, not keen on the prospect of a conflict with Britain, claimed to have only asserted their right by treaty. This was a line that found little favour in Westminster where a general mobilisation of the navy had been ordered. 'From this moment', wrote Johnson in an essay on the crisis, 'the whole nation can witness that no time was lost. The navy was surveyed, the ships refitted, and commanders appointed; and a powerful fleet was assembled, well manned and well stored.' Johnson thought it a folly that Britain would go to war over a portable storehouse in the 'deserts of the ocean' 7,000 miles away. Firing cannons at the British, driving them from the shore and removing the rudder were each inflammatory actions, he admitted, but they were injuries the British should bear.

If the rudder be to a ship what his tail is in fables to a fox, the part in which honour is placed, and of which the violation is never to be endured, I am sorry that the *Favourite* suffered an indignity, but cannot yet think it a cause for which nations should slaughter one another.[5]

The crisis soon passed. In January 1771 there was a conciliatory declaration by the Spanish, accompanied by a promise to restore Port Egmont. It was just as well. Johnson had spoken of British 'preparedness', but in reality the crisis had completely surprised the navy, which responded slowly. For this the old, faltering First Lord, Admiral Hawke, was blamed, and once peace had been secured he was quietly retired. In his place came, for a third time as First Lord, that old friend of Joseph Banks's, Lord Sandwich.

Tall, urbane, an enthusiast of cricket and music – he enjoyed pounding the drums at the Bach recitals at his home in Hinchingbrooke in Cambridgeshire – Sandwich was a veteran political operator. His name would pass into history in a strange sort of way, due to his fondness for eating salt beef between two slices of bread, but in his time Sandwich had a very different repute. From the 1760s he retained his notoriety as a rake and he lived openly (some said shamelessly) with his mistress, Martha Ray, who had borne him a succession of children over the last decade. If he continued to suffer the abuse of the press – Wilkes had written, 'Nature denied him wit, but gave him a species of buffoonery of the lowest kind'[6] – few doubted that, in reality, Sandwich was both a wise old fox and a safe pair of hands. Generally regarded as the ministry's best performer in the House of Lords, Sandwich was known for his mastery of the issues at hand, a coolness of demeanour and the ability to lay rhetorical blows. Easing into his new job in January 1771, there soon came news to excite even him. They were reports of *Endeavour*.

On 5 January 1771 a handful of lines appeared in the shipping columns, announcing that contrary to all rumour, *Endeavour* had arrived in the Dutch East Indies with Solander and Banks safe.[7] It was an unverified account that left everyone impatient. Five months passed until, on 11 May, more definite intelligence was carried from India House to Sandwich at the Admiralty, confirming that *Endeavour* had arrived at Batavia on 10 October 1771, 'and was repairing in order to return to England'.[8] This news soon bridged the gap between private and public spheres. A letter from Sydney Parkinson, 'principal drawer to Mr Banks', was published, relating the 'great hardships' they had experienced, and vaguely outlining the arc of the voyage. 'They have picked up a vast number of plants', the report ran, 'and other curiosities, and are expected in England some time next month.'[9]

Jane Gomeldon was one of those to receive a letter from Parkinson. 'My dear cousin', it began, 'Fain would I have excused myself from writing, could I have found any excuse, I am so hurried and fluttered about here; but, when I considered what a pleasure it would give thee to hear of our safe arrival here, I thought it would be unjust to withhold it.' Parkinson's letter was necessarily short. 'Were I to enter even into general things, I should not finish I do not know when', he excused himself. But within the narrow limits of several hundred words, he acquainted one of his fondest friends with his unlikely story. 'We had many hair-breadth escapes' off the coast of New Holland, he wrote. 'I have spared no pains during the voyage, to pick up every thing that is curious for thee; and I flatter myself that I shall make a considerable addition to thy museum.'[10]

Parkinson wrote these words on 16 October 1770, a week after they had anchored in Batavia, the main anchorage in the Dutch East Indies. In European minds this was a seductive place, rich in colour, wealth and spices. This was not what *Endeavour*'s crew found. Banks was disconcerted from the beginning. A boat rowed out to greet them. The officer aboard, wrote Banks, 'and his people were almost as Spectres, no good omen of the healthyness of the countrey we were arrived at'[11]. Conversely *Endeavour*'s crew might have been called 'rosy and plump, for we had not a sick man among us'. Only the ship herself was a desperate case. The leaks had multiplied since they left New Holland. She was now making from six to twelve inches of water an hour. Her keel was in a frightful state, the false keel was half missing and she still bore her old wound under the starboard chains.

All this had made a stay in Batavia a necessity. Cook had been horrified at what he saw on 8 November. In addition to the injuries they anticipated, they found the teredo worms had bored several floor pieces almost through, 'so that it was a Matter of Surprise to every one who saw her bottom how we had kept her above water; and yet in this condition we had saild some hundreds of Leagues in as dangerous a Navigation as is in any part of the world, happy in being ignorant of the continual danger we were in'.[12]

As the repairs had begun the sailors and gentlemen drifted ashore. Banks had hired a house and two carriages. Having established a temporary home he sent for Tupaia. Their *arioi* friend had stayed aboard *Endeavour*, being sick with a 'bilious' complaint. Once ashore his spirits soared at the sight of:

Houses, Carriages, streets, in short, every thing were to him sights which he had often heard describd but never well under-

stood, so he lookd upon them all with more than wonder, almost
mad with the numberless novelties which diverted his attention
from one to the other he danc'd about the streets examining
every thing to the best of his abilities.[13]

It was but a brief happy interlude. Tupaia had left Ra'iātea fifteen
months before. In this time he had lost the status and purpose of his
previous life. Along with his servant or travelling companion, Taiato,
he had persisted in his language lessons with Green the astronomer,
making, Parkinson reckoned, 'great progress in the English tongue'.
But Tupaia had also been physically weakened. Suffering from incip-
ient scurvy all the way up the New Holland coast, he had recovered
at Endeavour River – spending the six-week stay angling in the shallows – but his illness had returned as soon as they were at sea. In
Batavia, where everyone they met seemed to caution them about the
'extreme unwholesomeness' of the air, Tupaia's 'broken constitution'
stood little chance.

But he had not been the first to succumb. Most of the crew were
lodged at a location called Cooper's Island where they were seized by
a putrid dysentery. Monkhouse, the surgeon, died first. Following him
was one of the ship's boys, then a steward of the gun room. As
October 1770 ended and November began, the days began to fill with
fresh reports of new victims. Banks's two surviving servants, Peter
and James, developed intermitting fevers 'and Dr Solander a constant
nervous one'. Banks blamed 'the numberless dirty Canals which intersect the town in all directions'. Tupaia's opinion was much the same.
He asked to return to the ship so he could 'breathe a freeer air', but
by the end of October he had been sinking too.

On 9 November Taiato, who had become the 'darling of the ship's
company', reached the final stage of his illness. 'He frequently said
to those of us who were his intimates', Parkinson wrote, '*Tyau mate
oee*, "My friends, I am dying."'[14] Parkinson had drawn Taiato – a short,
full-cheeked boy with black curly hair, playing a nose flute – in Tahiti.
All these months later he was left to watch as Taiato accepted every
medicine prescribed him. But it was without success. Taiato's death
'so much affected' Tupaia, Banks wrote, 'there was little hopes of
his surviving him many days'. Whereas Taiato had been an optimistic
patient, Tupaia was a defeated one. He refused everything. He 'gave
himself up to grief', Parkinson wrote, 'regretting, in the highest

degree, that he had left his own country' and crying out inconsolably for his lost friend, *'Taiyota! Taiyota!'* Tupaia died on 11 November.

As *Endeavour* grew stronger in the yard, her crew grew weaker in their beds. Both Banks and Solander had progressive, dismal fevers, and retreated to a country house to recover. And even when the ship got underway again in January, bound for England, the illness travelled with them. As Cook struck south-west into the Indian Ocean 'the people', wrote Banks, 'in general grew worse and many had now the dysentery or bloody flux.'[15] In the days to come Herman Spöring died, as did Charles Green the astronomer and, on 26 January 1771, with something in the order of 1,300 illustrations completed, his journal still earnestly progressing, and with his tender letter to Jane Gomeldon not yet delivered, so too did Sydney Parkinson.

On 12 July 1771, *Endeavour* anchored in the Downs and Cook sent an instant dispatch to the Admiralty, reporting their arrival and his intention to come 'at once' to Whitehall 'with journals, charts &c'. His sailing duties at last at an end, a burst of administration was now required before he could leave the ship a free man, and begin the final leg of his circumnavigation to Mile End. There were the journals to collect and submit to the Admiralty; letters for the Victualling Board on the effectiveness of the sauerkraut, and muster books for the Navy Board listing in cool, crisp columns the names of those who returned and those who had not. The deaths had not ended in the Indian Ocean. Molyneux, the promising sailing master who had been so busy on the reefs of New Holland, 'a young man of good parts', wrote Cook, who 'had unfortunately given himself up to extravecancy and intemperance', had died after the Cape of Good Hope.[16] Then six weeks before home, Hicks, Cook's second in command, had finally succumbed to 'a Consumption which he was not free from when we saild from England'.[17]

The last life to be lost was not a human one, but that of Banks's greyhound 'Lady', who, a strangely affecting entry in Banks's journal tells us, was 'found dead in my Cabbin laying upon a stool on which she generaly slept', a fortnight before home:

> She had been remarkably well for some days, in the night she shriekd out very loud so that we who slept in the great Cabbin heard her, but becoming quiet immediately no one regarded it.[18]

Banks wondered at so instantaneous a death, but it was the story of another of the animals – this time a survivor – that thrilled the papers. Within a week of their return the *General Evening Post* printed a paean to the ship's goat. Brought aboard to provide milk for the crew, the goat was already a veteran at the time of her enlistment, having spent three years in the West Indies and been round the world with Wallis in the *Dolphin*. Now a double circumnavigator, the newspapers were pleased to report, 'She never went dry during the whole of the voyage.' In gratitude, the authorities had decided 'to reward her services by placing her in a good English pasture for the rest of her life.' Greater honours awaited. Soon the goat would be sanctified in verse by Johnson:

> In fame scarce second to the nurse of Jove,
> This Goat, who twice the world had travers'd round,
> Deserving both her master's care and love,
> Ease and perpetual pasture now has found.[19]

The rest of the ship's company were able to share in the goat's glory as they dispersed from the Thames into the London streets. Cook's privilege was to forward a list of names to the Admiralty, those who had performed exceptionally and so were deserving of promotion. Some feats had already made it into Cook's journal – the midshipman Jonathan Monkhouse's work with the fothering sail being one; though he, too, had died on the homeward passage – but now Cook had chance to write explicitly about the good conduct of Pickersgill, who had succeeded Molyneux as *Endeavour*'s master. Cook thought him 'deserving of a Lieuts Commission', a nomination that was honoured.

The public, though, would not hear any of these names. From May onwards, as *Endeavour* had entered the western approaches, letters written at the Cape of Good Hope outpaced her. First the Admiralty, then the families of the crew and finally the general public realised that this was the greatest South Seas voyage since Anson's. By the time *Endeavour* came alongside at Deptford, the newspapers were impatiently trying to establish and arrange in any fashion the facts of what had happened. With Cook busy completing his duties and Banks and Solander occupied with the unloading of their massive collections, the papers interrogated the sailors for any detail they could. Solander, best known of the travellers, was reported to have been gravely ill but recovering fast. There were stories of Tupaia and his boy – 'Natives of George's Island' – who had perished at Batavia but who had been 'amazingly struck with the sight of Coaches and Horses, having never seen either Horses, Cows or Sheep ... They were extremely surprised also at the Sight of themselves and Company in a Looking Glass.' Charles Green's demise was dramatised too. One newspaper claimed that 'in a fit of phrensy he got up in the night and put his legs out of the portholes, which was the occasion of his death'. If this was not fanciful enough, the high peak of magnification was reached by the *Public Advertiser* on 7 August, who reported that 'Mr Banks and Dr Solander have made more curious Discoveries in the way of Astronomy, and Natural History, than at any one Time have been presented to the learned World for these fifty years past.'[20]

Banks would do little to quench these rumours, despite the fact that he had been mostly indifferent about the Transit of Venus. He had never had a public profile before July 1771. Even in early reports of their return his name had trailed second to Solander's. But from August onwards the names 'Mr Banks and Dr Solander' framed almost every *Endeavour* story. Theirs was a symbiotic relationship of the 'ingenious gentlemen', and they were now circumnavigators, eligible to a club of elite voyagers including Francis Drake, William Dampier and George Anson. And Banks was not grizzled and past forty. He was twenty-eight, handsome, eloquent and appealingly rich.

Of all the stories from the voyage, it was the size and scope of their natural-history collections that were the most thrilling. 'No less than seventeen thousand plants, of a kind never before seen in this kingdom', wrote the *Westminster Journal*. The *Public Advertiser* revealed that some of them had already been planted in the 'Royal Garden at Richmond, and thrive very well'. John Ellis, always quick with the gossip, had written to Linnaeus on 16 July that Banks and Solander had returned 'after so many perils, laden with the greatest treasure of Natural History that ever was brought into any country at one time by two persons'.[21] On 8 August, in Uppsala, Linnaeus composed, in Latin, the most admiring of letters to 'Immortalis Banks'. 'None, from the earth's foundation, has ventured such great things; none has ever been so generous; none, at any time, has so exposed himself to all dangers as you alone have.' He signed off, 'Farewell, man without equals.'[22]

Cook was left with the more moderate 'approbation' of the Admiralty. 'Resolved', ran their minutes on 1 August, that Cook 'be acquainted [that] the Board extremely well approve of the whole of his Proceedings, and have great satisfaction in the account he gives of the good behaviour of his officers and men, and of the chearfullness and alertness with which they went through the fatigues and dangers of the Voyage.' Each of these words must have been ringed with gold for Cook. And an honour greater than any before granted to a Whitby sailing master followed. Banks's and Solander's celebrity had already led to an audience with King George III on 10 August at St James's. The king, having invested in the voyage after the Royal Society's 'Memorial' of 1768 – had taken an interest in its progress. Now, on 14 August, Cook himself was introduced by Sandwich. At the same occasion an even more wished-for award was conferred. He was presented with his captain's commission. He would now legitimately be 'Captain Cook'.

Cook's name was to be lost in the glow of the naturalists'. 'The people who are most talk'd of at present are Mr Banks and Dr Solander', judged Lady Mary Coke – salonesse, socialite and arbiter of fashion – their voyage had been 'very amusing'. But not every word said of Banks was complimentary. Having mentioned nothing of it throughout the voyage, it now became clear that he had left a promise of marriage behind with a young lady called Harriet Blosset. Having arrived home at the height of the season, Banks appeared to have forgotten his bearings as a gentleman. 'I saw Mr Morrice this morning', Lady Mary Coke wrote on 14 August:

He was excessively drole according to custom, and said he hoped Mr Banks, who since his return has desired Miss Blosset will excuse his marrying her, will pay her for the materials of all the work'd waistcoats She made for him during the time he was sailing round the World. Everybody agrees that She passed those three years in retirement, but whether She imploy'd herself in working waistcoats for Mr Banks I can't tell you, but if She loved him I pity her disappointment.[23]

If any social situation in Georgian London equated to being becalmed on the edge of a reef, then Banks had discovered it. This was a delicate scenario made infinitely worse by Banks's handling of it. Everyone agreed that his was ungallant behaviour. Arriving back in London, Banks had simply ignored Miss Blosset, while going about town meeting old friends. Soon the news was out that Blosset had been sewing for a scoundrel. After a week of the indignity she decided that she could tolerate his behaviour no longer. She struck out for London having sent a letter to Banks in New Burlington Street, demanding an 'interview of explanation'. Daines Barrington, a friend of Banks's, heard the ensuing tale, which he set down in a half-amused, half-scandalised letter:

> To this Mr Bankes answer'd by a letter of 2 or 3 sheets professing love &c but that he found he was of too volatile a temper to marry.
>
> The answer as you may suppose rather astonished & some how or other after this there was an interview when Miss Bl: swoon'd &c & Mr Bankes was so affected that Marriage was again concluded upon. Notwithstanding this however a short time afterwards he writes a second letter to the same purport with the former, & leaves poor Miss Bl: in the most distressing as well as ridiculous situation imaginable.

It would take Jane Austen to fully portray the interview between Banks and Blosset, the span of which – Barrington discovered – 'lasted from ten O'clock at Night to ten the next Morning'. By the time the bells of Grosvenor Chapel rang the next day, Banks had declared he was ready to marry 'immediately'. But wise to his volatile moods, Blosset delayed. 'If he was of the same mind a fortnight hence, she would gladly attend him to church.' The inevitable letter came three or four days later from New Burlington Street, 'desiring to be off'.[24]

In other circumstances the Blosset affair may have left a deeper stain on Banks's character. But Banks's fortunes were too far in the ascendancy to be checked. Young, urbane, good-looking with a dash of the dangerous and the exotic, that summer Banks experienced an early-modern version of what later would be called 'celebrity'. The fashionable talked about his adventures. He was soon to be painted by Benjamin West and Joshua Reynolds, shown as the intellectual man of action or the dreaming romantic, wrapped in Tahitian bark cloth or resting his arm on a table filled with scientific papers. His journal, inevitably, was polished into voyaging literature. Lord Sandwich selected Dr John Hawkesworth, one of the best London writers, to complete the job. Then there were the honorary doctorates from Oxford for Banks and Solander and the ever-closer relationship with the king. Banks became such a favourite at court that in September the *Public Advertiser* felt compelled to protest, 'it is too great a Liberty to take with such sacred Characters, to suppose they would Day after Day stare at the Pictures of some useless Weeds, or gape over the Slippers and Habits of poor Savages, fit only to add to the like Curiosities at Don Saltaro's Coffee-house'.[25]

Already the contents of the ship had dispersed, starting a process of fragmentation that would take parts of *Endeavour*'s massive collections into private houses, museums, libraries and universities. But as that exuberant summer tailed away into autumn, on 28 September 1771 there was a final moment of synthesis. Sandwich, the First Lord, held a 'Splendid entertainment' at his house in the Admiralty on Whitehall for all the principal people 'belonging to the *Endeavour*'.[26]

Amid the excitement it was, perhaps, difficult to pinpoint exactly what the *Endeavour* voyage had achieved. Nothing new had really been found. The transit observations had been gathered, but not impeccably so. It was clear that plenty of curiosities had been carried home in boxes and jars, but what was the worth of these plants and spears in a country that, more than anything, was craving fossil fuels and new technologies? To gather all these plants many lives had been lost and no southern continent – one of the chief objectives of the voyage – had been found. As Johnson said to Boswell, 'they have found very little, only one new animal, I think', the *kanguru*. 'But many insects, Sir', Boswell replied.[27]

This was a hard verdict. With the transit observations it is difficult to see how Cook and Green could have done any better with the apparatus available to them. The 'black drop effect' they experienced was not particular to them, but rather a blight for every observer. As for the various collections, it took decades for people to come to terms with the scale of what had been brought home. One recent publication has tallied up Banks's haul: '5 mammals; 107+ birds; 248+ fishes; 370+ arthropods; 206+ molluscs; 6 echinoderms; 9 salps; 30 medusae and some other animals'. On top of this were 30,400 botanical specimens, of which 1,400 were previously unknown to Western science.[28] Everyone knew about Linnaeus's herbarium at Uppsala. On *Endeavour*'s return in 1771 she contained a herbarium that outdid Linnaeus's in scope, diversity and size. All told, this one single voyage enhanced the list of plant species collected in the *Species plantarum* of 1762–3 by around a fifth.[29]

Other personal collections augmented Banks's vast one. For Cook the most important were his charts, views of coasts and maps of anchorages that had piled up as they went. Among them the most exciting were the charts of Tahiti, New Zealand and the east coast of New Holland. Botany Bay would not be forgotten. In the immediate aftermath, though, New Zealand was acknowledged as a discovery, 'truly one of the highest consequence'. That the Dutch might have explored the islands a century and a half before but did not, presented the British with an opportunity many were eager to seize.

Arousing as much interest was the story of *Endeavour*'s near disaster on the reef. For some the escape – the calm weather, the nearby harbour, the abundance of turtle, the friendly breeze – was providential. It is an interesting insight into the development of Western philosophy that such an interpretation was not universally accepted. John Hawkesworth, compiler of the official account, theorised that it was a 'mere natural event'.

> If it was not a mere natural event, but produced by an extraordinary interposition, correcting a defect in the constitution of nature, tending to mischief, it will lie upon those who maintain the position, to shew, why an extraordinary interposition did not take place rather to prevent the ship's striking, than to prevent her being beaten to pieces after she had struck: a very slight impulse upon the ship's course would have caused her to steer clear of the rock, and if all things were not equally easy to Omnipotence, we should say that this might have been done with less difficulty than a calm could be produced by suspending the general laws of Nature which had brought on the gale.[30]

This passage is reminiscent of Banks's phrase 'almost providential'. Those are two revealing words. Having faced death and been fortunately spared, Banks still can't quite bring himself to believe that God had anything to do with it. This was the age of enquiry and knowledge, and superstition was being driven away. But which voyager a century, or even a generation before, would have denied the inference

that they were divinely favoured? In Banks and Hawkesworth we see
the progress of Western thought. It was not God, it was luck.

The voyage provided more subject for discussion. On Sunday 18
August, six weeks after their return, Banks and Solander dined with
the new president of the Royal Society, John Pringle, and Benjamin
Franklin. Franklin wrote an intriguing account of their conversation.
He was most interested of all in the people the naturalists had met.
Those 'of Otahitee (George's Island) are civilized in a great degree',
Franklin heard. There was praise too for the Māori, 'a brave and
sensible People', though the inhabitants of New Holland were beyond
their understanding. They told Franklin an affecting story. One day
they had found four children in a hut on the New Holland coast. It
seemed, they thought, a good opportunity to establish relations. Seeing
some other people at a distance who were shy and would not engage,
'we adorn'd the Children with Ribbands and Beads, and left with them
a Number of little Trinkets and some other useful Things'. Banks and
Solander had then retired to a distance, to let events unfold. They
had, at length, returned to the hut to find all the presents discarded
on the floor. The story intrigued Franklin.

> We call this Stupidity. But if we were dispos'd to compliment
> them, we might say, Behold a Nation of Philosophers! such as
> him whom we celebrate for saying as he went thro' a Fair, *How
> many things there are in the World that I don't want!*[31]

Franklin was not among those to get carried away with Banks's
return. There is surprisingly little in his papers on *Endeavour* that summer.
Perhaps his attention was consumed by the ongoing disorder in America,
or maybe he shared some of his friend Dalrymple's sense of unfairness
that all the glory had been deflected away from him. Dalrymple had
been one of the most eager to hear news of the voyage. A central
question – one that remained unanswered for many – had bothered
him. How had Cook escaped the reefs and corals off New Holland?

Dalrymple soon got his answer. He met Banks soon after
Endeavour's return and he learned that they had searched for and
located a strait that Dalrymple had mentioned in his book of historic
voyages. Dalrymple knew at once that Cook 'could only have got
[this] from me'. This 'Torres Strait' had allowed *Endeavour* to pass
between New Holland and New Guinea. The story was difficult for

Dalrymple to stomach. This idea that he had not only mapped out the parameters of the voyage, but had then come to rescue the hapless crew gnawed at him. Now he was forced to endure the fanfare of their homecoming with every curiosity save the one he wanted them to find. 'I did then, and still do, believe that a *Southern Continent does exist*', he declared.[32]

Dalrymple's anger was bottled up for eighteen months following *Endeavour*'s return. But after reading Hawkesworth's account of the voyage, his fury exploded. Several letters addressed to Hawkesworth from Dalrymple emerged. They were productions of epic hostility, liberally enlivened with italics and capitals to better convey the warmth of his fury. He took aim at his foes, the unnamed Admiralty mandarins who had defeated him by stratagem back in 1768. And there was ammunition spare for Cook too, whom he thought negligent as an explorer. One of Cook's journal entries aggravated him wildly. When *Endeavour* was on her run north-west from Cape Horn to Tahiti, tell-tale signs of land had accumulated, but Cook had written 'It was a general opinion that there was Land to windward, *but I did not think myself at liberty to search for what I was not sure to find.*'[33]

This sentence was too much for Dalrymple to bear. 'Such a declaration, if not foisted in by you, would almost preclude me from taking any further notice of C. Cook's conduct or opinions', he wrote. Dalrymple may have forgotten that Cook was hurrying towards Tahiti to study the transit – the principal objective, and one he hardly would be excused disregarding for some seabirds. But it was, to Dalrymple, an unpardonable offence. To negligence he added the charge of wanton violence, rounding off his public letter:

> In the mean while I *wish* YOU *more candour*, and resign *myself to Providence*, although, *in the wisdom of its dispensations*, I was prevented, by the *secondary influence* of *narrow minded men,* from compleating the Discovery of, and establishing an amicable intercourse with, a *Southern Continent*; which, notwithstanding your sagacious reasonings, I still think, from my own experience, in such like voyages, *may be done* without *committing murder.*[34]

He was not alone in feeling unease at what had happened in Poverty Bay. Hawkesworth tackled the question of violence head-on. He expressed 'regret' at what had happened, but believed there was a sad inevitability to such confrontations. History was in motion, people were caught between forces. The pursuit of knowledge and commerce were pushing Europeans outwards, and it was logical that those they met endeavoured 'to repress the invaders of their country'. If those who resisted were not 'overpowered, the attempt must be relinquished'. The lesson for Hawkesworth was that those entrusted with the delicate task of voyaging must not be 'men who are liable to provocation by sudden injury, to unpremeditated violence by sudden danger, to error by the defect of judgment or the strength of passion'.[35]

In the immediate aftermath of *Endeavour*'s return the Admiralty realised that they had been fortunate with their crew. Gore and Hicks had been fine sailors, and Pickersgill, Molyneux and Jonathan Monkhouse had all contributed to the safe management of the ship too. Banks and Solander were a more obvious success. It was more chance than design that had flung the philosophers and the sailors together and little forethought had been given to the social dynamics of their addition by anyone but Hawke. But for a little inconvenience aboard, the voyage had been enormously enhanced by their erudition, their methodological approach, their desire to chronicle and to collect.

Banks, in particular, had infused the voyage with his playful, probing, fun-loving personality. As loudly as his achievements were being blared from newspaper columns in 1771, he had done something in excess of what people comprehended even then. He had created an archetype. Whenever ships sailed on exploration voyages afterwards, they would carry a naturalist as a matter of course, who would often have something of Banks about them. They would be bright, cheerful, clever, game, often just down from Oxbridge, and boisterous in their resolution to experience the world. In time a twinkling list of naturalists would follow Banks: Georg Forster, Alfred Wallace, Charles Darwin and Joseph Hooker; the list is perhaps still going with Sir David Attenborough today.

No one had any notion of this historical significance in the 1770s. But people did get to appreciate another of Banks's innovations. In 1773 the collected papers of Sydney Parkinson were published, as one of the earliest eyewitness accounts of *Endeavour*'s voyage. They introduced the public to Parkinson, a young, earnest, thoughtful voyager, whose fear of death was always finely balanced by his desire to experience the world around him. The 'fair copy' of Parkinson's journal disappeared sometime on the homeward passage – something that

occasioned a dispute between Parkinson's elder brother and Banks –
but what did make it into print in his *A Journal of a Voyage to the South
Seas* gave the British public a far clearer perspective of life in the Pacific
islands. Brightening the pages were selections from Parkinson's artistic
work – enticing visual depictions of tattooed warriors, unfamiliar
landscapes and exotic plants. These were only a fraction of Parkinson's
massive output, which stretched well beyond a thousand works. As
Banks pioneered the voyaging naturalist, Parkinson shaped the role
of the voyaging painter.

Above all of these was Cook. In 1771 the Admiralty could hardly
have been more pleased with him. The list of accomplishments stood
for itself, but it was his manner of going about things that was equally
striking. In an excitable age Cook had demonstrated that he had much
of the stoic about him. He had acted with cool resolution in the
calamity on the reef. He had been uncorrupted by the pleasures of
Tahiti. He had not got carried away with his successes, as Wallis and
Byron had, but had kept diligently to his orders. Even in Batavia when
everyone else had succumbed to maladies, Cook had seemed immune.
Perhaps the Admiralty's greatest discovery on the *Endeavour* voyage
was Cook himself.

Promotions, honours and respect were granted the ship's company,
but nothing was immediately done for *Endeavour* herself. A generation
later, when thinking about Cook's ships, the Admiralty mandarin Sir
John Barrow wrote that he would have had them 'laid up in a dock'
until they had 'wasted away plank by plank'. This is what Queen
Elizabeth I had done with Sir Francis Drake's *Golden Hind*, Barrow
recorded. '[Drake's] ship was preserved with great care, for many
years, in the dock-yard of Deptford; and when time had gradually
reduced her to such a state of decay that she could no longer be held
together, a chair was constructed from some of the soundest parts
and presented to the University of Oxford, as a relic that was still
worthy of further preservation.'[36]

There was nothing like this for *Endeavour*. By the time of Lord
Sandwich's entertainment at the Admiralty in September, she had
already been recommissioned for service elsewhere. If Cook and
Banks were to sail again, they needed to find a new ship. Plans for
another voyage were already afoot. There was one obvious zone of
interest that remained to be explored. This was a stretch of the mid-

Pacific, at high latitudes. It was the final lingering place that a continent could be found. Cook's *Endeavour* journal ended with a
suggestion that they return to the friendly anchorage at Queen
Charlotte's Sound in New Zealand, and his plan was quickly adopted.
On 25 September the Admiralty instructed the Navy Board to
'purchase two proper vessels of about 400 tons for service in remote
parts'. This time Cook was to have his choice. If imitation is the
highest form of flattery, no better can be said of *Endeavour* than
during that autumn Cook went to the Thames and selected two barks
of similar design: *Marquis of Granby*, 450 tons, and *Marquis of
Rockingham*, 336 tons. They were both colliers built by Thomas
Fishburn. Far from being an obscure business on a provincial river,
Fishburn's shipyard was becoming something of a Georgian Cape
Canaveral: a launch site for expeditions to new worlds.

The plan was to sail in the spring, and by November the usual
flurry of communications was relaying between the Admiralty, the
Navy Board and the Victualling Office. Names were proposed. *Drake*
for the *Marquis of Granby*, *Raleigh* for the *Marquis of Rockingham*, though
these were soon amended. *Drake* became *Resolution* and *Raleigh* became
Adventure, Sandwich sanctioning the changes after a 'hint' from one
of his colleagues, who pointed out that the Spanish 'hold in detesta-
tion those two names [Drake and Raleigh] and will believe we do it
on purpose to insult them'.

This discussion was one of scores that occupied Sandwich and Cook
over the autumn and winter of 1771. The abundance of letters, memo-
randums, orders and notes between them can be studied today, but
they were concealed from the public at the time, who were left to
garner what information they could from the newspapers. This version
of the voyage's fitting-out was quite different. It was a separate telling
of the same story that could be traced back to 26 August 1771, and a
report in the *Gazetteer and New Daily Advertiser*, that proclaimed 'Mr
Banks is to have two ships from government to pursue his discoveries
in the South Seas, and will sail upon his second voyage next March.'[37]

The public interest in the summer of 1771 did not only irritate
Dalrymple, it left Banks hungry for more. He had one small voyage
and one great voyage behind him as evidence of his pedigree as a
traveller. More laurels, Banks convinced himself, awaited. This next
voyage promised a return to Tahiti and a reacquaintance with friends
(and flames), but otherwise it augured more snow than sunshine, with

the proposed route taking them deep into the high latitudes. He was not daunted by this. 'O how Glorious would it be to set my heel upon ye Pole!', Banks exclaimed at Christmas 1771, 'and turn myself round 360 degrees in a second.'[38]

As far as the newspapers were concerned, the next voyage was to be a Banks and Solander reprise, and they reported it as such. According to the *Reading Mercury*, it was anticipated 'that Messrs Banks and Solander in their next voyage to the South Seas, will be ordered to proceed by the North-west passage, the Spanish Ambassador having peremptorily declared to our Ministry, that his Master will not suffer them to pass by the Falkland Islands'. More details came from the *Kentish Gazette*, which revealed on Christmas Eve that 'Dr Solander and Mr Banks had a private conference with his Majesty on Wednesday evening at St James's: they were closeted for near two hours. It is supposed they received some instructions relative to their intended voyage.' Another 'very long conference' took place with Banks, Solander, Lord Sandwich and Lord North in early January, 'relating to their intended voyage'.

Banks was financing his part of the voyage again, and having experienced the limitations on *Endeavour*, he was anxious to tackle the shortcomings. Applications to join Banks's latest enterprise arrived by the hundredweight at New Burlington Street. By the spring Banks's addition to the *Resolution*'s company had risen to fourteen. Naturally there was him and Solander. Then to capture the seductive elegance of the Pacific in oil he contracted Johan Zoffany, the German neoclassical painter, as the lead artist. Also in the suite were two other draughtsmen – both in the Parkinson mould – a surgeon, six servants and – a fact that has never been forgotten – two French-horn players.

Banks had been irritated to find Cook had purchased two more colliers without consulting him. He believed they were not big enough. *Resolution* was hardly larger than *Endeavour*, yet his suite was twice the number. It was too late for Banks to do anything about the ship, but he had insisted that alterations be made – against the advice of the Navy Board and Cook's old patron, Hugh Palliser, who was now comptroller of the navy. The amendments to *Resolution* focussed on the traditional officers' quarters and the great cabin. Fishburn would have been baffled to see the plan that was proposed. Everything in the upper works was to be raised a foot. A new deck was ordered and a 'round house' was to be constructed over the great cabin, a place for Cook and the principal officers away from the great cabin that would remain Banks's domain.

These alterations were completed at Deptford as Banks assembled his team in the early spring. Allied with reports in the newspapers, this contorted ship became an attraction in herself, Cook recording that 'out of Idle curiosity' people of 'all ranks' came to view her, 'Ladies as well as gentlemen, for scarce a day past on which she was not crowded with strangers who came on board for no other purpose but to see the Ship in which Mr Banks was to sail round the world.' On 2 May, with the departure imminent, and all Banks's provisions and equipment being loaded onto the *Resolution*, Cook led a review of the ship headed by Sandwich, 'after which a grand entertainment was given to the Nobility and Gentry who attended on the occasion'.

On 13 May 1772 *Resolution* sailed from Deptford. The plan was to have a pilot take her downriver, then for Cook to guide her into the anchorage at the Downs. Fully loaded with provisions and men, they sailed east into the morning sun with 'a moderate breeze with the wind from ENE to ESE'. This should have been an easy prelude to their departure, but it turned out very differently. Having spent as much as £10,000 on fitting the ship out, it was disconcerting to see how poorly *Resolution* sailed. All the light colliers were 'working down the river, some with top gallant sails and *all* their whole top sail and staysails', Cook wrote, but at the same time they 'could not with safety (though the wind was steady and without flurries) carry out single Reeft Topsails with the Jib'. Time and again *Resolution* fell off the wind, and she crouched so low in the water that she was listing almost as much as *Endeavour* had when punctured with the coral rock off New Holland. It was a shameful performance. This was a ship they hoped to sail to the end of the world. As soon as he was able, Cook drafted a letter to the Navy Board:

The Pilot desires me to inform you that he cannot think of taking her further than the Nore* with security to the ship or without hazarding his reputation in the attempt, unless with a fair wind.

---

*   The Nore is a hazardous sandbank in the Thames Estuary where the river meets the North Sea.

I thought it my duty to give you the earliest notice of our situation. I beg leave to offer you my own private opinion and to assure you that I think her an exceeding dangerous and unsafe ship.[39]

In nautical parlance *Resolution* was 'crank', or 'so exceeding crank' as Cook expanded in a later letter: 'I beg leave to offer it as my opinion that she is too deep in the water to carry sail, being loaded below her bearings, and that by cutting down part of her upper works, shorting her masts and exchanging her guns from 6 to 4 pounders would lighten her to a proper depth of water and make her very fit to proceed on the voyage.'

It is inconceivable that Cook, who had been raised among the yards at Whitby and knew the balances and the lines of colliers like few others, would not have anticipated this. The troubles – he made this crystal clear – had come from Banks's alterations. That Cook must have known what was coming leaves him open to a charge of subterfuge, one that Banks soon levelled at him. As for Banks himself, the great house of cards that he had spent eight months building was about to come tumbling down.

Banks was to hear the wretched state of affairs from Charles Clerke, who had sailed with him on *Endeavour*. 'She is so very bad, that the Pilot declares, he will not run the risk of his Character so far, as to take charge of her, father than the Nore, without a fair Wind', he explained. Clerke nonetheless displayed admirable *esprit de corps*:

Hope you known me too well, to impute my giving this intelligence to any ridiculous apprehensions for myself, by God I'll go to Sea in a Grog Tub if desir'd, or in the Resolution as soon as you please; but must say, I do think her by far the most unsafe Ship I ever saw or heard of; however, if you think proper to embark for the South Pole in a Ship, which a Pilot, (who I think is, by no means a timorous man) will not undertake to carry down the River; all I can say is, that you shall be most chearfully attended, so long as we can keep her above Water.[40]

The true misery of Banks's situation was made plain on 20 May, when the Admiralty ordered the *Resolution* returned to her original condition. For Banks this was public humiliation. Temperamentally disposed to outbursts of passion, Banks now acted in a manner so foolish it would long be remembered in the Georgian navy. On 28 May he ordered all of his equipment, his people and provisions off *Resolution*, because he 'declined' to take the voyage.

His decision was communicated to the Admiralty in an intemperate and poorly judged letter to Sandwich. Banks wrote with a mixture of entitlement, false modesty and high arrogance. He implied that he had only taken the voyage at the request of 'others'; that he had 'pledged' himself 'to all Europe'; that he had funded generously where others had not. 'Shall I then my lord who have engagd to leave all that can make life agreable in my own country and throw on one side all the Pleasures to be reapd from three of the best years of my life merely to compass this undertaking pregnant enough with dangers and difficulties ... be sent off in a doubtfull ship with accommodations rather worse than those which at first I absolutely refusd.' Banks now arrived at his main charge: one particularly offensive to any sea officer. He asserted that the ship was 'unsafe merely in conformity to the official opinion of the navy board who purchasd her without ever consulting me'. For Sandwich this was intolerable. That Banks had increasingly treated the Admiralty as a subservient office was bad enough, but to suggest he knew more of the workings, preparation and management of ships was pure self-righteousness.

Sandwich sent a grave reply on 2 June. Banks had threatened a public letter and Sandwich advised him against this, 'as it will probably make it necessary that some answer should be given ... for it is a heavy charge against this Board to suppose that they mean to send a number of men to sea in an unhealthy ship'. It was logic Banks could not counter.

The same day Sandwich composed his riposte, Cook too was writing to New Burlington Street. 'The Cook & two French Horn men are at liberty to go when ever they please', does not rank as one of Cook's most insightful lines, but it is a memorable one. Elsewhere Cook summarised:

Mr Banks unfortunate for himself set out upon too large a Plan a Plan that was incompatible with a Scheme of discovery at the Antipodes; had he confined himself to the same plan as he set out upon last Voyage, attended only to his own persutes and not interfered with the choice, equipmint and even Direction of the

Ships things that he was not a competent judge of, he would have found every one concerned in the expedition ever ready to oblige him, for my self I can declare it: instead of finding fault with the Ship he ought to have considered that the Endeavour Bark was just such another, whose good quallities enabled me to remain so much longer in the South Sea then any one had been able to do before, and gave him an oppertunity to acquire that reputation the Publick has so liberally and with great justice bestowed upon him.[41]

The affair occasioned another intriguing paper. So long an admirer of Cook's, Hugh Palliser had watched Banks's plans explode. Palliser was steeped in the sea. He had enlisted in the 1730s, had fought in the wars of the 1740s and 1750s, and had been involved in numerous single ship engagements. Palliser's instinct was for pragmatism. In this spirit he wrote a memorandum, *Thoughts upon the Kind of Ships proper to be employed on Discoveries in distant Parts of the Globe*. It enumerated on the perils of the distant sea voyage, most particularly 'running ashore upon desart, uninhabited or perhaps savage Coast[s]'. The ideal ship, he reckoned, 'must be one of a large Burthen, and of a small Draught of Water, with a Body that will bear to take the Ground, and of a *Size* which in case of necessity may be safely and conveniently laid on shore to repair any accidental Damages or Defect'.

On the whole, I am firmly of Opinion that Ships of no other Kind are so proper for Discoveries in distant unknown Parts, as the *Endeavour* (formerly employed) was: – for no Ships of any other Kind can contain Stores and Provisions sufficient (in propor-tion to their Complements) for the purpose, considering the Length of Time it may be necessary they should last, and if they could contain sufficient Quantities. yet on arriving at the Parts for Discovery, they would still from the Nature of their Construction and *Size*, be less fit and applicable for the purpose: Hence I conclude it is, that so little Progress has hitherto been made in Discovery in the Southern Hemisphere: for all Ships which attempted the Business before the *Endeavour*, were unfit for it, altho' those employed did the utmost in their Power: As soon as Mons. Bougainville came in sight of a part of the new discovered coast which Capᵗ Cook compleatly explored, he fled from it as fast as possible and durst not approach it with the Ship he was in: –

It was upon these Considerations that the *Endeavour* Bark was chosen for that Voyage (the first of the King so employed) and notwithstanding those on board her who are not proper Judges found fault with her during the whole Voyage, yet it was to these properties in her that they owe their Preservation, and that enabled Capt Cook to stay in those Seas so much longer than any other Ship ever did or could do.[42]

Sandwich thought much the same. Jotting down a few words of advice for Banks, who had vowed to begin a new voyage of exploration, all of his own, he suggested:

Upon the whole I hope that for the advantage of the curious part of Mankind, your zeal for distant voyages will not yet cease, I heartily wish you success in all your undertakings ... and as I have a sincere regard for your wellfare and consequently for your preservation, I earnestly entreat that that ship may not be an old Man of War or an old Indiaman but a New Collier.[43]

It did not take the newspapers long to get hold of the story. On 29 May, the day after Banks's angry letter to Sandwich, they reported that 'The intended Voyage of Mr Banks and Dr Solander to the South Seas, it is now said, is entirely laid aside.' Various reasons were forwarded in the days to come – that it gave 'umbrage' to the Spanish king, 'for want of necessary accommodation' – but the material fact remained the same. Banks was not going. Returned to her original state, *Resolution* was soon on her way to Plymouth for final preparations – once again, sailing like a true Whitby collier.

On 12 July, Banks's fall was confirmed in true British style with a mischievous Fleet Street caricature. *The Fly Catching Macaroni* shows Banks dressed in all the gaudy finery of a Pall Mall gentleman, standing astride an upturned globe as if he was straddling a fairground ride. Having gained a perilous balance, Banks's eyes are fixed on the top-left corner of the print where a lone butterfly flaps past. The action is frozen at the decisive moment, as Banks flails and swots at the creature with his catching nets. To inflate the sense of absurdity, the artist has added a pair of ass's ears to the subject's head. 'I rove from Pole to

Pole, you ask me why,' poses the caption, 'I tell you Truth, to catch a – Fly.'[44]

Banks would see nothing of the South Pole, though Cook would get close on his first voyage in HMS *Resolution* – an expedition the historian Glyndwr Williams has called 'arguably the greatest, most perfect of all seaborne voyages of exploration'.[45] On his outward passage he paused at the Cape of Good Hope to begin the process of mending his friendship with Banks. 'Dear Sir', he began, 'Some Cross circumstances which happened at the latter part of the equipment of the *Resolution* created, I have reason to think, a coolness betwixt you and I, but I can by no means think it was sufficient to me to break of all correspondence with a Man I am under m[a]ny obligations to.' Hoping to lighten the mood, Cook found safety in more humdrum matters:

> I am in your debt for the Pickled and dryed Salmon which you left on board, which a little time ago was most excellant, but the eight Casks of Pickled salted fish I kept for my self proved so bad that even the Hoggs would not eat it.[46]

There was no estrangement between Cook and Banks, who retained a mutual regard for the remainder of their lives. Banks, in particular, hung Nathaniel Dance's iconic three-quarter-length portrait of Cook over the fireplace of his library in later years, doubtless glancing towards it at moments of indecision. As for another old friend, HM Bark *Endeavour*, even by the time *Resolution* was purchased in November 1771, she was already long gone.

II

The Frozen Serpent of the South

Lord Sandwich had long got a bad press. Public attitudes towards him had been shaped by an unforgettable episode on 15 November 1763. Everyone knew the story. It came towards the end of the Wilkes affair. The government, in which Sandwich was a Secretary of State, had explored every legal method to destroy Wilkes. Failing, Sandwich had conceived a plan to shame him in public. Sandwich knew Wilkes. They socialised in the same circles and may even have been friends. Through this familiarity, Sandwich had learned about an obscene, blasphemous poem, part-authored by Wilkes, called 'An Essay on Woman'. This was a bawdy parody of Alexander Pope's 'An Essay on Man'. It continued as it began:

> Awake, my Fanny, leave all meaner things,
> This morn shall prove what rapture swiving brings.
> Let us (since life can little more supply
> Than just a few good Fucks, and then we die)[1]

Thrown carelessly together in the 1750s, in 1763 Wilkes had come across the poem again. He had asked his printer to run a few copies off the press for the amusement of friends. Particularly risqué were some insinuations about the Bishop of Gloucester's wife. Sandwich had obtained a copy. Realising its explosive potential he brought it to the Lords on 15 November. He rose and told his fellow lords that 'he had a paper in his hand abusing in the grossest manner, the Bishop of Gloucester'. The poem, he went on, 'was so infamous, so full of filthy language as well as the most horrid blasphemies that he was ashamed to read the whole to their lordships'. 'Read on! Read on!', the cry echoed around the chamber. Sandwich did. The effect was deadly.[2]

Sandwich might have achieved his short-term objective of embarrassing Wilkes. But he also damaged himself in ways he had not anticipated. Everyone knew Sandwich's personal life was far from spotless. Aside from living openly with a mistress, rumours of his clandestine assignations around the West End were rife. For him to play the role of the outraged moralist smacked of sanctimony. By outing Wilkes in so public a forum, he violated the social code that a gentleman's private life should never be exposed to the public. That Sandwich had transgressed this rule was made all the worse by the dignity of his rank. He was no petty, backstabbing squire. He was an earl.

Long after the fuss over 'An Essay on Woman' subsided, the reek of Sandwich's hypocrisy remained. Lord le Despenser reflected the general opinion, he 'never before heard the devil preach a sermon against sin.' Having earned the reputation of a man with an incredible capacity for treachery, he soon acquired the nickname that stuck: 'Jemmy Twitcher', the infamous turncoat in John Gay's *Beggar's Opera*. If Jesus had his Judas, and Caesar had his Brutus, Wilkes had his Sandwich. The cries 'Jemmy Twitcher! Jemmy Twitcher!' chased Sandwich's coach along London's streets and his name through the newspaper columns for years after.

By the 1770s, this was an old story. Sandwich had learned to endure 'with equal good-humour the freedom with which his friends attacked him, and the satire of his opponents', wrote Walpole.[3] The taunts were made more tolerable, perhaps, because his political career had not suffered. This was paramount as Sandwich was not a rich man. To maintain his position among London's aristocratic elite, it was important for him to retain a high-ranking government position. Though the king harboured some doubts about Sandwich's murky reputation, it was hard to ignore someone of his administrative calibre. 'No man in the Administration was so much master of business, so quick, or so shrewd', Walpole observed. To these talents, Sandwich had the double appeal of being a member of the hawkish and powerful Bedford faction, who had argued for a hard-line policy against the colonies and against the repeal of the Stamp Act. These views brought him in harmony with the king's. It had been to no one's surprise when Sandwich was appointed First Lord by North in 1771. The Admiralty, wrote Walpole, was 'the favourite object of Lord Sandwich's ambition; and his passion for maritime affairs, his activity, industry and flowing complaisance, endeared him to the profession'.[4]

North had been anxious about the state of the navy for some time. Replacing Hawke – who retired in poor health – Sandwich had found an alarming situation. He never laid the blame on Hawke, but Sandwich later stated that the navy had lapsed into 'the most ruinous condition'.[5] Less than six months' oak or timber 'of any kinds' was left in the yards, and many of the line-of-battle ships were in such a wretched state they were fit for nothing but scrap. Returning to his familiar office and chambers at the Admiralty on Whitehall, Sandwich set to work to transform the anaemic navy. From 1771 his mornings began in a burst of letter writing that was usually finished by breakfast. He wanted lists, figures, facts. These were used as the foundation for a raft of reforms, for simplifying supply chains, finding new sources of oak, and making the yards more productive. Whatever taunts he endured about his private life, no one could lay any charge against Sandwich's professional conduct.

Sandwich was often to be found writing by candlelight, spells of conscientiousness from which the habit of eating a 'sandwich' appear to come. But he was not entirely desk-bound. To see that his orders were carried out he resumed an old habit of visiting the yards person-ally. These inspections became a feature of dockyard life. His tall, loping frame was increasingly to be seen peering at hulls and disap-pearing into hatches. By the summer of 1772, his enthusiasm was already being commented upon. 'While the noble Jockies of the King's cabinet council were squandering away their time at Newmarket and the watering-places', wrote the *Kentish Gazette*, 'Sandwich was doing honour to himself and serving his country'.

His Lordship, in the course of a few weeks, has reviewed the navy in so effectual a manner as has not been known since the last peace. Not content with a general view of the King's ships and stores, he descended to the most minute enquiries into the regulations of the work and workmen, carefully recorded every thing in his journal, and laid the whole before his Majesty.[6]

Sandwich toured the towering first-rates like HMS *Victory*, with their three tiers of gun decks; the brilliant new seventy-fours and sixty-fours and the older fifties. He got to know the glamorous frig-ates: the fast-sailers with their coppered bottoms that excelled in the chase. Then, on 18 August 1772, his inspections brought him to that curious old collier from Whitby that James Cook had sailed around the world. She was lying at her moorings at Woolwich dockyard.

Endeavour had not been idle since her return in 1771. No sooner had Cook brought her to the Thames than the Admiralty had advised the Navy Board that she was not to be 'dismantled farther than absolutely necessary'. She had returned at an opportune moment. The crisis on the Falklands may have passed, but issues had been outstanding. Most important had been the reclaiming of Port Egmont from the Spanish. In April 1771 the *Juno* frigate, a sloop called *Hound* and the *Florida* transport, had sailed with a force of 300 to oversee this. As no provisions could be expected, it was important a storeship follow as soon as possible. *Endeavour* had appeared on cue. She underwent a swift overhaul. Her complement was trimmed from the ninety-four of Cook's voyage to a more workmanlike thirty-five, and a new commander, James Gordon, was found. By September Gordon's crew was in place. By October he represented *Endeavour* as ready for sea. On 19 November 1771 she was plying west through the Channel.

The round trip took nine months. Gordon returned into the Channel at the start of August 1772, attracting some attention as the ship 'in which Dr Solander and Mr Banks sailed round the world'. Added to that accomplishment was another. 'She left England Dec 5, 1771. Thus she was not quite eight months going and coming, which is the quickest passage ever known', reported the papers.[7] By mid-August *Endeavour* was working up the Thames. On 16 August she came alongside at Woolwich. Two days later Sandwich and the comptroller of the navy, Hugh Palliser, paid her a visit.

Dwarfed by the mighty men-of-war in the royal dockyard, *Endeavour* hardly looked like anything special. But having spent so much time with Banks over the past year, Sandwich knew stories about this collier few others on the wharves did. This was a chance for him to go beneath to examine the planking on her starboard side, where the reef had cut through the oak, and to linger in the great cabin for a minute, where Banks and Solander had made sense of their botanical discoveries. But Sandwich's instincts, like those of his time, were pragmatic and analytic rather than sentimental. *Endeavour* was no museum. Instead she remained a useful, if peculiar, part of his reckoning. The collier was now eight years old. By a rough calculation, in these years she had travelled something like 70,000 miles, crossing the Atlantic, Pacific and Indian oceans. How much more life did she have in her? The calculation was always whether the expense of repair and upkeep justified the benefit of having a large-capacity Whitby bark in his fleet.

Sandwich left *Endeavour* confident enough to pass her for another voyage to the Falklands. There had been a change in the government's policy. It was never sustainable to retain a large garrison on a remote island in the south Atlantic, incapable of providing subsistence. So far the settlement had hung by a frail thread. If the transport struck a rock, then it would disappear into a thousand fathoms of grey ocean leaving the garrison to starve. But not wanting to abandon a place they had fought so desperately to keep, the decision had been taken to replace the *Hound* – she had remained as a patrol – and her men with a smaller force. *Endeavour* was to transport a whole new garrison with food and materials for a year. She would leave them behind on the island, along with a thirty-six-ton 'shallop' called HMS *Penguin*. A light, coasting craft, the *Penguin* had been designed and constructed at Woolwich. It now existed in flat-pack form – strakes, keels, rudder, spars and all – and was ready to be packed into *Endeavour*'s hold until it could be assembled on arrival.

Shallops were an antiquated form of sailing craft: light, dextrous and quick. They had been used extensively on coastal surveys and a young Joseph Banks had once taken a cruise in one at Chateaux Bay on the Labrador coast, an unnerving experience he vowed never to repeat. The *Penguin* was to be an evolution on this type, usefully light at thirty-six tons but capable of some force with ten swivels – small cannons mounted on pivots. While providing some defence, the hope was that the *Penguin* would give the men some latitude for exploring the bays or even escaping in case of some disaster. Lieutenant Samuel Clayton, a second officer, had been appointed to the command of the little *Penguin*, and he was to have the title of 'Commanding Officer at Falkland's Island' when they arrived. Everything was ready by mid-November 1772. Reaching the Nore and taking on a party of marines, a total of ninety-two men and provisions were now aboard *Endeavour*, just a fraction less than in 1768.

A great deal of Gordon's written material survives today. We have his journals and logs, and the frequent letters he wrote to the Navy Board, among which are his diligently compiled weekly 'State of

Endeavour', which details the progress of enlisted men and ongoing repairs. But within the mass it is difficult to discern an authentic feel for Gordon's character. His letters are terse and formal, suggesting the natural reticence of a man impatient to get on with the job. After Cook's inquisitive journals, Gordon's callow correspondence is enough to create the impression of a man without flair or imagination. Yet it is not fair to compare the two. Gordon's remit was much narrower. He was not employed in the business of exploration but in the practical matter of transportation. Gordon did as he was told. He was probably entirely representative of a type of middling naval officer, who having progressed so far had found his level. Gordon never demonstrates any interest in *Endeavour*'s former life. Only once did he mention Cook. There was a 'want' of a fireplace in his cabin, he complained, 'there was one formerly in this ship but it was taken away in the ship that fitted in this yard and went out with Capt Cook'.[8]

In expressing his views about the fireplace, Gordon was reflecting a truth. *Endeavour* was ostensibly the same vessel as the one that had sailed in 1768. But like the fire in the captain's cabin, the glow of her previous life had gone. The scientific instruments had been taken ashore. There stood no Charles Green on the quarterdeck, badgering the midshipmen to improve their measurements. Gone were Banks and Solander and Parkinson. Having been so enhanced by the improvements of 1768, *Endeavour*'s reduction was all the more pronounced. Reading Gordon's stark account of their passage south to the Falklands in 1772 and 1773, one wonders how many celestial events occurred that Green would have noticed; or how many birds paused for a rest on the rigging that Banks would have seized; or how many shoals were sighted that Cook would have charted. Of Gordon himself, we have only a passing verdict. He was eager 'to make the best of his way for the place of our destination, without touching any where unless in case of absolute necessity'.[9]

Manning this latest expedition to the Falklands had proved troublesome. On 14 September, Lieutenant Clayton had informed the Navy Board that 'No Surgeon's Mate has appeared' and that one was promptly needed.[10] A candidate was soon found, a man called Bernard Penrose, who rather than simply making up the numbers, transpired to be the most interesting of all those who sailed in 1772. Penrose kept a carefully observed, high-spirited journal of his travels. It was later published, winning the approval of the *Gentleman's Magazine* for his 'great propriety of character'.[11] After Hawkesworth's and Parkinson's books in 1773, there was a new vogue for travel literature. People were particularly interested in the subjective experience of travel and the emotional responses that it elicited. The reading public had long been entertained by breathless accounts of dramatic voyages, but Penrose's account would offer them something different. Penrose's travels were not to be a peripatetic procession across the oceans, but an account of survival 'in the manner of Robinson Crusoe', on a bleak and barren Atlantic island.

On 28 February 1773, Penrose got his first sight of the low grey coastline around the settlement at Port Egmont. They were warmly greeted by the *Hound*'s men, who having seen *Endeavour* were delighted by the prospect of fresh food. When they learned they were to be relieved entirely and carried home to Britain, there was disbelief. This 'at first could scarce be credited', wrote Penrose. There was no replacement ship, and 'no one dreamt of the *Penguin* lying in embryo' in *Endeavour*'s hold. Once the orders were understood, though, 'as elegant an entertainment as the circumstances of the place would afford' was held by the *Hound*'s captain. With thoughts of England in their minds, the *Hound*'s men helped the unloading of *Endeavour* with 'undissembled' cheerfulness.[12] The carpenters brought from Woolwich began setting, scarping and hammering the *Penguin* into shape on the beach, the chink of the caulkers' hammers adding a punctuating ring to the breaking of waves and the shrieks of seabirds.

Before Penrose and the *Penguin*'s men lay an indistinct, daunting period of time. They were to be left as an isolated social cell, fending for themselves. Penrose was not lacking conviction. The reoccupation of these islands, he contended, 'has shewn the world that nothing can deter Great Britain from asserting her rights; and though the object in question may in the end not prove worth the tenure, yet the discovery should be the result of our own experience, and not the effect of credulous timidity overawed by foreign menaces':

we consoled ourselves with the solid reflection, that we were colonists, not shipwrecked adventurers; that we were under the eye of administration, who would take care to supply us with necessaries; and that in case of the worst, we had a new vessel, not large indeed, but capable of carrying us to a friendly port.[13]

Six weeks after her arrival, on 17 April 1773, *Endeavour* weighed and Gordon stood out to sea. Penrose and forty-six companions were left to begin their lives as settlers, 'in full possession of our extensive territory'.[14]

With few accounts and hardly any images, the Falklands existed in the European imagination as the saturnine twin of George's Island. One was in the twinkling Pacific, the other in the dreary Atlantic. At George's Island was an abundance of everything: of life, of food, of plants and greenery. The Falklands were the diametric opposite. They were sparse, rugged, pummelled by Cape Horn gales, and devoid of human life. For centuries since they had first been sighted – by the English explorer John Davis in the 1590s – the islands had been avoided by European explorers. Even the privateers who operated off the coast of South America in the seventeenth century had left them alone.

It was only with the *Dolphin*'s visit in 1765 that attitudes changed. Rather than mere desolation, Byron's men identified some positive attributes. The place they called Port Egmont seemed to have potential. It had three entrances and was large enough 'to receive the whole royal navy of England'. The landscape behind was filled with fowls, too, so by the time the *Dolphin* left, 'A stranger would scarcely forbear smiling at seeing our ship ... for never was any poulterer's shop in Leadenhall market so plentifully supplied.'[15]

In the eight years since Byron's visit, a determined effort had been made to turn his vision into some sort of reality. In 1773 Port Egmont remained too grand a name for the tenuous settlement that existed, but at least there was something. The 'ornament and defence' was a timber-framed blockhouse. Armed with four guns, it importantly fulfilled a legal necessity of having a permanent structure, but as had recently been shown, it offered little defensive clout. More practically it housed the various supplies of materials and provisions, and served as a focal point around which several 'inferior' buildings stood. These were 'erected by the unskilful hands of marine architects', made of foraged stones, rocks and sods from the shore, 'and thatched for the most part with Penguin grass'. In the most 'splendid', Penrose affirmed, with a dash of pride, 'the Captain of the *Hound* had taken up residence while he was Governor of the place, and in this dwelling he was succeeded by our commander, Lieutenant Clayton'.

In front was the sea. Behind was a sparse, undulating landscape, mostly filled by vast swells of the 'Penguin grass' – 'a very coarse species, rising to the height of six or seven and sometimes ten feet' – through which the early settlers had been forced to wade. Seaweed had been gathered to use as a manure that was raked into the black earth. Some potatoes, cabbages, broccoli, carrots, turnips, parsley, spinach, lettuce, 'and some few but very fine cauliflowers' had been planted and were doing tolerably well. Only cucumbers, beets and radishes had frustrated their 'utmost art', Penrose observed. Clayton's men inherited the vegetable garden, the tending of which along with the unpacking and the upkeep of the buildings kept them busy initially. To instil some order, Clayton implemented a weekly routine. Six days were to be spent at Port Egmont in preparation for the winter or on expeditions in the shallop, but Saturdays were set aside as a day of indulgence, as a chance to 'wash their linnen, repair their cloaths, and to think of their friends in England'.[16]

These Saturdays were often spent on exploration forays. Traversing the craggy bays and crossing the empty heaths, Penrose and his companions found 'an infinity of penguins', standing upright on the beaches. The sheer mass of them struck Penrose. In London there was a fascination with unusual creatures. People could visit Ashton Lever's exotic 'Holophusikon' in Leicester Square to gawp at the peculiar productions of nature. Lever had birds of paradise, hummingbirds, pelicans, flamingos, peacocks and a penguin among his attractions. A lonely penguin among the sedan chairs and carriages of London might have fascinated, but these colonies of penguins in their natural environment were a sight to behold. Penrose watched as they constructed their nests and paired for protection. Nothing, though, could save their eggs from the sailors. The birds were equally defenceless. 'If ever we wished to kill them as a supply for our hogs, we had nothing more to do than to drive a flock together, which we could with the greatest ease, and then in an instant knock down as many as we wanted.'[17]

The Georgian attitude towards animals was entirely different to today's. Yet even with the period relish for blood, one can detect a disturbed moral undertone to Penrose's accounts. The killing was too easy. Strolling through the penguin towns – they assigned each colony the name of a British town to impose order on the landscape – Penrose found himself experiencing an odd sensation. The 'awful idea struck him': the 'desertion of these islands by the human species'. There was

Parkinson made this striking portrait of a Māori man during *Endeavour*'s visit to New Zealand in 1769/70. It was published in Parkinson's posthumous journal in 1773 and it provided European audiences with one of the first pictures of the indigenous people of New Zealand.

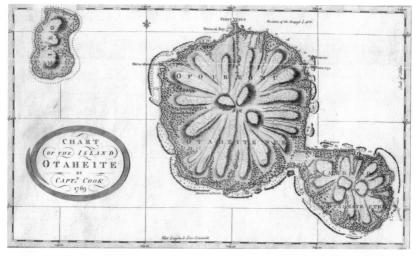

Top: Stories about Tahiti, 'a sweet, zephyr land', captured European imaginations in the 1760s and 1770s. Here is Cook's chart of a place originally named 'King George's Island' by the British.

Bottom: After the collision with the Great Barrier Reef – an 'alarming and I may say terrible Circumstance' – Cook beached *Endeavour* on the banks of the Waalumbaal Birri, today known as the Endeavour River in Queensland.

Top: After joining *Endeavour*'s crew Tupaia greatly aided communications with indigenous populations. Here he sketches a decisive moment of exchange as Banks and a Māori man barter over a crayfish.

Bottom: Reports of the 'kanguru' delighted Europeans. James Boswell reveals that Samuel Johnson once tried to mimic one: 'He stood erect, put out his hands like feelers, and, gathering up the tails of his huge brown coat so as to resemble the pouch of the animal, made two or three vigorous bounds across the room.'

Top left: William Brougham Monkhouse, *Endeavour*'s surgeon, kept a detailed account of the fraught first meetings between the Europeans and the Māori in Poverty Bay.

Bottom left: Robert Molyneux was *Endeavour*'s sailing master and was closely involved in Cook's attempts to escape the treacherous reefs off New Holland in 1770.

Top right: : John Gore, third lieutenant on *Endeavour*, was a superb sailor and a veteran of two previous South Sea voyages.

Bottom right: Sydney Parkinson: the able, assiduous Quaker. He had 'the greatest sympathy for the peoples of the Pacific'.

Capt. James Cook
of the Endeavour.

Wouvard del. The FLY CATCHING MACARONI. *1772*

Top left: James Cook. Enigmatic, complex, driven.

Bottom left: Joseph Banks, the courageous adventurer, shrouded and surrounded by artefacts from the voyage during his first taste of celebrity in 1771.

Top right: Lord Sandwich, First Lord of the Admiralty and a polarising figure. 'No man had so many public enemies who had so few private', wrote Horace Walpole.

Bottom right: Banks and his fellow natural philosophers were also subject to ridicule by the popular press. This caricature lampoons a collecting culture that has run out of control.

THE STATE BLACKSMITHS
Forging fetters for the Americans

Published according to Act of Parliament 1st March 1776.

Left: As the Industrial Revolution gets underway this caricature plays on the English reputation for practical genius. King George, Lord Sandwich and Lord North are among the establishment figures forging fetters for their subjects in America.

Bottom: The fleet of almost 500 ships in New York harbour in 1776 was the greatest land and sea force the British had ever assembled. It would remain so until D-Day in 1944.

Opposite right: After the success of the New York campaign in 1776, British naval operations turned to Newport in Rhode Island. This chart was made in 1777 and shows Narragansett Bay's complicated geography. The following year Rhode Island became the focus of the first joint French–US operation against the British.

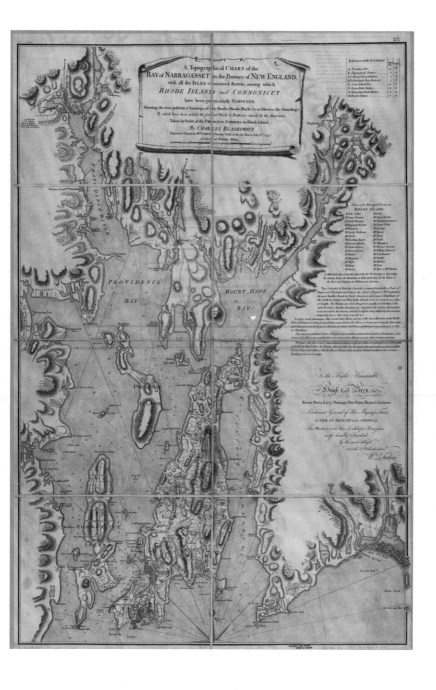

CLOSE ENCOUNTERS OF THE FIRST KIND.

Reg Mombassa

Endeavour has a complex legacy. For some the ship and Cook's first South Seas expedition stand as an inspiring combination of science and exploration. Others view *Endeavour*'s arrival as heralding a long period of destruction and dispossession. Here the Australian/New Zealand artist Reg Mombassa depicts *Endeavour* as an alien spacecraft, arriving to terrorise those on the beach below.

chilling emptiness in the air. A 'general stillness' prevailed in the towns. As 'we took our walks among them, in order to provide ourselves with eggs, we were regarded indeed as intruders, with side-long glances', Penrose wrote. This quietness; the penguins looking askance at their killers; the sense of solitude and imprisonment: all of these are present in Penrose's descriptions. This feels like an early appearance of the Gothic aesthetic that rose in the years ahead. Between Penrose's description of the Falklands and the Gothic novels of the 1790s, there is much in common. The islands are waxwork-still. The furious ocean beats. Raptors wheel in the sky. The seals slither on the beach past the ribcages of dead whales. Statuesque penguins gaze back at their killers with cold vacant eyes.

Sometimes nature attacked. Penrose described the island's population of sea lions, with their 'short and broad' faces, 'like that of a bulldog but infinitely more savage'. He had seen for himself how their teeth were well capable of snapping a large club in two. The sailors on the *Hound* had learned a bloodier lesson. One of their number had attacked a 'very large one' with his hand spike. Slipping as he aimed his blow, the lion had whipped around, seized him, 'and tore his right leg entirely off just below the knee'. The sailor had been hurried to the blockhouse, 'but only lived to undergo an amputation'. As soon as the animal had tasted the sailor's blood, Penrose reported, 'he set up a most hideous roar, and retired to the sea'.[18]

It is likely that Edmund Burke read Penrose's description of the Falkland Islands. In a Commons speech Burke conferred a memorable name on this hostile place: 'The Frozen Serpent of the South'. Had Burke visited he would have had more to say. People in the 1770s were increasingly intrigued by marginal landscapes: mountains, moorlands, deserts and islands. Many saw these bleak vistas through Burke's fashionable writings on the 'sublime'. To Burke the sublime was 'the strongest emotion' the 'mind is capable of feeling'.[19] The sublime was experienced near crashing waterfalls, by peering over frightful precipices or dizzying overhangs. At the Falklands a sublime landscape was found twenty miles from Port Egmont, on an isolated clifftop the sailors called Flower-de-Luce Point. This was a spectacular setting, high over a coastline hollowed into numerous caves and subterranean passages, 'by the violence of the waves setting in from the open ocean', where they watched the endless chain of breaking waves, sounding and whitening:

a romantic excursion it was in the highest degree. The grandeur of the scene was truly picturesque; the sea always ran here prodigiously high, and poured in such a terrible surf, that it was impossible for a boat to land. The wildness of the cliffs over-hanging the beach, together with the various echoes reverberated from them, of the grouls of sea-lions, the screams of various birds, and the thundering of the breakers, struck the mind with an idea of awful magnificence.[20]

Then there were other amusements. Their favourite was 'marooning', an imitation of the punishment meted out on the buccaneers' infamous voyages a century before. In these 'six select hands' were given a boat, some bedding, bread, brandy, a few pieces of beef and pork and some muskets, then were dispatched to a distant shoreline. These maroon-ings took Penrose to islands, coves and creeks that no human had ever seen. Their rowing boats cutting through the cold, glassy water, they stayed out in the frosty air for three or four days at a stretch before returning to Port Egmont, pockets filled with all they had scavenged, shot or found. Penrose skirted around tales of disharmony. He wrote undaunted of the 'state of tranquillity', their cheerful repose only occasionally interrupted by an accident, 'such as swamping a boat; meeting with cross winds' and other 'trifling mortifications'. But so far from home, so vulnerable to accidents, their situation was always precarious. On 6 November 1773, even Penrose's rosy pen turned bleak, as the settlers were 'alarmed with an incident, that threw us all into the greatest consternation'.[21]

November marked the bridge between spring and the onset of the southern summer. For the settlers it was a time of plenty with the egg season providing them with all they could need. On 6 November a group ventured out to one of the egg towns. While there they stopped to boil a kettle over a fire they had built on the grass. It was a foolish idea. The grass 'being dry as tinder' was ignited by a spark. Before it could be extinguished, flames were travelling across the ground.

The egg town was four miles from the blockhouse. The sailors hurried back, and Clayton immediately dispatched a party 'to endeavour to extinguish it'. But before they returned the fire had progressed out of proportion. The next day, 7 November, was ominous. By the afternoon the settlers could see that the fire had advanced 'with great celerity towards our settlement'. They had little means of tackling it. A curtain of flames leapt and reared over the hills, leaving the sailors in a helpless state of distress and terror. Their best hope was a change in the weather. In the meantime there was nothing they could do but start the process of evacuating and saving all they could.

Their first thought was the *Penguin* herself. Not being used, she had been beached at high tide and secured by a series of supports. As their only means of escape, it was essential she be floated into the bay. Her ballast was heaved ashore. Her powder, sails and provisions were fetched out of the blockhouse. While this was happening they realised their terrible luck. The *Penguin* was 'neaped'. That day brought one of the month's two 'neap' tides, when the water level remained lower because of a weakened gravitational pull. The difference was crucial. Three feet separated the sea from the *Penguin*'s hull and, as this sickening fact became plain, Penrose turned to see the flames 'advancing fast round the hills of our gardens'. With no other choice, every man was now deployed to fight the fire.

But to their bad luck with the tides, the *Penguins* were soon able to add their misfortune with the weather. The next day the breeze freshened, 'and blew the heath again into a most furious blaze'. Having already battled for several days, the sailors were forced to begin anew. Everything flammable – spirits, oil, the casks of pitch, tar and resin – were hauled to the beach. Flimsy barricades were constructed from shovelled earth. The grass was scythed down to starve the flames. As night fell:

> It was indeed a most dreadful scene, the conflagration raged on every side with the utmost fury, and the horror of it was increased by the darkness of the night. The wind blowing at the same time almost an hurricane, carried the burning heath to a very great distance, and beat down the smoak upon us some times to so great a degree, that we were nearly suffocated.[22]

In the end the barren landscape saved them. Had it been filled with trees, then the fire might have burned for weeks. As it was, just short of their encampment after an exhausting, ruinous week, 'the flames abated for want of matter to supply them'. Looking around Penrose saw weakened bodies, scorched limbs, blackened clothes and faces. As they rested, the fire smouldered, until it was finally extinguished by a fierce rainstorm. No one had died, Penrose wrote, though 'many sea lions, indeed, and an innumerable quantity of penguins were destroyed, as the wind was so fresh, that the heat was set in a blaze in various places at once; and the poor animals being surrounded, knew not which way to retreat'.[23]

The Port Egmont fire of 1773 demonstrates the precarious nature of living in an infant colony. *Endeavour* might easily have sailed back in 1774 to find the blockhouse reduced to a charred shell and the men standing in rags or wrapped in sealskins on the shore. Vulnerable to the weather, to illness, starvation and chills, this would have been the implosion of the colony. But there were many other ways for settlements to fail. Boredom or the collapse of discipline were equally fatal. These were the next challenges the *Penguin*'s men had to endure. By January 1774, they were longing for home. With *Endeavour* expected at any time, two midshipmen and one of the common hands were sent to keep a lookout on a hill called Keppel's Island, one of the highest points on the island.

In his published account, Penrose is careful never to question the purpose of the settlement. But anyone who experienced the isolation he did must have dwelt on the point of it. The salient question was whether these colonies were worth the effort. The trouble with colonies, as the British were discovering, did not end when they were established. Stories of the exhaustive toil, clearing the 'impenetrable forests' of Virginia or of John Smith's endless work, surveying Chesapeake Bay in a shallop in the early 1600s, were not yet forgotten and they held particular significance for the *Penguin*'s crew as they explored the bays of the Falklands. Just as Penrose and his fellow sailors scanned the horizon for signs of *Endeavour*, the American colonies looked back across the Atlantic for support and had been doing so for 150 years. This was how the colonial anatomy operated. Great Britain was like the heart of the body, pumping out vital matter: settlers, money, armies, laws – and all the things a society needed to establish itself and grow. 'A Colony is to the Mother-country as a member to the body', Samuel Johnson put it, 'deriving its actions and its strength from the general principle of vitality.' To most it seemed entirely logical that if colonies 'were governed by English laws, entitled to English dignities, regulated by English counsels, and protected by English arms ... it seems to follow by consequence not easily avoided, that they are subject to English government, and chargeable by English taxation.'[24]

This conception of the colonial anatomy had been called into question over the past decade. For many in Britain, Johnson's portrayal was the correct one. The anatomical order must not be interfered with. Even if a colony should grow as fast and as prosperous as those in America had done, they should retain loyalty to the system that had nursed them through infancy and protected them into adulthood. The snarls those in Great Britain had heard coming across the Atlantic for ten years were, therefore, the sounds from a dog ripping at the colonial body: biting the hand that fed him.

The argument over taxation could never be understood independently from this conception of what a mother country and what a colony actually were. To hear 'provincials' speak of being abandoned to slavery by the taxes the government laid upon them was absurd. Colonial Americans were taxed much less than their counterparts in the three home kingdoms, so their arguments smacked of hauteur. Instead of complaining about the government's actions, the Americans should be grateful that they had the protection of Parliament, which as every true Briton knew was the ultimate safeguard of liberty against monarchical tyranny and had remained so since the revolutionary settlement of 1689. This, including a Bill of Rights and a Toleration Act, curbed the powers of the Crown in stark contrast to the absolute monarchies of continental Europe. As one Englishman, Ambrose Serle, later put it:

Who will believe in future Times, that the Inhabitants of this Country, living under the mildest & most relaxed Government in the World, extending their Commerce & enriching themselves daily under that Government, and protected hitherto not only without Expence to themselves, but with the most liberal & indulgent Bounties, should so lose all Sense of Honor, Interest, and Duty, to their Parent State, as both to refuse Assistance to the Charges it incurs on their Behalf, and to attempt its utter Ruin & Subversion?[25]

'I almost wish that the Colonies had never existed', Serle concluded. 'It will be vain to prohibit the use of the word *slavery*', moaned Johnson, 'but I could wish it more discreetly uttered; it is driven out at one time too hard into our ears by the loud hurricane of Pennsylvanian eloquence.'[26]

The other side of the argument was equally trenchant. As Edmund Burke put it in the Commons, few could have envisaged the human miracle that had happened in North America in little more than a century. He asked his fellow MPs to imagine themselves transported to the year 1700. Now, look westwards, across the Atlantic:

> There is America – which at this day serves for little more than
> to amuse you with stories of savage men and uncouth manners;
> yet shall, before you taste death, show itself equal to the whole
> of that commerce which now attracts the envy of the world.
> Whatever England has been growing to by a progressive increase
> of improvement, brought in by varieties of people, by succession
> of civilizing conquests and civilizing settlements in a series of
> seventeen hundred years you shall see as much added to her by
> America in the course of a single life.[27]

To have anticipated such growth, Burke claimed, would 'require all the sanguine credulity of youth, and all the fervid glow of enthusiasm'. But the growth had happened. And it had happened, Burke contended, due to the industry and attitude of the American people. Every year the colonists increased in population, in size and in wealth. How absurd did it seem, then, that they had no parliamentary representative? What kind of system exists in which an entire people are subject to taxation without having any say in it at all?

This, broadly, had been the disagreement in 1764 when George Grenville had introduced the Sugar Act, and it was still the argument in 1774. Within those years events had ebbed and flowed. The Stamp Act had been enacted in 1765 and repealed the following year. The Townshend Acts had been introduced in 1767 and then repealed – with the exception of the duty on tea – after the appointment of North in 1770. Franklin had had a ringside seat in Westminster, watching the bungling to and fro and becoming increasingly exasperated at the government's inability to find a political solution to the quarrel. Often he had made use of the press to offer hints for a route to peace or defend the 'American' point of view. In September 1773 his *Rules by Which a Great Empire May Be Reduced to a Small One* were printed in the *Public Advertiser*. The first rule began:

In the first Place, Gentlemen, you are to consider, that a great
Empire, like a great Cake, is most easily diminished at the Edges.
Turn your Attention therefore first to your remotest Provinces;
that as you get rid of them, the next may follow in Order.[28]

Adrift in the south Atlantic, at the very rim of Franklin's cake,
Penrose did not have the chance to read the full list of Franklin's
'rules', nor was he a witness to the latest troubles with the Massachusetts
Bay Colony. North might have rescinded the loathed Townshend duties
in 1770, but he had been compelled to retain one, as an expression of
Parliament's right to tax. For several years this duty of three pence in
the pound had been paid without complaint. Then in May 1773 North's
government had passed the Tea Act. This statute was intended to
assist the beleaguered East India Company by presenting them with
a monopoly on the colonial tea trade. Its consequences were momentous. The Tea Act was interpreted as a fresh attempt to assert
Westminster's supremacy over the colonies. Although the Tea Act
actually reduced the total cost Americans were asked to pay – Lord
North later stated that it would have been 'impossible ... to foretell
that the Americans would resist at being able to drink their tea at
nine-pence in the pound cheaper' – its deeper significance was not
missed.[29] By agreeing to the tax, the colonists were submitting to
parliamentary taxation. In the summer and autumn of 1773 opposition
to the legislation was mobilised yet again.

As the sailors fought the egg-town fire, three East Indiamen sailed
towards Boston harbour with their holds loaded with chests of tea.
The ships arrived to find angry broadsides pasted up at the wharves.
'The hour of destruction, or manly opposition to the machinations
of Tyranny stares you in the face', one broadside warned.[30] On 16
December a band of dissidents, disguised as Mohawk Indians, boarded
the ships and threw all 342 chests overboard.

Reports that the East India Company's property had been 'riot-
ously destroyed' crossed the Atlantic by January 1774. Europe and
America drew breath for Britain's response. The *Middlesex Journal*
demanded the hanging of a hundred 'puritanical rebels in Boston'.
There were calls in the Commons for an immediate and violent
response. In January an order was given to prevent the exportation
of small arms to America. An Act of Parliament followed, shutting
the customs house at Boston and blockading the port. In the spring

a lieutenant general, Thomas Gage, was appointed commander-in-chief of the British forces in America as well as governor of the Massachusetts Bay Colony. More 'coercive' legislation followed for 'the better regulating of the government' of Massachusetts and for the suppression of riots. Called the 'Intolerable Acts' in the colonies, it seemed that many were being punished for the behaviour of a few. What had simmered for a decade, now flamed. A sermon came echoing from an American pulpit, *'O! Thou Lord of the East & of the West, & of ye South! Defend us against Lord North!'*[31] This was the wicked tyranny Catharine Macaulay had spent a decade writing about. Known as a friend to liberty in London, Macaulay soon received a letter from Abigail Adams, deploring the 'complicated miseries and distresses brought upon us by the late inhumane acts of the British parliament':

> We are invaded with fleets and Armies, our commerce not only obstructed, but totally ruined, the courts of Justice shut, many driven out from the Metropolis, thousands reduced to want, or dependent upon the charity of their neighbors for a daily supply of food, all the Horrours of a civil war threatening us on one hand, and the chains of Slavery ready forged for us on the other ... You will think ... that we are in great confusion and disorder – but it is far otherways. Tho there are but few who are unfealing or insensible to the general calamity, by far the greater part support it with that firmness, that fortitude, that undaunted resolution which ever attends those who are conscious that they are the injured and not the *injurer*, and that they are engaged in a righteous cause in which they fear not to 'bare their bold Breasts and pour their generous Blood'.[32]

In comparison with what was to come, the squabbles over the Falklands soon passed into history as a triviality. Port Egmont had been a plaything with some implications for trade and exploration. But the American question was quite different. It went right to the heart of what Britain was.

The lookout party waited on Keppel's Island for months for *Endeavour* to appear. Then, on St George's Day, 23 April, 'when she was least expected, we had the satisfactory surprize of seeing the *Endeavour* standing into the harbour', Penrose wrote. Many had watched her approach, but few had ever been so overjoyed at the prospect. 'It may be easily conceived we felt great pleasure at the sight of this ship', he continued, 'even when we only imagined she brought us refreshments, and intelligence from our distant friends.' But *Endeavour* brought happier news than this. 'Our sensations were beyond description', Penrose concluded, 'when the orders were communicated to us, which commanded us to evacuate the island and to return to England.'[33]

No time was lost. The stores were all pulled out of the blockhouse and loaded. The dwelling houses were emptied and the *Penguin* was ripped to pieces, her timbers so frail that they were good for nothing but the galley stove. The labour was intense. It continued day after day 'till the Store Ship was full, and could take no more'. Then, on 20 May, the two crews gathered beside the hollowed-out settlement to take their official leave. The sailors stood in file and the marines were drawn to attention as an inscription, engraved on a slab of lead, 'was affixed to the door of the blockhouse':

Be it known to all nations,
     That Falkland's Island, with this fort, the storehouses, wharfs, harbours, bay, and creeks thereunto belonging, are the sole right and property of His most Sacred Majesty George the Third, King of Great Britain, France, and Ireland, Defender of the Faith, &c. In witness whereof this plate is set up, and his Britannic Majesty's colours left flying as a mark of possession by S. W. Clayton, commanding officer at Falkland's Island, AD 1774.[34]

This was the concluding stage of a colonial retreat that had been kept secret in Europe. The turnaround at Port Egmont took less than a month and on 21 May *Endeavour* sailed north into the Atlantic. It would be a boisterous passage home. The Falklands had barely sunk into the grey ocean behind them when the skies darkened and the wind came on to blow. Those aboard wondered 'whether it would not be prudent to turn back', but 'the strong desire to return to England, however, operated with all its force'.[35]

They very nearly suffered for their rashness. For twelve days storms howled around *Endeavour*. Looking at the logs and the journals of this, the return leg of *Endeavour*'s third and final Atlantic relay, there is the impression of her being sailed on the very edge. Sailors were blown from the shrouds. One island after another was missed as they raced northwards over enormous seas. Battened down inside, they were not even able to light a fire to heat the provisions, being obliged to subsist on undressed pork and beef. The pace was unremitting. In less than a fortnight they crossed 405 leagues. This was exhilarating sailing, even for a sharp-lined, freshly tallowed frigate, let alone a heavily burdened, hard-pressed, put-upon Whitby collier. It was ten years since she had left Fishburn's yard, five since she had sailed from Tahiti. In 1774, *Endeavour* left the southern hemisphere – which she had explored more rigorously than any vessel in recorded history – for the final time.

Penrose and the rest of HMS *Penguin* disembarked on 19 September 1774. The Thames was the same busy river as ever, the tide carrying in East and West Indiamen, continental traders and north-country colliers as it always did. A few miles upstream London seemed the same restless capital they had left in 1772. Yet the mood had changed. The papers were filled with bellicose statements from the government and anxious letters, privately sent by the residents in Massachusetts but reprinted for the benefit of the public. 'Whatever your Opinion may be of us in America', one letter from Boston went, 'I will assure you that King George III has not better Subjects; let us but enjoy the true Liberty of our chartered Rights, we are no Encouragers of Riot, on the contrary Lovers of Peace and Justice.'

> this Tea is the Bone of Contention; Evil has been predicted, but, should that be the Case, you will, you must share in the Calamity, and curse the Iron Hand of Oppression.[36]

The letters from Boston told the human experience of Parliament's legislation. Since the harbour was closed, trials were 'felt most severely – All Trade and Business is at a stand'. A personal letter addressed to General Gage, who was enforcing the coercive acts, cautioned him against breaking the ancient bonds binding Britain to America. He 'may be assured, that this tie once broken, no other will ever be found sufficient to bring the two Countries together'.[37]

By making an example of Massachusetts, North's government had hoped to throttle the life out of the dissident movement. Already by

September 1774 it seemed as if efforts to ostracise the colony as a renegade territory were failing. In May 1774, Virginia had voted that an attack on one was an attack on all of them. In June 'a political solemn league and covenant' had been entered into by the thirteen colonies. Delegates had arranged to meet in Philadelphia, and were doing so as *Endeavour* returned to the Thames. Benjamin Franklin had followed everything from Craven Street. In September he wrote to his friend, the Boston lawyer Thomas Cushing, 'I rejoice to find that the whole Continent have so justly, wisely, and unanimously taken up our Cause as their own. This is an unexpected Blow to the Ministry, who rely'd upon our being neglected by every other Colony.'

They are now a little disconcerted, but I hear yet from that Quarter no Talk of retreating or changing of Measures. The Language of those about the Court rather is, that the King must now go on, whatever may be the Consequence. On the other hand our Friends are increasing and endeavouring to *unite*.[38]

It was a decade since Franklin had returned to London. In some ways his life had gone on as pleasantly as ever. He continued to attend Royal Society meetings and he used his lodging at Craven Street as his base for travelling tours to Scotland, Ireland, France and the English countryside. Now sixty-eight, Franklin might have been sliding into a blithe dotage had not politics interfered. His sympathy had long been on the American side of the argument and he was aggravated by the ministry's immoral blundering behaviour. This had harmed his public standing. Mentions of 'Dr Franklin' as 'the great American philosopher' could, by 1774, be read in two ways. To many in the government, Craven Street had come to be seen as something of an unofficial American Embassy in London. It had long been taken as fact by Franklin that his letters home were intercepted and read. 'Dr Franklin, as a Natural Philosopher,' pondered the *Kentish Gazette*, 'may perhaps be able to convince us, that there is something in the air of America, which inspires an extraordinary wisdom, together with an extraordinary rectitude of principle.'[39]

To avoid confrontation Franklin had withdrawn from politics. 'I made no Justification of my self from the Charges brought against me', he told his son William, 'I made no Return of the Injury by abusing my Adversaries; but held a cool sullen Silence, reserving my self to some future Opportunity.'[40] It seemed unlikely that any such opportunity would materialise. That autumn North called a surprise general election, which bolstered his majority. The haste with which the election was called made Franklin suspicious. He reasoned, rightly, that the government had wanted to avoid the expected back-lash that would follow non-importation measures from America. With trade depressed, it 'would probably have been a means of Outing many of the Court Candidates', Franklin speculated.[41] Emerging from the vote well, North was secure for another seven years. It meant that the government had the political stability it needed to deal with America.

And yet just when all seemed hopeless, something unexpected had materialised. Franklin had always sought a political solution and dreaded the prospect of a descent into violence. With the coercive measures making the situation worse, the next step would surely be civil war. As desperate to avoid this as Franklin was William Pitt, now Lord Chatham, the greatest political figure of the previous generation. By 1774 Chatham was physically weakened and politically withdrawn. But memories of Britain's triumph – largely due to his strategies – in the Seven Years War could never be eradicated. In May 1774 Chatham had broken his long political silence on America, speaking in the Lords against North. Then in August an unexpected courtship of Franklin had begun. Franklin had met Chatham and the two had discussed solutions. It was an unusual but historically potent pairing: the towering statesman of the age and one of the greatest Americans on this side of the Atlantic, both allied to avert what they had come to view as a catastrophe.

As Parliament paused for the election in the autumn and early winter, Franklin and Chatham remained in contact. Chatham's idea was to exert all of his political influence against the government in a speech early in the new parliament. In the meantime they awaited news from Philadelphia. Reports from the 'Continental Congress' eventually reached Franklin in mid-December. 'The first Impression made by them on People in general was greatly in our favour', he wrote. The colonies had reasserted their allegiance to the Crown, but had reinforced their position on Parliament's right to tax. As the government had feared, they had decided to pursue a policy of non-importation of British goods, and it was said that militias were being organised to prepare for 'forcible resistance'. Franklin sent Chatham news of the congress's proceedings 'as soon as I receiv'd them.' On 26 December 1774, they met again:

> He received me with an affectionate kind of Respect that from so great a Man was extreamly engaging. But the Opinion he express'd of the Congress was still more so. They had acted, he said with so much Temper, Moderation and Wisdom, that he thought it the most honourable Assembly of Statesmen since those of the ancient Greeks and Romans in the most virtuous Times.[42]

There was no hiding the compact between Chatham and Franklin. Not only did Franklin visit Chatham at the end of the month, Chatham even came to Franklin's lodgings at Craven Street, 'his Equipage waiting at the Door, and being there while People were coming from Church it was much taken notice of and talk'd of', wrote Franklin. 'Such a Visit from so great a Man, on so important a Business, flattered not a little my Vanity.'[43]

Chatham's plan for reconciliation involved concession on both sides. Parliament would retain their rights to govern imperial trade and quarter troops in America. But the right to impose taxes would be transmitted to the various colonial legislators. All their hopes rested on one date, 30 January 1775, when Chatham's chance to make his case in the Lords arrived. That day he invited Franklin to watch from the gallery. Franklin later wrote how Chatham, in a most 'excellent Speech, introduc'd, explain'd, and supported his Plan'. The initial response was encouraging. Lord Dartmouth, Secretary of State for America, conceded that Chatham's argument contained 'Matter of such Weight and Magnitude, as to require much Consideration', and he proposed that rather than having an immediate vote on its contents, he 'would be willing it should lie upon the Table for Consideration'.[44] This was the best that Chatham and Franklin could have hoped for.

In the chamber on 30 January along with Chatham, Dartmouth and Franklin, was Lord Sandwich. In an episode Franklin never forgot, he watched as Sandwich 'rose, and in a petulant, vehement Speech oppos'd [the bill] being receiv'd at all, and gave his Opinion that it ought to be immediately REJECTED with the Contempt it deserv'd'.

[He] could never believe it the Production of any British Peer. That it appear'd to him rather the Work of some American; and turning his Face towards me, who was leaning on the bar, said, he fancied he had in his Eye the Person who drew it up, one of the bitterest and most mischievous Enemies this Country had ever known. This drew the Eyes of many Lords upon me: but as I had no Inducement to take it to myself, I kept my Countenance as immovable as if my Features had been made of Wood.[45]

This was the acerbic Sandwich of public infamy, rounding on a foe in the Lords and humiliating him in the most public way. But this was not quite Jemmy Twitcher. This time popular opinion was behind Sandwich. Many of the peers shared Sandwich's exasperation towards America, and after his intercession Chatham's bill was thrown out before its second reading. Franklin left appalled. It was not so much Sandwich's personal attack that offended him. It was the 'total Ignorance of the Subject in some, the Prejudice and Passion of others'. He left having formed an 'exceeding mean Opinion of their Abilities', abilities that 'made their Claim of Sovereignty over three Millions of virtuous sensible People in America, seem the greatest of Absurdities, since they appear'd to have scarce Discretion enough to govern a Herd of Swine'.[46]

Slim as hopes had been, 30 January 1775 had offered a final chance for peace. After that date, Franklin never believed reconciliation possible. As the winter of 1775 softened into spring, events progressed at a pace. Soon Massachusetts was declared in a state of rebellion and British forces were being prepared to sail for Boston. This was reported alongside news of Sandwich's revitalised navy. If it had been in a wretched state in 1771, now the situation was much improved. Fourscore ships of the line were in service with more on the stocks, 'with a proportional number of inferior rates, all either stout, clean ships, or vessels newly built'. If more ships were required, then three years' seasoned timber was in the yards, ready to be put into production at a few days' notice. Whatever happened, Sandwich said, he felt sure he was able 'to supply government with such a naval force, as would at once protect us at home, and be sufficient to enforce its measures respecting America'.[47]

There were reports from America, too. One told that the American ladies 'after the manner of the Roman females' were collecting and sending jewels to Philadelphia, so that when the congress met, they could have the use of them: 'for the support of the glorious cause of liberty'. The women were said to 'farther declare, that if their persons should be wanted, they would, fearless of danger, take the field against the enemies'. In Craven Street, Franklin was dismantling his London life. March 1775 was spent in a succession of goodbye visits to friends, in the payment of debts and the packing of luggage. He did, however, have time to visit the Lords on 15 March to witness one final debate. He had hoped to see Lord Camden – the old Lord Chancellor – speak in favour of the Americans. Instead he was forced to hear more of Sandwich's invective.

> The noble lord mentions the impracticability of conquering America; I cannot think the noble lord can be serious on this matter. Suppose the colonies do abound in men, what does that signify? They are raw, undisciplined, cowardly men. I wish instead of 40 or 50,000 of these brave fellows, they would produce in the field at least 200,000, the more the better, the easier would be the conquest; if they did not run away, they would starve themselves into compliance with our measures.[48]

'I was much disgusted', Franklin wrote to his son, 'by many base Reflections on American Courage, Religion, Understanding, &c, in which we were treated with the utmost Contempt, as the lowest of Mankind, and almost of a different Species from the English of Britain.' Franklin stormed back to Craven Street, and drew up an intemperate memorial to the government, demanding compensation for the inhabitants of Boston damaged by the closure of their port. Showing the memorial to a friend, Thomas Walpole, Franklin wrote that 'he lookt at it and at me several Times alternately, as if he apprehended me a little out of my Senses'. Franklin thought better of sending it.[49]

Within a week, on 21 March 1775, Franklin was boarding the packet that would take him from Portsmouth to Philadelphia. Once at sea he pulled out his pen, and 'having now a little Leisure for Writing', he began an account for his son, 'I will endeavour, as I promised you, to recollect what Particulars I can of the Negotiations I have lately been concern'd in, with regard to the Misunderstandings between Great Britain and America.'[50] His retrospective of the extraordinary six months of negotiation with Lord Chatham is one of the most poignant works he ever wrote.

Franklin was on the Atlantic on 19 April when the first shots were fired at Lexington and Concord. The next day the frigate HMS *Cerberus* – named after the three-headed dog of Greek mythology – left England carrying the generals, William Howe, Henry Clinton and John Burgoyne. More ships would follow: sixty-four-gun ships, frigates, sloops, fireships and scores of transports. Among them all was a Whitby collier, her famous past concealed under a completely new identity.

The Collier Fleet

By the mid-1770s Whitby's shipbuilding trade was flourishing. No 'sea-port town in England', wrote Lionel Charlton, builds the 'number of merchant ships annually equal to those we launch and fit out at Whitby'.[1] A typical year saw twenty-four or twenty-five new ships launched into the Esk. Almost always they would join the swelling flocks of barks and cats, bound to the coal wharves at Newcastle and thereafter to London. Less than twenty colliers had sailed in convoy with the *Earl of Pembroke* on her first voyage in 1764, but already by the 1770s there seemed something quaint about so small a fleet. Hundreds of sail soon clustered in the lower reaches of the Thames Estuary, waiting for a tide to carry them upriver. At the start of the sailing season in 1775 the newly launched colliers, with their sanded decks, gleaming sides, freshly stitched canvas and bright Union Jacks fluttering from their ensign staffs, were carried on their passage up the Thames past an unusually shabby old bark, lashed alongside near the Woolwich dockyard.

On 17 March 1775, as Franklin was gathering up his belongings at Craven Street, a man called George Brodrick was corresponding with the Navy Board. Brodrick was one of those innumerable Thames-side operators: ear to the ground, alert to profit. In the last month he had seen adverts listing *Endeavour* for sale. Looking over the old storeship he had seen four hand pumps, 'with their proper Geer'. These were the pumps that had worked through the night on 10 June 1770 – had they not existed, perhaps British Australia would not have either – but returning to the storeship later, Brodrick had found the pumps and the gear stripped away. Irritated, Brodrick wrote to the Navy Board. The storeship 'had a large quantity of water in the Hold, which without the pumps cannot be got out'.[2]

Brodrick's letter painted a sorry picture. The rot had long set in. During her years of voyages to and fro across the Atlantic, Gordon might not have cosseted her but he had kept her in a seaworthy state. But since her last return from the Falklands no new purpose for *Endeavour* had been found and the funds for her upkeep had dried up. Neglect was fatal to ships. An accident might appear much worse, but abandonment was the surest way to ruin a vessel. In January 1774, for instance, *Endeavour* had been driven ashore at Sheerness in an alarming episode; nothing bad had come of it and Gordon soon had her sailing again. In comparison the entire winter laid up in the Thames had proved ruinous. Water was seeping in through broken seams in her outer carcass. The hold was now a basin of filthy river water. Oak was valued for its strength but it did not stand constant submersion. It was only a matter of time before the rot spread from her floor pieces and outer planking, into her knees and futtocks. Then that really would be the end. In February 1775 a survey had been carried out by the Woolwich Yard officers. A letter had come back to Stephens, the Admiralty secretary, that *Endeavour* needed 'a middling to large repair' which would take six weeks. Unwilling to put up the money, she had been advertised for sale.[3]

Endeavour's story may have ended here. Exhausted, she could easily have been broken down for timber. She was a not inconsequential size at 368 tons – bear this figure in mind – and she contained a correspondingly large amount of oak. Ship breakers were adept at salvaging valuable pieces to sell on. Also appealing were *Endeavour*'s unusual embellishments: the doors to her cot cabins, some old furniture, her stove and interior wood that might be clawed out for further profits.

Brodrick, though, seems not to have been a scrap merchant. What precisely happened to *Endeavour* from March to November 1775 is not entirely certain. The last of the Royal Navy records confirm that she was sold for £645 on 7 March 1775.[4] Brodrick was clearly involved in the transaction. He might have been acting on behalf of the new owner, or he may even have been the owner himself. Shortly afterwards come two tantalising mentions in the shipping catalogue Lloyd's Register. On 6 May an *Endeavour* sailed for Newfoundland from Poole in Dorset with the master's name 'Blanchard'.[5] Although there were many merchants' ships named *Endeavour*, the connection with the name 'Blanchard' is significant for reasons that will become evident.

A second mention comes on 27 October, 1775, when an *Endeavour* arrived back at Gravesend after a voyage to Archangel in the Russian Empire. This ship had been sailing in company with another called

Constant Friends, the master's name, 'Brodrick'.[6] More than 3,000 miles separate Newfoundland and Archangel and it seems unlikely *Endeavour* visited both. The summer of 1775, then, is an ill-defined moment in *Endeavour*'s life. No longer a ship of the Royal Navy, all that can be said for certain is that she, like events around her, remained in motion.

News of the violent confrontations at Lexington and Concord had reached Britain by the start of June 1775. On 1 July, King George III wrote to Sandwich. 'I am of his opinion that when once those rebels have felt a smart blow, they will submit; and no situation can ever change my fixed resolution either to bring the colonies to a due obedience to the legislature of the mother country or to cast them off!'[7]

The time for peace treaties or conferences had concluded. Many relished the prospect of the conflict to come. 'The nation (except some factious and interested opponents)', Sandwich wrote to one of his admirals, 'are in a manner unanimous in their resolution to crush the unnatural rebellion that has broken out in America by force of arms, which to our great concern we find now to be the only expedient left.' After a decade's bickering, there seemed some relief that lines had finally been drawn. But if the argument was to be decided by the military, then great logistical problems faced the British. Edmund Burke had pointed out the obvious in the Commons: 'three thousand miles of ocean lie between you and them. No contrivance can prevent the effect of this distance in weakening government. Seas roll and months pass between the order and the execution; and the want of a speedy explanation of a single point is enough to defeat the whole system.'[8]

The truth of Burke's words was already being demonstrated. Vice Admiral Samuel Graves, commander-in-chief of the Royal Navy in North America, had little idea about what he was expected to do. In Britain his ineffectiveness was already irritating the public, and Sandwich spent much of the summer months writing jockeying letters, exhorting Graves to 'exert yourself to the utmost' and 'show the rebels the weight of an English fleet'.[9] He repeated to Graves the maxim: 'you may be blamed for doing too little, but can never be censured for doing too much'.[10] The absence of any clarity over British objectives, though, and the small size of his fleet, hampered Graves. Just one warship, a few frigates and a dozen sloops had been in America when he arrived on the station in April 1774. Little more had arrived since. As the king was writing to Sandwich of 'smart blows', Hugh Palliser was totting up a 'disposition of the force', needed to 'annoy the rebellious provinces'. He thought twenty-two ships were needed for Boston – including three fifties – three for the strategic harbour at Rhode Island, then two fifties, three frigates and three sloops at New York. As marvellous as this sounded on paper in Whitehall, none of this existed for Graves.[11]

Sandwich's naval reforms had been going forward well but he realised the danger of dividing his squadrons. The heaviest line-of-battle ships needed to stay in home waters, in case France or Spain, or a combined force, decided to capitalise on Britain's overseas distractions. Warships were one problem, but an altogether more thorny one was troops. The king had resolved to put down the American rebellion in much the same manner his grandfather had quelled the Highland revolt of 1746. The rebels were to be obliterated. The British would attack like sharks before the rebellion gathered life. This year's campaigning season might have been over, but George III wanted the next, 1776, to stand in history alongside other victorious years, 1415 or 1759, as one of decisive British success. To achieve this he needed a formidable army. British regulars alone numbered less than 20,000, and so were insufficient for the task. Naturally, then, the king looked abroad for reinforcements. Catherine the Great of Russia rebuffed him, but the traditional recruiting grounds in Germany bore fruit. By December 1775 contracts were all but signed with Charles I, Duke of Brunswick and the landgrave of Hesse-Kessel. Between them they agreed to supply the British with around 16,000 troops.

But here again was Burke's snag. George II might have seen his army march to the north of Scotland, but it was something entirely different to transport an army across 3,000 miles of ocean to the scene of battle. An army was no light load. It was not only soldiers and weapons, but it meant tents, barrack furniture, coals and candles, specialist clothing, bags of flour and oats, casks of water and horses. 'Our army ... is healthy, brave and zealous', wrote Admiral James Gambier, but 'Twelve hundred leagues with its natural difficulties demand a solemn thought – the means and expense.'[12]

Usually the Admiralty did not trouble itself with transportation matters, but the vital nature of preparations during the winter of 1775–6 meant that Sandwich and, in particular, Palliser became actively involved. Only in February 1776 did the full extent of the challenge become clear. An army of almost 30,000 infantry and 1,000 horses was to be delivered to the North American shores for the beginning of the campaign season in the spring. A total of around 80,000 tons of transports were needed for the task.[13] It was, perhaps, the steepest logistical challenge of the entire Georgian age. To meet it Sandwich and Palliser fell back on a tested tactic: hiring high-capacity colliers on short-term contracts. Finding a sufficient number of weatherly vessels, though, proved troublesome. To do so was vital. If the transport fleet was lost in unseaworthy ships, the whole campaign would be over before it had begun.

Sandwich, though, was optimistic. In a letter of 30 December 1775, he admitted:

Our disgraces have been great & repeated in America, but I am clear in the opinion I allways had, that they are entirely owing to our having begun too late, and having suffered ourselves to be amused by what were called concilliatory measures; fleets and armies, admirals & generals, can do very little without ships, troops, and orders; & the consequence of their having gotten them by slow degrees has been that we have been on the defensive the whole campaign ... It is however our business to look forward & not to lose our time in complaints, the next campaign promises fair.[14]

Notices from the Admiralty were soon circulating in the northern ports, offering ten shillings a ton for the hire of colliers or other cargo vessels as transports, for six months certain. Lured by the bounty, day after day masters reported to Deptford, offering potential ships. To look through the yard's books from late 1775 into early 1776 is to see the intensity of the work. Surveys were made: oak planking was inspected for faithfulness, rigging was examined, dimensions were jotted down, descriptions of vessels were sketched for administrative purposes. There was no time for deck plans or drawings. There were just two salient questions: was a ship seaworthy, and when could it enter service?

Still needing more tonnage, Sandwich looked further afield. In January he wrote to the king: 'a thought has occurred ... a large number of Transports may be procured at Hamburgh', an idea Palliser 'greatly approves'.[15] In February Sandwich extended the search to

Bremen and Lübeck. And then another agent was dispatched to Holland. 'We flatter ourselves', Sandwich told the king, 'that as soon as it is known that we are determined to deal with foreigners, we shall get the better of the combination among the owners of Ships at home.'

At Deptford the work was relentless. The yard books show vessels being offered for charter each day. Inspections were immediately carried out, but they were not indiscriminate. A sizeable number of potential transports were rejected because of their structural defects. On 6 December the yard officers wrote 'We have Surveyed the *Endeavour* Bark', but found her to be 'the same that was lately sold from Woolwich':

> the Officers of which Yard having we apprehend, prior to her being Sold, reported her Defects such as to render her unfit for His Majesty's Service, and it appearing to us, that no Material Repair has been given her since, We cannot under these circumstances recommend her as a proper Ship, to be employed as a Transport.[16]

Among the four sets of initials at the foot of the letter, once again there is an 'AH', presumably of Adam Hayes. Hayes was still the master shipwright at Deptford. He could hardly have failed to recognise the bark that he had helped convert in 1768. He, uniquely so, saw the entire progression of the ship's life. He had known the *Earl of Pembroke*, Milner's bright, sturdy collier. He had seen Cook's *Endeavour*, loaded with philosophical equipment and provisions for the South Seas. And now he witnessed the third major transformation in her life.

By the end of 1775 *Endeavour* was owned by a man called James Mather. Mather was one of three brothers from London's East End who were active in the Greenland whale fishery and in supplying chartered storeships to the Royal Navy. *Endeavour* may have been defective and tired, but she was not beyond repair. After her rejection in early December, *Endeavour* was taken to a shipwright called William Watson. Three weeks after she had been rejected, on 27 December the yard officers examined the collier again.

> Age uncertain, she is now under Repair, has many Timbers Rotten, and Wm Watson, the Builder, believes she was built

somewhere to the Northward, she appears to be Old and defective.[17]

This brief note catches events in progress. The bark was not only being paid with pitch, repatched, dubbed, scrubbed and, perhaps, fitted with new spars, she was also being given a fresh identity. At some point over the Christmas week the decision was taken to eradicate the hindrance of a blemished name. If *Endeavour* was now remembered chiefly for her faults, then something different was required. As Thomas Milner had known in Whitby a decade before, a name could act as a political statement if needed. In this spirit a name appropriate to the time and to the service was selected: *Lord Sandwich*.

This shift in identity is documented in another of the Deptford yard books. It reads: '*Lord Sandwich* 2d: unfit for Service She was Sold out of service Called *Endeavour* Bark refused before.' The sleight of hand would wrong-foot historians for centuries to come. Administratively speaking, *Endeavour* simply vanished in the Thames in 1775. The proof that *Endeavour* and *Lord Sandwich* were one and the same vessel, though, is not confined to a single line in the Deptford books. On 5 February 1776 a new survey was performed on the *Lord Sandwich*.

Ships Name	Masters Names	Burthen	Height Between Decks		
			Afore	Mids	Abaft
Lord Sandwich	*John Blanchard*	368 71/94	7ft .6in	7ft. 9in	7ft. 11in.

Here is evidence that cannot be refuted. When Milner sold the *Earl of Pembroke* to the navy in 1768, a similar survey had been carried out. On 27 March 1768 her burthen in tons had also been recorded as 368[71/94] tons. The between-deck measurements – afore, amid and abaft – for the *Earl of Pembroke* in 1768 are also identical to those of the *Lord Sandwich* in 1776.[18] In an age before standardisation, the likelihood of two vessels having precisely the same measurements is negligible. The Deptford survey of 5 February goes on to describe *Lord Sandwich* as a bark, 'built at Whitby, and rep'd lately in the River, Bottom Sheathed, has rises to her Quarter Deck and Forecastle, is roomly and has good accommodation'.[19]

A subsequent examination was carried out on 9 February. This repeats the tonnage 368[71/94] for *Lord Sandwich*. After this the yard officials felt confident enough to inform the Navy Board 'we find her compleated, fitted and stored ... and having all her Men onboard was ready to enter into Pay'.[20]

Leafing over the reports on his Whitehall desk, Sandwich might have smiled at the ship's name. He was wily enough to spot a clever diplomatic ploy when he saw one. But he could not have guessed that his own name was only a veneer. History often conceals facts. Sometimes, however, through a long lens, it is possible to discern things that were entirely hidden to those closest to the scene. Reading the few lines of description, there was no way Sandwich could have detected that this was a bark that he knew intimately. All that mattered was that another 368 tons had been chalked off the total they needed to find.

For the *Lord Sandwich* – as *Endeavour* must now be called – February 1776 marked the most unexpected of new beginnings. Looking back it is striking to see how the arc of this ship's life resembled the rise of the political strife in America. Her launch in 1764 came just months after the Sugar Act. Her purchase in 1768 happened as the colonists reacted to the Townshend duties. She approached New Holland as the Boston Massacre was taking place, and returned from her last voyage as the first Continental Congress opened. Now, after so long running in parallel, the bark's life would interweave with events in America. In February 1776 she sailed down the Thames for the last time. Patched and plugged, she was no longer the weatherly ship of old that had completed one of the most iconic of solitary voyages. This next as *Lord Sandwich* would be entirely different in character, but it would turn out to be almost as historically significant.

In the words of one of his colleagues, the spring of 1776 advanced on Sandwich with 'hasty strides'. On the south coast at Portsmouth, the warships, transports and auxiliary troops were expected to gather in April or May, so that the Atlantic crossing could be made in time for campaigns in summer and late autumn. News of the invasion force was reported in the newspapers alongside the accounts from America of a fiery polemic 'lately published', and attributed to one of the chief Boston agitators, Samuel Adams. Though it was not yet known, *Common Sense* was actually written by Thomas Paine, an Englishman who had travelled to Philadelphia some years before with a letter of recommendation from Benjamin Franklin. Paine had left Old England behind and he implored all other British Americans to do the same.

Small islands not capable of protecting themselves, are the proper objects for kingdoms to take under their care; but there is something very absurd, in supposing a continent to be perpetually governed by an island. In no instance hath nature made the satellite larger than its primary planet, and as England and America, with respect to each other, reverses the common order of nature, it is evident they belong to different systems: England to Europe, America to itself.[21]

Common Sense was quoted at length in the British newspapers. Most significantly it showed the personal animosity levelled at King George III himself. The quarrel had begun as a parliamentary one, but the king's active encouragement in the suppressive measures and in his hiring of foreign mercenaries had outed him as a vile tyrant, a cruel and wicked tormentor of his subjects. Paine likened the king to 'the principal ruffian of some restless gang'. Did the monarch guard against civil war? Plainly not. 'The whole history of England disowns the fact. Thirty kings and two minors have reigned in that distracted kingdom since the conquest, in which time there have been (including the Revolution) no less than eight civil wars and nineteen rebellions.' In 1776, Paine exhorted, 'The sun never shined on a cause of greater worth.' The 'United Colonies' had a chance 'to make the world over again'. 'We are endeavouring, and will steadily continue to endeavour, to separate and dissolve a connection which hath already filled our land with blood.'[22]

There were other signs that the Americans would not prove as timid as the British hoped. On the evening of 2 May, Sandwich was summoned to an emergency meeting of Cabinet by the Secretary of State for America, Lord George Germain. The news had reached London that General Howe – commander-in-chief of British armed forces – had been 'obliged' to abandon Boston, 'for want of Provisions and from the position of the Enemy'. The full story – that Howe had been brilliantly outflanked by a provincial army led by General George Washington – was not included in Germain's first letter to the king. This was perplexing for Sandwich. The previous autumn he had replaced Graves with Admiral Shuldham, who had assumed command only in January. It turned out that Shuldham's first task was to evacuate Boston along with Howe's 6,000 men to Halifax in Nova Scotia. With Boston fallen, the strategic focus shifted, inevitably, to New York.

Standing on the southernmost tip of Manhattan Island, like a toe at the end of a foot, New York had been a focal point in colonial America ever since the British had wrested it from the Dutch a century before. The population of 20,000 – twice the size of Whitby – lived in a little collection of orderly streets that stretched back from the shores of a massive deep-water bay. When the Dutch had first sailed into this bay in the early seventeenth century, they had been elated. Here was a 'convenient haven from all winds, wherein a thousand ships may ride in safety'. The harbour's position at the bottom of the Hudson River made it even more appealing. If British forces in Canada could secure the northern end of the corridor and a naval fleet could evict Washington's forces from New York, then the British would be able to drive a wedge between the New England colonies and those in the south.

To further season New York's appeal was its social composition. Two-thirds of the private property was believed to be Tory-owned with Queens County known in particular as a royalist stronghold. Until 1775 New York had been Britain's military base and many in the army knew the woods, streams, marshes and rocky hills of Manhattan well. One officer claimed that Manhattan had 'the finest & most romantic Landskip that the Imagination can conceive'. With theatres and balls in the city, and hunting in the countryside, half an hour's ride away, New York's appeal was complete.

With the Hudson or North River on one side, the East River on the other and the harbour to the south, it was obvious that whoever had naval advantage would be able to surround Manhattan on three sides. Did that make it impossible to defend? General Charles Lee of the Continental Army believed so. He wrote to Washington that the best they could do was to turn the city itself into 'an advantageous field of battle'.[23] Washington was more hopeful. He arrived in New York from Boston in mid-April and established his military headquarters on Broadway, the main thoroughfare. He was soon busy constructing defences. Washington had the advantage of time, but as everyone knew, he had no ships to compete with Britain's. Since May 1775 the sixty-four-gun HMS *Asia* had been patrolling the harbour at will. 'We expect a very bloody summer at New York', Washington wrote to his brother on 31 May.[24]

Having recently replaced Admiral Graves with Shuldham, in February Sandwich had written to Shuldham with the 'disagreeable' news he too was to be replaced, or as Shuldham put it, made 'the football of Fortune'.[25] With the size of Britain's fleet escalating, a figure with gravitas was to command. Vice Admiral Lord Richard Howe was the elder brother of General William Howe who was already leading the army. Lord Howe had a famous fighting reputation. He had entered the navy at thirteen, had sailed in Anson's fabled fleet in 1740, had fired the first shots of the Seven Years War and had played a starring role in the Battle of Quiberon Bay. When war with Spain over the Falklands seemed certain, Howe had been appointed commander-in-chief of the Mediterranean fleet in response. The news that he was to command the navy in America had been announced with expectation. 'Lord Howe is to have the command of the fleet against the Americans', rang an article in the *London Chronicle*, 'his brother being commander by land, the most spirited conduct is expected next campaign'.[26]

As Washington chased one Howe out of Boston, papers in England were tracking the progress of the other brother to Spithead where he was to go aboard his flagship, the newly launched HMS *Eagle*, a fine man-of-war of sixty-four guns. Rattling along the London Road too were four wagons 'laden with money' from the Bank of England 'for payment of his Majesty's ships and the transports'.[27] The French, keeping a careful surveillance on preparations, were impressed. 'It is not a small task to transport to America in a short time' ran an intelligence report prepared for the foreign minister, the Count de Vergennes, '34 thousand troops, cavalry, ammunition, victuals, artillery, wagons, pack horses and all the paraphernalia required for the operations of such a large army which will land far away on an enemy shore, among fanatic people determined to destroy everything they will not be able to defend.'[28]

The scale was extraordinary but by April 1776 sufficient transports had been found for preparations to go ahead. To some it was amazing that such energy had been poured into so destructive a project. One satirical woodcut, *The State Blacksmith Forging Fetters for the Americans*, played on this. It showed members of the British government busily forging the chains that would shackle their subjects. North, Lord Mansfield and King George were hard with work, linking together the chains. Sandwich was at the centre of the mischief. He grips a hammer in one hand, an anchor in the other. Dark things were being planned from the gloom of the shop.

This is how Sandwich was viewed across the Atlantic, where his infamy matched that of Jemmy Twitcher's at home. It was little wonder that a skirmish on the Delaware in May 1776 was reported with such glee, when HMS *Roebuck* was driven ashore. The *Roebuck* 'was built last summer under the particular patronage of Lord Sandwich, whose favorite she is. – The Captain is also of his particular appointment', went one newspaper piece. '*Quere*, What must his Lordship say of his ship, when he hears that she was beat by the "cowardly Americans" who have nothing but rusty guns, broomsticks, &c?'[29]

Nor was Sandwich's conduct above suspicion at home. On 10 May 1776, the old Scottish philosopher David Hume was travelling by coach from Scotland to London when, at an inn near Newbury, he came across a party comprising Sandwich, Joseph Banks, 'and two or three Ladies of Pleasure', entertaining themselves on a fishing lake. The tone of the diversion struck Hume wholly at odds with the political atmosphere. He watched the sport as Sandwich 'caught trouts near twenty inches long, which gave him incredible Satisfaction'. How incomprehensible, Hume pondered:

> That the First Lord of the Admiralty, who is absolute and uncon-
> trouled Master in his Department, shou'd, at a time when the
> Fate of the British Empire is in dependence, and in dependence
> on him, find so much Leizure, Tranquility, Presence of Mind
> and Magnanimity, as to have Amusement in trouting during three
> Weeks near sixty Miles from the scene of Business, and during
> the most critical Season of the Year. There needs but this single
> Fact to decide the Fate of the Nation.[30]

Hume's was a noble but flawed reading of the situation. Sandwich had actually done his utmost to prepare the British response. His work had begun back in 1771 when he had vowed to reinvigorate a weary navy. His reforms may not have been completed, but he had had some success. For months he had been office-bound. Now, whatever could have been done had been done. Writing to the king on 23 May he reported 'It is with particular satisfaction that Lord Sandwich can now observe to your Majesty that this great work of compleating the transports is now brought to a conclusion with less delay and difficulty than might have been apprehended.'[31]

*

Since the Middle Ages the German people had retained a reputation as a 'pugnacious and warloving people'. Their disposition for valour, wrote one solider, 'is woven into the spirit of the nation and stems from its very origin'.[32] Fractured into its many principalities, this character was thought to be found nowhere more potently than in Hessen-Kassel. Situated in the German interior, among rough, wild hills and forests, the men of Hessen-Kassel were known as unusually 'stout and strongly built', features arising from a 'cold but wholesome' environment, and food that was 'not luxurious but nourishing'. The ruling princes of Hessen-Kassel, the landgraves, had long turned their physical prowess to profit on the market, raising auxiliary armies to be rented out to the powers of Europe. For 'Hessians', soldiering was a way of life.

> The Hessian knows that he is born to be a soldier; from his youth he hears of nothing else. The farmer who bears arms tells the son his adventures, and the lad, eager to tread in the footsteps of the elder, trains his feeble arms early to the use of formidable weapons; so when he has reached the size necessary to take a place in the valiant ranks, he is quickly formed into a soldier.[33]

Throughout the eighteenth century the landgraves' best customer had been the British Crown. With a desperate need for troops in late 1775, it had surprised no one that George III had come calling again. Aiming to secure 4,000–5,000, the British had been delighted at the Hessian response. As many as 12,000 were ready to serve. Events had progressed at speed. By December 1775 a draft treaty was sent to London and by February it was concluded. 'There is not common sense in protracting a war of this sort', Lord Germain reasoned, 'I should be for exerting the utmost force of this Kingdom to finish the rebellion in one campaign.'[34]

Pitting the drilled, effective, experienced Hessians against Washington's assemblage of farmers, tradesmen and boys, many of them barely armed at all, was thought the best way of concluding the campaign rapidly. In mid-March 1776 the chartered transports began to sail from Deptford for the River Weser. On 23 March the mustered troops started to come aboard. Three weeks of delay followed. A thousand more Hessians had turned out than were initially anticipated with the result that two regiments had to be left behind.

Having heard plenty about Hessian soldiers in the papers, the inhabitants of Portsmouth were able to see them for themselves in early
May as they arrived at Spithead.

Among the First Hessian Division was a man called Albert Pfister,
who wrote an account of their voyage. For all they flourished on the
battlefield, Pfister demonstrates that Hessians were timorous sailors.
Ever since their mobilisation the soldiers had fretted about the prospect
of the 'terrible ocean'. The dangers they foresaw soon arose. A fleet
of a hundred ships, almost ninety per cent of which were transports,
sailed under sealed orders on 6 May, shepherded by Commodore
William Hotham in the fifty-gun *Preston*. The fleet had barely left
Portsmouth when 'an adverse and violent storm' whipped up, throwing
all into confusion. 'No one could stand upright in the cabins, everything was tossed about pell-mell and sailors fell overboard and could
not be saved', Pfister wrote.[35]

Pfister's description of the early days of the voyage recorded his
initial human response to this unfamiliar piece of engineering. He
was alive to the vibrations of his transport. He felt the exaggerated
rolls or heaves of her body, as her shallow hull rocked in harmony
with the ocean. This, as it had for Banks, made many Hessians seasick.
But Pfister experienced the charms of sailing too. One night, after the
winds had lapsed into a 'perfect calm', he stood in the moonlight as
his transport climbed waves that 'rose to an astonishing height', her
bows lifting towards the sky, before they crested the wave and raced
down the back slope. He watched as 'foam sparkled' and 'lightning
flashed and quivered on the waves'.[36]

Picturing Pfister standing in the moonlight, an Atlantic breeze on
his face, looking towards the strobing forks of light, it feels like we
are looking at a Romantic of the years to come. But this was no
Romantic solitude. All it took was for the sun to rise in the morning
for the great fleet to appear again. Ships were strewn across the water.
Leading the way was HMS *Preston* and Commodore Hotham, then
there were four thirty-six-gun frigates and two fireships.[37] These
fighting ships guarded about ninety transports that carried, all told,
about 12,500 land troops. Pfister was 'astonished' at this show of naval
might. 'Who may be the master of the ocean', he wrote, 'was made
evident when a Danish and later two Swedish East Indian ships were
passing through the fleet.'[38] As they came into firing range, the
merchants struck their flag and topsails in a sort of maritime curtsy.

The British fleet must have presented an awesome sight to the Swedish and Danish crews. In total size this naval force was barely smaller than the Spanish Armada of 1588. Gazing at it, the Scandinavian merchants would have known the outline of colliers from the northern seas, and they would also have been able to detect a looseness in their handling. Sailing colliers was always a matter of confidence. In careful hands they were dextrous enough, as Cook had demonstrated. But when manned with inexperienced crews, the commonplace became hazardous. Pfister saw one transport, *Good Intent*, ram into the bows of the *Claudina*, leaving a gash above the cabin. Others sailed so poorly they 'oftentimes had to be taken in tow by the war vessels'. Another, *Speedwell*, was making so much water that Pfister thought it 'doomed to sink'.[39]

But if the collier fleet looked ragged to the Scandinavian merchants, the trim order of the Royal Navy was not far behind. Five days after Hotham had sailed with the transports, Admiral Howe had left Portsmouth in the *Eagle*. 'Made great Progress with a fair Wind all Night', wrote Howe's secretary, Ambrose Serle, on 15 May. 'For the most part, we gained 7 and 8 Knots an Hour. The Ship rolled much, which made several of our People very sick: As to myself, I was very well, but could not do much Business.'

Serle would be an important eyewitness to the clashes that would follow. While he journalised in his spare time, in his working hours he kept on top of Howe's administration. Keen-eyed, Serle maintained a regular list of the ships under Howe's command. Perhaps it was Serle who wrote out the list of 'Eighty-five Sail' of transports sailing with Commodore Hotham. Eleventh on this list, carrying 206 Hessian soldiers of 'Du Corps', was *Lord Sandwich*, 368 tons, being commanded by a master called William Author.[40] Just one *Lord Sandwich* features on Howe's list, a fact that forges another link, proving that as Pfister was being tossed and jostled on his transport, not very far away was the old *Endeavour*.

Pfister was not alone in describing the Hessians' Atlantic crossing. One of his fellow travellers was the poet and adventurer Johann Gottfried Seume, whose primary concern was the wretchedness of the food. 'Today bacon and peas – peas and bacon tomorrow', he commenced a philippic about conditions aboard. Only occasionally, Seume complained, would this monotony be interrupted by porridge, peeled barley or pudding 'made of musty flour, half salt and half sweet water and of very ancient mutton suet'. The biscuits were riven with worms and so impenetrably hard they had to be split open with cannonballs:

> We were told (and not without some probability of truth) that these biscuits were French, and that the English, during the Seven Years War had taken them from French ships. Since that time they had been stored in some magazine in Portsmouth and that they were now being used to feed the Germans who were to kill the French under Rochambeau and Lafayette in America.[41]

The Hessians had been loaded in the transports with such density they had felt like 'salted herrings' themselves. The bunks were intended to hold six men, 'but after four had entered, the remaining two could only find room by pressing in'. The soldiers were obliged to lie straight as a flagstaff, and, 'after having roasted and sweated sufficiently on one side, the man who had the place to the extreme right would call: round about turn! and all would simultaneously turn to the other side.' Statistics suggest Seume wasn't exaggerating. The 206 Hessians crammed aboard *Lord Sandwich* – which did not include the sailing contingent – was more than double the maximum *Endeavour* carried. Few could have prepared for such physical discomfort. As outsiders, Seume and Pfister were attentive to things sailors would consider too commonplace to mention. They write of glowing galley fires, steaming kettles, sodden clothing and bed linen and the ghastly cramped lower decks. Hanging like fruit bats at night and doubled up by day, the best place to be was up on deck, but this could be disquieting too. Climbing up on 20 May, Pfister saw a grey sky and felt a freshening wind. Despite the sailors' protests that it was 'simply good fresh air', he noticed the galley fire being struck out, the sails being drawn in and the uppermost parts of the mast being fetched down.[42]

The dramatic centrepiece of Pfister's account was what he rather grandly called the Whitsuntide Storm. He wrote of ships being scattered like leaves on the breeze. Inside his transport all is chaos. Everything 'though tied fast' is broken loose and catapulted 'helter-skelter'. The Hessians were sent flying too, 'and there was no end to the spells of seasickness and of misery made ridiculous'. By 27 May:

The raging sea was playing with the gigantic structure of the ships as with a toy; sailors were swallowed up by the waters, others committed suicide and soldiers who ventured to go on deck fell down unconscious because of the force of the waves. Only one consolation remained, namely, the clarified atmosphere; but on the third day of Whitsuntide dark gloomy clouds and torrents of rain darkened the whole firmament, the winds seemed to be let loose, sounding like roaring thunder, all nature seemed to have united in bringing to young America a terrible funeral feast.[43]

So long seen through James Cook's understated pen – he often described such storms as 'blowing weather' – Pfister depicts life at sea with melodrama fit for the stage. Such an attitude is understandable for someone unaccustomed to the sailors' life and unfamiliar with the violence a collier could withstand – Cook had once written of *Endeavour*, 'No Sea can hurt her laying Too under a Main Sail or Mizeon ballanc'd' – but there is an additional distinction in attitude between the rational responses of the British sailor and those religious ones of the Hessian soldiers. 'Stout Calvinists', Pfister describes how they started 'pleading' for 'the protection of heaven', as if 'a furious wrathful indignation rages in the American pulpit scattering its curses and, praying to God and Saviour, dedicated the fleet to destruction'.

With a loud and deafening roar the huge waves wash over the ships; the decks and every port-hole had to be made extra tight. The soldiers were lying in the lower compartments as if buried alive in coffins, gasping in the darkness after air and water; from moment to moment the most of them, quiet and depressed, expected to go out of this dark night into the eternal day of heaven.[44]

Pfister's Whitsuntide Storm soon blew itself out, but it left Hotham with the devil of a job gathering up all the ships. Fifteen transports disappeared entirely. The destruction of the fleet by storm was one of the events Sandwich dreaded. It so nearly happened.

By the end of June 1776, 'with many a change of wind and weather, of calm and turbulent sea, of joyous or anxious feeling', Hotham had brought the fleet to the banks of Newfoundland. The plan had been to rendezvous with General Howe, but Howe was already gone. He had left behind an order for the fleet to meet him instead at the Sandy Hook lighthouse, off New York.

As the fleet turned south and Pfister watched 'the sharp glow of Halifax lighthouse' recede 'like a star gradually fading away', 500 miles away Ambrose Serle with Lord Howe on HMS *Eagle* was coasting past Long Island. 'It appeared to rise into easy Hills, wch were every where clothed with Trees.' On 12 July 1776, Serle woke to a brilliant sunlit morning and the 'beautiful Prospect of the Coast of New Jersey', with woods and houses plainly visible behind the white shingle of the shore.[45]

Howe's flagship had experienced the same foul Atlantic weather. HMS *Eagle* had been 'tossed from Billow to Billow, and sported about by the Winds & the Waves like a Feather', terrifying Serle, leaving him fearing for the Hessian transports.[46] Even when the storm had died away, violent gusts continued to buffet them. One day as Serle had walked on deck a sailor called William Englefield had fallen from the main-top, landing 'within a few Feet' of where Serle stood. His skull had been stove in on one side and 'All the Booms, on wch he was dashed, were stained with Blood', Serle wrote.[47]

As well as distressing sights there had been uplifting ones. Serle had been staggered by the icebergs they saw with one 'at least as large as Westminster Abbey'.[48] He had relished the entertainment of dolphins playing alongside as they came into soundings off the North American coast. 'The Smell of the Land & of the Spruce-trees was very pleasant', he wrote, 'after so long Voyage, in which we had no better Effluvia than the Hold of a crouded Ship, or at best the Smell of Ropes & Tar.'[49] Then there were the many flying fish, which Serle had read about. These fish were said to 'fly against the Wind' by the natural philosophers.[50] This observation led Serle's mind to the American rebels. He had thought long about the subject. His verdict was that the 'rebels' were scoundrels and ingrates. Like the flying fish they were launching themselves into the headwinds of history. 'That the Turbulence and Malignity of a few factious Spirits should affect the Lives of Thousands', Serle pondered, 'and the Welfare of Tens of Thousands', was a melancholy reflection indeed.[51]

On the afternoon of 12 July, the *Eagle* navigated the dangerous passage through Sandy Hook, and came to anchor off Staten Island.

Nothing could exceed the Joy, that appeared throughout the Fleet and Army upon our Arrival. We were saluted by all the Ships of War in the Harbour, by the Cheers of the Sailors all along the Ships, and by those of the Soldiers on the Shore. A finer Scene could not be exhibited, both of Country, Ships, and men, all heightened by one of the brightest Days that can be imagined.[52]

The *Eagle* was not long anchored before General Howe was aboard, acquainting his brother with the latest news. Admiral Howe had harboured hopes of defusing the conflict and before he had sailed from Portsmouth had secured for both him and his brother the power to act as peace commissioners. But that day Admiral Howe learned that the last chance for a negotiated settlement had recently passed. On 4 July the Continental Congress in Philadelphia had taken an irrevocable step and declared the colonies independent from Great Britain. No longer could the struggle be termed a quarrel or a rebellion. As John Adams put it, the colonies had entered into 'the very midst of a Revolution, the most compleat, unexpected, and remarkable of any in the History of Nations'. For Serle, gazing across the bay to New York, this was proof of the 'Villainy & the Madness of these deluded People'. The *Eagle* lay 'in full View of New York, and of the Rebels' Head Quarters', Serle wrote. General Washington, he added, 'is now made their Generalissimo with full Powers'.[53]

A short distance across the harbour, the mood in New York was tense but excitable. Receiving the news of independence on 8 July, Washington had ordered it to be read in public before his troops and the people of the city. After the reading, a mob had surged down Broadway towards Bowling Green, shouting huzzas and beating drums. The statue of George III erected to celebrate the repeal of the Stamp Act was heaved down. The crowd hacked at the statue, mutilating its body. The king's head was set on a spike outside a tavern while the remainder of the statue, so the story went, was carried away to Lichfield, Connecticut, where 4,000 pounds of lead were melted down 'to be run up into Musquet balls for the use of the Yankees'.[54]

This jubilation was tempered by the appearance of the ships. On Saturday 29 June, General Howe's fleet of a hundred sail had started to arrive from Halifax. Washington's army had watched as they fell 'into great confusion, all dropping upon one another', as they tried to pass the treacherous sandbars at Sandy Hook. Perhaps now a strategic truth at last became apparent. New York was encircled by 'deep navigable water', but this was only accessible through two choke points: past these sandbars at Sandy Hook or through the notorious Hell Gate passage into the East River. Neither of these locations had been fortified. Now it was too late.

Watching Howe's fleet arrive, one of Washington's militiamen on Staten Island wrote, 'I was upstairs in an outhouse and I spied as I peeped out the Bay something resembling a wood of pine trees trimmed ... I declare at my noticing this, that I could not believe my eyes ... I thought all London was afloat.'[55] On 4 July, the *New York Journal* reported:

> Last Saturday arrived at the Hook (like the swarm of Locusts, escaped from the bottomless pit) a fleet said to be 130 sail of ships and vessels from Halifax, having on board General Howe, &c. sent out by the Tyrants of Great Britain, after destroying the English constitution here, on the pious design of enslaving the British Colonies and plundering their property at pleasure, or murdering them at once, and taking possession of all, as Ahab did of Naboth's vineyard.[56]

The *Eagle* and several other warships had since added to this number. Peering through his perspective glass, Serle surveyed New York on 12 July. 'The Rebels appeared very numerous, & are supposed to be near 30,000; but from the Mode of raising them, no great matters are to be expected.'[57]

Among Pfister's company of soldiers, morale had plummeted after the change of destinations from Halifax to Sandy Hook. To have suffered so long, only to find that they were to endure more, was sufficient to make them restless. The first object of their rage was General Howe, whom they blamed for changing plans. He had, Pfister wrote with asperity, 'begun his career with blunders and perplexities'. Now he had started for Halifax 'inopportunely', then 'changed his mind during the trip, and at last aimed for New York'. This additional leg would add at least a fortnight, Pfister foresaw, and possibly more to the length of the voyage, meaning that the Hessians would have spent nearly a hundred days at sea, 'which was even at that time very rare'.[58]

To alleviate the threat of disease, a regime of constant cleaning had been put in place on the transports. The decks were scrubbed each day, fresh air was pumped beneath, bedding was aired on deck and the linens were disinfected in steaming vinegar. But nothing could be done about the dwindling supplies of rotting food. In the days after leaving Halifax, the first symptoms of scurvy began to show. Pfister put the malady down to 'tainted humours', and described how the Hessians sought to physic themselves with the chewing of tobacco, a habit learned from watching the English sailors, and also by swigging sea water. It was all to no avail. 'The disease reigned supreme', Pfister wrote. Made thirsty by the salty water and sweating in the growing summer heat, the soldiers were horrified to find that the water 'which in the whole fleet had been stored in oaken casks' was growing 'undrinkable and finally putrid'.

Entering his third month at sea, Pfister's account grows woozy and elegiac. He gazed, awestruck, at 'the threatening, gigantic cone of a water spout', as it whipped up the waters around one of the transports. The air grew thick. St Elmo's Fire – the sign of a highly charged atmosphere – shone at the tops of masts and on the yardarms. Pfister saw the glow, 'feared as an apparition of a warning spirit'. On 12 July the weather broke spectacularly, 'in a most fearful thunder storm'. The following morning a strong wind 'tore to pieces the sails on several ships' but it also dispersed the black clouds. A calm succeeded. Across the stillness of the fleet, Pfister heard the singing of hymns. It was a Sunday, he realised. As the services finished, a dense sea fog enveloped the transports and rain began to fall. 'All at once there was a great outcry in the fleet', Pfister wrote.

> Two ships, the *Hartley* (with Knyphausen soldiers under Captain von Biesenrod) and *Lord Sandwich* (on board of which was Colonel von Wurmb and a part of the life guards) could be seen colliding because of the great waves, causing each other considerable damage.[59]

Watching in alarm as the two transports crunched against each other, Pfister could not have known that he was committing to history the last direct eyewitness account of *Lord Sandwich* at sea.

The scene disturbed Pfister and more was to come. Made furious by their mistreatment, the discipline of those on board began to suffer.

A duel was fought on one ship. On another the sailors mutinied and had to be arrested before the cutlasses and pistols could be served out. This, at least, was an aberration. Pfister was heartened by the industry of the sailors he saw. From the damp fogs to the storms and into the blazing heat of summer, their toil was unremitting. Pfister marvelled at their 'ever agility', as they sprang from the shrouds and hared up and down the ratlines. 'As a spider that moves about as swiftly as the arrow in her web', he wrote, 'so the sailors were going up and down the rope ladder of the masts and through the rigging, hanging only at their feet, tying the tackle and binding the sails.'

Three weeks of wanton and fretful weather followed, until on 10 August, the transports' sails were filled by 'a most speedy wind'. With 'high towering sails' they at last made good time, splitting the waves and currents off New England. By 11 August the 'charming coast of Long Island' was before them. The next morning the English flag was unfurled across the fleet, and Sandy Hook – that long-wished-for rendezvous – rose out of the western horizon, with its white lighthouse. Staten Island lay behind.

A veritable painting spread itself out before the eyes of these newcomers, most charming after so many dangers had been encountered and after so long a denial of a glance on the beautiful smiling landscapes, teeming with inhabitants, exalted and majestic, the shores studded with troops, the tents of a friendly and a hostile camp, of a forest of masts of 500 ships, and the many hundred boats which so vigilantly were watching the hostile shores—here a belligerent power assembled, such as America had never seen before in order to have a combat, which in the destiny of the world gave its immeasurable decision.[60]

Serle watched the transport fleet anchor off Staten Island on 12 August 1776. 'We were gladdened with the Sight of the grand Fleet in the offing', he scribbled. 'The Joy of the Navy & Army was almost like that of a Victory.' One by one the colliers navigated the sandbars at Sandy Hook. So great was the mass of ships, and so long the queue they formed, that it took the entire day for the whole fleet to cross the bar. 'So large a Fleet made a fine Appearance on entering the Harbour', Serle wrote, 'with the Sails crouded, Colours flying, Guns saluting, and the Soldiers both in the Ships and on the Shore continually shouting. The Rebels (as we perceived by the Glasses) flocked out of their lurking Holes to see a Picture, by no means agreeable to them.'

Running his glass over the collier fleet, Washington and his military commanders in New York could only reflect that this was the worst they could ever have expected. Britain had thrown all of their forces against the one place he had resolved to defend. In New York harbour there was now amassed the most powerful naval force that Britain – or England before her – had ever sent into combat. In fact Sandwich's 1776 fleet remained the greatest land and sea force assembled by Great Britain until the D-Day landings in World War Two.

Gazing timorously across the bay from lower Manhattan, Joseph Reed, the lawyer turned revolutionary, wrote home to his wife, 'When I look down and see the prodigious fleet they have collected, the preparations they have made, and consider the vast expenses incurred, I cannot help being astonished that a people should come 3,000 miles at such risk, trouble and expense, to rob, plunder and destroy another people because they will not lay their lives and fortunes at their feet.'[61]

When sailing in the Pacific as *Endeavour*, the ship had emitted a mystic air. Often her power came from her strangeness, her unknown capacities or from incomplete understandings of her technology. By contrast, in New York people were all too aware of the significance of these transports. As they watched the Hessians disembark with their equipment and munitions, everyone understood what was to come. The potency of this fleet has long been acknowledged. *Endeavour*'s presence within it never really has. The bark had seen so many vistas, from the coal staithes on the Tyne, the glinting waters in Matavai Bay, the Deptford Yard, Batavia Roads and the remote colonial outpost at Port Egmont. But no scene was a theatre quite like this. 'We expect to be attacked every tide', confessed one New Yorker on 12 August.

'We have now a gallant Fleet here', Serle wrote two days after *Lord Sandwich*'s arrival.[62] 'Besides Sloops, Bombs, Fireships, armed Vessels, &c. The whole Fleet consists of about 350 Sail. Such a Fleet was never seen together in America before; wch is allowed on all Hands.' That night a great formal dinner was held on the *Eagle*. In attendance was a list of names that would pass into history. There was Admiral Howe, his brother General Howe, Lord Cornwallis, General Grant, Sir Peter Parker and the Hessian commander General Heister. 'Our Army now consists of about 24,000 men', Serle confirmed, 'in a most remarkable State of good Health & in high Spirits. On the other Hand, the Rebels are sickly & die very fast.'[63]

Five days after *Lord Sandwich*'s arrival, on 17 August 1776, Washington issued a proclamation:

WHEREAS a Bombardment and Attack upon the City of New-York, by our cruel, and inveterate Enemy, may be hourly expected: And as there are great Numbers of Women, Children, and Infirm Persons, yet remaining in the City, whose Continuance will rather be prejudicial than advantageous to the Army, and their Persons exposed to great Danger and Hazard: I Do therefore recommend it to all such Persons, as they value their own Safety and Preservation, to remove with all Expedition, out of the said Town, at this critical Period, trusting, that with the Blessing of Heaven upon the American Arms, they may soon return to it in perfect Security.[64]

Events now happened apace. On 25 August Serle watched the 'main Body of the Hessians' cross the channel to Long Island.[65] Two days later Washington's army was routed at what became known as the Battle of Brooklyn, the biggest battle of the revolutionary war. On 15 September General Howe invaded Manhattan Island at the Battle of Kips Bay and New York fell to the British. On 16 November a Hessian-led attack stormed Fort Washington at the north of Manhattan. Almost 3,000 troops of the Continental Army were captured and those remaining were forced to retreat into the Jerseys. Although General Howe failed to completely destroy his army, for Washington it was the most desperate moment of the entire war. General Hugh, Lord Percy, writing to Lord George Germain, summarised: 'this business is pretty near over'.[66]

Serle was equally expectant. 'All Philadelphia, we heard this morning, is in Confusion from the Expectation of a Visit; and many of the Inhabitants are moving out of Town with their Effects', he wrote on 22 November.[67]

Serle realised that Howe had other targets in mind too. On 28 November, he watched as 'Most of the lighter Transports laden with Troops passed up the East River, in order to go through Hell-Gate into Connecticut Sound', to begin their next operation.[68] A month later in London, on 30 December, the king sat down to compose a congratulatory letter. 1776 had gone as well as he could have hoped. 'Lord Sandwich', he began, 'The accounts from the Admiral and General are the more agreable as they exceed the most sanguine expectations.' With a new year beckoning, the king anticipated more good news. 'The possession of Rhode Island cannot fail of success.'[69]

Ghosts

Narragansett Bay cleaves into the south New England coastline. To examine Charles Blaskowitz's 1777 map of the bay is to see a fractured, unsettled geography. It looks as if an axe has been swung into the continental land mass leaving two deep gashes and forming a great tidal basin of about 250 square miles. Strewn with scores of irregularly shaped islands, Narragansett Bay's Atlantic entrance is made complicated by the two biggest of these: Conanicut or Jamestown and Aquidneck or Rhode Island, from which the colony's wider name comes. Conanicut and Aquidneck choke Narragansett's opening. Running north to south like isthmuses, they create three distinctive channels, each of which had its own specific character. In the 1770s the deepest water was known to be found in the Middle Channel: an even twenty fathoms that guided vessels through a narrow passage past a commanding prominence called Brenton Point into the sheltered waters beside the city of Newport. This was to Blaskowitz's mind 'one of the finest Harbours in the World'.[1]

'I have always understood that Rhode Island and other places in rebellion are open to the sea', Sandwich had hinted to Admiral Graves as far back as August 1775.[2] Graves had been replaced before he had an opportunity to act on the advice, but Newport had never strayed far from British minds. In December 1775, Sandwich had received a detailed intelligence briefing, reaffirming 'the particular advantageous situation' of the bay. Each of Narragansett's three passages, it stated, were deep and wide enough to admit warships. In winter, because of the brisk currents, there was little danger of the bay being blocked up with ice. With frigates guarding the entrances, the bulk of the navy stationed within, and a small strong garrison controlling Newport, the British could feel secure. 'The rebels will never venture upon an island where their retreat would be sure of being cut off.' It concluded:

'You will please to observe this bay runs 30 miles up into the country to a town called Providence, through which place all the provisions come for the supply of the rebel army at Boston.'[3]

What Sandwich had been told in 1775, Howe had been thinking a year later. It wasn't the geography alone that tempted the British. Its climate was known as 'the most healthy' in the colonies, bracing but never bitter in winter and free from 'the violent and excessive heats' of the south, 'being allayed by the cool and temperate breezes that come from the sea'.[4] Closing their eyes and breathing in this tonic air, a British officer might have been at home in Kent or Suffolk. Familiar too were the breads, beef and ciders produced locally and declared 'excellent'. These staples fed a Newport that, over the past thirty years, had emerged as one of the colonial boom towns, its fleet expanding as dramatically as Whitby's, from about a hundred vessels in 1741 to '352 vessels in the coasting trade and 183 ships to foreign ports' in 1764.[5]

With a pre-rebellion population of about 10,000 – level with Whitby's – Newport's ships had increasingly been seen in distant seas. They carried home Gloucester cheese, wines from Tenerife and Madeira, chocolate, coffee, indigo and raw sugar from the Caribbean, the last of which was frequently refined into loaves by the slaves who were owned and sold in Newport, part of a far more disturbing trade. All these were brought alongside at the wharves that skirted Newport's waterfront, each poking out into the bay like the fingers of a hand. For decades locals had watched the expansion of the maritime economy: the merchant vessels drawing alongside with their goods unloaded and carted away for sale along with the crabs, oysters and lobsters 'several feet long' fished from the bay.[6]

With its enterprise and balance of Old World and New World characteristics – Newport's main thoroughfare was called Thames Street – it encapsulated the imperial fantasies of men like Dalrymple: different to the Mother Country, yet familiar enough for comfort. But the British knew there was hostility in Newport too. Although there was a rump of embedded Tories, the local Patriots had been loud and abrasive since 1765. Tipped into a fury by the Stamp Act, a decade's raucous factionalism had reigned. The loyalist 'Newport Junto' had been subject to incredible abuse. Attempting to defend the government's stance in print, one of the Junto had elicited the following reply. 'Ambitious, of the Character of Author', it blazed:

his Writings abound with little Witticisms, quaint Similies, Poetical Flourishes and Bombastick Flatulences … & gives out with a Grace the Low Stuff-the Idle Nonsense-the Contemplous Rhan-Rhan & the unanswerable Pugh-Pugh of the Combination.[7]

Since 1766, 18 March had been kept as a day of celebration and bell-ringing to mark the repeal of the Stamp Act, with parades to the Liberty Tree. Solomon Southwick, printer of the *Rhode Island Mercury*, had become infamous even in Britain for his masthead, 'Undaunted by TYRANTS −we'll die or be FREE'. For Ambrose Serle, such belligerence was maddening. He wrote acridly of the 'Temper of the Inhabitants of this Island'. They:

are vulgar in their Behaviour, yet affect what they think Politeness, which is a sort of Rudeness that suits so ill with it, that they are never more irksome than when they offer to be civil. Generosity of Spirit is certainly not among their Virtues: They don't seem to feel an exalted Sentiment, nor are they troubled with refined Sensibilities.[8]

The thinking of Serle and other English Tories was shaped by the unforgiveable burning of the custom schooner *Gaspee* in 1772. It had been one of the first hostilities between the countries and, ever since, the British had watched Rhode Island carefully. As soon as news of violence at Lexington had arrived, a truculent naval officer called James Wallace had tormented the bay in the *Rose*. In April 1775 he had threatened to 'fire upon the Town & lay it in Ashes' should any troops march in support of the rebels. 'An inhuman Wretch!' and 'The infamous Capt Wallace' were names applied to Wallace.[9] He torched property, intercepted merchants and once, in 'One of his mad Fits', had drawn 'all three of the Men of War before the town of Newport and swore with the most bitter Imprecations that he would burn it'.[10] None of this altered the temper of Rhode Island. The colony had declared its independence in May 1776, two months before the others.

Howe had launched his operation on Rhode Island in November 1776. His orders were passed to Sir Peter Parker, in the fifty-gun HMS *Chatham*. On 8 December, at three in the afternoon, the whole fleet were led into Narragansett Bay by Captain Wallace, now commanding HMS *Experiment*. They met no opposition. Passing two makeshift forts, 'without guns', Wallace intercepted a brig carrying hogsheads, staves and beeswax, and they watched as three 'Rebel privateers' sailed for Providence, 'that nest of pirates'. Having got his fleet into position, the landings went ahead. A force of around 7,000 British and Hessians, led by Lieutenant General George Clinton, went ashore north of Newport. They met 'the least opposition'. Most of the local population had already gone.[11]

As the soldiers splashed onto Aquidneck Island, the most dramatic story belonged to Solomon Southwick, printer of the *Rhode Island Mercury*. Having spent the morning frantically burying his printing press and type in a garden, he fled with his wife, who carried their child in her arms. Reaching a boat, they 'were just putting off from the shore into a very rough sea, occasioned by a high wind, when a party of soldiers who were in pursuit of them came in sight.' The Southwick family were saved by a royalist relative, who managed to delay the troops for a vital instant. It gave Solomon:

time to get a few rods from the shore before the party arrived at the spot they had just quitted. The boat was yet within reach of their shot. The soldiers fired at them but without effect. The passengers fortunately received no injury, and were soon wafted to a place of safety.[12]

This was all of little moment to the British. It took six weeks for dispatches to cross the Atlantic. News of the victory was published in a *London Gazette Extraordinary* on 21 January 1777. George III was as thrilled as anyone. 'I am very much pleased with the good news you have sent unto me, which secures an excellent port for the ships', he wrote to Sandwich.[13]

It had been late November when Parker's fleet left for Newport. As before, Hotham was to lead the transports in the *Preston*, with two frigates, *Brune* and *Mercury*, and the fourteen-gun *Kingfisher*. Again Howe had ensured that a list of 'ships to be employed' was compiled before operations began. Among the transports in Hotham's fleet was *Lord Sandwich*, once again carrying her old cargo of Hessian soldiers.

Not wanting to risk the transports in the open ocean, Parker had divided his squadron. Hotham's fleet sailed north from Staten Island towards Manhattan, taking the right fork and entering the East River.

This would be the bark's last substantial seagoing voyage, and for everything that she had encountered before, it is difficult to imagine a more iconic passage. Today Manhattan's identity is defined by its towering skyscrapers, its grid arrangement and the pump and pulse of its brash mercantile character. In 1776 the landscape that the *Lord Sandwich* sailed past held different significances.

At the tip of the island stood the charred ruins of New York, desolate in the grey of November after the driving fire of 21 September that had destroyed almost a thousand buildings. Entering the East River the *Lord Sandwich* crossed the site of Washington's last-gasp retreat after the Battle of Brooklyn. Here, on the 'remarkably still' night of 29 August, all 9,000 of Washington's soldiers – with their tents and weaponry – had been evacuated in secret across the East River to Manhattan in one of the most startling and consequential military manoeuvres of the war.

A short distance up the East River, on the larboard bow, was the deep-water cove called Kips Bay where the British had begun their invasion of Manhattan on 15 September. In the cornfields beyond, just eighty yards from the advancing redcoats, Washington was said to have thrown his hat to the ground in despair at the sight of his retreating forces, shouting out, 'Are these the men with which I am to defend America?'[14] Through these cornfields behind Kips Bay ran the Old Post Road, connecting New York to Harlem Heights and the scene for the last decisive encounter, at Fort Washington.

After Kips Bay there were the notorious, tremulous shallows at Hell Gate passage. Crossing these, the *Lord Sandwich* then entered the sinuous waterways that conducted her to Flushing Bay, Hampstead Bay and, finally, into Long Island Sound.

Knowing he would never get his heavy warships through such a passage, Parker had taken the bulk of his fleet out through the Narrows and past Sandy Hook into the Atlantic. Within four days Parker had joined Hotham's fleet, and in three days more they were at Newport. As the *Lord Sandwich*'s anchor rattled out, splashing into the cold waters of Narragansett Bay, it was time again for her sails to be reefed then stripped, her Hessian soldiers and their equipment disembarked.

This ship's coming had always symbolised change. In Deptford she had altered conceptions about what an exploration vessel should be. In the South Seas she had interfered with the rhythms, social hierarchies and belief systems of ancient societies. At the Falklands, her arrival had marked the division between a time of scarcity and a time of plenty. At Newport she symbolised a complete shift in power structures within the city. First Aquidneck and then Conanicut Islands were occupied. The old establishment and social make-up was gone. The new hierarchy was now the British military, supported by Hessian soldiers and local loyalists. Frigates were stationed at every entrance to the bay.

Peering into their own harbour, Newport's sailing masters could interpret this fleet with a professional eye. They might gaze longest at HMS *Asia*, the first of Thomas Slade's sixty-fours, with her pure elegant lines and her 500 men bustling like ants over every inch of her. Her two long tiers of guns were capable, they all knew, of throwing such a weight of metal across the water that a century's industry at Newport would be reduced to cinders in minutes. The dextrous frigates might catch the eye, too, already probing on ahead into the farther reaches of the bay in search of privateers.

Few, though, would have looked long at the *Lord Sandwich*. Arriving in Newport it is unlikely that she appeared like anything other than a tawdry merchantman, with old cordage, torn or patched sails, splintering deck, yards askew and with as many pumping beneath as sailing above. By December 1776 many of the transports had already been ordered home by Howe. Perhaps one of the reasons *Lord Sandwich* did not return, is that she could never have completed the crossing.

All this was apparent to the discerning. More striking to everyone else was her name. For years the New England newspapers had reprinted Sandwich's attacks against them. Now they were faced with the taunting presence of a *Lord Sandwich* in the bay, as obstinate and ineradicable as the words of his speeches.

To the historian she emits a different power. Embedded within her timbers, hiding in plain view, was a history that none in her immediate vicinity could see. No one could know how far this shabby transport had sailed or what wonders she had seen. Mentions of her hereafter, by Serle or Howe or in the newspapers, are ringed with dissonance. She was a masquerade. The *Lord Sandwich* had a dark exterior, but an enlightened core. Already by 1776 her real worth was not to be measured in guns like the *Asia*, or in tons or even in the number of Hessian soldiers she carried. It was to be measured in the secrets she held.

The occupation of Newport was spun as a deliverance to virtue by the British papers. 'The people of Rhode Island have been almost ruined since the Commencement of the American War', ran a report in the *General Evening Post*, 'their lucrative Branch of Commerce with the West-Indies has been of course destroyed, and out of 135 Vessels, which they fitted out within these last two Years, 70 of them have been lost and taken, and the rest have had very ill Success.' Liberated to resume their lives as true-born Britons, the inhabitants were said to be 'quite happy in having the Opportunity of swearing Allegiance of his Majesty'.[15]

This news might have been swallowed whole in London by those who Burke called, rather immoderately, 'vulgar and mechanical politicians', but the unremittingly positive tone of the pieces suggested to others that propaganda was at work. Anyone could look at a military map and conceive that it was not going to be easy to maintain a place like Newport that was surrounded by Patriot troops on all sides. The initial invasion had gone well but now came the problem Burke had so eloquently put in his 1775 speech 'On Conciliation'. 'The use of force alone is but *temporary*. It may subdue for a moment but it does not remove the necessity of subduing again; and a nation is not to be governed, which is perpetually to be conquered.'[16]

While Aquidneck and Conanicut Island looked to British eyes like specks of virtue, to many in America they were cancerous cells in the body of New England. A British fleet might be based in Newport harbour, but beyond in the green fields of Connecticut or on the Massachusetts coast, Patriot troops were only a few miles away. As the Hessians occupied their defensive positions in December 1776, they heard the whistle of artillery shot, something that kept them in a state of continual alarm. The waters were patrolled by British frigates by day, but with muffled oars it was easy for whaleboats to evade detection on dark nights. With Washington's forces stretched in the Jerseys, no military operations were expected. But there was always the threat of surprise operations to destroy armaments or capture prisoners.

The social dynamics within Newport were messy. The binary camps – Patriots/Tories, loyalists/rebels – were a simplification that neglected the important third category of those who remained ambiguous, disinterested or uncommitted. With as much as half of Newport's pre-revolutionary population having fled by the time the British arrived, a rump of about 5,000 was augmented by an initial force of

7,000 that dropped in the six months after the invasion to 4,000. These shifts from the settled, organic, diverse Newport of before to a temporary, incoherent one confused the simplest things. Living arrangements were upended as Hessian or British soldiers were quartered with families. Power structures were subverted as the respectable gentry of the port were forced into subservience. Food went first to the soldiers, who burned so much firewood that trees, fences and even some houses were pulled down to maintain the supply.

The fraught existence of Mary Almy, who kept a boarding house in Newport, exemplified how confusing the complexities could be. A lifelong Newport resident, she was descended from one of the early governors. Her brother in-law was Augustus Johnston, one of the members of the Newport Junto – for which crime Johnson earned the description 'a little round, fat, oily Man of God'[17] – and she remained steadfast in her loyalty to the Crown. Yet her husband, Benjamin Almy, had fled Newport in 1775 to join the Patriot forces inland. Her family divided, Almy simply got on with the business of running her business, simultaneously rooting for the British and wishing her husband well. 'When I look over the list of my friends on both sides of the question', Almy would sigh, 'my heart shudders at the thought, what numbers must be slain, both so obstinate, so determined.'[18]

In such an environment, how could the British truly know the secrets of people's hearts? They did their best, obliging them to make public oaths in the aftermath of the invasion. But for intolerant figures like Serle, wary of 'that low Cunning, which is the Characteristic of the New England People', what value could be placed on these? With her husband away serving Washington, maybe even Mary Almy was a subversive? These were unknowables to nag at the British garrison keepers. Suspicious as they were, they could hardly have guessed at the clandestine networks of women that developed during the occupation. Exploiting their ability to move freely, Patriot-supporting women would bring messages baked in loaves of bread, carrying supplies and sometimes weapons. One of the paradoxes of the British occupation was that it presented Newport's women the chance to escape the restrictions of their usually prescribed gendered roles.

Strolling along Newport's wharves, with the might of the navy riding at anchor in the bay, and the swathe of sailors, tavern-keepers, merchants, fishwives and grocers milling in front of them, the British developed a paranoia. Who was friendly and who was not? In no one did this disquietude live more than Major General Richard Prescott. A fifty-two-year-old veteran of the War of the Austrian Succession, Prescott was choleric, restless and still furious at the treatment he had received as a prisoner of the American forces in Philadelphia. He had sailed as part of Clinton's invading party in December and at the start of 1777 he had found himself second in command at Newport beneath General Hugh, Lord Percy. Prescott walked into Newport a man in a rage. He interrogated residents in public. Quakers, the mildest of all the religious denominations, were expected to defer to him by tipping their broad hats. When they failed to do so, Prescott bristled at the affront. One was challenged, 'Why he did not take his hat off!' The reply came back, 'it was against his principle to show those signs of respect to man'.[19] At this Prescott ordered a servant to throw the hat to the floor. Another Quaker, guilty of the same offence, was rushed up against a wall by Prescott. He did worse in private. Soon after the invasion a continental ship was seized and one of the prisoners was hauled in front of the British military commanders.

Says Prescott, 'What are you?' 'I have been a lieutenant of a privateer.' 'A lieutenant of a privateer, ha! Damn your blood, one of the damn'd thieves,' and immediately made up to him and hit him a knock in the jaws, and said he should be hanged … [Prescott] added, 'Yes, damn you, I have been a prisoner among you and know how I was treated'; and hit him another knock. Lord Percy desired [Prescott] not to proceed in that way, as he [the lieutenant] was a prisoner; [Prescott] told the prisoner he should be chained neck and heels, and be fed with nothing but oatmeal and water, and while he lived his life should be miserable, and hit him another knock, which Lord Percy again disapproved of, and ordered him to be put into prison, which he said was enough without blows or irons.[20]

When Lord Percy was called back to England in May 1777, Prescott was left behind in Newport, in complete control. Between 1764 and 1768 Thomas Milner had filled the *Earl of Pembroke* with coals. Between 1768 and 1771, Joseph Banks had filled *Endeavour* with plants. From

January 1777 onwards, Richard Prescott began to fill *Lord Sandwich* with prisoners.

As warfare became an increasingly protracted and sophisticated business in the eighteenth century, so the taking of prisoners became a more complex affair. To catch an enemy combatant was not simply to remove them from the theatre of battle, it was to gain a commodity that might be traded when the time came. Mirroring the stratification of social class, the different ranks of seniority had correspondingly different monetary values. It was a principle that held on either side and one that, from the moment they arrived in Narragansett Bay, the British applied themselves. With Newport as their naval base throughout winter, it became the natural unloading port for prisoners of recently captured prizes. From January 1777 prisoners from captured merchantmen were unloaded at Newport's wharves by returning frigates, ready to be sent to the Newport City gaol on Marlborough Street – 'a substantial brick edifice', known locally as the 'Provost'.[21] Soon, inevitably, the Provost was full and the British looked for new accommodations.

A tired sailor but still roomy as ever, it had not taken long for *Lord Sandwich* to be put to her new purpose. With her unusual combination of trim stern cabins and generously spaced interior deck, she offered Prescott and the naval commander Sir Peter Parker a structure that somewhat mimicked the architectural make-up of a prison with distinct, partitioned spaces for gaolers and prisoners. The main interior deck was easily secured with hatches and with its shallow draft the *Lord Sandwich* could be kept both near enough to the shore to make her easily accessible to the harbour boats, yet she could equally be manoeuvred further out into the bay in the event of an insurgent attack or any other security threat.

Six weeks after *Lord Sandwich*'s arrival in Newport she took her first prisoners aboard. These were around fifty prisoners captured by the frigate HMS *Greyhound*. In January 1777 these were the first to be held aboard the ship since Cook had abducted the Māori boys at Poverty Bay in 1769. Terrified as they had been, those boys had met a far better reception than these American prisoners did eight years later. Once clapped beneath they were left to subsist among mice and rats on short rations in the January winds. Newport may have been admired for its summer climate, but the winters brought icy breezes and violent snowstorms from the north.

People ashore were soon talking about the vile conditions in the floating gaols. The *Providence Gazette* of 7 March 1777 carried a report from a local doctor, who spoke of the 'deplorable conditions' of prisoners exchanged from the prison ships. They were 'run over with vermin, half rotten with scurvy and putrid fever. Some of their extremities were frozen and almost rotten through neglect.' Locked in the damp, cold ship, the prisoners were denied sunlight, were 'upbraided' with 'the epithet of damn'd Yankee Rebels', and forced to receive 'the kicks, cuffs and bruises of the soldiery'. The report concluded with an observation:

This is the treatment free born Americans suffer, who have the misfortune to fall into the hands of Britons, a nation formerly not less celebrated for humanity than bravery. But alas! How plainly does their conduct demonstrate them to be lost to all sense of honor and humanity.[22]

As spring succeeded winter, a new set of hardships replaced the last. The warm air was, if anything, worse. The prisoners were allowed fresh air during the day, but they were 'driven below deck into the steaming hold' in the evening, 'with the grating laid over the opening'. Kept above the stinking, leaking hold, fevers, fluxes, colics, asthmas and consumptions were dreaded. 'It is an established fact', wrote J. H. Röding, the author of the *Universal Marine Dictionary*, 'that bad air, resulting from perspiration, is lighter than clean air. Therefore, such will always rise and swim about the latter like oil and water. One can easily convince oneself of that in a sick bay, as [the] higher as one goes up in it, [the] more irritable the smell becomes.'[23] As temperatures rose, in Newport harbour the air inside the prison ships grew hot and foul.

The *Lord Sandwich* had become a perversion of everything *Endeavour* had represented. *Endeavour* had always been characterised by action. She had crossed the Atlantic time and again, she had sailed the South Seas and Indian Ocean. All this time sailors had teemed over her masts, yards and decks: reefing, furling, setting, drawing, tightening, heaving, loosening, knotting, spinning yarn. The naturalists Banks and Solander had leapt from gunwale to gunwale, all to satisfy the thrill of a moment, to catch a glimpse of a rare plumage or an iridescent sparkle on the waves. To be confined aboard at Rio was Banks's idea of hell. By 1777 this had all gone. *Lord Sandwich* was now locked in her station: anchors down, sails struck, hatches bolted, sentries posted, spirits suppressed. The people locked inside her hold resembled ghosts. She resembled a ghost herself.

The summer of 1777 was tense in Newport. On 4 July cannon fire boomed from Providence as the first anniversary of independence was marked. 'As the evening was very still and fine', one soldier wrote, the echo down the bay 'had a very grand effect, the report of each being repeated three of four times'.[24]

A week later, on 11 July, the British woke to the staggering news that General Prescott and one of his aides – the nephew of the secretary of war Lord Barrington – had been abducted in the night from his private residence. A party of forty Patriot soldiers had rowed noiselessly from the mainland overnight, had surprised the sentry at Prescott's rural retreat and bundled him away. 'Sir, you have made a damn'd bold push tonight', Prescott had addressed his captor when the raid was over.[25] It was the most audacious and complete triumph. One Patriot officer wrote disbelievingly:

> History scarcely affords such an instance, and it must be a most mortifying scene to General Prescott when he reflects that he was taken on an island in the midst of the British fleet and his army, and that without the discharge of a single gun.[26]

Prescott's capture reinforced the paranoia. In October 1777 the British received intelligence that a new attack was imminent, with subversive cells ready to be activated within the city. To pre-empt events, a blacklist of suspected rebels was compiled. Sixty-one 'friends to liberty' were herded aboard *Lord Sandwich*, 'for refusing to sign an oath pledging to defend the town against attacks from the revolutionaries'.[27]

The October 1777 imprisonments brought the last notable figure aboard. John Townsend, a Newport cabinetmaker, had already established a reputation, and he would go on to produce a remarkable range of furniture and earn renown as the American Chippendale. Known for his 'precision, elegance, and fastidious attention to detail', Townsend was carried aboard Fishburn's bark and imprisoned with sixty or so others. It is difficult to think of two more contrasting craftsmen than Fishburn and Townsend. One was bluntly practical, working in stout English oak. The other epitomised Georgian elegance, celebrated for his embellishments, for the graceful curves and the mirrored shine of his Caribbean mahogany. Locked away in the oaky gloom, Townsend and Fishburn were briefly united in a physical space. Running his eyes over the internal works of the *Lord Sandwich*, Townsend would have encountered a style more simple and straight-forward than anything he ever produced. It is a haunting picture: the master cabinetmaker, locked away inside a wooden prison.

'Heavens! what a scene of wretchedness before this once happy and flourishing island', Mary Almy wrote in 1778. It was not only the ship and the prisoners that had been hollowed out and reduced to spectres of their former selves; the city itself was ruined. Ambrose Serle saw the hardship for himself on Sunday 3 January 1778, as he toured the port. All the prejudices of the English had long lived inside Serle. He found the misery he had anticipated:

> 'Tis built almost entirely with Wood, & makes but a mean appearance. It has one long Street, out of wch run several Lanes, The whole miserably paved, and, at this time, extremely dirty. The public Buildings are but ordinary; and the Style of the Town perfectly suits the Genius of the People, who for Fraud, Smuggling & Rebellion are not to be exceeded in No. [i.e. North] America. There are some Exceptions, but too few to take off the general Stigma.[28]

Serle had arrived in Newport two days before in HMS *Eagle*. Howe had made for Rhode Island to meet Admiral Peter Parker and General Robert Pigot, the replacement for Prescott, 'a very worthy officer', Serle thought. While few in Newport would have been thrilled to meet Serle, Howe's arrival brought unexpected benefits. Howe was disturbed at what he found on the prison ships. He ordered that all those incarcerated were to be released without prior exchanges being agreed. Plans were immediately put in progress for the prisoners to be conveyed to Patriot positions at nearby Bristol or Warwick Neck.

Lord Sandwich was allotted the task of carrying the prisoners. On 11 March 1778, the collier sailed for the last recorded time. Under a flag of truce she ventured fifteen miles up Narragansett Bay to Bristol, unloaded 157 prisoners, and returned. Just how she made her way is uncertain. For fifteen months she had lain at anchor in Newport harbour. It is possible she was lightly rigged with an old sail across half a mast. Perhaps she was towed by one of the frigates or even sculled at a fraction of her old pace.

It had been a long fourteen years since Milner had taken the *Earl of Pembroke* to sea as a precise, weatherly sailer. Had she stayed with Milner in Whitby, the *Earl of Pembroke* might have sailed into the next century, to be numbered among the old maids of the sea like Thomas Fishburn's long-lived *Liberty and Property* in Whitby as the new titans of iron made their appearance in the 1850s. None in Whitby could have foreseen what the *Earl of Pembroke*'s last horrid cargo would be. When brought off at Bristol the *Lord Sandwich*'s prisoners were described as:

> sick and much emaciated, owing to the horrid treatment they received during their captivity, a detail of which, or a view of the present hopeless condition, might excite compassion and resentment in the breast of a Saracen or a savage of any other country than Britain. Many of these unhappy persons had their limbs froze in the severity of the winter, and, if they survive, will probably remain cripples during life.[29]

Four prisoners were dead before they landed. The *Providence Gazette* added that 'many more, it is thought must unavoidably fall victims to the deliberate and wanton cruelty of our merciless adversaries'.

From a prosperous, socially and religiously diverse merchant town, Newport had been hollowed out by the conflict. Serle believed that the rebels had only themselves to blame. Escaping the dreary streets and deserted wharves one 'serene & comfortably warm' day during his visit, Serle ventured out to the southern extremity of Aquidneck Island, where the rolling waves of the Atlantic Ocean crashed over 'romantic' rocks. Climbing to the summit of these, Serle discovered 'a beautiful View of the Sea, Town, Harbor, & adjacent Country'.[30] The brisk sea air, the black rocks and green fields combined to form an exhilarating vista: waves rising and falling in one direction; scattered islands and headlands in the other.

Like Prescott, during his time in Newport Serle could not escape his feeling of paranoia, or his scorn for the 'rebels' he blamed for tearing the British Empire apart. High on the rocks, the Atlantic wind tussling his hair, Serle experienced the simultaneous feelings of being freed by nature and hemmed in by politics. Gazing inland, he knew the Patriot forces were only a matter of miles away. Sure enough by the spring of 1778 they would be gathering for an invasion of Aquidneck Island. The sea, the bay and all the waterways though, Serle might have reasoned, would remain Britain's. There was only one possible thing that could change that.

In 1776, as the huge transport fleet sailed across the Atlantic a satirical illustration was published in Britain. *The Present State of Europe and America, or the Man in the Moon taking a View of the English Armada*, pictured events in the northern hemisphere from the point of view of an interested bystander: 'The Man on the Moon'. To highlight the derangement of politics, the geography was contorted so America stands east of Old England and France to her west. The English fleet bobs mid-ocean. Great armies await them on the North American battlefields. George III glares at the rebel forces from behind his ships, but he does not notice – as the Man on the Moon does – that French armies are gathering behind. George III is about to be startled by the lusty crow of a Gallic cockerel.

The illustration projected a political situation that was familiar to everybody. The French had been humiliated at the Treaty of Paris in 1763. Their empire reduced and surrendered to their ancient rival, they had long awaited a chance of redress. The prospect of the French joining the Americans had worried British politicians for years. As more of the British military capacity was sucked into quelling the troubles, the more precarious their situation had become. When Ambrose Serle climbed over the rocks on Aquidneck Island and the *Lord Sandwich* made her final voyage to Bristol, the alarming news was being received in London that the colonists had agreed and signed a treaty of friendship and commerce with the French. As far as the king was concerned, the treaty was 'certainly equivalent' to a declara-tion of war. The development would leave Britain, in the opinion of the historian Andrew Jackson O'Shaughnessy, 'more isolated than at any other time in its history, even more than in 1940'.[31]

Horror-struck by the news and having lost all faith in his ability to conduct the war, in Westminster Lord North attempted to resign. He implored the king to immediately begin negotiations with members of the opposition. In reply George III called North's actions as 'disgraceful to me and [a] destruction to my kingdom, and Family'.[32]

At the Admiralty, meanwhile, intelligence briefings informed Sandwich that France's naval preparations were 'carrying on both at Brest and Toulon with the utmost diligence and vigour'. The majestic flagship *La Bretagne*, with its 110 guns, was rumoured to be fitting out at Brest. 'Great numbers of men are constantly at work building new ships and arming and equipping every ship that is fit for service.'[33] The reports plunged Sandwich into an awful dilemma. For two years Howe had been in North America. His ships and men were tired. Bit by bit his forces had been divided in convoying and cruising operations. Should this newly fitted-out French fleet strike without warning, the consequences would be dire. Reinforcing Howe was one solution. But doing this would mean leaving a weakened home force exposed to attack from the main French fleet at Brest.

News about the Franco-American pact was made public on 13 March. Within a week the French ambassador was obliged to leave Whitehall. Soon an order was sent to the Thames to detain all French vessels. In the anxious weeks that followed Sandwich did everything to discover the truth of what was happening in France. Reports came back that Franklin, Silas Deane and Arthur Lee were meeting with Louis XVI and the Count de Vergennes, the Secretary of State, at Versailles. More reports confirmed that the French fleet certainly was fitting out at Toulon, and that it was going to be commanded by a favourite of Queen Marie Antoinette's, the Comte d'Estaing. George III was as involved as anyone in the guessing game. He fired off daily letters to Sandwich with his latest theories about French movements and objectives. 'I have not the smallest doubt', he wrote in April, 'that d'Estaing's fleet is gone with Deane ... to attack either Philadelphia or New York.'[34]

To better evaluate the situation, Sandwich lapsed into third-person analysis: his best way of making sense of a confusing situation. He began writing documents headed 'Lord Sandwich's opinion'. In these he reasoned that it was 'unsafe' to remove ships from the Channel. 'Our principal object must be our defence at home', he concluded. Doing nothing, though, meant leaving Howe to his fate. Scout vessels were deployed to watch the Strait of Gibraltar. April passed, then May.

At the start of June the news reached Britain that d'Estaing had led a massive fleet through the strait and westwards through the Atlantic.

This was a force of no little size. Leading it was d'Estaing's flagship, *Le Languedoc*, with its three gun decks and ninety guns. In support was an eighty, six seventies – including one captained by the South Seas explorer de Bougainville – three sixty-fours, a thirty and numerous frigates. This was the force Washington, Franklin and thousands of other Patriots had dreamed about. It was more than a match for Howe. On learning this news, after weeks of hesitation, Sandwich finally ordered a British fleet – led by another old South Seas hand, Commodore Byron once of the *Dolphin* – in pursuit.

D'Estaing was presented with a golden chance in 1778. He had the advantage of firepower, men and freshness, as well as the possibility of taking the British by surprise. But d'Estaing's progress across the Atlantic was leisurely. Many of his vessels were ponderous sailers, weighed down by the enormous press of guns. Time was wasted, chasing merchantmen and practising manoeuvres. In all it took almost as long for d'Estaing's fleet to cross the Atlantic as it had the transport fleet two years before. 'D'Estaing's great object was the surprize of the fleet in the Delaware', wrote the *Annual Register*, but by the time he arrived in July, Howe's fleet had fallen back to New York.[35] Following them, d'Estaing could not find a pilot brave enough to lead the heavy French ships through the Sandy Hook channel. A quirk of geography had delivered Howe. Whether the huge warships might have crossed into New York harbour became a matter of hydrological conjecture:

A diversity of opinion seems to prevail, on the practicability of the great ships of the French fleet passing in force through the strait, and over the bar. Some are of opinion, that it might have been attempted with prudence. If so, it may be considered as a happiness on all sides, that D'Estaing was not possessed of that spirit of enterprize which would have been equal to so arduous an attempt; that the terror of the British flag was yet in no degree weakened; and that the name of the noble Commander who opposed him, added some weight to that effect. D'Estaing accordingly cast anchor on the Jersey side, about four miles without the Hook, and in the vicinity of the small town of Shrewsbury.[36]

As it was, Howe's British fleet remained safely embraced by the harbour. With New York tantalisingly out of grasp, Washington had been as frustrated as anyone. For eleven days d'Estaing's French fleet

lay off the Jersey coast. Letters were rowed back and forth from
Washington to d'Estaing. Eventually it was settled. New York was to
be set aside for another day. D'Estaing was to sail eastwards, to
Newport, Rhode Island.

The *Lord Sandwich* was created in the shadows. Records of her earliest
life are threadbare and fleeting. Her end, though, could hardly have
been more central to the historical narrative. At the end of July the
attentions of so many were converging on the strip of water where
she rode at anchor outside Newport. North of Aquidneck Island at
Providence, General John Sullivan, commander of the troops at Rhode
Island, had begun his final preparations for invasion. 'Everything
depends almost upon the success of this expedition', Major General
Nathanael Greene had written to him. 'Your friends are anxious, your
enemies are watching. *I charge you to be victorious.*'[37] At his headquarters,
Washington waited for news from Newport. In London, so did Lord
Sandwich. At St James's Palace, so did King George.

General Pigot, the British commander at Rhode Island, received
warning a French fleet was sailing towards them on 26 July. He immediately set out to convert Aquidneck Island into a fortress capable of
the most 'vigorous and obstinate defence'. He ordered artillery positions and redoubts to be built on either side of the Middle Channel.
The British and Hessian troops were joined in their work by sailors,
so that all was 'in constant readiness, at the first signal'.

The most vivid account of events during the next days was left by
Mary Almy. She wrote of how 'Every sailor was equipt with a musket
that could get one; he that could not, had a billet of wood, an old
broom, or any club they could find'.[38] She wrote of people exhausted
by stress and physical toil: 'the fatigues of body and mind with a
thousand perplexities that attend such an uncommon care, made them
ready to meet their fate, let it be for life or death'. With the invasion
imminent, Almy was struck by the idea of her husband being among
the invading army:

> The boys endeavor to put on an air of manliness, and strive to
> assist, but slip up to the girls, in a whisper, 'Who do you think
> will hurt you? Ain't your papa coming with them?' Indeed this
> cut me to the soul. After three years a lost wanderer, and could
> not meet a welcome.[39]

Almy saw the French on 29 July. As the enormous ships of d'Estaing's fleet came to anchor off Brenton's Point, Newport buzzed with life. Almy conveyed the scene in a chain of run-on sentences. The pavements were almost 'all torn up with the swiftness of the light-horse, momentary intelligence; every idle person that loved news, this was his day. As every ear was open to the marvelous, when night came my heart ached with the many falsehoods that my ear had paid attention to the day long.'

The three entrances to the bay, so long governed by British frigates, became French highways. Almy watched as the sloop *Kingfisher* was burnt to keep it out of French hands. To exacerbate the feeling of order subverted, on 31 July a stifling fog overspread the bay, burying Newport. 'All in terror till it clears off', wrote Almy. The fog had lifted by 1 August, when she wrote:

> All the fleet in motion; everything in consternation; the inhabitants much distressed; the batteries all spirited; all warlike preparation; the streets filled with carts and ordnance stores: every busy soul harnessing, tackling and loading with comb[ustible] matter, to supply every deficiency that their former negligence had made necessary, and by night they were so ready, that the foolhardy part would wish for nothing more than a movement of the French fleet into the harbor. But I lay down, earnestly praying they would never come so near.[40]

General Pigot, though, was not going to rely on prayers alone. He decided to make the Newport shoreline as difficult to approach as possible. To do so he planned to make use of the prison ships. His idea was to ruin Newport harbour by scuttling them across the shallows, a tactic Washington had used in the Hudson River during the British operations in 1776. The hulls of the sunken ships would be aggravating enough. With masts, spars and related debris scattered over the bottom too, the irritation would be all the worse. It would make landing difficult, and if the city should fall then it would frustrate shipping for months to come.

On 3 August a British officer, Captain Brisbane, was handed an order to have five of the transports

> sunk in the passage between Goat Island and the Blue Rocks, to prevent the Approach of the Enemy too near the North Battery,

so as to attack it with Advantage. And Five more Transports are proceeding out, in order to be sunk between Goat Island and Rose Island for the same Purpose.[41]

Having digested its contents, Brisbane set about executing his orders. We know little more. The best we can do is imagine Brisbane's march with a party of marines or a group of soldiers from the British head-quarters, along the mill and bustle of Thames Street and down towards the long wharf where the harbour boats lie.

It is only a short pull from the wharf to the spot where the *Lord Sandwich* rides easily on the harbour swell, somewhere between Goat Island and the North Battery. In a few minutes Brisbane and his men come alongside. Brisbane heaves himself up the wooden slats, over the gunwale and his feet fall flat against the main deck.

The *Lord Sandwich* is an eerily quiet space in the centre of the action: the still centre of the turning world. The carved face of the old sailor still gazes out from the windlass palls, but now it does so across an empty ship. All the prisoners have been taken ashore. There are only ghosts aboard now. High in the maintop a Polynesian priest is crouched in contemplation. Beneath him on the forecastle Whitby apprentices play, throwing lumps of coal high across the deck. Hidden away behind a cabin door in the stern quarters, a shy artist is hunched over his journal.

As Brisbane sets about his destructive work, a tall lieutenant moni-tors him from the quarterdeck. He knows that within a matter of hours this bark will be at rest on the sea floor. Beneath the place where the lieutenant stands, clustered in the great cabin, two botanists carry on regardless. They are gathered around a long table that is piled high with books and is strewn with papers. In a gloomy, oaky atmosphere, one of them is frozen in profile, holding some strange new wonder up towards the light.

On 29 August 1778, the Battle of Rhode Island took place. It concluded the first joint military operation between France and the United States of America, and it ended inconclusively. The American forces withdrew to the mainland. The British remained on Aquidneck Island for another year.

On 30 November 1778, Joseph Banks was elected president of the Royal Society. He held the position for forty-one years until his death on 19 June 1820.

On 14 February 1779, on his third voyage of exploration, James Cook was killed in a skirmish at Kealakekua Bay, Hawaii. The *Resolution*'s surgeon, David Samwell, who witnessed Cook's final moments, wrote: 'not being able to swim he endeavoured to scramble on the Rock when a fellow gave him a blow on the head with a large Club and he was seen alive no more'.

On 19 April 1779 a motion was made in the House of Commons calling for the removal of Lord Sandwich as First Lord of the Admiralty. Sandwich survived until the fall of North's government in 1782, the year before the end of the war.

On 13 May 1787 a British fleet of eleven ships (later given the name 'The First Fleet') sailed from Portsmouth bound for Botany Bay in New South Wales to establish a new overseas colony. Among the vessels was a Whitby-built transport of 378 tons. It was called *Fishburn*.

Epilogue: Endeavours

In 1967 a Christmas card featuring *Endeavour* went on sale in Australia in anticipation of the bicentenary of 'Captain Cook's' famous voyage. For the manufacturers, it was a safe choice. *Endeavour* had long since been elevated to the status of national symbol, playing a starring role in the foundation story of modern Australia. It was the acorn from which the nation had prospered. Pictures of the ship had come to represent ideals of freedom, courage and independence. The ship also symbolised nostalgic bonds to Britain and older histories. The issue with the Christmas card, as one Melbourne resident recognised at once, was that *Endeavour*'s portrayal was 'all wrong'.[1]

In his own quiet and independent way, Ray Parkin was one of the great Australians of his generation. Born into a working-class family in Collingwood, Melbourne in 1910, he had spent days watching the hubbub of maritime activity in Port Philip Bay as a boy. There among the paddle steamers and turbine-driven liners, it was occasionally possible to see an old square-rigged sailing ship. A natural artist, Parkin had sketched their elegant lines and pleasing forms. Parkin had left school at fourteen. Four years later he had joined the Royal Australian Navy. In 1942 he had been a petty officer aboard HMAS *Perth* when she was torpedoed by the Japanese at the Battle of Sunda Strait. For ten hours Parkin had survived in the burning sea, 'squinting and blinking' as 'the dollops of oil-fuel flung' in his face.[2] He later recalled that at one point he had nearly given up, only to realise he 'didn't know how to die, [so] had to start swimming again'.[3] About half the *Perth*'s complement were dead by the time Parkin scrambled up a beach, 'streaked in tones from the deepest sepia to raw sienna'.[4] This visual detail was characteristic. The author Laurens van der Post met Parkin shortly afterwards in a Japanese prisoner-of-war camp. He was convinced Parkin 'was born an artist before life turned him into a quartermaster'. 'Not once', he added, 'in those rather terrible weeks did I notice any sign of decline in his urge constantly to make, shape and create things.'[5]

As well as sketching, Parkin wrote. His first literary attempt, a romantic novel, had been lost in the *Perth*. But after the war, he started again. Realising that 'life wasn't romantic', he condensed his experiences of war and imprisonment into a trilogy of memoirs that he wrote in his spare time when not working as a tally clerk at Melbourne docks. Reading Parkin's writing – vivid, spare, wise – Laurens van der Post was so struck he recommended them to his publishing contacts in Britain. All three were acquired by Leonard Woolf for the Hogarth Press and edited by Cecil Day Lewis in London, about whom Parkin was once asked 'Wasn't he the Poet Laureate?' 'Yes he was,' Parkin replied, 'but he didn't change anything in the book.'[6]

At Christmas 1967 Parkin's zest for precision was stimulated again. What was really known about *Endeavour*? Ever since Samuel Atkins had started the trend in the 1790s, artists had had a tendency to 'improve' her to satisfy aesthetic or narrative demands. Her bluff bows would often be sharpened. She would sometimes be lengthened, loaded with more cannons or sails – all things befitting of an icon. Parkin had no time for this. He knew colliers well. 'Ships of this type were still operating halfway through the nineteenth century', he later wrote. He thought it was unfair they were regularly compared with the 'glamorised' Victorian clippers like *Cutty Sark*. These clippers, he argued, were 'comparatively few, over-specialised and, as a class, of short duration'.[7] Collier barks, conversely, had survived so long that in his childhood he had known people who had sailed them. He sensed, without yet knowing, that *Endeavour* had qualities few appreciated.

Further aggravated by the 'flood of opportunistic journalese' on *Endeavour* in the bicentenary in 1968, Parkin set off on an endeavour of his own. He decided to collate all the surviving plans and drafts and to scour them for detail. He aimed to do precisely what the card had not: recreate *Endeavour*'s material reality with clarity. First he obtained an entire list of *Endeavour*'s 'scantlings' – an itemised list of each piece of wood with its breadth and thickness. Parkin began to arrange these, jigsaw-like, in drawings of his own. After his retirement in 1975 he travelled to London to analyse archival materials at Greenwich and the Reading Room of the British Museum. To reanimate life aboard he requested microfilms of the ship's log and all the surviving journals. Back home in Melbourne these were printed in full, 'yielding some 1,160 metres', which he then cut out and arranged chronologically so that on any given day, at any time, he could glance at a panorama of maritime activity aboard.[8]

Years passed as Parkin worked at his drafts. 'The more one learns of these times the less one is patronising', he mused. At 'about 3.3 breadths to her length', he judged *Endeavour* intelligently proportioned. The bark that began to appear in his sketches was not the 'dull creature' Admiral Wharton had once derided. Instead she was a machine cleverly adapted to her purpose. What else could have done her job so well? He realised that her flat bottom was an essential feature, allowing her to sit upright on sands or riverbanks as she did at Endeavour River. Her boxy-shape and bulldog's nose may not have been aesthetically pleasing but certainly they were signs of strength. Then there other, tiny, details. He reckoned the curious convex lines beneath her hull were expert design flourishes, that made her more attentive to her helm.

From a structural reanimation, Parkin's project expanded to become a work of philosophy. 'Perhaps no tool has ever influenced the user more throughout history than the ship', Parkin pondered. 'It is not a handheld device to be taken up and put down at will. Paradoxically it is a tool by which the *user* is held. It will serve him only in proportion to *his* service to *it*.' He thought of the sailors, their bodies in constant physical dialogue with oak timbers and hempen sailcloth:

> On the darkest nights he felt, through the soles of his mostly bare feet, or through this hand's grip changing grasp aloft, the roll, scend and pitch of the whole fabric. Last instant, this instant, the next instant – these plotted an intuitive graph within him that became a useable rhythm. Just as he knew where to scratch himself accurately in the dark, so he developed this wider proprioceptive sense about the ship herself. The tension on a rope, the spring of a spar, the creak of a block, the heel of the ship, the wind in his face, the tune in the rigging, the signs of the sea and sky, the centrifugal force on deck or aloft as the stars flew by – all this, and more, flowed through him.[9]

This interplay between man and machine fascinated Parkin. The relationship demanded much from either side, but once the sailor had 'programmed' his mind to control the vessel, the result was something eloquent and almost spiritual. 'The word *soul* has been used with ships', he wrote, 'but if the sailor ever used it he meant *essence* – the distillation of experiences shared.' Once locked into this relationship, the ship became a sort of biographical tool: revealing character. 'The ship can call forth qualities above and beyond the norm', he wrote. 'It explores the ultimate in the user and may give him in return a lasting self-respect – or a terrible insight. It may call forth his unsuspected best, or reveal his worst.'[10]

Of all the characters *Endeavour* revealed, none was more starkly exposed than Cook's. Parkin realised that the understanding and interplay between the captain and ship had been something special. In combination they had demonstrated just how much a person could achieve. It's tempting to think that Parkin saw something of himself in Cook. Although divided by time, they were boys from the waterfront with an aptitude for draughtsmanship, who had gone to sea and learned to survive *in extremis* through stoicism. Cook had always been content with his Whitby collier. Parkin recognised what a powerful tool she was too.

For thirteen years Parkin worked on his *Endeavour* project. He completed cutaway and profile charts, pictures of *Endeavour*'s boats, anchors, cables and sailing rigs, and depictions of her at various moments of the voyage. Three years alone were spent defining the appearance of her stern. To support these drafts, Parkin produced reflective chapters on 'The Captain', 'Scurvy and Provisions', 'The Ship's Company'. As little was known of *Endeavour* before or after Cook's circumnavigation Parkin restricted his focus to the years 1768–71. His central preoccupation was *Endeavour*'s cruise along the New Holland coast in 1770, which he reconstructed in hour-by-hour detail. The result was so vast and various that no one who saw it believed it was publishable. Another seventeen years passed (making thirty years in all) before Parkin's *HM Bark Endeavour: her place in Australian History*, was acquired by an imprint of Melbourne University Press in 1997. He was eighty-eight years old. Marketed for $150, it raced through three editions in two years, won the Douglas Stewart Prize for non-fiction, and became one of the most idiosyncratic, brilliant publishing tales of its time.

Parkin's *Endeavour* project is memorable, but it is not unique. There is an enduring magic connected to *Endeavour*'s story that continues to propel people into ambitious projects. It is almost as if the force of the untethered, freewheeling, expansive Georgian society to which the ship belonged is so powerful that it is capable of reaching across generations, transferring its energy, and making more endeavourers of new people in different times or places. Parkin's thirty years on *Endeavour* is eclipsed by the thirty-three years the New Zealand biologist Averil Lysaght spent on Joseph Banks and the members of his travelling suite. In 1980, the year before Lysaght's death, she wrote reflectively of her genesis moment. It had happened one rainy Saturday in 1948 at the Alexander Turnbull Library in Wellington. 'Quite by chance' she had opened a transcript of Banks's *Endeavour* journal. She instantly felt the force of his personality and boldness of his scheme come shining out. 'I determined then and there', Lysaght wrote, 'I would spend the rest of my life working on Joseph Banks and his papers.'[11] Lysaght was as good as her word, producing her 'monumental', *Joseph Banks in Newfoundland and Labrador, 1766* (1972).

But even her efforts seem diminutive when set beside those of James Cook's great biographer, J. C. Beaglehole. Beaglehole's research and writing on Cook and his three voyages is widely regarded as one of the scholarly achievements of the twentieth century. Each of Cook's three edited journals (published in four volumes between 1955–67) stretches across the bookshelf at around a thousand pages. They are crammed with introductions, explanatory notes, footnotes, appendices, maps and illustrations – all fittingly eighteenth century in scope – but even they were intended only as a 'preliminary step' for his great biography *The Life of Captain James Cook* that was published posthumously in 1974. Of Cook's three voyages, *Endeavour*'s was the one that always took Beaglehole's breath away. 'Really that voyage makes most of the other Great Occasions of the 18th Century seem pretty silly', he wrote in a letter. 'What is Dr Johnson, what is Voltaire, what is Burke or Pope or Chatham by the side of Cook?'[12]

Beaglehole, like Lysaght, experienced a moment of intense connection with the story before he set out on his grand project. It came in 1935. He had been hiking across New Zealand's North Island, arriving at 'Cook's Beach', near Whitianga, where *Endeavour* had once anchored. Beaglehole had 'dossed down for the night' in an untenanted shack, waking to 'one of those mornings we get sometimes, absolutely pure and crystalline, the sea and the sand as pure as the air and the early sun'.

I walked along the beach by the side of the sea, round the magnificent curve ... up to the edge of what Cook called the Oyster river. On the other side of the stream two or three Maori figures appeared and looked at me: otherwise the whole bay, from the sea in to the hills, was empty and silent. And yet I felt something. It was nothing to do with a half-stirring breeze, or the gradually warming sun, though it was a sort of faint tingling of the mind ... I don't want to use that old expression, 'the trembling of a veil', but it really was as if a veil had suddenly trembled, an invisible veil; and on the other side, just outside my vision, was a ship, and a boat rowing towards the shore; and somewhere or other, just floating beyond the reach of my ear, was the sound of words. I almost, before I turned back, caught sight of the *Endeavour*; I almost heard the voices of eighteenth-century sailors.[13]

The span of *Endeavour*'s life, 1764–78, forms a crucial mini epoch in the development of Western society. It opens just after the Treaty of Paris amid the first stir of problems in America. It ends with France's entry to the war and the beginning of the process of reimaging empire: from British America to British Australia. In 1778, the year *Endeavour* was scuttled, Carl Linnaeus died in Sweden and the Earl of Chatham died in Britain. These were the leading political and scientific figures of the preceding generation. Their loss, along with Cook's (in 1779), then Solander's (1782) and Sandwich's (1792), signalled the end of an era in history as a new dominant political figure, William Pitt the Younger, rose to power and the terror of revolution caused European societies to turn inwards.

Looking back it is striking to see how Western society was shaped in these short fourteen years. The date of Wilkes's victory at Middlesex in 1768 has been pinpointed as the beginning of the democratic movement. In 1769 Watt's steam engine was patented. In 1770 Hargreaves's spinning jenny followed. Six years on, Adam Smith's *Wealth of Nations* provided capitalist societies with a practical theoretical framework in the same year that the United States of America – the greatest capitalist society of them all – was founded. Behind all this progress lay the bold and enterprising spirit that was hardwired into the culture. In these years life was lived on a grand scale and played out in a major key. 'Endeavour' was a word people often reached for to express this.

Wilkes used it on the hustings, Cook used it on the reef and Penrose used it when Port Egmont was on fire. To endeavour meant to exert everything: to stretch mind and body out towards a goal that was only just within reach. The impulse infected everyone. As George III once wrote, 'We must stretch every nerve to defend ourselves, and must run some risks, for if we are to play only a cautious game ruin will inevitably ensue.'[14]

Later generations marvelled at the fluidity of this society, with its high-flown ideas, intellectual impetuosity and fashion for risk-taking. Elizabeth Stone in *Chronicles of Fashion* (1846) wrote with disbelief about the tales of bets 'as to which two drops of rain coursing down the window pane would soonest reach the bottom; or which of two maggots would achieve in a certain given time the greatest distance across the cheese board'.[15] The frivolity astounded her, but it at least generated stories. In 1881 Robert Louis Stevenson let his imagination wander back to the previous century. He drew a map of an island – 'the shape of it took my fancy beyond expression'. He 'ticketed' his creation, 'Treasure Island', and the 'brown faces and bright weapons' of characters 'peeped out upon me from unexpected quarters'.[16] He chose Squire Trelawney as the name for his lead projector. He might equally have selected 'Alexander Dalrymple'.

Stevenson ploughed many of the characteristics of the age – strength, courage, quickness, magnificent geniality – into his arch villain Long John Silver. Here were the ingredients for a classic adventure story: a shipload of British projectors on a scheme to a distant island. In the years after *Treasure Island*'s release, Stevenson witnessed for himself the destructive consequences of such eighteenth-century impetuosity. Travelling to the South Seas in the 1880s he saw an imperialist machine in malevolent motion. The *pahi* which Parkinson had drawn coasting in the shallows, alongside the Tahitian surfers, carrying breadfruit to the markets, were now forced to share the water with ironclad battleships or belching steamers. Stevenson saw how cultures had been eroded or destroyed by missionary zeal and how populations had been ravaged by European diseases. Here was the tainted dystopia James Dunbar, professor of philosophy at the University of Aberdeen, had foreseen in 1782: 'the natives of the happy island', he had written, 'so cruelly abused, will have cause to lament for ages, that any European vessel ever touched their shores'.[17] Already for many the foaming white of *Endeavour*'s wake was drawing a line not only across water but through time: dividing a coherent, undisturbed past, from a fractious, messy present. As Stevenson wrote:

> The seven sleepers of Polynesia stand, still but half aroused, in the midst of the century of competition. And the island races, comparable to a shopful of crockery launched upon the stream of time, now fail to make their desperate voyage among pots of brass and adamant.[18]

Stevenson's argument was illustrated nowhere better than the foreshore at Tūranganui-a-Kiwa, where in 1769 Cook and the unknown Māori man had touched noses for the first time. In 1877 the Te Toka-a-Taiau rock that marked the location of the encounter, with all of its rich cultural heritage and historical meaning, was dynamited by the local harbour board in an effort to improve access to the newly renamed port of Gisborne. Such vandalism was typical of those Stevenson termed an 'irregular invasion of adventurers' that 'began to swarm around the isles of the Pacific' in the nineteenth century. Stevenson was quick to divide *Endeavour*'s voyage from the worst of these. But it was equally clear that with their sea charts and scientific surveys, and with the ritual planting of Union Jacks on new shores, Cook and Banks had established the platform for the aggressive process of colonisation that followed. The legacy of this is still being felt today.

To many people of the Pacific, as time passed *Endeavour* has become a powerful emblem of colonialism. Seeking to make sense of the ensuing histories of violence and dispossession and attempting to reclaim their own narratives, people have often looked backwards to those ephemeral and complex moments of first encounter. One of the most poignant reflective processes began in 2010 when a group of Australian artists, academics and songwriters set out to explore alternative perspectives of *Endeavour*'s cruise up eastern Australia in 1770. The members of *East Coast Encounter: re-imagining 1770*, worked in the spirit of the historian Judith Binney's post-colonial plea, that 'dialogue must be between each other: that is, it must transcend both self-representation and those European notions of claiming uniquely to possess the historical language which establishes an analytical truth'.[19]

A book and an exhibition emerged. *East Coast Encounter* included works of art that were challenging, brash, rich. A powerful connection to the original history came in Gemma Cronin's 'Badtjala Song', an evocative account of *Endeavour* – as the bad water spirit, or sand crab – sailing past Fraser Island or K'gari. Essays – 'Through Our Eyes' and 'Captain Cook came very cheeky, you know' – explored Aboriginal and Torres Strait Islander attitudes relating to those initial moments of contact. *East Coast Encounter* also served as a reminder that few objects in history have such a gulf between their material reality and their cultural meaning as Thomas Fishburn's bark. The most striking depiction of the ship came in a charcoal and coloured-pencil illustration called *Close Encounters of the First Kind* by the artist Reg Mombassa. Mombassa transformed *Endeavour* from an oaky coal collier into a metallic alien spacecraft, its body dominated by a massive eye. Equipped with skulls, RAF insignia, clanking chains and telegraph poles, it hovers in his composition above one of the east coast's sandy coves, massive in proportion to the silhouetted figures below. It depicts brute, pervasive civilisation in much the same manner Rousseau had in the 1750s.

This is *Endeavour*'s disturbing edge. If it is a potently creative force, then it is also capable of destroying. Many in the West have continued, however, to draw on its positive connotations. It is a source of inspiration; a driving impulse as people seek to explore the very limits of human capacity. In 1928 the aviator Captain Ray Hinchliffe and his co-pilot the Hon. Elsie Mackay, daughter of the Count of Inchcape, made their sensational attempt to fly across the Atlantic. Their Stinson Detroiter monoplane, distinguished by a 'dead black fuselage and brilliant gold wings', had its name *Endeavour* painted on its undercarriage. Evading the press, Hinchliffe and Mackay took off in secrecy from Cranwell Aerodrome, Lincolnshire, on 13 March 1928. Mackay, who was attempting to be the first female pilot to cross the Atlantic, was described by one friend as 'a tremendously plucky person'.[20] Reports stated that the pair had left Grantham with a packet of sandwiches in the early morning. *Endeavour* was glimpsed 400 miles to the west of Ireland. Captain Hinchliffe and Elsie Mackay were never seen again.

Having featured in the exploration age and the aviation age, it was natural that *Endeavour* should next appear in the space age. In 1971 the command module on the *Apollo 15* mission to the moon was given the call sign 'Endeavour'. Then in May 1989 President George H. W. Bush announced that the new space shuttle – commissioned to replace the ill-fated *Challenger* – had been named the SS *Endeavour*. 'For the first time', explained NASA's press report, 'an orbiter was named through a national competition involving students in elementary and secondary schools. They were asked to select a name based upon an exploratory or research sea vessel.'[21] They picked *Endeavour* as an ideal combination of science and exploration. In a rare concession to British spelling, they even retained the 'u'.

In the late 1960s six of *Endeavour*'s cannons and much of the ballast were recovered from the Great Barrier Reef where they had lain, encrusted in coral, for two centuries. These were distributed to museums in America, New Zealand, Britain and Australia. Even more in demand were wooden relics from the actual ship. There was not a universally accepted account of what had happened to her. Some claimed she had returned to the coal trade after the circumnavigation; others that she had been used as a prison hulk near Waterloo Bridge. The most commonly held belief was that she had finished her life in Newport, Rhode Island as an exhausted French whaler called *La Liberté*. This was the version John Dix heard on his visit in 1852. The theory had been established in the 1820s, when – it is not clear quite how – *La Liberté* had been identified as Cook's old ship. As she had rotted by Sherman's Wharf in Newport, people had come to gaze. Some had chopped away parts of her carcass as tangible mementos, either for themselves or to sell. To support the provenance of the artefacts, two documents were attested by John B. Gilpin, the British consul at Rhode Island. A letter was also written in 1828 by George Howard, a member of the New York Marine Society. It was addressed to institutions in Liverpool and London:

> The piece of wood which accompanies this [letter] is a part of the original keel of the ship *Endeavour* in which Capt James Cook first circumnavigated the globe in the years 1769, 1770 and 1771. The ship arrived at New Port [*sic*], Rhode Island, in distress from a whaling voyage and was condemned as unseaworthy in the year 1793, was purchased and broken up by Captain John Cahoone of the Revenue cutter *Vigilant*, and pieces of her deposited in many of our public institutions and private collections.[22]

A scrap of *Endeavour* was acquired by the British consul at Newport. Another was gifted to the novelist J. Fenimore Cooper. *Endeavour*'s whole stern post was seen by Dix in 1852, providing the subject for his poem 'An Ocean Fragment'. The aviation pioneer and yachtsman Thomas Sopwith was presented with a piece after his America's Cup attempt (in the yacht *Endeavour*) in the 1930s. As Cook's status grew in the twentieth century, people became more eager to obtain their own connection with the story. More artefacts arrived in Sydney at the Australian National Maritime Museum and at Greenwich.

Other pieces travelled even further. With the command module's call sign 'Endeavour', it seemed appropriate for a fragment of Cook's ship to travel as a keepsake with the *Apollo 15* astronauts. In the summer of 1971, a piece went to the moon. Having rounded Cape Horn, charted the Society Islands, New Zealand and survived the Great Barrier Reef, this piece of oak was now gliding on further voyages over the Sea of Tranquillity, the Apennine Peaks and coming to a new landing site on the rim of the Hadley Rille. Not only had it been there as Banks and Solander visited new shores, but it was there as Commander David Scott and Pilot James Irwin explored the unknown themselves. Except Scott and Irwin were not looking for plants, but pieces of primordial crust.

More fragments of the stern post would follow. When SS *Endeavour* was launched in 1992, NASA's *Space News Roundup* reported:

> As the British captain sailed across the South Pacific in 1768, he may have wondered about sailing among the stars with which he marked his journey, but he probably never dreamed a space-craft that would streak through the heavens above would be christened after the ship on which decks he stood.
>
> The spirit of Cook will travel with the Space Shuttle *Endeavour* on its maiden voyage symbolically represented by a small piece of stern post from Cook's *Endeavour*, on loan to NASA from the Graduate School of Oceanography at the University of Rhode Island.[23]

It was an arresting image: Tupaia, Cook and Green, all gazing upwards on a cold South Seas night, never imagining how far it would one day be possible to travel. 'I wonder what Captain Cook would have thought about a piece of the ship orbiting the earth', Andrew Thomas, Australia's first astronaut, said after he took another scrap into orbit himself in 1996.[24] The same year a member of the public approached the Australian National Maritime Museum offering to sell a block from *Endeavour*'s keel. They were forwarded to Mike Connell, the Australian government's official maritime valuer, who examined the piece.

'I was nervous as soon as I saw it', Connell said.[25]

One of the disquieting things for Connell was the lack of supporting evidence establishing the link between the ship and object. To build a better case he decided to conduct a research project of his own. He asked one of his colleagues, Desmond Liddy, for help and together they trawled the archives for mentions of *Endeavour*. After 1775 they found nothing. She seemed to have vanished from the bustle of the Thames into the oblivion of time. At length they caught the scent of a trail.

In the autumn 1970 edition of *New Zealand Marine News*, a maritime historian called N. A. Maffey had unearthed a curious detail. Maffey was sceptical about the Newport claim. 'Memory can play queer tricks on people over such a period', he wrote. Documents contained more reliable truths. Several years before Maffey had been examining some early copies of Lloyd's Register, which had just been reprinted. In them he noticed that a ship called *Endeavour* had been renamed *Lord Sandwich* in February 1776. The ship had been built at Whitby in 1764 and it was roughly the same tonnage as Cook's exploration vessel. Additionally it had been sheathed and repaired in the king's yard, which was something that 'could have only happened to one of His Majesty's Ships'. Maffey found that this ship had been engaged as a transport, but it had then vanished 'so her ultimate fate still remains obscure'.[26] Connell and Liddy investigated Maffey's claims. They received confirmation from Lloyd's Register that there had been a handwritten amendment to the records for 1775–6, showing the transfer of ownership from the navy to a private owner, along with the alteration of *Endeavour* to *Lord Sandwich*. This vessel had been surveyed in 1776, then later had been listed 'LO Trnsp' or 'transport of troops, prisoners or convicts, out of London'. This was as far as they took the matter. Among all the other theories, this was just another. They thought it was as likely as anything that *Endeavour* was 'hulked and left to decay naturally in the River Thames'.[27]

But Connell and Liddy made another finding too. Acting on a tip from a correspondent in Massachusetts, they had unearthed a different explanation for Newport's *La Liberté*. John Barrow, the distinguished Admiralty administrator of the late Georgian age, had actually seen

La Liberté for himself. As a young man in 1792, Barrow had been travelling to the British Embassy in China when his vessel had called at
the Cape Verde Islands. They had been followed into the anchorage
by four whalers belonging to Dunkirk.

> One of them was the old *Resolution* of Captain Cooke, now
> transformed to a smuggling whaler under the French name of
> *La Liberté*; and, what was still worse, bearing the French repub-
> lican flag. I am not ashamed to confess that my feelings were
> considerably hurt in witnessing this degradation of an object so
> intimately connected with that great man. Such a feeling, though
> excited by an inanimate object, is not, I trust, either uncommon
> or unnatural … Few, I believe, will envy that man's feelings, who
> can see without emotion the house in which he was born, and
> in which he spent his happiest years, either wholly demolished
> or degraded to some unworthy purpose. The *Resolution* was the
> house of our immortal Cooke and, out of respect for his memory,
> I would have laid her up in a dock, till she had wasted away
> plank by plank.[28]

Barrow was an impeccable witness. He became the force behind
the Arctic expeditions of John Ross and John Franklin and a member
of the Royal Society. He was known for his mastery of naval affairs
and therefore his identification of *La Liberté* as *Resolution* is vital. To
someone like Barrow, *Resolution* and *Endeavour* were different enough,
in size and decoration. But as John Dix shows in his 'An Ocean
Fragment', it was easy to muddle the facts of Cook's voyages. It seems
probable that this happened at Newport in the 1820s. Connell and
Liddy had no doubt. 'After evaluating all the evidence, it can now be
concluded with certainty that the vessel wrecked in Newport, Rhode
Island was James Cook's Sloop *Resolution* and not the *Endeavour*', their
paper ended.[29] It was a tantalising claim. If so, the remains of one of
Fishburn's colliers had travelled into space after all. It was just the
wrong one.

As Mike Connell and Desmond Liddy left the *Endeavour* story, a
new researcher entered it. D. K. Abbass of the Rhode Island Marine
Archaeology Project had already been working on the historical ship-
wrecks of Narragansett Bay for several years when she heard of the
Connell/Liddy research. The name *Lord Sandwich* was instantly

familiar as the name of the infamous prison ship of the British occupation. Intrigued to explore whether *Endeavour* and *Lord Sandwich* were
connected, she travelled to the Public Records Office in London to
examine the Deptford Yard records from the crucial period at the end
of 1775 and the beginning of 1776. After a week's study she emerged
with five distinct pieces of primary source evidence, charting each
step in *Endeavour*'s transformation. When these were added to the
additional evidence in Lloyd's Register, the connection between
Endeavour and *Lord Sandwich* was plain for all to see. Aside from an
eyewitness account, it is hard to think of better testimony the Georgian
world was capable of bequeathing. For the first time it was possible
to know what Sandwich or Cook or Banks or even J. C. Beaglehole
did not. There was an extraordinary coincidence. *Endeavour* and
Resolution, built on the same tiny patch of Whitby shoreline, both
circumnavigators, both essential to the Cook story, had finished their
lives yards from one another.[30]

Abbass published her discoveries in the journal of the Newport
Historical Society in 1999. Ever since she has spearheaded the Rhode
Island Marine Archaeology's (RIMAP's) search for the bark's remains.
Remote sensors have probed the bottom of Newport harbour to
pinpoint oak frames and other telling debris. With around 200 vessels
lost in Rhode Island waters during the Revolutionary War, the search
has been complex. But supported by grants from the Australian government and by teams of local volunteers, their own grand project
continued year after year. As more documentary evidence has emerged
from the British archives, the search has narrowed. A breakthrough
came in May 2016 when RIMAP announced that they had established
beyond doubt that the *Lord Sandwich* had been scuttled in a specific
location, just off Goat Island, as part of a cluster of five vessels. Then,
just over two years later, on 19 September 2018, the *Sydney Morning
Herald* splashed with the long-awaited headline: 'HMB Endeavour
found: one of the greatest maritime mysteries of all time solved.'[31]

While conveying the excitement of the latest development, the
headline masked a more nuanced story. From the five potential wreck
sites, the *Lord Sandwich*'s location had been further whittled down –
through an analysis of the profile of each vessel – to just one. This,
though, was not quite the same as objectively proving this wreck to
be the *Lord Sandwich*. Conclusive evidence, as Abbass pointed out,
would only come with the retrieval of artefacts and the scientific

evaluation of the salvaged materials. This – Abbass is hopeful that controlled excavations can begin in 2019 – will be challenging and expensive. But if a link can be forged between the surviving timbers and, perhaps, a Yorkshire oak tree, then the combined team of Australian and American marine archaeologists will certainly have found one of the most significant objects of the whole Enlightenment Age.

During her life important events always revolved around *Endeavour*. It is intriguing to think of them continuing to do so as she rests in Newport. She would have been there as John F. Kennedy and Jacqueline Lee Bouvier celebrated their wedding at nearby Hammersmith Farm in 1953, or when Bob Dylan outraged the folk music world by 'going electric' at the Newport Folk Festival in 1965. For such a politically charged object it seems appropriate that former Secretary of State John Kerry's yacht is often to be glimpsed nearby. Australians, mean- while, have a poignant reflection of their own. When John Bertrand won the America's Cup in *Australia II* in 1983, he may very well have skimmed right across *Endeavour*'s wreck site.

As for the endeavouring spirit, what of that? It's tempting to think we are a people with many more things but many less dreams, in a risk-averse society when it takes years for even a modest policy to be implemented and dozens of emails for a decision to be reached. But occasionally you will hear about a man with a mighty beard from Cheltenham swimming through walls of jellyfish on his way from Land's End to John O'Groats. Or you will read about Malala Yousafzai's ambition to secure an education for every child in the world, or Elon Musk's scheme to build a 3D tunnel under LA so cars can whizz from place to place at 130mph to beat the congestion. Or you will hear a politician catch an old mood in a new century, as Barack Obama did not so long ago. 'The future rewards those who press on. I don't have time to feel sorry for myself. I don't have time to complain. I'm going to press on.'[32]

Acknowledgements

Anyone who plunges into the mid-eighteenth-century world this book deals with finds a fabulous array of historical characters, scenes and ideas awaiting them. Making sense of them 250 years later has proved to be an immense and enjoyable challenge and it is one I would never have been able to confront without the support and encouragement of a whole ship's company of academics, writers, librarians and friends in countries across the world.

For enabling me to follow *Endeavour* to distant shores, from the dreamy coves of Queen Charlotte's Sound to Botany Bay and the Great Barrier Reef, I am enormously grateful to the Winston Churchill Memorial Trust. I was awarded a Churchill Fellowship in 2016 to travel to Australia and New Zealand, which helped me meet academics, museum curators and members of the diverse communities connected to the story. The experience enriched this book. Thank you Julia Weston, Sara Canullo, Harj Garcha, Sara Venerus and Tristan Lawrence in London. For their advice, encouragement and guidance while I was on my travels, I would like to thank Professor Iain McCalman, Professor David Philip Miller, Dr Maria Nugent, Dr Kate Fullagar, Professor John Maynard, Dr Nigel Erskine, Colleen Miller, Helen Tiernan, Robyn and Alan Cadwallader, Adam Davey, Beverley Payne, Cenk Baban and Laura King, Raymond Morgan at Breaker Bay and the crew of the *R. Tucker Thompson* in the Bay of Islands who showed me the thrills of skylarking in the tops.

Back home in the northern hemisphere I have benefited greatly from the wisdom and generosity of Professor Simon Schaffer of the University of Cambridge. In Whitby I am grateful to Dr Sophie Forgan at the Captain Cook Museum and also to Michael Yates and Alan Appleton. At Greenwich I am indebted to Dr Richard Dunn. David Simpson, Peter Gibbs and Matthew Biggs have all injected a Banksian vigour and geniality into my botanical research. At Newport, Rhode

Island I received the kindest welcome and the finest of tailored tours from Tom and Corky Buckley. To my old seafaring friend Nigel Pickford, too, I am indebted for his tips about the elusive Mr Bird.

At an early stage of the writing Peter Francis at Gladstone's Library provided me with a week's accommodation – the very best of all presents. At Hawarden, too, thank you to Louisa Yates, Gary Butler and their indefatigable team of interns who helped me impose some order into my notes just as they were expanding to Johnsonian proportions. I am grateful to the other libraries that this project took me to: the British Library, Royal Society Library, the State Library of New South Wales, the National Library of Australia in Canberra and, most of all, the London Library, where much of this book was written. Thank you, too, to Gwyneth Endersby at the North Yorkshire County Records Office in Northallerton.

I am especially grateful to Sarah Bakewell and Mike Jay for the many enjoyable conversations, for fielding so many questions, for constantly nudging me in intriguing directions and, most of all, for reading a draft of this book. Their advice was immensely helpful, though it goes without saying that any surviving mortifications (as Cook might term them) are entirely my own.

This book would have been nothing at all had Juliet Brooke not allowed me to write it in the first place. I'm as indebted as ever to her for commissioning it and her deft editorial skill and support. At Chatto & Windus Becky Hardie and Greg Clowes guided this book shrewdly towards publication. I am also grateful to Clara Farmer and to Lucie Cuthbertson-Twiggs. My warmest thanks to Sophie Harris and Suzanne Dean for creating Chatto's superb jacket image and to Matt Broughton for his excellent work on the maps, images and endpapers. My thanks too to Ileene Smith and all at Farrar, Straus & Giroux in New York; to Nikki Christer and Meredith Curnow in Sydney; to David Milner for his insightful editorial work; to my endeavouring agent Annabel Merullo, and Laura McNeil, Alexandra Cliff and everyone else at Peters, Fraser & Dunlop.

Anyone who works on this story owes a debt of gratitude to the Rhode Island Marine Archaeology Project, the Australian Maritime Museum and, particularly, to Dr Kathy Abbass for confirming the link between *Endeavour* and *Lord Sandwich*. Their combined efforts to locate and recover what they can in Narragansett

Bay are ongoing. The latest progress can be followed at http://www.rimap.org/channels/rimap-endeavour.

I spent many years as a boy gazing out from the sands of Filey Bay, wondering about the ships that used to once sail by. That I have had the opportunity to write this book is due to my parents who have encouraged my love of history and storytelling ever since. My biggest debts are to them and also to my wonderful wife Claire and our boisterous little boy Thomas. One of them has done everything to support this book and it is to her it is dedicated. The other has tried his very best to frustrate its progress. To them both, for brightening all days and all endeavours, thank you.

Select Bibliography

Key reference works

J. C. Beaglehole (ed.), *The Endeavour Journal of Joseph Banks 1768–1771*, 2 Vols. (London: Angus & Robertson, 1962)

J. C. Beaglehole (ed.), *The Journals of Captain James Cook on his Voyages of Discovery: The Voyage of the Endeavour 1768–1771* (Cambridge: Cambridge University Press for the Hakluyt Society, 1955)

Sydney Parkinson, *A Journal of a Voyage to the South Seas, in His Majesty's Ship, the Endeavour* (London: printed for Stansfield Parkinson, 1773)

Primary sources

Anthony Addington, *An Essay on the Sea-Scurvy* (Reading: C. Micklewright, 1753)

Mary Almy, *Mrs Almy's Journal in Newport Historical Magazine*, Vol. 1 (Newport: Newport Historical Publishing, 1880)

Anon, *The North Briton* (London: W. Bingley, 1769)

Anon, *A Journal of a Voyage round the World, in His Majesty's Ship Endeavour* (London: T. Becket and P. A. de Hondt, 1771)

Anon, *Pen and Ink Sketches of Eminent English Literary Personages* (London: J. S. Pratt, 1850)

Anon, *Transatlantic Tracings and Popular Pictures from American Subjects* (London: W. Tweedie, 1853)

G. R. Barnes and J. H. Owen, *The Private papers of John, Earl of Sandwich, First Lord of the Admiralty 1771–1782*. Vol. 1, August 1770-March 1778 (Publications of the Navy Records Society, v. LXIX, 1932)

John Barrow, *A Voyage to Cochinchina in the years 1792 and 1793* (London: T. Cadell and W. Davies, 1806)

James Boswell, *The Life of Samuel Johnson, LL.D*, Vol. 1 (London: Henry Baldwin, 1791)

Burke: Select Works, Vol. 1 (Clark: The Lawbrook Exchange, 2005)

Edmund Burke, *A Philosophical Enquiry into the Origin of our Ideas of the Sublime and Beautiful* (London: R. & J. Dodsley, 1759)

Hugh Carrington (ed.), *The Discovery of Tahiti: A Journal of the Second Voyage of HMS Dolphin Round the World by George Robertson 1766–68* (London: Hakluyt Society, 1948)

Lionel Charlton, *The History of Whitby, and of Whitby-Abbey* (London: A. Ward, 1779)

Rev. Sir John Cullum, *The History and Antiquities of Hawstead in the County of Suffolk* (London: J. Nichols, 1784)

Alexander Dalrymple, *An Account of the Discoveries Made in the South Pacifick Ocean, Previous to 1764* (London: privately printed)

Mr Dalrymple's Observations on Dr Hawkesworth's Preface to the Second Edition. (London: privately printed)

Daniel Defoe, *An Essay Upon Projects* (London: Thom. Cockerill, 1697)

Andrew Duncan, *A Short Account of the Life of Sir Joseph Banks* (Edinburgh: Archibald Constable & Co., 1821)

John Evelyn, *The Diary of John Evelyn* (London: Everyman, 2006)

Roger Fisher, *Heart of Oak: the British Bulwark* (London: J. Johnson, 1763)

George Forster, *A Voyage Around the World*, Vol. 2 (London: B White, 1778)

The Papers of Benjamin Franklin (New Haven: Yale University Press, 1972)

Edward Gibbon, *The History of the Decline and Fall of the Roman Empire* Vol. VIII. (Philadelphia: Abraham Small, 1816)

John Harris, *Navigantium atque Ifinerantium Bibliotheca, or a complete collection of voyages and travels* (London: T Woodward, 1744)

Samuel Johnson, *Selected Essays* (London: Penguin, 2003)

Samuel Johnson, *Taxation No Tyranny: An Answer to the Resolutions and Addresses of the American Congress* (London: T. Cadell, 1775)

James Lee, *An Introduction to Botany.* Second Edition (London: J. & R. Tonson, 1765)

Catharine Macaulay, *Loose Remarks on certain positions to be found in Mr. Hobbes's Philosophical Rudiments* (London: T. Davies, 1767)

John Marra, *Journal of the Resolution's Voyage in 1772, 1773, 1774 and 1775* (London: F. Newberry, 1776)

Mr. Marshall, *The Rural Economy of Yorkshire*, Vol. 1 (London: T. Cadell, 1788)

William Mountaine, *The Seaman's Vade-Mecum and Defensive War by Sea* (London: W. & J. Mount, 1756)

Naval Documents of the American Revolution, Vols. 3–6 (Washington: US Navy Department, 1968–1972)

Thomas Paine, *Common Sense* (London: Penguin, 2005)

Papers Relative to the Late Negotiations with Spain; and the taking of Falkland's Island from the English (London: J. Almon, 1772)

Parliamentary History of England from the earliest period to the year 1803, Vol. 18 (London: Hansard, 1813)

Bernard Penrose, *An Account of the Last Expedition to Port Egmont, in Falkland's Islands in the Year 1772* (London: J. Johnson, 1775)

Albert Pfister, *The Voyage of the First Hessian Army from Portsmouth to New York 1776* (New York: Chas. Fred. Heartman, 1915)

Thomas Pierson, *Roseberry Topping: a poem* (Stockton: Jennett & Co., 1847)

Erich Pontoppidan, *The Natural History of Norway* (London: A. Linde, 1755)

Rev. J. Ray, *A Complete Collection of English Proverbs* (London: T. & J. Allman, 1818)

R. Richardson, *The Dolphin's Journal Epitomized in a Poetical Essay* (London: Privately published, 1768)

Jean-Jacques Rousseau, *The Social Contract* (London: Penguin, 2004)

John James Rousseau, *A Discourse upon the Origin and Foundation of the Inequality among Mankind* (London: R. and J. Dodsley, 1764)

Ambrose Serle, *The American Journal of Ambrose Serle, Secretary to Lord Howe 1776–1778* (San Marino: Huntington Library Publications, 1940)

Tobias Smollett, *Roderick Random* (London: Penguin, 1995)

Ezra Stiles, *The Literary Diary of Ezra Stiles*, Vol. 1 (New York: Charles Scribner's Sons)

William Sutherland, *The Ship-builder's Assistant, or some Essays Towards Compleating the Art of Marine Architecture* (London: Thomas Page, William and Fisher Mount, 1726)

Henry Taylor, *Memoirs of the Principal Events in the Life of Henry Taylor of North Shields* (North Shields: T. Appleby)

Mr. Tuke, Junior *General View of the Agriculture of the North-Riding of Yorkshire* (London: W. Bulmer & Co., 1794)

Richard Walter, *A Voyage Around the World in the Years MDCCXL, I, II, III, IV by George Anson* (London: John and Paul Knapton, 1748)

William Watson, *The Poetical Remains with other Detached Pieces of the Late F. Gibson* (London: R. Rogers, 1807)

Rev. Gilbert White, *The Natural History of Selborne* (Edinburgh: Constable & Co., 1829)

Rev. George Young, *A History of Whitby and Streoneshalh Abbey*, Vol. 2 (Whitby: Clark & Medd, 1817)

Secondary materials

Robert Greenhalgh Albion, *Forests and Sea Power: the timber problem of the Royal Navy 1652–1862* (Cambridge, MA: Harvard University Press, 1926)

Alan Appleton, *Whitby Timeline* (privately published)

Rodney Atwood, *The Hessians* (Cambridge: Cambridge University Press, 1980)

Peter Aughton, *Endeavour: the story of Captain Cook's first great epic voyage* (London: Cassell & Co, 1999)

Stephen Baines, *Captain Cook's Merchant Ships* (Stroud: The History Press, 2015)

R.E.R. Banks, B. Elliott, J.G. Hawkes, D. King-Hele, G. Ll. Lucas (eds.), *Sir Joseph Banks a global perspective* (London: Royal Botanic Gardens Kew, 1994)

Rosalin Barker, *The Rise of An Early Modern Shipping Industry: Whitby's Golden Fleet, 1600–1750* (Woodbridge: Boydell Press, 2011)

David Barrie, *Sextant: a voyage guided by the stars and the men who mapped the world's oceans* (London: William Collins, 2015)

J. C. Beaglehole, *The Life of Captain James Cook* (London: Adam & Charles Black, 1974)

Judith Binney, *Redemption Songs: A Life of Te Kooti Arikirangi Te Turuki* (Wellington: Bridget Williams Books, 1995)

John Brewer, *Sentimental Murder: Love and Madness in the Eighteenth Century* (London: Harper Perennial, 2005)

D. J. Carr, *Sydney Parkinson: Artist of Cook's 'Endeavour' Voyage* (London: Croom Helm Ltd, 1984)

Harold Carter, *Sir Joseph Banks* (London: British Museum, 1988)

Arthur Cash, *John Wilkes: the scandalous father of civil liberty* (New Haven: Yale University Press, 2006)

Neil Chambers (ed.), *Endeavouring Banks: Exploring collections from the Endeavour Voyage* (London: Paul Holberton Publishing, 2016)

Neil Chambers, *The Scientific Correspondence of Sir Joseph Banks*, Vol. 1 (London: Routledge, 2007)

Maurice Cranston, *Jean-Jacques: the early life and work of Jean-Jacques Rousseau 1712–1754* (Chicago: University of Chicago Press, 1991)

Paul F. Dearden, *The Rhode Island Campaign of 1778: inauspicious dawn of alliance* (Providence: Rhode Island Bicentennial Foundation, 1987)

Greg Dening, *Mr Bligh's Bad Language: Passion, Power and Theatre on the Bounty* (Cambridge: Cambridge University Press, 1992)

Joan Druett, *Tupaia: Captain Cook's Polynesian Navigator* (Santa Barbara: Praegar, 2011)

East Coast Encounter (Collingwood: One Day Hill, 2014)

Richard England, *Schoonerman* (London: Hollis & Carter, 1981)

Patricia Fara, *Sex, Botany and Empire: The Story of Carl Linnaeus and Joseph Banks* (London: Icon Books, 2003)

Howard Tyrrell Fry, *Alexander Dalrymple, 1737–1808, and the expansion of British trade* (London: Frank Cass & Co., 1970)

Kate Fullagar, *The Savage Visit* (Berkeley: University of California Press, 2012)

John Gascoigne, *Joseph Banks and the English Enlightenment: Useful Knowledge and Polite Culture* (Cambridge: Cambridge University Press, 1994)

John Gascoigne, *Captain Cook: voyager between worlds* (London: Hambledon, 2007)

George Goodwin, *Benjamin Franklin in London* (London: Weidenfeld & Nicolson, 2016)

Rongowhakaata (R.W) Halbert, *Horouta: The History of the Horouta Canoe, Gisborne and East Coast* (Auckland: Reed Books, 1999)

Gabriel Hemery and Sarah Simblet, *The New Sylva: a discourse of forest & orchard trees for the twenty-first century* (London: Bloomsbury, 2014)

Bridget Hill, *The Republican Virago: Life and Times of Catharine Macaulay* (Oxford: Clarendon Press, 1992)

Jonathan Lamb, *Scurvy: the disease of discovery* (Princeton: Princeton University Press, 2016)

Margarette Lincoln, *Science and Exploration in the Pacific: European voyagers to southern oceans in the eighteenth century* (Woodbridge: Boydell Press, 1998)

Averil M. Lysaght, *Joseph Banks in Newfoundland and Labrador, 1766: His Diary, Manuscripts and Collections* (London: Faber & Faber, 1971)

Christian M. McBurney, *Kidnapping the Enemy: Special operations to capture generals Charles Lee & Richard Prescott* (Yardley: Westholme Publishing, 2013)

Iain McCalman, *The Reef: A passionate history* (New York: Scientific American, 2013)

David McCullough, *1776* (New York: Simon & Schuster, 2005)

David R. MacGregor, *Merchant Sailing Ships: Sovereignty of Sail 1775–1815* (London: Conway Maritime Press, 1985)

Joseph Angus Mackay, *Historic Poverty Bay and the East Coast* (Gisborne: Joseph Angus Mackay, 1949)

Frank McLynn, *Captain Cook: Master of the seas* (London: Yale University Press, 2011)

Karl Heinz Marquardt, *Captain Cook's Endeavour* (London: Conway Maritime Press, 1995)

Karl Heinz Marquardt, *HM Bark Endeavour: What do we really know about the Ship* (available at: http://karl-heinz-marquardt.com)

Robert Middlekauff, *The Glorious Cause: The American Revolution, 1763–1789* (Oxford: Oxford University Press, 2005)

Edmund Sears Morgan & Helen Morgan, *The Stamp Act Crisis: Prologue to Revolution* (Chapel Hill: University of North Carolina Press, 1953)

Maria Nugent, *Captain Cook was Here* (Cambridge: Cambridge University Press, 2009)

Andrew Jackson O'Shaughnessy, *The Men Who Lost America* (London: Oneworld, 2013)

Lincoln Paine, *Sea and Civilisation* (New York: Vintage Books, 2013)

Ray Parkin, *HM Bark Endeavour: her place in Australian history* (Melbourne: Melbourne University Press, 1997)

Ray Parkin, *Out of the Smoke: The story of sail* (London: The Hogarth Press, 1960)

Roy Porter, *English Society in the 18th Century* (London: Penguin, 1991)

Roy Porter, *Enlightenment* (London: Penguin, 2001)

Oliver Rackham, *Trees & Woodland in the British Landscape* (London: Phoenix Press, 2001)

N. A. M. Roger, *The Wooden World: anatomy of the Georgian Navy* (London: Fontana Press, 1988)

N. A. M. Roger, *The Insatiable Earl: A life of John Montagu, Fourth Earl of Sandwich* (New York: W. W. Norton, 1994)

George Rude, *Wilkes and Liberty: A social study of 1763 to 1774* (Oxford: Clarendon Press, 1962)

John Rushton and Brian Walker, *Dalby: Valley of Change* (Scarborough: Newby Books, 2009)

Anne Salmond, *Two Worlds: First Meetings Between Maori and Europeans 1642–1772* (Honolulu: University of Hawaii Press, 1991)

Anne Salmond, *The Trial of the Cannibal Dog* (New Haven: Yale University Press, 2003)

Anne Salmond, *Aphrodite's Island: the European discovery of Tahiti* (Auckland: Viking, 2009)

Barnet Schecter, *The Battle for New York* (London: Jonathan Cape, 2003)

David Syrett, *Shipping and the American War 1775–83* (London: The Athlone Press, 1970)

Nicholas Thomas, *Discoveries: The Voyages of Captain Cook* (London: Penguin, 2004)

Andrew White, *A History of Whitby* (Chichester: Phillimore, 1993)

Glyn Williams, *The Prize of all the Oceans: The triumph and tragedy of Anson's voyage around the world* (London: HarperCollins, 1999)

Ben Wilson, *Empire of the Deep: The rise and fall of the British navy* (London: Weidenfeld & Nicolson, 2013)

Andrea Wulf, *The Brother Gardeners: Botany, Empire and the Birth of an Obsession* (London: Windmill Books, 2011)

Andrea Wulf, *Chasing Venus: The race to measure the heavens* (New York: Vintage Books, 2012)

Picture Credits

FIRST PLATE SECTION

p.1: *Landscape with a Hut in an Oak Tree and the 'Man in the Moon' Inn* by Anthony Devis (1729–1816) (© Harris Museum, Art Gallery & Library, Preston, England).

p.2: *Watercolour of Whitby* (*c.*1790), attributed to John Bird (© Captain Cook Museum); 'Henry Simpson's apprentice workbook', early 1700s (held at the Whitby Literary and Philosophical Society).

p.3: 'An exact Plan and Survey of a Farm of Land lying in the Cars near Ruswarp. belonging to Mr J Mellar' (1761) by Lionel Charlton (© North Yorkshire County Record Office).

p.4: *Shields, on the River Tyne* (1823) by J. M. W. Turner (1775–1851) (© Tate Britain); *The Bark, Earl of Pembroke, later Endeavour, leaving Whitby Harbour in 1768* (*c.*1790) by Thomas Luny (1759–1837) (© National Library of Australia).

p.5: (Clockwise from top left) *Portrait of Alexander Dalrymple* (1765) by John Thomas Seton (© National Museums of Scotland); *John Wilkes* (1764) by James Watson (© National Portrait Gallery, London); *Benjamin Franklin* after Joseph Siffred Duplessis, based on a work of 1783 (© National Portrait Gallery, London); *Catharine Macaulay* (1775) by Robert Edge Pine (© National Portrait Gallery, London).

p.6: *Endeavour, off the coast of Tierra del Fuego* (1769) by Alexander Buchan (© British Library Board. All Rights Reserved / Bridgeman Images); *The Three Sat on One Tree Hill* (1768–80) by Sydney Parkinson (© British Library Board. All Rights Reserved / Bridgeman Images).

p.7: 'Observations made, by appointment of the Royal Society, at King George's Island in the South Sea; by Mr. Charles Green, formerly Assistant at the Royal Observatory at Greenwich, and Lieut. James Cook, of his Majesty's Ship the Endeavour' (*Philosophical Transactions*, vol. 61, 1771) by Charles Green and James Cook (© The Royal Society); *A scene in Tahiti with two war canoes and a sailing canoe, Captain James Cook's First Voyage* (1768–70) by Tupaia (*c.*1725–70) (© British Library Board. All Rights Reserved / Bridgeman Images).

p.8: *Artocarpus altilis, breadfruit tree* by Sydney Parkinson (© The Trustees of the Natural History Museum, London).

SECOND PLATE SECTION

p.9: *Portrait of a New Zealand man* (1769) by Sydney Parkinson (© British Library Board. All Rights Reserved / Bridgeman Images).

p.10: *Chart of the Island of Otaheite* (1769) by James Cook (private collection); *Captain Cook having been shipwrecked in his Voyage round the World, has the Endeavour repaired in an Harbour on one of the Hope Islands* (private collection).

p.11: *A Maori bartering a crayfish with an English naval officer* (1768–70) by Tupaia (© British Library Board. All Rights Reserved / Bridgeman Images); *The Kongouro from New Holland* (1772) by George Stubbs (© National Maritime Museum, Greenwich, London).

p.12: (Clockwise from top left) *Portrait of Surgeon William Brougham Monkhouse* (1768), artist unknown (© National Library of Australia); *Portrait of Captain John Gore* (1780) by John Webber (© National Library of Australia); *Portrait of Sydney Parkinson* (© The Trustees of the Natural History Museum, London); *Portrait of Robert Molyneux* (c.1760), artist unknown (© Hocken Collections, Uare Taoka o Hākena, University of Otago).

p.13: (Clockwise from top left) *James Cook* (1775–76) by William Hodges (© National Maritime Museum, Greenwich, London); *John Montagu, 4th Earl of Sandwich*, after Johan Joseph Zoffany, based on a work of c.1764 (© National Portrait Gallery, London); 'The Fly Catching Macaroni'(1772), artist unknown (© Trustees of the British Museum); *Joseph Banks* (1773) by Benjamin West (© The Collection: Art and Archaeology in Lincolnshire, Usher Gallery, Lincoln).

p.14: 'The state blacksmiths forging fetter for the Americans'(1776), artist unknown (© Trustees of the British Museum); *View of the Narrows between Long Island & Staaten Island with our fleet at anchor & Lord Howe coming in – taken from the height above the Water* (1776) by Archibald Robertson (Spencer Collection, The New York Public Library).

p.15: 'A topographical chart of the bay of Narraganset in the province of New England, with all the isles contained therein, among which Rhode Island and Connonicut have been particularly surveyed, shewing the true position & bearings of the banks, shoals, rocks &c. as likewise the soundings: To which have been added the several works & batteries raised by the Americans. Taken by order of the principal farmers on Rhode Island' (1777) by Charles Blaskowitz and William Faden (© Library of Congress, Geography and Map Division).

p.16: *Close Encounters of the First Kind* (2013) by Reg Mombassa (© Reg Mombassa).

Every effort has been made to trace or contact copyright holders. The publishers will be pleased to make good any omissions or rectify any mistakes brought to their attention, at the earliest opportunity.

Notes

Prologue: Endeavours of the Mind

1. Anon, *Pen and Ink Sketches of Eminent English Literary Personages* (London: J. S. Pratt, 1850) p. ix
2. Anon, *Transatlantic Tracings and Popular Pictures from American Subjects* (London: W. Tweedie, 1853) p. 56
3. Ibid., p. 88
4. Ibid.
5. Ibid., p. 27
6. Ibid., p. 90
7. Ibid., p. 91
8. Ibid., p. 98
9. Emily Brontë, *Wuthering Heights* (London: Smith, Elder & Co., 1870) p. 113
10. *Oxford English Dictionary*, 2nd edn, Vol. 6 (Oxford: Oxford University Press, 1989) p. 226
11. Theresa May, The government's negotiating objectives for exiting the EU: PM speech, https://www.gov.uk/government/speeches/the-governments-negotiating-objectives-for-exiting-the-eu-pm-speech
12. Thomas Hobbes, *Leviathan, or The Matter, Forme, & Power of a Commonwealth ecclesiastical and civil* (London: Andrew Crooks, 1651) p. 1
13. Andrea Wulf, *Chasing Venus: The race to measure the heavens* (New York: Vintage Books, 2012) p. 41
14. James Boswell, *The Life of Samuel Johnson, LL.D*, Vol. 1 (London: Henry Baldwin, 1791) p. 101
15. David McCullough, *1776* (New York: Simon & Schuster, 2005) p. 93
16. Roy Porter, *English Society in the 18th Century* (London: Penguin, 1991) p. 206
17. N. A. M. Roger, *The Insatiable Earl: A life of John Montagu, Fourth Earl of Sandwich* (New York: W. W. Norton, 1994) p. 77
18. *Newcastle Chronicle*, Saturday 13 June 1761. Also, Robert Black, *The Jockey Club and its Founders* (London: Smith, Elder & Co., 1891) p. 133

19. Arthur Cash, *John Wilkes: the scandalous father of civil liberty* (New Haven: Yale University Press, 2006) p. 16

20. Ibid., p. 4

21. Neil Murray, 'Signs of Habitation', in *East Coast Encounter* (Collingwood: One Day Hill, 2014) p. 22

22. Greg Dening, *Mr Bligh's Bad Language: Passion, Power and Theatre on the Bounty* (Cambridge: Cambridge University Press, 1992) p. 27

Chapter 1: Acorns

1. Roger Fisher, *Heart of Oak: the British Bulwark* (London: J. Johnson, 1763) p. 38

2. Ibid., p. 46

3. Ibid., p. 37

4. Rev. Gilbert White, *The Natural History of Selborne* (Edinburgh: Constable & Co., 1829) p. 9

5. Rev. Sir John Cullum, *The History and Antiquities of Hawstead in the County of Suffolk* (London: J. Nichols, 1784) p. 2

6. *The History of Ancient Greece; from the earliest times, till it became a Roman Province* (Edinburgh: J. Bruce, 1768) p. 76

7. Oliver Rackham, *Trees & Woodland in the British Landscape* (London: Phoenix Press, 2001) p. 15

8. Fisher, p. 93

9. Robert Greenhalgh Albion, *Forests and Sea Power: the timber problem of the Royal Navy 1652–1862* (Cambridge: Harvard University Press, 1926) p. 99

10. John Evelyn, *The Diary of John Evelyn* (London: Everyman, 2006) p. 376

11. John Evelyn, *Sylva, or a Discourse of Forest Trees*, 2nd edn (London: Jo. Martyn & Ja. Allestry, 1670) p. 14

12. Ibid., p. 18

13. Ibid., dedication

14. Ibid., p. 24

15. William Mountaine, *The Seaman's Vade-Mecum and Defensive War by Sea* (London: W. & J. Mount, 1756) p. 144

16. Albion, p. 17

17. Mr Marshall, *The Rural Economy of Yorkshire*, Vol. 1 (London: T. Cadell, 1788) p. 1

18. Ibid., p. 4

19. William Camden, *Britannia (1607), with an English translation by Philemon Holland*, a hypertext critical edition by Dana F. Sutton (The University of California, Irvine: posted 14 June 2004)

20. Lionel Charlton, *The History of Whitby, and of Whitby-Abbey* (London: A. Ward, 1779) p. 308
21. Marshall, p. 9
22. Rev. George Young, *A History of Whitby and Streoneshalh Abbey*, Vol. 2 (Whitby: Clark & Medd, 1817) p. 554
23. Charlton, p. 74
24. Marshall, p. 124
25. Ibid., p. 18
26. Charlton, p. 338
27. *Newcastle Courant*, Saturday 10 April 1762
28. Mr Tuke Jr, *General View of the Agriculture of the North-Riding of Yorkshire* (London: W. Bulmer & Co., 1794) p. 16
29. Marshall, p. 287
30. *Caledonian Mercury*, Thursday 20 November 1740
31. Evelyn, *Sylva*, p. 15
32. Tuke Jr, p. 90
33. Evelyn, *Sylva*, p. 23

Chapter 2: Enigmas

1. Rev. J. Ray, *A Complete Collection of English Proverbs* (London: T & J Allman, 1818) p. 177
2. *The Yorkshire Archaeological Journal*, Vol. 17 (Leeds: John Whitehead & Son, 1903) p. 42
3. Lionel Charlton, *The History of Whitby, and of Whitby-Abbey* (London: A. Ward, 1779) p. 335
4. 'An Account of the fossile Bones of an Alligator, found at the Sea-shore, near Whitby in Yorkshire. In a Letter to John Fothergill, M. D. from Capt. William Chapman', *Philosophical Transactions Vol. L. Part II. For the Year 1758* (London: L. Davis & C. Reymers, 1759) p. 691
5. Ibid., p. 354
6. Ibid., p. 356
7. William Watson, *The Poetical Remains with other Detached Pieces of the Late F. Gibson* (London: R. Rogers, 1807) p. vii
8. Rev. George Young, *A History of Whitby and Streoneshalh Abbey*, Vol. 2 (Whitby: Clark & Medd, 1817) p. 869
9. William Watson, *The Poetical Remains with other Detached Pieces of the Late F. Gibson* (London: R. Rogers, 1807) p. vii
10. Ibid., p. 71

11. James Boswell, *The Life of Samuel Johnson, LL.D*, Vol. 1 (London: Henry Baldwin, 1791) p. 14

12. NYCRO, Mic 2003/213

13. Young, p. 869

14. Ibid.

15. These details come in a private communication from Mike Yates of the Whitby Literary and Philosophical Society

16. William Sutherland, *The Ship-builder's Assistant, or some Essays Towards Compleating the Art of Marine Architecture* (London: Thomas Page, William and Fisher Mount, 1726) p. 38

17. *Newcastle Courant*, 9 November 1734

18. *Public Advertiser*, 15 December 1758

19. Charlton, p. 358

20. Young, p. 550

21. Watson, p. ix

22. Alison Adburgham, *Women in Print: Writing Women and Women's Magazines from the Restoration to the Accession of Victoria First Edition* (London: Allen & Unwin, 1972)

23. Alexi Baker, 'Jane Squire (bap. 1686, d. 1743)', *Oxford Dictionary of National Biography*, https://doi-org.ezproxy2.londonlibrary.co.uk/10.1093/ref:odnb/45826

24. *The Ladies Diary: or Woman's Almanack, for the year of our Lord 1761* (London: A Wilde) p. 33

25. Ibid., p. 36

26. *The Gentleman's Diary or Mathematical Repository, 1761* (London: Company of Stationers, 1761) p. 19

27. Ibid., p. 21

28. Shelley Costa, *The 'Ladies Diary': Gender, Mathematics, and Civil Society in Early-Eighteenth-Century England* in *Science and Civil Society*, Vol. 17 (Chicago: University of Chicago Press, 2002) p. 58

29. Ray Parkin, *HM Bark Endeavour: her place in Australian history* (Melbourne: Melbourne University Press, 1997) p. 43

30. Charlton, p. 358

31. *Mechanics Magazine*, 21 March 1862

32. J. A. Leo Lemay, *The Life of Benjamin Franklin*, Vol. 2 (Philadelphia: University of Pennsylvania Press, 2006) p. 198

33. The best overview of the bark vs cat discussion is to be found in Karl Heinz Marquardt, *HM Bark Endeavour: What do we really know about the Ship* (available at: http://karl-heinz-marquardt.com)

34. John Evelyn, *Sylva, or a Discourse of Forest Trees*, 2nd edn (London: Jo. Martyn & Ja. Allestry, 1670) p. 20

35. Tobias Smollett, *Roderick Random* (London: Penguin, 1995) p. 426

2

6905NOTES

367. *Scots Magazine*, 5 December 1763
38. *Derby Mercury*, 16 December 1763
39. *Caledonian Mercury*, 21 December 1763
40. *Scots Magazine*, 5 December 1763
41. Charlton, p. xvii
42. Ibid., p. xii
43. Ibid., p. 314
44. *Daniel Defoe, An Essay Upon Projects* (London: Thom. Cockerill, 1697) p. 1
45. Ibid., p. 29
46. Ibid., p. 16
47. Ibid., p. 15
48. Charlton, p. 362
49. Mr Marshall, *The Rural Economy of Yorkshire*, Vol. 1 (London: T. Cadell, 1788) p. 287
50. Stephen Baines, *Captain Cook's Merchant Ships* (Stroud: The History Press) p. 170
51. *Gazetteer and London Daily Advertiser*, 21 April 1764
52. Samuel Taylor Coleridge, *The Major Works* (Oxford: Oxford University Press, 2008) p. 49

Chapter 3: Cross Currents

1. Erich Pontoppidan, *The Natural History of Norway* (London: A. Linde, 1755) p. 211
2. Ibid., p. 211
3. Ray Parkin, *HM Bark Endeavour: her place in Australian history* (Melbourne: Melbourne University Press, 1997) p. 74
4. Robert Middlekauff, *The Glorious Cause: The American Revolution, 1763–1789* (Oxford: Oxford University Press, 2005) p. 138
5. N. A. M. Roger, *The Wooden World: anatomy of the Georgian Navy* (London: Fontana Press, 1988) p. 50
6. *Caledonian Mercury*, 8 July 1756
7. *Ipswich Journal*, 15 August 1761
8. *Aberdeen Journal*, 8 December 1760
9. J. C. Beaglehole, *The Life of Captain James Cook* (London: Adam & Charles Black, 1974) p. 45
10. Henry Taylor, *Memoirs of the Principal Events in the Life of Henry Taylor of North Shields* (North Shields: T. Appleby) p. 157
11. Stephen Baines, *Captain Cook's Merchant Ships* (Stroud: The History Press, 2015)

12. Roger, p. 116
13. NYCRO. *Thomas Milner – Receipt from Thomas Milner [bearing his mark] to John Richardson for £1 15s for his last voyage in the ship Brotherly Love.* ZW VI 20/1
14. Roy Porter, *Enlightenment* (London: Penguin, 2001) p. 76
15. Rosalin Barker, *The Rise of An Early Modern Shipping Industry: Whitby's Golden Fleet, 1600–1750* (Woodbridge: Boydell Press, 2011) p. 56
16. Richard England, *Schoonerman* (London: Hollis & Carter, 1981) p. 113
17. Taylor, p. iv
18. Lionel Charlton, *The History of Whitby, and of Whitby-Abbey* (London: A. Ward, 1779) p. 361
19. Taylor, p. 1
20. Ibid., p. 158
21. Ibid., pp. 4–5
22. A. F. Humble, 'An Old Whitby Collier', *The Mariner's Mirror* (1975) 61:1, 51–60, DOI: 10.1080/00253359.1975.10658005
23. Taylor, p. 57
24. *Public Advertiser*, 7 August 1764
25. Porter, *Enlightenment*, p. 40
26. Roy Porter, *English Society in the 18th Century* (London: Penguin, 1991) p.186
27. *The Papers of Benjamin Franklin*, Vol. 11 (New Haven: Yale University Press, 1967) p. 517
28. Ibid., p. 521
29. R. B. Mowat, *Americans in England* (Cambridge: Houghton Mifflin Company, 1935) p. 31
30. Walter Isaacson, *Benjamin Franklin: an American life* (New York: Simon & Schuster, 2003) p. 50
31. Porter, *Enlightenment*, p. 11
32. George Goodwin, *Benjamin Franklin in London* (London: Weidenfeld & Nicolson, 2016) p. 97
33. *The London Chronicle for 1763*, Vol. 14 (London: J. Wilkie, 1763) p. 435
34. Catharine Macaulay, *Loose Remarks on certain positions to be found in Mr. Hobbes's Philosophical Rudiments* (London: T. Davies, 1767) p. 38
35. *The Adventurer*, 16 October 1753
36. Robert Middlekauff, *The Glorious Cause: The American Revolution, 1763–1789* (Oxford: Oxford University Press, 2005) p. 61
37. Arthur Cash, *John Wilkes: the scandalous father of civil liberty* (New Haven: Yale University Press, 2006) p. 55
38. *The North Briton* (London: W. Bingley, 1769) p. 4
39. Ibid., pp. 17–18
40. *Annual Register, or a view of the history, politics and literature for the year 1764* (London: J. Dodsley, 1764) p. 25

41. Goodwin, p. 155
42. Edmund Sears Morgan and Helen Morgan, *The Stamp Act Crisis: Prologue to Revolution* (Chapel Hill: University of North Carolina Press, 1953) p. 27
43. Sarah Vickery, 'Handwritten History, 1765–1867: Correspondence of Great Americans from the Collections of the Newport Historical Society', *Newport History*, Vol. 80, Iss. 264, p. 35
44. Howard Tyrrell Fry, *Alexander Dalrymple, 1737–1808, and the expansion of British trade* (London: Frank Cass & Co., 1970) p. xviii
45. Ibid., pp. 114–15

Chapter 4: Mr Birds Ways

1. RS. Royal Society Club account slips. RSC/2/2
2. Alexander Dalrymple, *An Account of the Discoveries Made in the South Pacifick Ocean, Previous to 1764* (London: privately printed) p. 6
3. Ibid., p. 23
4. Alexander Dalrymple, *A Plan for Extending the Commerce of this Kingdom, and of the East-India-Company* (London: J. Nourse, 1769) p. 1
5. *Annual Register, or a view of the history, politics and literature for the year 1768* (London: J. Dodsley, 1768) p. 58
6. Ibid.
7. Dalrymple, *An Account*, pp. iii–iv
8. *The Naval Chronicle for 1816*, Vol. 35 (London: Joyce Gold, 1816) p. 180
9. Ibid., p. 182
10. Ibid.
11. *The Politicians Dictionary; or a summary of political knowledge*, Vol. 2 (London: Geo. Allen, 1775) p. 233
12. Ibid., p. 228
13. Ibid.
14. Ibid., p. 251
15. Dalrymple, *An Account*, p. iv
16. Ibid.
17. Ibid., p. 94
18. *The Works of Samuel Johnson L.L.D*, Vol. 4 (Philadelphia: William Brown, 1825) p. 299
19. Dom Pernety, *The History of a Voyage to the Malouine (or Falkland) Islands, Made in 1763 and 1764* (London: T. Jefferies, 1771) p. vi
20. Anon, *A Voyage Around the World, in his Majesty's Ship the Dolphin* (London: J. Newberry, 1767) p. 76
21. *The Works of Samuel Johnson*, p. 295

22. J. C. Beaglehole (ed.), *The Journals of Captain James Cook on his Voyages of Discovery: The Voyage of the Endeavour 1768–1771* (Cambridge: Cambridge University Press for the Hakluyt Society, 1955) p. 511

23. RS. *Letter from Alexander Dalrymple, London, to Dr Charles Morton, Secretary, Royal Society.* 7 December, 1767. MM/3/14

24. Ibid., 23 January 1766

25. Robert Middlekauff, *The Glorious Cause: The American Revolution, 1763–1789* (Oxford: Oxford University Press, 2005) p. 137

26. *The North Briton* (London: W. Bingley, 1769) p. xliii

27. Ibid., p. xlv

28. *The Papers of Benjamin Franklin*, Vol. 15. (New Haven: Yale University Press, 1972) p. 82

29. Beaglehole (ed.), p. 604

30. Howard Tyrrell Fry, *Alexander Dalrymple, 1737–1808, and the expansion of British trade* (London: Frank Cass & Co., 1970) p. 119

31. Beaglehole (ed.), p. 605

32. Ibid.

33. 'Memoirs of Alexander Dalrymple', *The European Magazine and London Review for November 1802* (London: J. Sewell, 1802) p. 325

34. Alexander Dalrymple, *Mr Dalrymple's Observations on Dr Hawkesworth's Preface to the Second Edition* (London, 1773) p. 19

35. Beaglehole (ed.), p. 606

36. *The North Briton*, p. xlvi

37. Ibid., p. xlvii

38. *The Papers of Benjamin Franklin*, p. 99

39. *Annual Register, or a view of the history, politics and literature for the year 1768* (London: J. Dodsley, 1768) p. 92

40. Fry, p. 135

41. *Mr Dalrymple's Observations on Dr. Hawkesworth's Preface to the Second Edition*, p. 19

42. Beaglehole (ed.), p. 513

43. 'Memoirs of Alexander Dalrymple', p. 325

Chapter 5: Land of Liberty

1. J. C. Beaglehole (ed.), *The Journals of Captain James Cook on his Voyages of Discovery: The Voyage of the Endeavour 1768–1771* (Cambridge: Cambridge University Press for the Hakluyt Society, 1955) p. 606

2. *The North Briton* (London: W. Bingley, 1769) p. xlvii

3. *The Papers of Benjamin Franklin*, Vol. 15 (New Haven: Yale University Press, 1972) p. 99

4.   *The Whitehall Evening Post Or London Intelligencer*, 18. Jan.–1. Feb. 1755

5.   Beaglehole (ed.), p. 608

6.   *Annual Register, or a view of the history, politics and literature for the year 1768* (London: J. Dodsley, 1768) p. 202

7.   Ibid., p. 203

8.   Jean-Jacques Rousseau, *The Social Contract* (London: Penguin, 2004) p. 2

9.   *Annual Register*, p. 190

10.   Bridget Hill, *The Republican Virago: Life and Times of Catharine Macaulay* (Oxford: Clarendon Press, 1992) p. 56

11.   *The North Briton* (London: W. Bingley, 1769) p. xlviii

12.   Ibid., p. lii

13.   Ibid., p. l

14.   Arthur Cash, *John Wilkes: the scandalous father of civil liberty* (New Haven: Yale University Press, 2006) p. 217

15.   *Newcastle Courant*, 7 May 1768

16.   Cash, p. 217

17.   *Annual Register*, p. 105

18.   Cash, p. 221

19.   *The North Briton*, p. lxxviii

20.   *Annual Register*, p. 109

21.   *The North Briton*, p. lxxviii

22.   *The North Briton*, p. lxviii

23.   *Annual Register*, p. 106

24.   Andrew C. F. David and Colin Jones, *Documents, The Mariner's Mirror*, 85:3, 335–7, 1999, DOI: 10.1080/00253359.1999.10656754

25.   J. C. Beaglehole, *The Life of Captain James Cook* (London: Adam & Charles Black, 1974) p. 16

26.   Stephen Baines, *Captain Cook's Merchant Ships* (Stroud: The History Press) pp. 107–8

27.   Beaglehole (ed.), p. xxii

28.   Nicholas Thomas, *Discoveries: The Voyages of Captain Cook* (London: Penguin, 2004) p. 8

29.   Beaglehole (ed.), p. 607

30.   Ibid., p. 513

31.   Ibid., p. 608

32.   Ibid., p. 613

33.   Ibid., p. 612

34.   *Caledonian Mercury*, 30 May 1768

35.   Hugh Carrington (ed.), *The Discovery of Tahiti: A Journal of the Second Voyage of HMS Dolphin Round the World by George Robertson 1766–68* (London: Hakluyt Society, 1948) pp. 210–11

36. Robert Middlekauff, *The Glorious Cause: The American Revolution, 1763–1789* (Oxford: Oxford University Press, 2005) p. 153

37. *The Papers of Benjamin Franklin*, Vol. 15. (New Haven: Yale University Press, 1972) p. 13

38. Karl Heinz Marquardt, *Captain Cook's Endeavour* (London: Conway Maritime Press, 1995) p. 17

39. Cash, p. 232

40. *Kentish Gazette*, 8 November 1769

41. Rev. George Young, *The Life and Voyages of Captain James Cook* (London: Whittaker, Treacher & Co., 1836) pp. 111–12

Chapter 6: 'Take a Trip in disguise'

1. J. C. Beaglehole (ed.), *The Journals of Captain James Cook on his Voyages of Discovery. The Voyage of the Endeavour 1768–1771* (Cambridge: Cambridge University Press for the Hakluyt Society, 1955) p. 11

2. J. C. Beaglehole (ed.), *The Endeavour Journal of Joseph Banks 1768–1771*, Vol. 1 (London: Angus & Robertson, 1962) p. 167

3. Ibid., p. 171

4. Ibid.

5. Beaglehole (ed.), *The Journals of Captain James Cook*, p. 13

6. Beaglehole (ed.), *The Endeavour Journal of Joseph Banks*, Vol. 1, p. 31

7. Averil M. Lysaght, *Joseph Banks in Newfoundland and Labrador, 1766: His Diary, Manuscripts and Collections* (London: Faber & Faber, 1971) p. 44

8. Ibid., p. 234

9. Beaglehole (ed.), *The Endeavour Journal of Joseph Banks*, Vol. 1, p. 5

10. Edward Gibbon, *The History of the Decline and Fall of the Roman Empire*, Vol. 8 (Philadelphia: Abraham Small, 1816) p. 31

11. James Lee, *An Introduction to Botany*, 2nd edn (London: J. & R. Tonson, 1765) p. v

12. Andrea Wulf, *The Brother Gardeners: Botany, Empire and the Birth of an Obsession* (London: Windmill Books, 2011) p. 61

13. Lee, pp. iii–iv

14. Ibid., p. 232

15. Wulf, p. 117

16. Lee, p. iii

17. Carolyn Fry, *The Plant Hunters* (London: Andre Deutsch, 2009) p. 19

18. Lee, p. 243

19. Harold Carter, *Sir Joseph Banks* (London: British Museum, 1988) p. 62

20. Neil Chambers, *The Scientific Correspondence of Sir Joseph Banks*, Vol. 1 (London: Routledge, 2007) p. 2

21. John Brewer, *Sentimental Murder: Love and Madness in the Eighteenth Century* (London: Harper Perennial, 2005) p. 9

22. G. R. Barnes and J. H. Owen, *The Private papers of John, Earl of Sandwich, First Lord of the Admiralty 1771–1782, Volume 1, August 1770–March 1778* (Publications of the Navy Records Society, v. LXIX. 1932) p. xiii

23. Andrew Duncan, *A Short Account of the Life of Sir Joseph Banks* (London: 1821) p. 9

24. Averil M. Lysaght, *Joseph Banks in Newfoundland and Labrador, 1766: His Diary, Manuscripts and Collections* (London: Faber & Faber, 1971) p. 46

25. *The Atheneum; or Spirit of the English Magazine*, Vol. 8 (Boston: Munroe & Francis, 1821) p. 64

26. Beaglehole (ed.), *The Endeavour Journal of Joseph Banks*, Vol. 1, p. 158

27. Jonathan Lamb, *Scurvy: the disease of discovery* (Princeton: Princeton University Press, 2016) p. 82

28. J. C. Beaglehole (ed.), *The Endeavour Journal of Joseph Banks 1768–1771*, Vol. 2 (London: Angus & Robertson, 1962) p. 311

29. Beaglehole (ed.), *The Endeavour Journal of Joseph Banks*, Vol. 1, p. 153

30. Ibid., p. 30

31. Carter, p. 55

32. D. J. Carr, *Sydney Parkinson: Artist of Cook's 'Endeavour' Voyage* (London: Croom Helm Ltd, 1984) p. x

33. Neil Chambers, *The Letters Of Sir Joseph Banks, A Selection, 1768–1820* (London: Imperial College Press, 2000) p. 1

34. John Gascoigne, *Joseph Banks and the English Enlightenment: Useful Knowledge and Polite Culture* (Cambridge: Cambridge University Press, 1994) p. 61

35. Beaglehole (ed.), *The Endeavour Journal of Joseph Banks*, Vol. 1, p. 156

36. Greg Dening, *Mr Bligh's Bad Language: Passion, Power and Theatre on the Bounty* (Cambridge: Cambridge University Press, 1992) p. 77

37. Beaglehole (ed.), *The Endeavour Journal of Joseph Banks*, Vol. 1, pp. 176–7

38. Anon, *A Voyage Around the World, in his Majesty's Ship the Dolphin* (London: J. Newberry, 1767) p. 19

39. Beaglehole (ed.), *The Endeavour Journal of Joseph Banks*, Vol. 2, p. 311

40. William Mountaine, *The Seaman's Vade-Mecum and Defensive War by Sea* (London: W. & J. Mount, 1756) p. 42

41. Beaglehole (ed.), *The Journals of Captain James Cook*, p. 23

42. Beaglehole (ed.), *The Endeavour Journal of Joseph Banks*, Vol. 2, p. 312

43. Beaglehole (ed.), *The Journals of Captain James Cook*, p. 487

44. Beaglehole (ed.), *The Endeavour Journal of Joseph Banks*, Vol. 2, p. 315

45. Beaglehole (ed.), *The Journals of Captain James Cook*, p. 28

46. Ibid., p. 495

47. Beaglehole (ed.), *The Endeavour Journal of Joseph Banks*, Vol. 1, p. 194

48.   Ibid., p. 195
49.   Ibid., p. 212
50.   *The Works of Samuel Johnson L.L.D*, Vol. 4 (Philadelphia: William Brown, 1825) p. 301
51.   Beaglehole (ed.), *The Endeavour Journal of Joseph Banks*, Vol. 1, p. 213

Chapter 7: Airy Dreams

1.   Richard Walter, *A Voyage Around the World in the Years MDCCXL, I, II, III, IV by George Anson* (London: John and Paul Knapton, 1748) pp. 74–5
2.   J. C. Beaglehole (ed.), *The Endeavour Journal of Joseph Banks 1768–1771*, Vol. 1 (London: Angus & Robertson, 1962) p. 216
3.   Sydney Parkinson, *A Journal of a Voyage to the South Seas, in His Majesty's Ship, the Endeavour* (London: printed for Stansfield Parkinson, 1773) pp. 10–11
4.   Walter, pp. 79–80
5.   Parkinson, pp. 10–11
6.   Ibid., p. 5
7.   Walter, p. 75
8.   Parkinson, p. 11
9.   *Mechanics Magazine*, 21 March 1862
10. Beaglehole (ed.), *The Endeavour Journal of Joseph Banks*, Vol. 1, p. 235
11. Parkinson, p. vi
12. Ibid., Advertisement
13. Ibid., p. xi
14. Beaglehole (ed.), *The Endeavour Journal of Joseph Banks*, Vol. 1, p. 176
15. Parkinson, p. 4
16. D. J. Carr, 'The Books that sailed with the *Endeavour*', *Endeavour*, New Series, Vol. 7, No. 4, 1983
17. Anne Salmond, *Aphrodite's Island: The European discovery of Tahiti* (Auckland: Viking, 2009) p. 66
18. Hugh Carrington (ed.), *The Discovery of Tahiti: A Journal of the Second Voyage of HMS Dolphin Round the World by George Robertson 1766–68* (London: Hakluyt Society, 1948) p. 167
19. Anthony Addington, *An Essay on the Sea-Scurvy* (Reading: C. Micklewright, 1753) p.1
20. J. C. Beaglehole (ed.), *The Journals of Captain James Cook on his Voyages of Discovery. The Voyage of the Endeavour 1768–1771* (Cambridge: Cambridge University Press for the Hakluyt Society, 1955) p. 74
21. Beaglehole (ed.), *The Endeavour Journal of Joseph Banks*, Vol. 1, p. 242

22. Jonathan Lamb, *Scurvy: the disease of discovery* (Princeton: Princeton University Press, 2016) p. 59

23. Carrington (ed.), pp. 139–40

24. Parkinson, p. 13

25. *The Works of Samuel Johnson L.L.D*, Vol. 4 (Philadelphia: William Brown, 1825) p. 15

26. Beaglehole (ed.), *The Journals of Captain James Cook*, p. 79

27. Carrington (ed.), p. 154

28. Beaglehole (ed.), *The Journals of Captain James Cook*, p. 80

29. Parkinson, p. 28

30. Beaglehole (ed.), *The Endeavour Journal of Joseph Banks*, Vol. 1, p. 284

31. *Oxford Journal*, 10 June 1769

32. Beaglehole (ed.), *The Journals of Captain James Cook*, p. 98

33. James Cook, *Observations made, by appointment of the Royal Society, at King George's Island in the South Sea. Philosophical Transactions of the Royal Society*, 61 (1771), pp. 397–421

34. Parkinson, p. 55

35. Joseph Farrell, *Robert Louis Stevenson in Samoa* (London: MacLehose, 2017)

36. Parkinson, p. 14

37. D. J. Carr, *Sydney Parkinson: Artist of Cook's 'Endeavour' Voyage* (London: Croom Helm Ltd, 1984) p. xi

38. Parkinson, p. xi

39. Bernard Smith, 'The first European depictions', in Ian Donaldson and Tamsin Donaldson, *Seeing the First Australians* (Sydney: Allen & Unwin, 1985) pp. 28–9

40. Parkinson, p. 26

41. Ibid., p. 16

42. Ibid., p. 33

43. *Scots Magazine*, January 1766

44. Maurice Cranston, *Jean-Jacques: the early life and work of Jean-Jacques Rousseau 1712–1754* (Chicago: University of Chicago Press, 1991) p. 293

45. John James Rousseau, *A Discourse upon the Origin and Foundation of the Inequality among Mankind* (London: R. and J. Dodsley, 1764) p. 20

46. Ibid., p. 97

47. Cranston, p. 300

48. Parkinson, p. 24

49. Ibid., p. 23

50. Ibid., p. 26

51. Beaglehole (ed.), *The Endeavour Journal of Joseph Banks*, Vol. 1, p. 258

52. Parkinson, p. 27

53. Beaglehole (ed.), *The Endeavour Journal of Joseph Banks*, Vol. 1, p. 312
54. Ibid., pp. 313–14

Chapter 8: Perfect Strangers

1. Anne Salmond, *The Trial of the Cannibal Dog: Captain Cook in the South Seas* (London: Allen Lane, 2003) p. 37
2. J. C. Beaglehole (ed.), *The Endeavour Journal of Joseph Banks 1768–1771* Vol. 1 (London: Angus & Robertson, 1962) p. 379
3. *Annual Register, or a view of the history, politics and literature for the year 1777* (London: J. Dodsley, 1778) p. 64
4. Sydney Parkinson, *A Journal of a Voyage to the South Seas, in His Majesty's Ship, the Endeavour* (London: printed for Stansfield Parkinson, 1773) p. 73
5. Beaglehole (ed.), *The Endeavour Journal of Joseph Banks*, Vol. 1, p. 376
6. J. C. Beaglehole (ed.), *The Journals of Captain James Cook on his Voyages of Discovery. The Voyage of the Endeavour 1768–1771* (Cambridge: Cambridge University Press for the Hakluyt Society, 1955) p. 563
7. Anne Salmond, *Aphrodite's Island: the European discovery of Tahiti* (Auckland: Viking, 2009) p. 20
8. Beaglehole (ed.), *The Endeavour Journal of Joseph Banks*, Vol. 1, p. 307
9. Beaglehole (ed.), *The Journals of Captain James Cook*, p. 564
10. Beaglehole (ed.), *The Endeavour Journal of Joseph Banks*, Vol. 1, pp. 312–13
11. Nicholas Thomas, *Discoveries: The Voyages of Captain Cook* (London: Penguin, 2004) p. 81
12. Beaglehole (ed.), *The Endeavour Journal of Joseph Banks*, Vol. 1, p. 318
13. Ibid., p. 323
14. Beaglehole (ed.), *The Journals of Captain James Cook*, p. 117
15. Anon, *Monsters of the Deep and curiosities of ocean life* (London: T. Nelson & Sons, 1875) p. 283
16. Beaglehole (ed.), *The Journals of Captain James Cook*, p. 514
17. Averil M. Lysaght, *The journal of Joseph Banks in the Endeavour / with a commentary by A. M. Lysaght* (Guildford: Genesis Publications, 1980)
18. Parkinson, p. 67
19. Lincoln Paine, *Sea and Civilisation* (New York: Vintage Books, 2013) p. 14
20. Beaglehole (ed.), *The Journals of Captain James Cook*, p. 154
21. Beaglehole (ed.), *The Endeavour Journal of Joseph Banks*, Vol. 1, p. 368
22. *A Letter from Mr Dalrymple to Dr Hawkesworth* (London: 1773) p. 27
23. Hugh Carrington (ed.), *The Discovery of Tahiti: A Journal of the Second Voyage of HMS Dolphin Round the World by George Robertson 1766–68* (London: Hakluyt Society, 1948) pp. 234–5

24. Beaglehole (ed.), *The Journals of Captain James Cook*, p. cclxxxii

25. John Marra, *Journal of the Resolution's Voyage in 1772, 1773, 1774 and 1775* (London: F. Newberry, 1776) p. 219

26. Beaglehole (ed.), *The Endeavour Journal of Joseph Banks*, p. 396

27. Ibid., p. 399

28. Beaglehole (ed.), *The Journals of Captain James Cook*, p. 565

29. Ibid., p. 566

30. Rongowhakaata (R. W.) Halbert, *Horouta: the history of the Horouta Canoe, Gisborne and the East Coast* (Auckland: Reed Books, 1999) p. 26

31. Joseph Angus Mackay, *Historic Poverty Bay and the East Coast* (Gisborne: Joseph Angus Mackay, 1949) p. 21

32. Beaglehole (ed.), *The Journals of Captain James Cook*, p. 169

33. Ibid., pp. 565–6

34. Beaglehole (ed.), *The Endeavour Journal of Joseph Banks*, Vol. 1, p. 402

35. Beaglehole (ed.), *The Journals of Captain James Cook*, p. 568

36. Ibid., p. 171

37. Beaglehole (ed.), *The Endeavour Journal of Joseph Banks*, Vol. 1, p. 403

38. Beaglehole (ed.), *The Journals of Captain James Cook*, p. 171

39. Beaglehole (ed.), *The Endeavour Journal of Joseph Banks*, Vol. 1, p. 403

40. Ibid., p. 404

41. Beaglehole (ed.), *The Journals of Captain James Cook*, p. 172

42. Beaglehole (ed.), *The Endeavour Journal of Joseph Banks*, Vol. 1, p. 424

43. *A Letter from Mr. Dalrymple to Dr. Hawkesworth* (London: 1773) p. 27

44. Beaglehole (ed.), *The Endeavour Journal of Joseph Banks*, Vol. 1, p. 472

45. Ibid.

46. Beaglehole (ed.), *The Journals of Captain James Cook*, p. cxlix

47. Beaglehole (ed.), *The Endeavour Journal of Joseph Banks*, Vol. 1, p. 435

48. J. C. Beaglehole (ed.), *The Endeavour Journal of Joseph Banks 1768–1771*, Vol. 2 (London: Angus & Robertson, 1962) p. 34

49. George Forster, *A Voyage Around the World*, Vol. 2 (London: B. White, 1778) p. 477

50. Beaglehole (ed.), *The Endeavour Journal of Joseph Banks*, Vol. 1, p. 456

Chapter 9: 'That rainbow serpent place'

1. Thomas Pierson, *Roseberry Topping: a poem* (Stockton: Jennett & Co., 1847) p. 9

2. John Gascoigne, *Captain Cook: voyager between worlds* (London: Hambledon, 2007) p. 16

3. J. C. Beaglehole, *The Voyage of the Resolution and Adventure 1772–1775* (Cambridge: Hakluyt Society, 1961) p. 323

4.   J. C. Beaglehole (ed.), *The Journals of Captain James Cook on his Voyages of Discovery. The Voyage of the Endeavour 1768–1771* (Cambridge: Cambridge University Press for the Hakluyt Society, 1955) p. 300

5.   Anne Salmond, *The Trail of the Cannibal Dog: Captain Cook in the South Seas* (London: Allen Lane, 2003) p. 131

6.   Maria Nugent, *Captain Cook was Here* (Cambridge: Cambridge University Press, 2009) p. 110

7.   Eric Deeral, '*Ngarrbal-ngay wanhu? Nguba ngaadal wuwu-thirr*: Visitors who may need help', in *East Coast Encounter* (Collingwood: One Day Hill, 2014) p. 28

8.   Edmund Burke, *A Philosophical Enquiry into the Origin of our Ideas of the Sublime and Beautiful* (London: R. & J. Dodsley, 1759) p. 19

9.   Nugent, p. 111

10. Sydney Parkinson, *A Journal of a Voyage to the South Seas, in His Majesty's Ship, the Endeavour* (London: printed for Stansfield Parkinson, 1773) p. 56

11. Nugent, p. 114

12. J. C. Beaglehole (ed.), *The Endeavour Journal of Joseph Banks 1768–1771*, Vol. 2 (London: Angus & Robertson, 1962) p. 54

13. Glyndwr Williams, 'Far more happier than we Europeans: Reactions to the Australian aborigines on Cook's Voyage', *Journal of Historical Studies*, Vol. 19, Iss. 77 (1981)

14. Beaglehole (ed.), *The Endeavour Journal of Joseph Banks*, Vol. 2, p. 50

15. Parkinson, p. 135

16. John James Rousseau, *A Discourse upon the Origin and Foundation of the Inequality among Mankind* (London: R. and J. Dodsley, 1764) p. 21

17. Beaglehole (ed.), *The Endeavour Journal of Joseph Banks*, Vol. 2, p. 58

18. 'Badtjala Song', translated by Gemma Cronin, in *East Coast Encounter* (Collingwood: One Day Hill, 2014) p. 10

19. Parkinson, p. 136

20. Beaglehole (ed.), *The Endeavour Journal of Joseph Banks*, Vol. 2, p. 62

21. J. C. Beaglehole (ed.), *The Endeavour Journal of Joseph Banks 1768–1771*, Vol. 1 (London: Angus & Robertson, 1962) p. 447

22. Beaglehole (ed.), *The Journals of Captain James Cook*, p. 344

23. Parkinson, p. 142

24. Beaglehole (ed.), *The Endeavour Journal of Joseph Banks*, Vol. 2, p. 77

25. Ibid., p. 78

26. Parkinson, p. 142

27. Beaglehole (ed.), *The Journals of Captain James Cook*, p. 346

28. Ibid., pp. 350–1

29. Beaglehole (ed.), *The Endeavour Journal of Joseph Banks*, Vol. 2, p. 81

30. Ibid.

31. Ibid., p. 82

32. Parkinson, p. 141
33. Ibid.
34. Deeral, p. 28
35. Ibid., p. 31
36. Beaglehole (ed.), *The Journals of Captain James Cook*, p. 399
37. Gascoigne, p. 17
38. Beaglehole (ed.), *The Endeavour Journal of Joseph Banks*, Vol. 2, p. 145
39. Ibid., p. 84
40. Beaglehole (ed.), *The Journals of Captain James Cook*, pp. 351–2
41. Parkinson, p. 146
42. Beaglehole (ed.), *The Endeavour Journal of Joseph Banks*, Vol. 2, p. 87
43. Beaglehole (ed.), *The Journals of Captain James Cook*, p. 370
44. Ibid., p. 375
45. Ibid., p. 377
46. Beaglehole (ed.), *The Endeavour Journal of Joseph Banks*, Vol. 2, p. 105
47. Ibid.
48. Beaglehole (ed.), *The Journals of Captain James Cook*, p. 378
49. Beaglehole (ed.), *The Endeavour Journal of Joseph Banks*, Vol. 2, p. 107
50. Beaglehole (ed.), *The Journals of Captain James Cook*, p. 379
51. Ibid.

Chapter 10: 360°

1. *The Works of Samuel Johnson L.L.D*, Vol. 4 (Philadelphia: William Brown, 1825) p. 304
2. *Horace Walpole's Correspondence*, Vol. 23, pp. 239–40
3. *General Evening Post*, 25 September, 1770
4. J. C. Beaglehole (ed.), *The Endeavour Journal of Joseph Banks 1768–1771*, Vol. 1 (London: Angus & Robertson, 1962) p. 51
5. *The Works of Samuel Johnson L.L.D*, Vol. 4, p. 318
6. John Brewer, *Sentimental Murder: Love and Madness in the Eighteenth Century* (London: Harper Perennial, 2005) p. 106
7. *Middlesex Journal*, 5 January 1771
8. *Oxford Journal*, 11 May 1771
9. *London Evening Post*, 14 May 1771
10. J. C. Beaglehole (ed.), *The Endeavour Journal of Joseph Banks 1768–1771*, Vol. 2 (London: Angus & Robertson, 1962) p. 323
11. Ibid., p. 184
12. J. C. Beaglehole (ed.), *The Journals of Captain James Cook on his Voyages of Discovery. The Voyage of the Endeavour 1768–1771* (Cambridge: Cambridge University Press for the Hakluyt Society, 1955) pp. 437–8

13. Beaglehole (ed.), *The Endeavour Journal of Joseph Banks*, Vol. 2, p. 187

14. Sydney Parkinson, *A Journal of a Voyage to the South Seas, in His Majesty's Ship, the Endeavour* (London: printed for Stansfield Parkinson, 1773) p. 182

15. Beaglehole (ed.), *The Endeavour Journal of Joseph Banks*, Vol. 2, p. 242

16. Beaglehole (ed.), *The Journals of Captain James Cook*, p. 466

17. Ibid., p. 471

18. Beaglehole (ed.), *The Endeavour Journal of Joseph Banks*, Vol. 2, p. 274

19. James Boswell, *The Life of Samuel Johnson, LL.D*, Vol. 1 (London: Henry Baldwin, 1791) p. 351

20. Beaglehole (ed.), *The Journals of Captain James Cook*, pp. 649–51

21. Beaglehole (ed.), *The Endeavour Journal of Joseph Banks*, Vol. 1, p. 53

22. Neil Chambers, *The Scientific Correspondence of Sir Joseph Banks*, Vol. 1 (London: Routledge, 2007) pp. 42–3

23. Beaglehole (ed.), *The Endeavour Journal of Joseph Banks*, Vol. 1, p. 54

24. Ibid., pp. 55–6

25. *Public Advertiser*, 3 September 1771

26. *Kentish Gazette*, 28 September 1771

27. Boswell, p. 414

28. Neil Chambers (ed.), *Endeavouring Banks: Exploring collections from the Endeavour Voyage* (London: Paul Holberton Publishing, 2016) p. 208

29. Harold B. Carter, 'Sir Joseph Banks and the Royal Society', *Sir Joseph Banks a global perspective* (London: The Royal Botanic Gardens, Kew, 1994) p. 5

30. John Hawkesworth, *An Account of the Voyages Undertaken by the order of His Present Majesty for making Discoveries in the Southern Hemisphere* (London: W. Strahan, 1773) p. xxi

31. *The Papers of Benjamin Franklin*, Vol. 18 (New Haven: Yale University Press, 1974) p. 210

32. *A Letter from Mr. Dalrymple to Dr. Hawkesworth* (London: 1773) p. 2

33. Ibid., p. 23

34. Ibid., p. 32

35. Hawkesworth, p. xix

36. John Barrow, *A Voyage to Cochinchina in the years 1792 and 1793* (London: T. Cadell, 1806) pp. 64–5

37. *Gazetteer and New Daily Advertiser*, 26 August 1771

38. Beaglehole (ed.), *The Endeavour Journal of Joseph Banks* Vol. 2, p. 329

39. J. C. Beaglehole, *The Voyage of the Resolution and Adventure 1772–1775* (Cambridge: Hakluyt Society, 1961) p. 930

40. Ibid., p. 931

41. Ibid., p. 718

42. Beaglehole (ed.), *The Endeavour Journal of Joseph Banks*, Vol. 2, p. 347

43. Ibid., p. 355

44. Chambers (ed.), p. 279
45. Glyndwr Williams, 'Seamen and Philosophers in the South Seas in the Age of Captain Cook', *The Mariner's Mirror*, 65:1, 3–22 p. 14
46. J. C. Beaglehole, *The Life of Captain James Cook* (London: Adam & Charles Black, 1974) p. 310

Chapter 11: The Frozen Serpent of the South

1. John Brewer, *Sentimental Murder: Love and Madness in the Eighteenth Century* (London: HarperCollins, 2004) p. 104
2. Ibid., pp. 103–4
3. G. R. Barnes and J. H. Owen, *The Private papers of John, Earl of Sandwich, First Lord of the Admiralty 1771–1782*. Volume 1, August 1770–March 1778 (Publications of the Navy Records Society, v. LXIX. 1932) p. xiii
4. Ibid.
5. *Scots Magazine*, 1 March 1775
6. *Kentish Gazette*, 8 August 1772
7. Ibid.
8. NA. ADM 106/1209/304
9. Bernard Penrose, *An Account of the Last Expedition to Port Egmont, in Falkland's Islands in the Year 1772* (London: J. Johnson, 1775) p. 9
10. NA. ADM 106/1208/235
11. *Gentleman's Magazine*, February 1775
12. Penrose, p. 11
13. Ibid., p. 42
14. Ibid., p. 13
15. Anon, *A Voyage Around the World, in his Majesty's Ship the Dolphin* (London: J. Newberry, 1767) p. 73
16. Penrose, p. 44
17. Ibid., p. 49
18. Ibid., p. 27
19. Edmund Burke, *A Philosophical Enquiry into the Origin of our Ideas of the Sublime and Beautiful* (London: R. & J. Dodsley, 1759) p. 59
20. Penrose, pp. 54–5
21. Ibid., p. 58
22. Ibid., pp. 62–3
23. Ibid., p. 64
24. Samuel Johnson, *Taxation No Tyranny: An Answer to the Resolutions and Addresses of the American Congress* (London: T. Cadell, 1775) p. 17

25. Ambrose Serle, *The American Journal of Ambrose Serle, Secretary to Lord Howe 1776–1778* (San Marino: Huntington Library Publications, 1940) p. 58

26. Johnson, p. 39

27. *Burke: Select Works*, Vol. 1 (Clark, NJ: The Lawbrook Exchange, 2005) p. 173

28. Benjamin Franklin, 'Rules by Which a Great Empire May Be Reduced to a Small One', *Public Advertiser*, 11 September 1773

29. *Annual Register, or a view of the history, politics and literature for the year 1775* (London: J. Dodsley, 1776) p. 54

30. Sarah Vickery, 'Handwritten History, 1765–1867: Correspondence of Great Americans from the Collections of the Newport Historical Society', *Newport History*, Vol. 80, Iss. 264, p. 39

31. Andrew Jackson O'Shaughnessy, *The Men Who Lost America* (London: Oneworld, 2013) p. 54

32. Carla Hay, 'Catharine Macaulay and the American Revolution', *Historian*, Vol. 56, No. 2 (Winter 1994) p. 308

33. Penrose, p. 72

34. Ibid., p. 76

35. Ibid., p. 79

36. *Derby Mercury*, 15 April 1774

37. *Derby Mercury*, 26 August 1774

38. *The Papers of Benjamin Franklin*, Vol. 21 (New Haven: Yale University Press, 1978) p. 306

39. *Kentish Gazette*, 4 January 1775

40. *Franklin Papers*, Vol. 21, p. 546

41. Ibid., p. 326

42. Ibid., p. 569

43. Ibid., p. 579

44. Ibid., p. 581

45. Ibid.

46. Ibid., p. 583

47. *Scots Magazine*, 1 March 1775

48. *The Parliamentary History of England from the earliest period to the year 1803*, Vol. 18 (London: Hansard, 1813) p. 446

49. *Franklin Papers*, Vol. 21, p. 598

50. Ibid., p. 545

Chapter 12: The Collier Fleet

1. Lionel Charlton, *The History of Whitby, and of Whitby-Abbey* (London: A. Ward, 1779) p. 358

2. NA. ADM 106/1226/154. George Brodrick, 17 March 1775

3. CL. ADM 354/189/330 – Woolwich Officers to Philip Stephens

4. Mike Connell and Des Liddy, 'Cook's *Endeavour* Bark: did this vessel end its days in Newport?', *The Great Circle, Journal of the Australian Association for Maritime History*, Vol. 19, No. 1, p. 40

5. *New Lloyd's List*, No. 639, Tuesday 9 May 1775

6. *New Lloyd's List*, No. 689, Tuesday 31 October 1775

7. G. R. Barnes and J. H. Owen, *The Private papers of John, Earl of Sandwich, First Lord of the Admiralty 1771–1782, Vol. 1, August 1770–March 1778* (Publications of the Navy Records Society, v. LXIX, 1932) p. 63

8. *Burke: Select Works*, Vol. 1 (Clark, NJ: The Lawbrook Exchange, 2005) p. 183

9. Barnes and Owen, pp. 66–7

10. Ibid., p. 67

11. Ibid., p. 64

12. David Syrett, *Shipping and the American War 1775–83* (London: The Athlone Press, 1970) p. 182

13. Ibid., p. 197

14. William Bell Clark, *Naval Documents of the American Revolution*, Vol. 3 (Washington: US Navy Department, 1968) p. 463

15. Ibid., p. 504

16. NA. ADM 106/3402, op. cit., p. 377

17. Ibid., p. 388

18. Ray Parkin, *HM Bark Endeavour: her place in Australian history* (Melbourne: The Miegunyah Press, 1999) p. 4

19. D. K. Abbass, 'Endeavour and Resolution Revisited: Newport and Captain James Cook's Vessels', *Newport History*, Vol. 70 (1999)

20. NA. ADM 106/3402, op. cit., pp. 424–6

21. Thomas Paine, *Common Sense* (London: Penguin, 2005) p. 35

22. Ibid., p. 73

23. Barnet Schecter, *The Battle for New York: the city at the heart of the American Revolution* (London: Jonathan Cape, 2003) p. 76

24. Ibid., p. 93

25. Barnes and Owen, p. 44

26. William Bell Clark, *Naval Documents of the American Revolution*, Vol. 4 (Washington: US Navy Department, 1969) p. 885

27. Ibid., p. 1014

28. Ibid., p. 1098

29. William James Morgan, *Naval Documents of the American Revolution*, Vol. 5 (Washington: US Navy Department, 1970) p. 107

30. Ernest Campbell Mossner, *The Life of David Hume* (Oxford: Oxford University Press, 1980) p. 595

31. Clark, *Naval Documents of the American Revolution*, Vol. 4, p. 1137

32. Rodney Atwood, *The Hessians* (Cambridge: Cambridge University Press, 1980) p. 7

33. Ibid., pp. 19–20

34. Ibid., pp. 25–6

35. Albert Pfister, *The Voyage of the First Hessian Army from Portsmouth to New York 1776* (New York: Chas. Fred. Heartman, 1915) p.10

36. Ibid., p. 11

37. Ibid., p. 9

38. Ibid., p. 10

39. Ibid., p. 23

40. NA. ADM 1/487, Part I, p. 51

41. Pfister, p. 30

42. Ibid., p. 12

43. Ibid., p. 13

44. Ibid.

45. Serle, p. 28

46. Ibid., p. 9

47. Ibid., p. 12

48. Ibid., p. 14

49. Ibid., p. 20

50. Ibid., p. 24

51. Ibid., p. 25

52. Ibid., p. 28

53. Ibid., p. 30

54. Schecter, p. 102

55. Ibid., p. 99

56. Morgan, pp. 918–19

57. Serle, p. 31

58. Pfister, p. 23

59. Ibid., p. 25

60. Ibid., p. 29

61. David McCullough, *1776* (New York: Simon & Schuster, 2005) p. 149

62. Serle, p. 63

63. Ibid., p. 64

64. William James Morgan, *Naval Documents of the American Revolution*, Vol. 6 (Washington: US Navy Department, 1972) p. 217

65. Serle, p. 77

66. Andrew Jackson O'Shaughnessy, *The Men Who Lost America* (London: Oneworld, 2013) p. 95

67. Serle, p. 145
68. Ibid., p. 147
69. Barnes and Owen, p. 169

Chapter 13: Ghosts

1. Charles Blaskowitz, *A Topographical Chart of the Bay of Narragansett in the Province of New England* (London: Wm Faden, 1777)
2. G. R. Barnes and J. H. Owen, *The Private papers of John, Earl of Sandwich, First Lord of the Admiralty 1771–1782, Vol. 1, August 1770–March 1778* (Publications of the Navy Records Society, v. LXIX. 1932) p. 72
3. Ibid., pp. 172–3
4. Blaskowitz
5. Marian Mathison Desrosiers, 'Daily Fare and Exotic Cuisine in Mid-Eighteenth-Century Newport', *Newport History*, Vol. 85, Iss. 274, p. 2
6. Ibid., p. 13
7. Sarah Vickery, 'Handwritten History, 1765–1867: Correspondence of Great Americans from the Collections of the Newport Historical Society', *Newport History*, Vol. 85, Iss. 264, p. 35
8. Ambrose Serle, *The American Journal of Ambrose Serle, Secretary to Lord Howe 1776–1778* (San Marino: Huntington Library Publications, 1940) p. 279
9. Ezra Stiles, *The Literary Diary of Ezra Stiles*, Vol. 1 (New York: Charles Scribner's Sons) p. 610
10. Charles P. Neimeyer, 'Rhode Island Goes to War: The Battle of Rhode Island, 1776–1778', *Newport History*, Vol. 72, Iss. 249, p. 123
11. *Shrewsbury Chronicle*, 25 January 1777
12. Deirdre C. Phelps, 'Solomon Southwick, Patriotic Printer of Revolutionary Rhode Island', *Newport History*, Vol. 77, Iss. 259, p. 24
13. Barnes and Owen, p. 172
14. Barnet Schecter, *The Battle for New York: the city at the heart of the American Revolution* (London: Jonathan Cape, 2003) p. 186
15. *Drewry's Derby Mercury*, 24 January–31 January, 1777
16. *Burke: Select Works*, Vol. 1 (Clark, NJ: The Lawbrook Exchange, 2005) p. 177
17. Vickery, p. 35
18. Mary Almy, 'Mrs. Almy's Journal', *Newport Historical Magazine*, Vol. 1 (Newport: Newport Historical Publishing, 1880) p. 21

19. Christian M. McBurney, *Kidnapping the Enemy: special operations to capture generals Charles Lee & Richard Prescott* (Yardley: Westholme Publishing, 2013) p. 115

20. Ibid., p. 114

21. Christian M. McBurney, 'British Treatment of Prisoners During the Occupation of Newport, 1776–1779: Disease, Starvation and Death Stalk the Prison Ships', *Newport History*, Vol. 79, Iss. 263, p. 5

22. Ibid., p.7

23. Karl Heinz Marquardt, *Captain Cook's Endeavour* (London: Conway Maritime Press, 1995) p. 13

24. McBurney, *Kidnapping the Enemy*, p. 128

25. Ibid., p. 139

26. Ibid., p. 140

27. Donald F. Johnson, 'Occupied Newport: A Revolutionary City under British Rule', *Newport History*, Vol. 84, p. 12

28. Serle, p. 271

29. McBurney, 'British Treatment', p. 14

30. Serle, p. 272

31. Andrew Jackson O'Shaughnessy, *The Men Who Lost America* (London: Oneworld, 2013) p. 13

32. Ibid., p. 32

33. Barnes and Owen, p. 343

34. Ibid., p. 23

35. *Annual Register, or a view of the history, politics and literature for the year 1778* (London: J. Dodsley, 1779) p. 227

36. Ibid., p. 228

37. Paul F. Dearden, *The Rhode Island Campaign of 1778: inauspicious dawn of alliance* (Providence: Rhode Island Bicentennial Foundation, 1987) p. 38

38. Almy, p. 22

39. Ibid., p. 23

40. Ibid., p. 20

41. NA. ADM 1/488, *Correspondence of Admiral Howe, 1777 to 1779*

Epilogue: Endeavours

1. Tony Stephens, 'A "damnable struggle", but he won', *Sydney Morning Herald*, http://www.smh.com.au/news/obituaries/a-damnable-struggle-but-he-won/2005/06/30/1119724752332.html, accessed January 2018

2. Ray Parkin, *Out of the Smoke: the Story of a Sail* (London: Hogarth Press, 1960) p. 1

3. Martin Flanagan, 'Be content, frugal, said a wise man', *The Age*, https://www.theage.com.au/articles/2003/02/02/1044122261316.html, accessed January 2018

4. Parkin, *Out of the Smoke*, p. 6

5. Ibid., p. ix

6. John Clark, 'Ray Parkin', http://mrjohnclarke.com/tinkering/ray-parkin accessed January 2018

7. Ray Parkin, *HM Bark Endeavour: her place in Australian history* (Melbourne: The Miegunyah Press, 1999) p. 69

8. Ibid., p. 6

9. Ibid., p. 42

10. Ibid., p. 41

11. Averil Lysaght (ed.), *The journal of Joseph Banks in the Endeavour / with a commentary by A. M. Lysaght* (Guildford: Genesis Publications, 1980) p. 30

12. Tim Beaglehole, *A Life of J. C. Beaglehole New Zealand Scholar* (Wellington: Victoria University Press, 2006) p. 351

13. Ibid., p. 217

14. Andrew Jackson O'Shaughnessy, *The Men Who Lost America* (London: Oneworld, 2013) p. 36

15. Mrs Stone, *Chronicles of Fashion, from the time of Queen Elizabeth to the present day*, Vol. 2 (London: Richard Bentley, 1846) p. 76

16. Robert Louis Stevenson, *Treasure Island* (Oxford: Oxford University Press, 2011) p. xl

17. James Dunbar, *Essays on the History of Mankind in Rude and Uncultivated Ages* (Dublin: B. Smith, 1782) p. 229

18. Robert Louis Stevenson, *A footnote to history: eight years of trouble in Samoa* (London: Cassell, 1892)

19. Judith Binney, *Redemption Songs: A Life of Te Kooti Arikirangi Te Turuki* (Wellington: Bridget Williams Books, 1995) p. 5

20. *Northampton Chronicle and Echo*, 14 March 1928

21. 'Space Shuttle Overview: *Endeavour*', Kennedy Space Center, https://www.nasa.gov/centers/kennedy/shuttleoperations/orbiters/endeavour-info.html, accessed January 2018

22. Steve Meacham, 'Murky history of the sunken *Endeavour*', *Sydney Morning Herald*, http://www.smh.com.au/news/world/murky-history-of-the-sunken-endeavour/2006/06/15/1149964675875.html, accessed January 2018

23. *NASA Space News Roundup*, 8 May 1992

24. Kate Lyons, 'Four missions, 177 days in orbit, and a "glimpse into eternity": The little boy who became Australia's first astronaut ... and the little pieces of his country he took with him into The Final Frontier', *Daily Mail*,

http://www.dailymail.co.uk/news/article-2663279/Australias-astronaut-hangs-space-helmet-22-years.html, accessed January 2018

25. Meacham

26. N. A. Maffey, *New Zealand Maritime News*, Vol. 21, No. 4 (Autumn 1970) (New Zealand Ship and Marine Society) p. 131

27. Mike Connell and Des Liddy, 'Cook's *Endeavour* Bark: did this vessel end its days in Newport?', *The Great Circle, Journal of the Australian Association for Maritime History*, Vol. 19, No. 1, p. 47

28. John Barrow, *A Voyage to Cochinchina in the years 1792 and 1793* (London: T. Cadell, 1806) p. 64

29. Connell and Liddy

30. D. K. Abbass, 'Endeavour and Resolution Revisited: Newport and Captain James Cook's Vessels', *Newport History*, Vol. 70 (1999)

31. https://www.smh.com.au/world/north-america/hms-endeavour-found-one-of-the-greatest-maritime-mysteries-of-all-time-solved-20180919-p504lx.html

32. 'Obama at Black Caucus dinner: "I need your help"', CBS News, https://www.cbsnews.com/news/obama-at-black-caucus-dinner-i-need-your-help/, accessed January 2018

Index